# The Small Cities Book

## On the Cultural Future of Small Cities

# The Small Cities Book

## On the Cultural Future of Small Cities

edited by W.F. Garrett-Petts

New Star Books ◢ Vancouver ◢ 2005

New Star Books Ltd.
107 3477 Commercial Street
Vancouver, BC
V5N 4E8
Canada

1574 Gulf Rd., #1517
Point Roberts, WA 98281
USA

info@NewStarBooks.com
www.NewStarBooks.com

Publication of this work is made possible by grants from the Canada Council, the British Columbia Arts Council, the Department of Canadian Heritage Book Publishing Industry Development Program, and the Community-University Research Alliance component of the Social Sciences and Humanities Research Council of Canada.

Cover photograph by Helen MacDonald-Carlson
Printed and bound in Canada by Gauvin Press
Printed on 100% post-consumer recycled paper.

Library and Archives Canada Cataloguing in Publication

The small cities book : on the cultural future of small cities
W.F. Garrett-Petts, editor.

Includes bibliographical references and index.

ISBN 1-55420-009-1

1. Cities and towns–Social aspects.  2. City and town life. 3. Community life.
4. Globalization–Social aspects.  5. Kamloops (B.C.). Garrett-Petts, W.F. (William Francis), 1954-

HT153.S59 2005      307.76'3
C2005-900840-7

# Contents

# Acknowledgments

Early in Italo Calvino's *Invisible Cities*, Marco Polo tells tales of cities visited: "I could tell you how many steps make up the streets rising like stairways, and the degree of the arcades' curves, and what kind of zinc scales cover the roofs," he says, adding, "but I already know this would be the same as telling you nothing." The city, he concludes, "does not consist of this, but of relationships … " Books about cities, too, are more than a collection of discrete observations and facts; they are about relationships. Nine cultural agencies, 16 university researchers, an equal number of community partners, and over 30 student research assistants contributed directly or indirectly to this project. In particular, the book owes much to the leadership shown by the Kamloops Art Gallery and its director, Jann Bailey, who saw in the city of Kamloops stories about cultural relations that needed telling. Lon Dubinsky, also of the Gallery and my co-director for the Cultural Future of Small Cities research program, helped draw the contributors together — and these contributors also deserve acknowledgment for their scholarship, patience, and dedication to this collection.

New Star Books of Vancouver has been our other partner in this project. *The Small Cities Book* is intended as the first in a series of collaborations between Thompson Rivers University (formerly The University College of the Cariboo) and New Star, with the goal of establishing, in the near future, Thompson Rivers University Press.

I want to thank Melva McLean, former managing editor at New Star, for her guidance, her intelligent commentary, and ultimately her faith in this project; similarly, publisher Rolf Maurer offered his unwavering, enthusiastic support. Thanks also to the editorial assistance provided so ably by Bronwen Boulton, Henry Hubert, Dana Novak-Ludvig, Helen MacDonald-Carlson, David MacLennan, and Jim Reilly; and special thanks to the anonymous reviewers who refereed this publication.

The book's design results from the fine work of Howard Glossop and principal designer Dennis Keusch.

Finally, and in the spirit of acknowledging community relationships, thanks go to the Social Sciences and Humanities Research Council of Canada for its Community-University Alliances Research program, a visionary program dedicated to the proposition that universities and community organizations can work together, as equal partners, in the pursuit of new knowledge.

# "Working Well, Together": An Introduction to the Cultural Future of Small Cities

W.F. Garrett-Petts and Lon Dubinsky

*The Small Cities Book* is a collaborative exploration involving both university and community research partners. As we write this introduction, we are beginning our fourth year of a five-year research program initiated by the Kamloops Art Gallery and The University College of the Cariboo in Kamloops, British Columbia. The program is supported by a Community-University Research Alliances (CURA) grant from the Social Sciences and Humanities Research Council of Canada (SSHRC), and the collaboration focuses on the cultural future of small cities — on the city as a cultural formation and how cultural and arts organizations work together (or fail to work together) in a small city setting.

There's much talk of late about a "new deal" for cities. But when national governments speak about cities, they are thinking primarily of the Torontos and the Vancouvers. *The Small Cities Book* has been written with the conviction that now is the time for small cities to make the case for smaller-scale cultural development. If not by definition, then certainly by default, "culture" is associated with big city life: big cities are commonly equated with "big culture"; small cities with something less. The Cultural Future of Small Cities CURA seeks to pro-

vide a more nuanced view of what constitutes culture in a small Canadian city. In particular, the university researchers and community partners are exploring notions of social capital and community asset building: in this context, "community," "creativity," "cultural indicators and scale," "home and homelessness," "visual and verbal representation," and the need to define a local "sense of place" have emerged as important themes.

If smaller urban centres are to prosper and maintain their identities in the face of mass cultural influences and big-box retailing, they need to think critically about notions of scale, space, and place. To tell their own stories, small cities need to listen to the vernacular, to local examples and voices. Accordingly, *The Small Cities Book* localizes questions of globalization and cultural identity at the municipal level, seeking to explore the challenges and possibilities facing small cities like Kamloops. It is our aim to share knowledge about cultural expression and community development that is transferable to other cities of comparable size in British Columbia, Canada, and elsewhere.

Influential studies by Manuel Castells (*The City*; *The Information Age*) and Saskia Sassen and Kwame Appiah on global cities, as

1

well as those specifically about urbanization in Canada (John Caulfield and Linda Peake; Trudi Bunting and Pierre Fillion), offer a starting point for research in this area, but these studies require a levelling when applied to small cities. Much has also been written on rural community life in a Canadian and international context, as demonstrated variously by *The New Rural Economy Project 2* and by many edited proceedings and collections, such as those by Kenneth Beesley and R. D. Ramsey, and Bill Reimer and Grace Young. Yet, their emphasis tends to be on small towns or sparsely populated regions. In either case, experiences may be similar, but the conditions and configurations of small cities can be decidedly different, owing to, among other things, what Clifford Geertz terms "local knowledge," and to factors of scale and geography.

At the Small Cities Forum (an international symposium hosted by the CURA in May 2004), Thomas Paradis provided a wonderfully concise "top-ten" list of reasons to approach cultural development in small cities differently. As Paradis argues, "[i]n certain ways, smaller places share some commonalities with larger places.... Still, there are probably more differences than similarities between the small city and the metropolis." Accommodating to new migration patterns, establishing growth-oriented social and economic networks, linking local planning to community functions and identity, recognizing the challenges of integrating "newcomers," preserving a viable downtown, animating local history, resisting the forces of purely commercial gentrification, promoting the multiple faces and facets of the city, generating a strong sense of place, and taking advantage of scale to promote community involvement — these are the key areas where small cities and their larger metropolitan counterparts differ in terms of the need for special emphasis, planning, and cultural participa-

tion (Paradis). Indeed, small cities occupy what many observers have identified as a cultural "third space" (Bhabba), positioned as they are in the shadow of large cosmopolitan cities but still bound by rural history and traditions. The under-representation of small cities in the scholarly literature on cities generally, particularly with respect to cultural issues, is thus a key rationale for research — and for this present book.

## Kamloops as a Site for Community-Based Research

We focus on Kamloops and the region as a living laboratory. Kamloops is located in the southern interior of British Columbia in the Thompson-Nicola region, about four hours northeast of Vancouver on the Trans-Canada Highway to Calgary and two hours north of Kelowna in the Okanagan Valley, with which it is often compared or confused, to the chagrin of both cities. The relative isolation of Kamloops is one of its virtues, at least in the case of the arts, for large cities are just too distant to satisfy a cultural diet. Yet, isolation is not the sole condition for the sustainability of arts and culture: there is a degree of local involvement that is attributable to more than the city's geographical location. For over twenty years the city has had numerous thriving arts organizations such as the Kamloops Art Gallery, the Kamloops Museum and Archives, the Kamloops Symphony Orchestra, and Western Canada Theatre — cultural organizations which many cities of comparable size either do not have or cannot adequately sustain.

At the initial meeting of potential research partners in 2000, Jann Bailey, the director of the Kamloops Art Gallery, pointed out that, as a cultural community, "we are all doing it well but not together." Given this observation, the participants immediately recognized that they were beginning with a knowledge and appreciation of Kamloops' diverse cultural resources, as opposed to its deficiencies and drawbacks, thus possessing the fundamentals for what John Kretzmann and John McKnight have termed "asset-building community development." However, the participants were also being asked to consider the possible advantages of working more deliberately together and of sharing resources. This led to a consideration of the very purpose of collaboration for the partners and the community of Kamloops.

The group recognized that while partnership arrangements can have a dramatic impact on the life of a small city like Kamloops, the possibilities and challenges are even greater when a topic as complex as culture is the focal point. Accordingly, we built in a self-appraisal component that takes into account the diverse literature on cooperation and community development, as well as related work on strategy and organizational theory by scholars such as Henry Mintzberg and several of his colleagues who discuss collaboration as an organizational strategy and simultaneously reflect upon their own collaboration as co-authors (Mintzberg et al.). A series of pamphlets documenting group meetings and fieldwork activities, poster displays, research process journals, a website, and *The Small Cities Book* have become for us such self-reflexive opportunities, ones where we seek to enact the principles of community collaboration, documentation, and dialogue that mark the spirit and potential of community-university research alliances.

Over an eight-month period in 2000, consultations and discussions led to the emergence of a research and community-based initiative designed (1) to examine cultural life in Kamloops and (2) to consider the implications of our research for cities of comparable size in British Columbia, Canada, and abroad. The program began with nine partners: the Kamloops Gallery (KAG) as lead organization, The University College of the Cariboo (UCC), City of Kamloops, Forest Research Extension Partnership, Kamloops Museum and Archives, John Howard Society, Secwepemc Cultural Education Society, Stuart Wood School, and Western Canada Theatre. More recently, we have extended our partnerships to include the Kamloops Make Children First Learning Initiative, the Comox Valley Art Gallery, and, more informally, two other CURAs studying small and mid-sized cities — those at the University of Waterloo and the University of New Brunswick, Saint John. Our studies and related community initiatives consider (1) city, regional, and environmental planning; (2) the challenge of linking cultural resources to social development; (3) the role for local history and heritage in cultural development; and (4) modes and strategies for representing the small city. In *The Small Cities Book*, we have organized these studies into three thematic clusters: Cultural Formations and Possible Futures, Cultural Narratives and Representations, and Cultural Symbols and Identities.

To further ensure continuity and knowledge sharing, all researchers and community partners meet formally on a regular basis. The study also includes a strong student component with UCC students engaged as research assistants, in work-study projects or as interns in community organizations. Information sharing includes a newsletter, the website (www.cariboo.bc.ca/smallcities), and three major public events to showcase the research results: an exhibition at the Kamloops Art Gallery and other venues that will document the work of the research projects, and two Small Cities forums (one held in May 2004 and the second scheduled for May 2005). These week-long forums include panels, workshops, town meetings, design charrettes and cultural events addressing the cultural, social and economic challenges facing small cities.

3

As we near the end of our research program, we are beginning to appreciate the implications of Jann Bailey's observation that local individual arts and cultural organizations were "doing it well but not together." Community–university research alliances like ours bring communities together in ways that make all partners productively self-conscious about community development in general — and about the shape (and purpose) of "research" in particular. Community-based research is good for the local economy, providing employment, business opportunities for local suppliers, and enhanced learning opportunities for students. It improves our local research capacity and know-how by mobilizing a ready network of university consultants and community researchers.

Working together, however, means more than establishing shared projects and goals: it also means understanding and negotiating otherwise hidden or unspoken assumptions, procedures, and agendas. Partnerships, however well intended, involve some measure of gain and some measure of loss — that is, all the participants are beginning to recognize that we need to work differently if we are to work well and together.

A community-university research alliance, as outlined in the SSHRC guidelines, is conceived as an "entity based on an equal partnership between organizations from the community and the university." We are working towards equality, but initial differences of perspective, tradition, and purpose preclude any immediate creation of a utopian alliance. Community organizations and universities do not necessarily speak the same language or hold the same objectives and values. Moving ahead with the university's research agenda while remaining sensitive to community sensibilities and expertise remains a dimension crucial to this form of research.

Attention to collaboration as a mechanism and process has also led us to reconsider the very idea of community. As attested by the CURA program itself,[1] few would dispute the value, if not the increasing necessity, of fostering a sense of community for the purpose of fusing research and education with the public good, in small cities or large metropolitan areas. An expanding literature about the meaning of and possibilities for community now traverses many disciplines and fields in the arts, humanities, and social sciences. "Community" has also become a watchword for diverse collective endeavours and arrangements not necessarily tied to local or civic associations or structures, or to a specific group held together by a common aim or purpose, as was traditionally the case. Community is now writ large, as in "the global community"; but as Peter Katz and others have suggested, it also has become synonymous, yet often erroneously, with "network" and other technological configurations.

For our part, we have viewed and continue to view Kamloops and the surrounding Thompson region as constituting a defined community, a cultural and geographical place with implicit and explicit similarities and differences to other places, and having a diversity of cultural identities and interests. In this respect, our research continues to take its cue from Lucy Lippard, who has perhaps best articulated the possibilities for art and cultural expression in local situations. As she puts it, "Community doesn't mean understanding everything about everybody and resolving all the differences; it means knowing how to work within differences as they change and evolve" (127).

In addition to collaboration and community, the CURA research features, of course, culture. As Raymond Williams observes, "culture is one of the two or three most complicated words in the English language" (*Keywords* 87). Williams' early work (*Long Revolution*) and a specific study of the coun-

4

try and city (*The Country*), as well as work by others, such as Geertz and Carey, laid the foundation for what has become known as the "cultural turn" in the arts, humanities, and social sciences.[2] What has emerged is the encompassing field and approach called cultural studies. An academic sea change has occurred that now provides a framework and an appreciation for the legitimate and inter-disciplinary study of a range of texts, arte-facts, practices, and events, some of which are included in this book.

However, because culture now refers to a multitude of enactments and interpretative possibilities, issues about the very conditions and contours of cultural participation become equally pertinent. Bennett Berger, for example, asks what needs to be known about the relationship between cultural (and symbolic) choices that people make and the social locations in which they take place. Or to raise matters relevant to Kamloops and other comparable cities, we are prompted to ask: (1) What comprises a viable and sustain-able cultural life that has meaning and value for its citizens in an economic and political climate characterized by mega-structures and forces such as globalization? (2) To what extent do the local and the vernacular give way to these more cosmopolitan trends and standards? (3) What is the value to the com-munity in either celebrating or institutional-izing a local history?

Working from these questions, we recog-nize, both theoretically and thematically, the importance of social capital in creating and sustaining cultural activity. Robert Putnam, like others, such as Francis Fukuyama and Xavier Briggs, defines social capital as "fea-tures of social organizations, such as net-works, norms and trust relations that facili-tate coordination and cooperation for mutu-al benefit" ("The Prosperous" 35). Social cap-ital is thus the glue that binds communities; for individuals and groups with cultural interests and objectives it is an essential resource, given the collaborative aspects of creation. It also has significant ramifications for policy making, cultural and otherwise, for, as Putnam explains, "social capital is not a substitute for effective public policy but rather a prerequisite for it and in part a con-sequence of it" ("The Prosperous" 42). Yet Putnam contends that, in the United States at least, while there is enormous and unprece-dented capital accumulation in the form of money and goods, social capital is being eroded, with the result being less citizen par-ticipation in civic life. For confirmation, he points to the decline of voluntary associations and other social ties and alliances that bring people together. In his much-quoted dictum, people are increasingly "bowling alone."

Social capital is therefore a key resource and phenomenon reflected in the Small Cities CURA's very partnerships and studies. The attention to collaboration also provides a platform for seeing social capital in action within the context of a Canadian small city, including its forms and extent. As Alejandro Portes and Patricia Landolt point out, indi-viduals, groups, and places always face barri-ers to participation, cultural and otherwise, because they lack the resources. While social capital may be of concern to the public and private sectors, it is especially an issue for non-profit organizations, now commonly regarded as the "third sector," given their mandates, associations and diverse activities (Drucker). Putnam may well be correct about the decline of voluntary and communal activ-ity, yet the pressures on and expectations of the third sector for services are dramatically increasing (Banting; Rifkin). Thus, in the longer term, the Small Cities CURA hopes to provide some insight about the capacities of non-profit cultural organizations in small cities and about some of the challenges faced by the larger sector in which they are situated.

## Artists-as-Researchers

The research projects represented here do not employ a single methodology; rather they reveal a commitment to methodological diversity, where the fundamental criterion is to use the most appropriate form of inquiry for the topic under study. Some projects incorporate traditional archival and historical methods; others employ ethnographic approaches and action research; while some use a combination of methods. One unique feature of this endeavour has been the involvement of artists-as-researchers.

From the beginning — and with an art gallery as lead partner — the directors saw the potential for "displaying" research as an important means of public dissemination. Once the research program was underway, at the first major meeting of researchers and community partners, the group reviewed its goals for (1) collaboration and assessment, (2) new partners and alliances, (3) additional funding possibilities, and (4) communication and dissemination strategies. In addition, Dubinsky and Garrett-Petts presented a brief on the potential involvement of artists. Initially, including the artists was presented as an example of how new researchers could be drawn into the project, in this case through culminating exhibitions that documented the projects and presented artistic work reflecting major project concerns. While the exhibition is still planned, the program has moved to attach artists to projects as they arise. In the meeting, we noted that this enhanced use of artist-participants reflected the progress of several current projects, and was "generally supported by an increasing interest by the contemporary art world in what we might call 'community-based art.'" We envisaged "several possibilities ... each ... contingent upon agreement by the researcher(s), community partner and artist(s) for each project. For example, some artists might participate

fully as researchers with their work incorporated into, if not in some cases synonymous with, a specific project. In other cases, artists might work as more detached observers" (Dubinsky and Garrett-Petts 4–5).

We are now in the midst of refining the forms and models of collaboration involving artists, academic researchers, and community organizations. To date, as this book illustrates, we have engaged numerous artists to work with our community-based research teams, encouraging them to follow one of three inquiry models (see Bratton and Garrett-Petts). We are encouraged by the potential we see for linking creative inquiry to more traditional methods of research. As Neil Bradford said recently in a backgrounder report on the structure of creative cities, "The lifeblood of the arts is creativity, imagination, experimentation, and appreciation of difference. These are precisely the habits of mind and modes of expression urgently required across all sectors [including community-based research]." Bradford notes that in business management, it is reported that "competition is no longer about creating dominance in large, scale-intensive industries but about producing elegant, refined products in imagination-intensive industries." He quotes the *Harvard Business Review* in proclaiming the "breakthrough business idea for 2004" to be that the master of fine arts (MFA) degree has become the new MBA, the essential currency for a business career [qtd. in Schachter]. Urban planners and policy makers recognize "that artistic works can enable dialogue between diverse people and groups; that cultural heritage can become a focal point for regenerating derelict neighbourhoods or, indeed, for reinventing a whole city's 'sense of place'; and that by valuing self-expression, the arts and culture contribute to active citizenship" (1-2).

Artistic practice — and the presence of

working artists as co-researchers — thus offers the possibility of well-crafted critique, playful destabilization and an identifiable "third view," one not tied directly to either the university or the community partners (see bissett; Garrett-Petts and Lawrence; Gottfriedson; Hargrave; Kroetsch; MacLennan et al.; Turner; and van Herk for examples in this volume). As an aspiring learning community, we continue to pursue our initial purpose, but we have also turned to art and artists to help refine our terms of reference, to help redefine our working relations. The chapters that follow reflect this artistic inflection, and, we trust, encourage readers to consider the poems, exhibitions, photographic essays, and creative nonfiction that have emerged as complementary forms of research — as practice-based embodiments of a small city culture in action.

## The Small Cities Book

In more traditional forms of social research, Robert Mackinnon and Ross Nelson offer an historical and geographical overview of Kamloops and the region, showing how "the driving sectors of the local economy may have [changed over time], but not the underlying economic and power relationships" (43). Echoing the observations of Paradis on why we need to study small cities, they conclude that responses to the opportunities and challenges posed by globalization are "scale dependent."

Next, Lon Dubinsky, working with a multidisciplinary team, reviews how city planners can promote community involvement and "visioning." Several kinds of perceiving, casting and reflecting characteristic of the charrette process — a community visioning exercise — are identified as helping citizens speculate about and design the physical and aesthetic shape of their immediate environment. As co-director of the Small Cities CURA, but

also as an arts researcher based primarily in eastern Canada, Lon Dubinsky is both community insider and outsider, participant and observer. What he identifies in "The Culture of Participation" many locals might too easily take for granted; namely, that Kamloops reveals a substantial number "of long-standing commitments and connectedness and an involvement in the arts and heritage that is rooted in what has been termed a culture of participation stretching across sectors, age groups and city areas" (81). He concludes that volunteerism, and the many various forms that cultural participation takes, constitutes evidence that "social capital seems to be thriving rather than dwindling" (82). These observations lead him to introduce the proposition — one developed more fully in Ross Nelson's "A Cultural Hinterland?" — that the usual measures (indices) used for assessing cultural capital in large centres, especially those developed by Richard Florida, are inappropriate for judging small cities.

Cultural participation, for example, is not always correlated with positive economic development. As John Bratton and Will Garrett-Petts point out in "Art at Work":

> [a]ccording to the existing literature on large urban centres, the opportunity to establish strong community ties may actually deter some people from moving to small communities and thus inhibit growth: deep community involvement is said to be commonly rejected or avoided by itinerant knowledge-sector workers and members of the so-called "creative class," who characteristically prize personal flexibility and opportunity over community responsibility and commitment. (112)

In contrast, Bratton and Garrett-Petts find that the small city setting narrows the false divide between creativity and work — that

7

smaller cities show an openness to "explore the complementary relationship between the arts and sustainable innovation (the potential for arts to invigorate innovators) in the workplace" (112).

In the second thematic cluster of chapters, Aritha van Herk reminds us that the small city may be a "comforting oxymoron," but one rarely visible as the subject of creative representation. "We hide, here in Canada, in cities small enough to disappear," she says. "The secret of cities is their ability to disappear their citizens...." She warns of geographers whose "cartographical programs ... 'unclutter' maps by erasing the small cities and exaggerating the large." "The small city," she says, "speaks to its own intimate murmur, its habits precise as a local vernacular" (137).

David MacLennan, Donald Lawrence, Will Garrett-Petts, and Bonnie Yourk engage in a very different cartographical practice — story mapping — as a means of exploring and documenting the community's "lived experience grounded in the routines and spatial patterns of everyday life" (146). Their focus is on the vernacular, on an "intermediate space where image, embodied knowledge and discursive knowledge overlap" (148). The story mapping sessions are held, generally, in community halls or neighbourhood centres, with each participant invited to draw and speak about his or her own personal map of Kamloops. This study of the community from "the ground up" maps individual stories of belonging and detachment, while, at the same time, identifying and validating the vernacular theories that inform these stories. Garrett-Petts and Donald Lawrence extend this study, asking what happens when a community art exhibition is used as a vehicle for academic inquiry into the nature of the small city. Echoing van Herk, they note that "smaller cities seldom find themselves the subject of ... artistic representation." In

"Relocating the Homeless Mind," they explore "the place of the small city in the Canadian imaginary" (168).

Similarly, Ginny Ratsoy considers the small city as setting and trope in Canadian literature. She finds small cities associated with what she calls a "peripheral vision," a way of seeing exhibited by those situated on the margin but self-consciously aware of their relationship to the centre. "Precisely because of Kamloops' edge position," she concludes, "it becomes a place of possibility — of escape, refuge, and self discovery" (209).

The city's children also have stories to tell. In their linked chapters on the development of children's museums, Elisabeth Duckworth and Helen MacDonald-Carlson argue that "small city museums should remain true to their roots: they should strive to draw upon vernacular experiences, to invest exhibits and programs with local significance" (248). Here the voices and images of the community's children help to define a larger sense of place.

Virtually all the researchers and community partners, in one way or another, are interested in the means and strategies used to represent Kamloops and the Thompson region to itself and to areas beyond. They also observe informal interactions, such as people using parks or other public spaces, patterns of walking, frequenting restaurants and taverns, or attending performances and events that bring locals and visitors together. As artist-researcher Laura Hargrave reflects in her *River Walk Project*, "the act of physically traversing the land [is] in some way tied to the lasting quality of the memory" (170). Such interaction remains important for a vibrant and desirable city culture; it is part of the social capital that flows from formally constituted associations.

The final cluster of chapters opens with a detailed consideration of how cultural symbols are socially constructed and consumed.

Sherry Bennett looks at local outlaw figures as objects of tourism promotion, asking the intriguing question, "What makes historical figures either eminently marketable or mere archival curiosities" (256)? Her study suggests that figures still rooted in vernacular culture, those not easily "separated from private and personal association" (274), are thus less attractive to the tourism industry than more stereotypical figures (the generic outlaws of popular culture). But, she argues, if we fail to promote local history on the basis of "proximity and familiarity" (275), we silence the very stories that define who we are and what we have to offer others.

The work of Marianne and George Ignace on relations between street culture, the "Rez," and the city details a moving story involving both artistic celebration and personal loss. Like Bennett, these authors seek to resist the temptation of the stereotype; in "Tagging, Rapping, and the Voices of the Ancestors," they argue that for Aboriginal culture to carry on, "it must reinvent itself in continuously new ways and forms" (318). Kamloops as the small city has a central role to play, for not only does it connect the reserve to the city, but the city also "provides one of the real arenas for the seeking and finding of self-expression among [Aboriginal] youth" (318).

This middle position, situated somewhere between the local and the cosmopolitan, creates both opportunities and challenges for theatrical expression and production as well. James Hoffman and David Ross tell the story of how an iconic historical document from 1910 ("The Laurier Memorial") became the subject of intense artistic collaboration and struggle. *Ernestine Shuswap Gets Her Trout* — a play by Tomson Highway, which, as Hoffman notes, "powerfully replays a performance that was originally staged in 1910" (288), suggests a model for the development

of vital, political theatre specific to small city symbols, scripts, and circumstances.

In "Change and Resistance: Kamloops' Civic Symbols and Identity in the 1990s" Rachel Nash argues that symbolic representation is "not limited to official insignia, coats of arms and similar materials put out by chambers of commerce, city governments and various booster organizations. Civic self-representation occurs through a complex of different practices and mechanisms, including celebrations, mascots, and the language cities use to describe and promote themselves" (319). Nash focuses on Kamloops' centenary year, 1993, as a "symbolic moment" marking a positive shift in both the city's economic situation and cultural confidence. It is a moment when "the community attempted the delicate task of fashioning a contemporary image, without completely abandoning its long-term identity in the process" (320). Nash sees small cities as having "a relatively limited range of representational resources on which to draw. That is, the big or 'world-class' city is a rich and suggestive notion, as is the small town. In contrast, there are fewer established ways to discuss and describe the small city; the patterns are not as clear" (330). As all the chapters in this cluster argue, the challenge for small cities is "to develop and sustain existing local identities without resorting to generic abstractions" (330).

The local also includes the disenfranchised. Just as a city's varied history is important to understanding itself and its future, many of its community organizations now recognize the vital importance of enabling particular clienteles to give voice to their life experiences through various forms of cultural expression. Linda Deutschmann looks at the meagre social capital of marginalized groups. She also speaks to the "not in my backyard (NIMBY) syndrome," which, because of closer proximities, small cities must inevitably address with respect to housing and the provisions of various community services.

## Some Tentative Conclusions

*The Small Cities Book* identifies four keys to a culturally healthy small community: (1) a vital, culturally rich and diversified downtown core; (2) an authentic, publicly celebrated history; (3) a high level of cultural participation, including a tradition of volunteerism, growth coalitions, and leadership; and (4) a cultural policy that links the city's centre and heritage to its outlying areas and communities. Actions that diminish the downtown, obscure or ignore local history and heritage, discourage cultural participation, or fail to consider outlying areas in relation to the city's centre and heritage will, in the long term, erode the city's identity and the prospects for future development.

Economic development and cultural development, therefore, cannot be effectively separated, especially in a small city setting. Tourism promotion, for example, can have only limited success if it is not planned in coordination with the cultural sector. As Thomas Paradis outlines in his "top-ten" reasons why Kamloops is no Vancouver, "[a]ny constructed theme that is perceived as imposed on a community from an elite group of citizens or city leaders is not likely to attract positive attention." If not cast as legitimate expressions of a city's local character and history, festivals, events, and promotional publications become merely generic — a sign of the city's decline, not its development. The city without its own story to tell has nothing distinctive to promote.

Our preliminary findings thus confirm the importance of specific community-based activities in the arts and heritage. The presence of Dubinsky's "culture of participation"

in many sectors of the city is a key to economic and social sustainability. A recent Cultural Strategic Plan found that one third of the Kamloops population is actively engaged in artistic events, education, or practices. Studies show that cities that define themselves as creative, as so-called "learning communities," share a strategic advantage: creative cities become magnets for economic and cultural development. Our findings thus suggest we need to celebrate creative participation in all its forms (see especially chapters by Bratton and Garrett-Petts; Ignace and Ignace; Nelson).

Through this study we can begin to understand how small cities overlook or undervalue creativity. Many cities fall victim to fragmented cultural planning and decision making, allowing one municipal sector to win out at the expense of another: local arts councils vs. major cultural organizations, sports vs. the arts, economic development vs. cultural development. We've come to see these divisions as false dichotomies, the kind of either/or thinking and practice that remains far removed from the lived experience of the average citizen. Most of us take little time to distinguish among sports, recreation, the arts, and our work activities. One flows into the others, part of the array of choices available. Also, different people define these activities differently. The arts, for example, can be recreational for some and a business for others. Important is the range of opportunities for ourselves, our families, and our neighbours.

Traditional cultural categories — high and low culture, arts and recreation — are not a good fit with the small city landscape. Our investigations suggest that we need to recognize and nurture more permeable boundaries between and among sports and recreation, high arts, amateur artistic expression and culture, folk arts and ethnic celebrations, and education at all levels. Ironically, sports and recreation are key drivers behind Kamloops' high levels of arts funding: the city's investment in sports, in particular, has created a rhetorical situation allowing, historically, a strong case for compensatory funding in the arts.

The 1993 Canada Summer Games established a watershed moment in terms of city pride, participation, and vision. According to Recreation and Culture Manager Ron McColl, the city's successful bid for, and hosting of, the national games came at a time when Kamloops was searching for a shared sense of identity. As McColl points out, "National events go to the spirit of a community" (personal interview); they help articulate and generate lasting cultural capital. During the 1980s (as MacKinnon and Ross detail in their chapter on local adjustments in a staples economy), Kamloops was hard hit by recession and experienced a general cultural malaise. The city's mascot was a cute but uninspiring "Kami the Trout," and the annual festival was called "Spoolmak Days" (Kamloops spelled backwards). While the city and region had a long history of organizing and hosting important events — including the first provincial winter games in 1979; the first BC Festival of the Arts in 1985; the Yale-Cariboo Music Festival; and, important to the region, the provincial bull sale centred in Kamloops — the Canada Summer Games was "the first *national event* requiring the full participation of the city's citizens" (McColl).

The Summer Games were a huge economic success, leaving behind money and such new facilities as a rowing club, a sailing club, a competition pool, a track-and-field stadium, and so on. More important, though, was the legacy of community pride and organizational leadership, fostering a "what do we do next?" attitude. It's hardly coincidental that, by 1995, the Mayor's Task Force on the Arts felt confident enough to recommend that the city commit 1% of its tax base to arts and culture — a goal exceeded by 1998.[3]

What the city discovered was that its scale did not prohibit a national vision for culture broadly defined. In 1985, the city proclaimed itself "The Tournament Capital of B.C."; following the Summer Games, Kamloops branded itself "The Tournament Capital of Canada." But in addition to playing host to numerous national and international tournaments (such as the Ford World Curling Championships, the Strauss Cup, the Memorial Cup, the World Fly Fishing Championships, and much more), the city's cultural sector has premiered or otherwise initiated numerous artistic, theatrical, educational, and musical events of national import. In other words, the city manages to balance local development in sports *and* culture with national (and even international) achievements and aspirations.[4] A national vision is common across a range of cultural activities in the city, and the city's double vision, its largely successful fusion of the local with the national (the centre and the periphery), may turn out to be its defining characteristic. As Kamloops Mayor Mel Rothenburger suggests in the concluding chapter of this book, "In Kamloops, all of these issues and initiatives consciously or subconsciously emanate from our very name: 'Meeting of the Waters,' as translated from the Secwepemc language" (350).

Of course, such an heroic narrative of achievement is only part of the story: it is important not to over-romanticize the small city, for scale not only provides opportunities — it also magnifies misunderstandings, difficulties and disagreements. Stories circulate quickly in a small city: the tall tale is endemic to small places. In large measure, understanding how stories work *in* and *on* the small

11

city is a prerequisite for successful municipal development.

In a variety of modes, and from multiple disciplinary perspectives then, the following chapters explore municipal development as a narrative art. Our sense of a city's history, its presence, and its potential futures is expressed in stories — in our newspapers, annual reports, promotional materials, and planning documents; in formal debate and casual conversation with one another; in the many ways we represent the city verbally and visually to others. Place, people, and participation — the "3Ps" of the creative city — have become key narrative elements essential for community self-definition, development, growth, preservation, and promotion. As this book attests, such narratives involve multiple authors: civic leaders, community coalitions, bureaucrats, educators and social critics, children, entrepreneurs, outlaws, poets, artists and other risk-takers. To build successful cities, we need resources, enabling policy (championed and implemented at all levels of government), political will, collaboration, participation via multiple points of entry, and leadership. Above all, cities — especially small cities — need opportunities to articulate, acknowledge, compare, and harmonize their competing narratives of place: they need opportunities for moving shared visions into action.[5]

## Notes

1. The CURA program, established by SSHRC, offers grants to institutions and organizations requiring infrastructure support to coordinate "programs of activities and partnerships within a broadly-defined theme area." The CURA program's express purpose is to "support a diverse range of innovative research, training and related activities that will (1) enhance mutual learning and horizontal collaboration between community organizations and universities, (2) contribute to the social, cultural, and/or economic development of communities, (3) enrich research, teaching methods, and curricula in universities, and reinforce decision-making and problem-solving capacity in the community, and (4)

enhance students' education and employability through diverse opportunities to build their expertise and workforce skills in an appropriate research setting." SSHRC scheduled two competitions (one in 1999/2000 and one in 2000/01) to fund 37 CURAs; this pilot period covered 4 years, with a total budget of $22.6 million. The Cultural Future of Small Cities program was awarded funding for three years in April 2001; we received an additional two-year completion grant in 2004. CURA has now become a mainstream program accepting annual applications. See www.sshrc.ca/web/apply/program_descriptions/cura_e.asp

2. For a recent and comprehensive overview of these developments, see Victoria Bonnell and Lynn Hunt.

3. Today, the City of Kamloops contributes 1.96 % to Arts and Culture.

4. For example, in June 2004, the Canada Council for the Arts announced that Vancouver Aboriginal artist Rebecca Belmore will be Canada's official representative at the 2005 Venice Biennale of Visual Art, the world's oldest and most prestigious venue for the international display of contemporary art. The Kamloops Art Gallery and the University of British Columbia's Morris and Helen Belkin Gallery, which proposed Rebecca Belmore as the Biennale candidate, were the institutions selected in a nation-wide competition to represent Canadian visual arts at the event. The 51st edition of the Venice Biennale will take place in June 2005.

5. The notion of municipal development as a narrative art was first presented by Garrett-Petts at the *Creative Cities Structured Policy Dialogue* hosted by Canadian Policy Research Networks, Ottawa, June 14, 2004.

## Works Cited

Banting, Keith, ed. *The Nonprofit Sector in Canada: Roles and Relationships*. Montreal: McGill-Queens UP, 1999.

Beesley, Kenneth, and R.D.Ramsey, eds. *Rural Research in the Social Sciences and Humanities VI: Proceedings of the Sixth Annual Colloquium*. Truro: Rural Research Centre, Nova Scotia Agriculture College, 1999.

Berger, Bennett. *An Essay on Culture: Symbolic Structure and Social Structure*. Berkeley: U of California P, 1995.

Bhabha, Homi. *The Location of Culture*. New York: Routledge, 1994.

Bonnell, Victoria E. and Lynn Hunt, eds. *Beyond The Cultural Turn: New Directions in the Study of Society and Culture.* Berkeley: U of California P, 1999.

Bradford, Neil. *Creative Cities Structured Policy Dialogue Backgrounder.* Ottawa: Canadian Policy Research Networks [Project F-115], 2004.

Briggs, Xavier de Souza. "Social Capital and the Cities: Advice to Change Agents." *National Civic Review.* 86.2 (1997): 111–118.

Bunting, Trudi and Pierre Fillion, eds. *Canadian Cities in Transition: The Twenty-First Century.* Toronto: Oxford UP, 1999.

Canada Council for the Arts. "Rebecca Belmore will represent Canada at the 2005 Venice Biennale of Visual Art." Press Release. Ottawa. 17 June 2004. <http://www.canadacouncil.ca/news/releases/2004/sk127319685800468750.htm>

Carey, James. "Mass Communication Research and Cultural Studies: An American View." *Mass Communication and Society.* Ed. James Curran, Michael Gurevitch and Janet Woollacott. London: Edward Arnold and Open UP, 1977. 409–425.

Castells, Manuel. *The City and the Grassroots.* Berkeley: U of California P, 1985.

——. *The Information Age.* (3 vols). Oxford: Blackwell, 1999.

Caulfield, John, and Linda Peake. *City Lives and City Forms: Critical Research and Canadian Urbanism.* Toronto: U of Toronto P, 1996.

Drucker, Peter. *Managing in a Time of Great Change.* New York: Truman/Talley Books/Dutton, 1995.

Dubinsky, Lon, and W.F. Garrett-Petts. "Moving Ahead." Discussion paper presented at the August 2001 Meeting of the Cultural Future of Small Cities Project, Kamloops, BC. August, 2001.

Fukuyama, Francis. *Trust: The Social Virtues and the Creation of Prosperity.* New York: Free Press, 1995.

Geertz, Clifford. *Local Knowledge.* New York: Basic, 1983.

Katz, Peter. "The 70 Percent Place." *Government Technology.* May 2000: 8–9, 45–47.

Kemmis, Daniel. *Community and the Politics of Place.* Norman, OK: U of Oklahoma P, 1990.

——. *The Good City and the Good Life.* New York: Houghton, 1995.

Kretzmann, John P., and John L. McKnight.

*Building Communities from the Inside Out: A Path Towards Finding and Mobilizing a Community's Assets.* Chicago: Institute for Policy Research, Northwestern UP, 1993.

Lippard, Lucy. "Looking Around: Where We Are, Where We Could Be." *Mapping the Terrain: New Genre Public Art.* Ed. S. Lacy. Seattle: Bay Press, 1995. 114–130.

McColl, Ron. Personal Interview. Kamloops: 21 May 2004.

Mintzberg, Henry, Denise Dougherty, J. Jorgensen, and F. Westley. "Some Surprising Things About Collaboration." *Organizational Dynamics.* (Summer 1996): 60–72.

New Rural Economy Project2. 7 August 2004 <http://nre.concordia.ca/nre2.htm>

Paradis, Thomas. "The Top-Ten Reasons Kamloops is No Vancouver." A paper presented at The Small Cities Forum, Kamloops, B.C., May 9, 2004.

Portes, Alejandro and Patricia Landolt. "The Downside of Social Capital." *American Prospect* 26 (1996): 18–21.

Putnam, Robert. *Bowling Alone: The Collapse and Revival of American Community.* New York: Simon, 2000.

——. "The Prosperous Community: Social Capital and Public Life." *The American Prospect* 4.13 (Spring 1993): 35-42.

Reimer, Bill, and Grace Young, eds. "Development Strategies for Rural Canada: Evaluating Partners, Jobs and Communities." *Summary of Proceedings from the 5th Annual ARRG Conference.* Canadian Agricultural and Rural Restructuring Group, 1994.

Rifkin, Jeremy. "All Government is Derivative. (Interview with Steven Ferry)." *Government Technology.* (May 2000): 10–15, 25.

Sassen, Saskia, and Kwame Appiah. *Globalization and Discontents: Essays on the New Mobility of People and Money.* New York: New Press, 1999.

Schachter, Harvey. "Business Embarks on Design Revolution." *Globe and Mail* 19 March 2004: C1-C2.

Williams, Raymond. *The Country and The City.* New York: Oxford UP, 1975.

——. *Keywords: A Vocabulary of Culture and Society.* London: Oxford UP, 1983.

——. *The Long Revolution.* London: Penguin, 1961.

13

# This Part of the Country

## Robert Kroetsch

### 1. Kamloops: Late Arrival

Searching for the mountain,
we found a shoe.

After the first drought
we dreamed a river.
After the forecast city
we listened for rain.

The fallen roof and fireweed
conspire.
       Seeds too explode.

lamb and jackhammer in duet:
silence, breaking the drum:
the city, climbing, climbing.

Two rivers, then, coming together.

## 2. This Part of the Country

In this part of the country, the horizon is a glacier.

One morning the horses of the sun lost all direction.

David Thompson, that very afternoon, found west. He saw

a man on a sandbar, sluicing for pieces of light.

I saw George Bowering riding a yellow horse, that high country poet

wearing no gun. His horse had eyes the colour of bullets.

In this part of the country, sagebrush is a version of dance. You must

enter in slowly. This is where train robbers learn their moves.

I saw Roy Miki wading in Sheila Watson's river. He was fishing

with a line made of blue memory. The sky was tinder dry.

## 3. Blue River: Checking In

Somewhere west and south of Mt Robson

I forgot my name. This much I remember.

It was a long, white drive; I was alone.

The patient trees were shrouded in snow.


The woman behind the motel desk

said I would have to sign my name.

Snow had fallen, I explained, and it fell;

the road was not to be found.


We were both surprised by the dark.

Some days night is a voluntary silence.

Then one of us asked (was it she

or I?), So how did you get here?

## 4. *This Part of the Country*

Landscape is a diagram of the impossible. Why do we have to look at a tree to see the wind? How do we tell the frozen lake from future interrogations?

Today in Kamloops the snowline slid slowly all day long down into the valley of the North Thompson River. First my head turned a hummocky white. Then my shoulders became slopes for elegant white toboggans. Then all my fingers assumed the dignity of ice. It was a slow procedure. When I went to move my feet I couldn't find them.

Here in this part of the county the so-called visibility, from airplanes and avalanches alike, is the equivalent of zero. We measure our descent by exhalation, hoping to see each breath freeze as it escapes the mouth. Is that a question or an answer?

# Part I

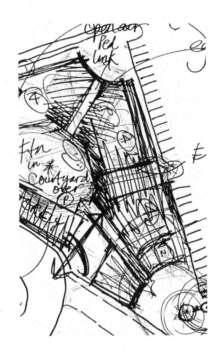

# Cultural Formations
# and Possible Futures

```
                    kamloops        ps

  k    k    k    k    k    k                    ala   almo
    as      as    sa   sam  am  k sssssssss              m    m
  s   s   s    salmo      a     k         kaaaaas
    mola  mala          almo  a  a  a   k   a  m  k aaa mo
      ama    ama   ama                                a
                          kam   kam   kam      loops   a
  oops   sa    sa    sa
                          sam   sam   sam    saml    saml
      lam   oop  soop
  pooooooooooooooooos      kam   sam   lam   loops  pool  s
        poooll    samllll   soop   poos   pool   loop

      kama    kama   ama  k   k   k   m loops  moops  l

    mop   mops   pom   pom   pam   pam   map   mop  a  mop

  sloops     pol  pom    pok    pos    poml  pam  sam  koop

    m   m   m   m   m   m                    mmmmmmmmmmmm
                                    mmmmm
        l   al   al   al   al                 oops   opl

  opl   opm      opn      opk    okamsamalloopsa

    loops    loops    ml    ka    kam   loops

    pool poops a   kal m   kol    oopa    poop a

        kam   kam   kam   kam    loops   loops  loops

    pool s    poolskam   poolsamk   amo   amo   moa

  sloops am   amo  kaml    amo  kaml   kam  kam  ola
            k       sam   sam   sam  k   sam  sam  sam  kaml
  am l  loops  mmm
                      amsko   amsko   ko   ko  oko   oka   oka
          salmon      ka   ka   ka   ka   kao   kaoooooo
    alm  almp  almps        kamloops    salmon    mon  sal
  lamps      las   laso    lasoo    sal  mon  man   sal
    amps                              mano   amo   amo
          ps mmmmmmmmmmmmmmm  k   a   l      samo  sano  sam
          k   k   k   k              an  so  an  so  an  so
                          pool  loop  sam  o  kalm
              kaml  k  k  k  s  s  s  al  al  al  man
    o   sal    ml  aml  loop  ssssss   pppp      oooooo
          m   m   m   aml   oml   opl  opl  apl  apl  lap
    sal  sal  mon   oops   soop
                              sam   am  amo    kaml


  may 3.03
```

---

bill bissett

# Urban and Economic Change in Kamloops: Postindustrial Adjustments in a Staples Economy

## Robert MacKinnon and Ross Nelson

**Introduction**

The growth of a global, postindustrial econo-my has emerged as a significant issue in geog-raphy (Harvey; Scott "The technopoles"; Dicken; Bryson et al.). Well documented are its impacts on the established manufacturing belts of North America and Europe (Massey and Allen; Scott "New industrial"; Rubenstein; Holmes), as well as on new centres of innova-tion and production (Hepworth; Scott "The technopoles"; Angel). Geographers have also begun to investigate how these economic changes found their way into resource exporting regions. Research by Barnes and Hayter indicates that new production tech-niques, changes in corporate control, and increased global competition can affect small communities in British Columbia's resource periphery. Physical isolation, a weakly devel-oped urban hierarchy, and a staples mentality have not insulated the province from the restructuring processes that characterize new, postindustrial economies elsewhere. Informed by this literature, this chapter explores how information and service-based industries have transformed the labour force and physical landscape of Kamloops, a rela-tively small city in the Interior of British Columbia.

Kamloops, like many urban centres in British Columbia's interior, has traditionally functioned as a processing and service centre for a resource economy. Over the last two decades, however, the city's economy, and thus its relationship with the surrounding region and external economies, has shifted. Resource industries are still important, but Kamloops is increasingly being shaped by multinational retailers and quaternary servic-es such as call centres, information processing facilities, advanced education, and health care. This shift, in turn, has come with "big city" urban processes like inner city decline and revitalization, new urbanist concepts, and high-technology industrial parks. The purpose of this chapter is to analyse the changing urban character of Kamloops. By focusing specifically on changes in Kamloops' labour force and economic landscape, this chapter documents and interprets a range of social, cultural, and economic adjustments still underway in this small, "hinterland city."

The chapter begins with a brief discussion of staples theory and its significance for understanding the geographic and economic relationships between Kamloops and the Vancouver-centred economic "core" of British Columbia. It then reviews the historical development of Kamloops against this background, dividing the city's recent history into two phases: the resource and transportation fuelled growth between 1945 and the economic recession of the early 1980s, and the subsequent rise of a tertiary and quaternary sector economy. The last section of the chapter examines how Kamloops' urban form has been shaped by this economic shift. The growth of the postindustrial economy is shown to have contributed to economic diversification in Kamloops, but this has not been without significant adjustments in the traditional role of Kamloops' central business district (CBD), as well as in the geographical balance of power within the community. It is argued that the impact of postindustrial forces in interior cities can differ markedly from those in Vancouver (and in other metropolitan cities) or in smaller resource-based communities in hinterland locations.

**A Staples Economy**

British Columbia is a classic example of a staples economy (Bradbury; McGillivray; Wood). A staples economy is one that is based on the export of raw or minimally processed natural resources (Barnes "Logics" 216). Wood (as logs, lumber and pulp), copper, and coal are the dominant staples in British Columbia. Other important staples include: gold, natural gas, fish, fruit, cattle, and wheat. As suggested by the well-known political economist, Harold Innis, staples-producing regions often fail to develop well-diversified economies because of the institutional nature of resource exploitation (Innis; Watkins). In British Columbia, large and often foreign-owned corporations have controlled resource development. Large firms have the necessary capital, technology, and infrastructure required to exploit staples in remote areas. However, with their focus on exporting resources to "home" markets, for-

eign firms have, at the same time, limited the growth of backward, forward, and final demand linkages in the economy (Parker).[1] Staples economies, as a result, are extremely vulnerable to boom-and-bust cycles. They also have extremely limited means to buffer the economic impacts created by external shifts in demand, technological change, and competing suppliers (Barnes "Logics").

British Columbia's well-known core-periphery structure is also a product of the province's staples economy (Bradbury). A core-periphery, or heartland-hinterland structure, is one in which the majority of the population, value-added processing, and control functions (government and private industry) are concentrated in a small area (the core) of a larger resource-producing region (the hinterland or periphery). Vancouver and the Georgia Strait urban region have functioned as British Columbia's core (see Figure 1). With nearly 2 million residents, the Vancouver Census Metropolitan Area has six times the population of the second largest city in British Columbia (Victoria), and is approximately 20 times the size of the largest community in the province's interior (Kelowna) (Statistics Canada). Vancouver also has a much more diverse and stable economy than the rest of the province (Davis and Hutton). The head offices of resource companies are located there, as well as a substantial percentage of the province's high-order economic and cultural functions (respectively, banking, insurance, and investment industries, and post-secondary education, the arts, and professional sports). Vancouver, as Hutton ("Vancouver") suggests, functions as the province's "downtown." As the terminus of the Canadian Pacific Railway and the British Columbia Railway, and with a deep-water port, Vancouver controls a large proportion of the resources moving out of, and the manufactured products into, British

Columbia. Over time, this natural advantage has been reinforced by the establishment of processing and service industries, which, in turn, have created agglomeration economies that inhibited economic and urban development in the resource periphery (Davis and Hutton).[2]

## Kamloops' Traditional Staples and Service Economy

Kamloops has a long and varied history as a staples and service centre. Located at the confluence of the North Thompson and South Thompson rivers, Kamloops has been variously described as "the forks," the "inland capital," and "the hub" of British Columbia's south central Interior (Morse 9, 11, Favrholdt *Kamloops* 47). The South Thompson River defines the only major east-west valley in southern British Columbia, while the North Thompson provides a direct connection to central British Columbia. In addition, the Okanagan Valley — located 75 kilometres to the southeast of the city — provides a direct connection to the Columbia River system, while the Nicola Valley, just 30 kilometres to the south, affords access to a large portion of the southern interior plateau. Thus, Kamloops has long had an important crossroads function. For the Secwepemc people, the meeting of these rivers has been an important gathering and overwintering location. Their winter homes dotted the banks of the Thompson, and the confluence of the North and South Thompson was an important trading location for them and for neighbouring peoples of the Fraser, Nicola, and Okanagan Valleys. Indeed, one theory says that the Secwepemc name for this location — *Cumcloups* — gradually evolved into the present-day name of the city (Favrholdt *Kamloops*).

The first European settlement was established in 1812 when the Pacific Fur Company and the Northwest Company established fur posts in the area. By the second decade of the 19th century, when the Hudson's Bay Company (HBC) had taken control of the export-oriented fur trade, Kamloops was situated in the middle of the company's cordilleran operations. Located roughly halfway between Fort Alexandria to the north and Fort Okanagan to the south, Kamloops was an important waypoint on the brigade trail, via which furs, horses, dried fish and other provisions and supplies were transported between the posts (Harris 39-41). This transit function further expanded when gold was discovered along the Fraser in 1858 and in the Cariboo and Big Bend regions in 1862 and 1865 respectively. People and supplies passed through Kamloops en route to these gold fields, and the settlement — still focused on the HBC post — became an important supply centre for the miners. American cattle drovers were among the first to establish ranches in the area in the 1860s, in direct response to the demand for meat created by the miners (McLean). The establishment of Indian reservations and the implementation of a regime of private property by the colonial government opened the traditional Secwepemc territory and adjacent lands to further cattle and sheep ranching and agricultural settlement (Weir; Favrholdt "Domesticating").

Thus, Kamloops gradually evolved from an Indian settlement and fur trading post to a "frontier village" (Morse 19). Still, the village remained a fledgling settlement until the arrival of the transcontinental railway in 1885. The Canadian Pacific Railway (CPR) not only linked Kamloops and the rest of the province to eastern Canada and to the Pacific — fulfilling the promise of Confederation — it was, and still is, a key element of the local landscape. The limited flat land along the South Thompson River has created an inti-

25

mate connection between the railway and the community. Initially the CPR tracks ran down the centre of Kamloops' main street, and they remain a significant edge or barrier between the downtown core and the South Thompson River. In 1891, water and electrical power systems were established, and, in 1893, the town received its municipal charter. At this date, approximately 1,000 people lived in the town, and only rudimentary services were available for citizens. As Kamloops evolved into an agricultural service, saw milling, and small-scale distribution centre, its population grew slowly. In 1914, Kamloops' citizens numbered 4,000 (Balf).

The town's importance as a transportation centre was reinforced in 1915 when the Canadian Northern Railway (later the Canadian National Railway) completed its trans-Canada line through Kamloops, and linked Kamloops to Edmonton via the North Thompson route. Fruit and vegetable farming, promoted in nearby North Kamloops and Brocklehurst by the B.C. Fruitlands Corporation, led to the development of a sizeable canning industry that produced apples and tomatoes for new markets accessible via the railway lines. Beans, potatoes, onions, and even hops were also produced for external markets; these remained important local crops until the 1950s (Hay and Favrholdt). In 1946, Kamloops and North Kamloops recorded a combined population of 11,300 (Favrholdt *Kamloops*).

Kamloops grew more rapidly after World War II, effectively doubling its population by 1961 (see Figure 2). More than half of this growth occurred on low-lying agricultural land beyond the city's legal boundaries. The largest of the new communities was North Kamloops. Abetted by the construction of new bridges across the Thompson River in 1923 and 1962, North Kamloops grew from a small agricultural village of less than 500

people in the 1920s to an incorporated town of 6,500 by 1962. The town added a further 5,000 residents by 1966, making North Kamloops the largest urban area in the region. Brocklehurst, Rayleigh, Westsyde, Valleyview, Dallas, and Barnhartvale were other incorporated and unincorporated communities in the immediate area. They collectively contributed 6,000 or so people to the amalgamated urban region in the 1960s (Moffat). (This demographic growth was undoubtedly stimulated by the establishment of a large pulp mill complex in Kamloops in 1965.)

The conversion of farmland was symptomatic of technological changes in fruit and vegetable production and of constraints imposed on urban development by the area's physical geography. Kamloops' small-scale fruit and vegetable industry could not compete with the large agri-businesses that were starting to appear at this time in the Okanagan and the United States, while general improvements in canning, refrigeration, transportation and marketing meant stiff, year-round competition even in local markets. The last Kamloops-area cannery ceased operation in 1959. As the viability of agriculture declined, and as the population grew, economic pressures to develop the lands along the rivers increased. The pressure was heightened by the scarcity of flat land suitable for residential and commercial development. Kamloops is situated in a narrow, steep-sided valley. Unstable silt bluffs and a 500-metre change in elevation to the plateau above limit upslope development, while flooding limits choices in the valley bottom. While economically logical, the conversion of farmland was not, according to at least one observer, a desirable or inevitable outcome. In an address to the Community Planning Association in Kamloops in 1952, J. Lewis Robinson, a professor of geography at the

University of British Columbia, encouraged local planners to preserve agricultural land by intensifying residential land use and, if necessary, "zoning agricultural land to protect it from [further] encroachment" (9). Robinson acknowledged that the city's future would likely be tied to "being the market and supply centre for southern B.C." (8). He argued, nevertheless, that as residential areas expanded into the region's limited agricultural lands, the city was "in danger of 'biting off the hand that feeds it'" (Robinson 10).

Kamloops' growth at this time, like that of other communities in the Interior, was spurred to a large degree by investments the British Columbia government made in the province's road network and "physical plant." These initiatives, and an increasing shortage of easily accessible timber on the coast, stimulated the Interior's forest industry and thus Kamloops' role as a service centre. Two sawmills were located in the city along with numerous small operations in the surrounding region. Government and other service sector employment, at an estimated 25% of the city's payroll in 1961, had become the leading contributor to the city's economic base (Black 88). Transportation also continued to play an important role. Employment in railway shops and in other transportation activities was estimated to account for nearly one-fifth of the city's payroll at this date. Retail and wholesale trade accounted for a similar proportion, while the manufacturing sector (sawmills plus a small oil refinery) generated 12%.

The origin of Kamloops' contemporary urban structure is rooted, to a large degree, in the resource boom of the 1960s and 1970s. Strong demand and rising commodity prices led to the construction of a sawmill and pulp mill complex on the south bank of the Thompson River, the expansion of the Royalite-Gulf Oil refinery in Brocklehurst,

and the extension of mining activities to the southwest and west of the city. The Weyerhaeuser pulp mill gradually became the city's single largest employer. It had over 800 people on staff when it opened its second mill in 1971. Further expansions increased staffing levels to almost 1,000 by 1980. The Bethlehem, Highmont, Lornex and Afton cluster of copper mines also contributed to the economy. The Afton mine, which began operating in 1979, was located only 12 kilometres west of the city centre (see Figure 3). It employed 300 workers. A small proportion of the 1,600 employed in the more distant mines in the Highland Valley lived in Kamloops. Nevertheless, these mines helped stimulate backward and forward linkages in the local economy. Heavy machinery suppliers (Finning), pipeline operators (Trans Mountain Pipe Lines), geotechnical firms (Placer Dome), exploration and drilling firms (Tonto), cement making (Lafarge), and a manufacturer of steel balls used to grind mined ore (Molycop) established bases in Kamloops.

These developments were clearly reflected in census returns. Between 1971 and 1981, employment in the primary sector more than doubled while the secondary sector (principally resource processing), transportation, and construction grew at rates similar to that of the labour force as a whole (see Figure 4). Employment in transportation continued to be the largest segment of the staples economy in absolute terms (see Figure 5). The greatest impact of the staples boom, however, was in the non-basic (services) sector.[3] High-wage, union jobs in the mines and mills translated into an increased demand for goods and services. In 1971 and in 1981, community, business and personal service employment was the largest segment of the city's labour force, increasing its share from approximately one-quarter in 1961 to one-third in 1981,

27

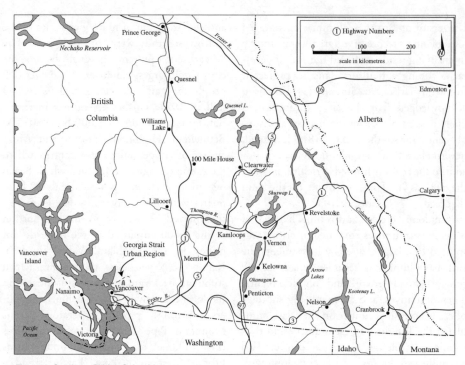

Figure 1: Southern British Columbia.

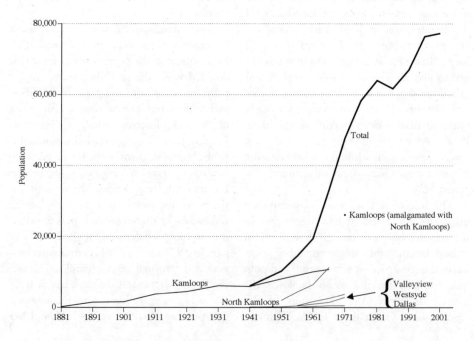

Figure 2:  Population growth, 1881-2001.

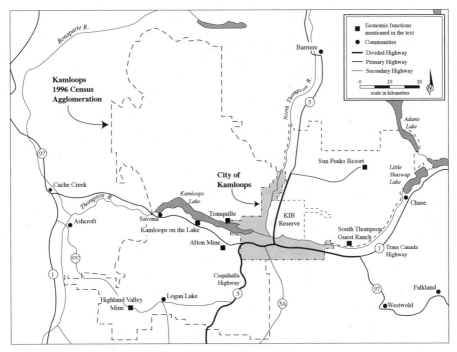

Figure 3: The Kamloops Region.

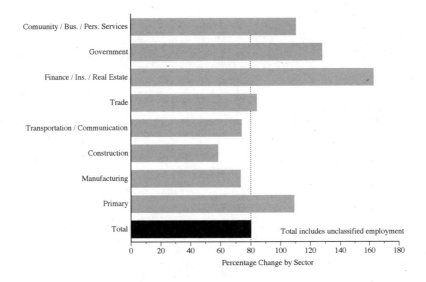

Figure 4: Sectoral change in Kamloops' labour force, 1971 to 1981.

29

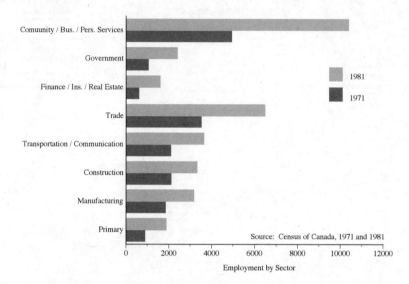

Figure 5: Kamloops' labour force, by industrial sector, 1971 and 1981.

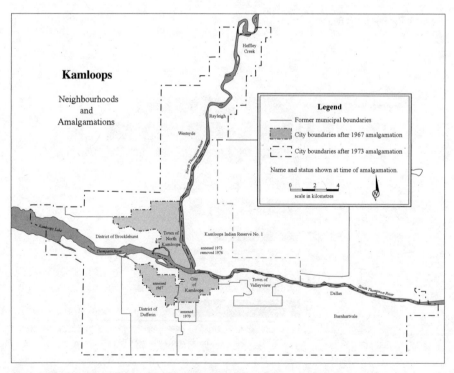

Figure 6: Municipal Boundaries of the City of Kamloops past and present.

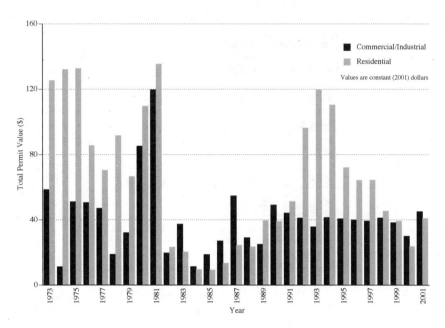

Figure 7: Residential and commercial construction, 1973 to 2001

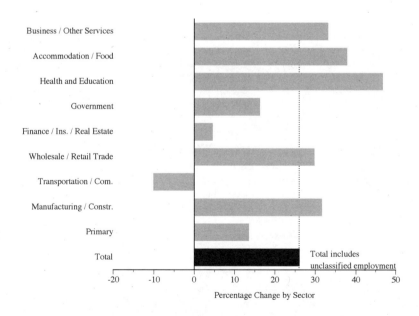

Figure 8: Sectoral change in Kamloops' labour force, 1986 to 1996.

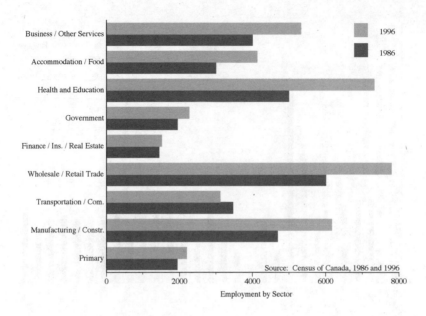

Figure 9: Kamloops' labour force, by industrial sector, 1986 and 1996.

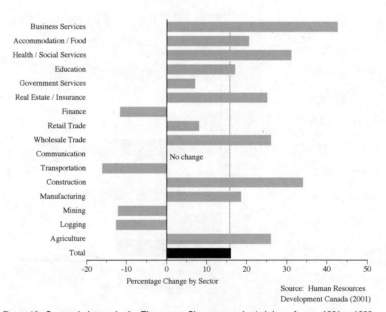

Figure 10: Sectoral change in the Thompson-Shuswap region's labour force, 1991 to 1996 .

32

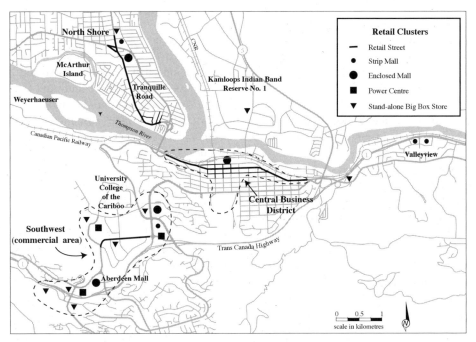

Figure 11: Principal retail areas in 2001.

representing more than 10,000 workers. Employment in the wholesale and retail trade held steady throughout this period at 20% of the city's workforce, while the smallest service sectors (government and finance, insurance, and real estate) recorded the greatest relative growth during the 1970s.

Growth in the service economy was reflected and abetted by the construction of four neighbourhood or regional malls, improvements to the highway network, and the opening or expansion of public sector (educational, medical, and legal) institutions. Cariboo College was one of several regional, two-year academic/vocational institutions established in the late 1960s and early 1970s in British Columbia. Its main campus was constructed on a bench on the southern edge of the city overlooking the confluence of the rivers. Satellite campuses in Williams Lake,

Merritt, Ashcroft, Lillooet, Clearwater, and 100 Mile House, as well as community offices in smaller centres, enlarged its student and faculty base. Kamloops' role as a regional service and distribution centre was further solidified by the completion of the Trans-Canada Highway (1962) through Rogers Pass, eliminating the circuitous Big Bend Highway and thereby significantly improving connections to Calgary and southern Alberta. A new highway to the north (Yellowhead, #5) similarly extended Kamloops' market range and improved links between the city and Edmonton (see Figures 1 and 3).

Vigorous growth in all sectors helped create a relatively diversified economy in this interior city. Indeed, a 1971 labour force study suggested that Kamloops, as well as a few other regional centres in British Columbia, had developed reasonably well-diversified economies (Li et al.). Kelowna, Prince George, Nanaimo, and Kamloops were identified as urban centres with levels of economic diversification that were not unlike that documented for the Vancouver-centred core region, whereas Trail, Powell River and Kitimat, for example, displayed much less diversification and more sector-specific specialization.[4]

Growth and economic diversification are fundamental goals of staples communities. However, extended periods of rapid development can also be a source of concern. After doubling between 1946 and 1961, the population more than doubled again to 47,800 by 1971 (see Figure 2). The legal boundaries of the city also expanded. North Kamloops and Kamloops amalgamated in 1967 (see Figure 6). In 1973, at the encouragement of the provincial government, the outlying municipalities of Dallas, Valleyview, and Westsyde, as well as the unincorporated communities of Brocklehurst, Dufferin, Rayleigh, Heffley Creek, and Barnthartvale joined the city. These changes extended the municipal limits 16 kilometres to the east of the downtown (to Campbell Creek) and nearly 32 kilometres to the north. In total, the city's boundaries enclosed 311 square kilometres (much of it semi-rural, agricultural, or hazard lands, with steep-sided, unstable slopes), making it one of the largest cities in British Columbia. The large spatial extent was in part dictated by the ungainly, linear configuration of existing settlement along the river valleys. Planners and civic officials, however, also wanted to ensure that there was space enough to accommodate anticipated growth. In the enlarged city's first official community plan, conservatively extrapolated growth rates (4% annual growth) suggested that the city's population would reach 75,000 by 1980, pass 100,000 by 1990, and top 160,000 by the year 2000 (City of Kamloops *Kamplan*). More aggressive estimates (6% annual growth) envisioned a city of 200,000 by the late 1980s. Planners also decided that new residential, commercial, and industrial developments should be concentrated initially in the southwest sector of the city to create a more compact urban region and thus a more economic and efficient infrastructure (roads, sewer, water, schools). This decision has proven important despite slower than anticipated growth. Kamloops' population increased at an average rate of 3% annually between 1971 and 1981 to a total just over 64,000. Since then, demographic growth has averaged 1.5% annually. The southwest sector has become, nevertheless, a principal focus of urban growth in the city. Adjacent to the university college and serviced by the Trans-Canada Highway, the southwest sector has left its staples-driven origins behind in the process of becoming the postindustrial (retail, education, and light-industrial) engine of Kamloops' current economy.

## Decline of the Staples Economy

A large service sector is not, by itself, a warranty against an economic downturn in a staples economy. According to economic base theory, the critical industries in an economy are those that draw in new money by exporting goods or services to other regions (basic activities). This direct monetary input can multiply when the new money subsequently circulates through industries that meet local demands (Kuby et al. 143). This process propelled Kamloops' economy during its golden years. However, the process can also work in reverse, as Kamloops and other communities in British Columbia's resource periphery demonstrated all too well in the early 1980s. A severe decline in the staples-exporting industries at this time multiplied through the economy, reducing employment in all sectors (Davis and Hutton; Barnes "External shocks").

Between 1982 and 1986, British Columbia suffered through a severe economic recession. Federal governments in industrial countries raised lending rates to 20% at this time in an attempt to curb double-digit inflation and cool down overheated economies (City of Kamloops *Kamloops* 2-3). The strategy worked, but the implications for British Columbia's staples economy were severe. The inflation-adjusted prices of lumber and copper fell by over 25% and 50% respectively, as shrinking industrial economies meant less demand for raw resources and thus lower commodity prices. In response, British Columbia's gross domestic product (GDP), which had grown at an annual average of 6.2% through the 1970s, fell hard. In 1982, the province's GDP dropped 10% (inflation adjusted). It was down a further 1% in 1983 and up only slightly in 1984. Marginally better results were recorded in the two following years; however, it took a strong performance in 1987 (+7%) for the province's GDP output to return to pre-recessionary levels.

The resource Interior of British Columbia was particularly hard hit as almost half of its regional districts lost population. Kamloops lost almost 2,500 residents — or approximately 4% of its total — between 1981 and 1986 (City of Kamloops, *Kamloops Tomorrow* 4-5). Housing starts collapsed from more than 1,100 per year in the early 1970s to fewer than 100 per year (see Figure 7) while all sectors of the economy lost workers. Manufacturing and construction employment fell over 25% and government services nearly 20%. Even jobs in the retail and finance, insurance and real estate industries shrank faster than the overall population as the unemployment rate rose from 7% to 15% (Statistics Canada).

The recession of the early 1980s was a catalyst for change in staples industries. When commodity prices recovered in the late 1980s, resource companies did not respond by rehiring workers. Concerned about future downturns, companies chose instead to invest in technology. The amalgamated Highland Valley copper mine, for example, currently employs only two-thirds of the workers employed at the mine in 1980. Nevertheless, the mine has maintained output by using capital-intensive equipment and technological systems, including both global positioning systems (GPS) and geographic information systems (GIS) that constantly monitor excavation and refining. Highland Valley was also able to introduce flexibility into its cost structure when the company, union, and provincial government agreed to a risk-sharing arrangement that tied wage and hydro rates to the price of copper (Cominco). Transportation, forestry, and utility companies have turned to similar technological solutions, as well as corporate restructuring, to reduce, or in some cases eliminate, both front-line and office workers. Weyerhaeuser, for instance, transferred most of its head office operations to Vancouver when its US parent acquired MacMillan Bloedel. BC Gas, BC Tel, and BC Hydro have also relocated or contracted out many of the functions they used to provide locally. In the mining sector, several companies have closed outright (Placer Dome's regional office) or, like home-grown Tonto Drilling, moved elsewhere (to Salt Lake City).

The magnitude of staples industries in Kamloops' current economy is not readily apparent in local census returns. Labour force statistics for Kamloops suggest that the primary and manufacturing sectors grew between 1986 and 1996, the latter at a faster rate than the overall labour force (see Figures 8 and 9). Part of the increase in the primary numbers is the result of intra-regional migration. Nearly half of Highland Valley's 1,100 employees now live in Kamloops. Miners have moved into the city in response to both new and improved highways and fears about the future of Logan Lake (the instant resource town created to serve the mine).[5] The mine closed for four months in 1999 due to low copper prices and is projected to cease operations in 2008. Detailed labour force statistics for the Thompson-Shuswap region reveal, more clearly than the Kamloops city data, the scale and nature of labour force change in Kamloops and its hinterland (see Figure 10). These figures indicate that while agriculture-related employment showed a slight increase between 1991 and 1996 — due primarily to the expansion of ginseng production in the South Thompson and Nicola Valleys — mining and forestry recorded sizable losses in employment in this period (-11.9 and -12.5% respectively, representing nearly 3,000 jobs in total). Similar losses were also recorded in the transportation category (-17%), reflecting the declining role of the railway in regional transportation.

Local and regional data are also indicative of structural changes in the manufacturing sector. In contrast to Fordist trends 40 years ago, but in line with post-Fordist theory, most new manufacturing enterprises were small in scale, relatively well diversified, and not necessarily tied to local resources or markets (BC Stats, Quarterly Regional Statistics).[6] New operations included two ginseng processing and export plants; a log home building operation; a specialized ticket printer supplying the BC Lottery Corporation as well as international customers (Pollard Banknote); and a microbrewery. "Bear Beer" was established in 1994; this was the first brewery to operate in the city since the 1920s. This company selected Kamloops because of local demographics and the city's proximity to other interior markets. Three years later, Bear Beer was producing

30,000 hectolitres of beer per year for the local market and for other breweries and outlets in the Pacific Northwest, western Canada, and even Asia. While the high-technology sector has not contributed substantially to secondary employment, it is being actively pursued. Technology Kamloops — a recently formed coalition of local politicians, educators and the business community — wants Kamloops to become one of only 30 cities in Canada to have a "community fibre network." The network would provide high-speed network capabilities to all citizens and businesses and thus help the city attract new "high-tech ventures" (Technology Kamloops).

## The New Postindustrial Economy

Service industries clearly have played an important role in Kamloops' economy for a long time. However, the decline of staples industries and their associated linkages, coupled with the rise of a global, postindustrial economy, has changed both the relative importance of staples and services and the character of the latter in the local economy. Perhaps the best illustration of shifts in the local economy is found in a government-sponsored analysis of local economic dependencies and impacts (BC Stats *BC Local*). According to this study, the public sector (education, health, justice, and government) is now the dominant sector in the Kamloops region (including Logan Lake and associated rural area). An estimated 27% of the "basic after-tax income is attributable to this sector" (BC Stats *BC Local* 23, 27). The primary sector, in comparison, generates 20% of the total (forestry 11%, mining 7%, and agriculture 2%) while transfer payments (16%) and investment income (10%) are also significant contributors (see Table 1). The study also indicates that Kamloops has one of the most diversified (and non-basic) economies in the Interior. Only urban areas in the Okanagan

## Cities

| Sector | Kamloops | Kelowna | Trail/ Rossland | Prince George | Williams Lake | Fort St. John | Port Hardy |
|---|---|---|---|---|---|---|---|
| Agriculture | 2 | 4 | 0 | 1 | 4 | 5 | 1 |
| Fishing | 0 | 0 | 0 | 0 | 0 | 0 | 5 |
| Forestry | 11 | 4 | 6 | 33 | 31 | 11 | 51 |
| Mining | 7 | 1 | 28 | 1 | 3 | 26 | 5 |
| Total Staples | 20 | 9 | 34 | 35 | 38 | 42 | 62 |
| Construction | 9 | 11 | 5 | 8 | 7 | 8 | 3 |
| Tourism | 6 | 6 | 4 | 4 | 7 | 7 | 7 |
| Public Sector | 27 | 21 | 23 | 24 | 22 | 19 | 16 |
| High Tech | 0 | 1 | 0 | 1 | 1 | 1 | 0 |
| Other Basic | 13 | 15 | 4 | 10 | 3 | 10 | 2 |
| Transfer/Investment | 26 | 36 | 30 | 18 | 22 | 15 | 10 |

Table 1: Basic sector income as a percent of total basic income, 1996.

and lower Fraser Valley equal or surpass Kamloops on these measures.

The general trend away from transportation and resource-related employment towards a more service-oriented employment base is also clear in labour force statistics. The health and education sectors registered the largest increase in employment between 1986 and 1996 and together constitute the second largest sector (after wholesale and retail trade) in the local economy (see Figure 8). Three of the five largest employers in Kamloops, furthermore, are found in this sector (see Table 2). Of particular importance is The University College of the Cariboo. In 1989, Cariboo College became a four-year degree-granting institution through partnership relationships with provincial universities, laying the foundation for considerable cultural and economic growth during the early 1990s (Wynn). The full- and part-time student population of the degree-granting institution

rose from fewer than 4,000 in 1989 to more than 7,000 in 1993 to approximately 9,000 at present. Together with the concomitant increase in staff and faculty, this growth provided a significant stimulus to the local housing market and to the overall economy. One estimate suggests that the 700 faculty and staff employed by The University College of the Cariboo in 1994/95, along with related indirect and direct expenditures by the institution, created 984 additional jobs and added $40 million to the local economy (Androkovich and Seldon 15). The University College of the Cariboo is also a key ingredient in efforts to attract high-technology businesses to the city, and in the promotion of the city's creative and cultural industries (Dubinsky and Garrett-Petts).

Quaternary and footloose service industries also began to establish new locations or expand existing operations in Kamloops during the late 1980s and the 1990s. Examples include the provincial lottery ticket centre (BC Lottery Corporation), a large planning, engineering, and consulting firm (Urban Systems), a call centre (Convergys), and, most recently, an aeronautical information provider (Nav Canada). These businesses have spurred the construction industry with major investments in new or existing properties, created backward linkages, and, particularly in the case of Convergys, expanded the labour market. Convergys is the major "tenant" in a suburban mall and employs 600 workers, making it the second largest private employer in Kamloops. The company was attracted to the city by federal and provincial training subsidies and, reportedly, by the "large number of skilled workers available" (*Kamloops This Week*). Unlike staples or manufacturing industries, call centres are not dependent on the location of physical resources or markets; their principal locational factor is labour. In search of pools of moderately skilled, yet inexpensive and committed labour (especially computer and communication systems workers), call centres have been attracted to peripheral areas in developed countries (Richardson and Marshall). In the case of Kamloops, the disappearance of jobs in staples industries has made call centre employment a necessary option for many workers.

Two other important ingredients in Kamloops' new, postindustrial economy are the retail and tourism sectors. Kamloops' central location in southern British Columbia has stimulated retail trade since its origins as a fur trading post. This situation has not changed. In fact, recent trends in the retail industry to larger (big box) and more specialized ("category killers") stores have increased the city's market range. Costco, Real Canadian Superstore, Wal-Mart, Michael's Crafts, Pier One Imports, Future Shop, Sport Mart, Toys "R" Us, Home

Hardware, Coast Mountain Sports, and Chapters Bookstores are some of the major national and international retail firms that have located in the city since the mid 1990s. Almost all of these stores, furthermore, are located in traditional malls, "power centres" or individual parcels in Kamloops' southwest sector (see Figure 11).[7] Planners directed development into the southwest in the 1970s, as noted earlier, in an attempt to create a more compact, serviceable city. Thus, this area has been the focus of most of the city's newer and more affluent residential subdivisions. Bisected by the Trans-Canada Highway, businesses are also attracted by the southwest's accessibility for consumers in outlying areas. Lured by low prices and greater selection, consumers regularly travel from Merritt, Ashcroft, Chase, the North Thompson communities, and even Williams Lake (three hours by car) to buy groceries and other low-order goods they once purchased exclusively in local markets (see Figures 1 and 3). This shopping and retail phenomenon has created its own linkages, as restaurants and motels have located nearby in an attempt to provide services to out-of-town, weekend shoppers.

Tourism is one of the growing sectors of the local economy. While it accounted for only 6% of the city's basic income in 1996, the tourism industry, as measured by employment in accommodation and food establishments, increased nearly 40% between 1986 and 1996, second only to health and education (BC Stats *BC Local*; see Figure 8). This increase, in part, reflects the efforts of local officials and organizations that vigorously promoted the city as a host for national and international sporting competitions. Since the early 1990s, Kamloops has hosted men's and women's provincial, national and world curling championships, the Canada Summer Games, the Memorial Cup, national colle-

| Employer | Employees |
| --- | --- |
| School District No. 73 | 1486 |
| Royal Inland Hospital | 1446 |
| Weyerhauser Canada | 920 |
| University College of the Cariboo | 800 |
| City of Kamloops | 650 |
| Convergys | 600 |
| Overlander Extended Care | 450 |
| Highland Valley Mine (Logan Lake) | 449* |
| Pollard Banknote | 320 |
| McDonalds Restaurants (5) | 315 |
| Canada Safeway | 306 |
| BC Lottery Corporation | 295 |
| Overwaitea | 262 |
| Ponderosa Lodge | 250 |
| Canadian Pacific Railway | 220 |
| Canada Post | 197 |
| Insurance Corporation of BC | 182 |
| Wal-Mart | 182 |
| Tolko Industries (sawmill) | 180 |
| Coopers Grocery | 178 |
| Costco Grocery | 178 |
| Real Canadian Superstore | 175 |
| Zellers | 157 |
| Paul Creek Slicing (Wood Processing) | 150 |
| Sears Canada | 150 |

* Employees living in Kamloops only. Source: Venture Kamloops, 2000.

Table 2. Major employers in Kamloops, 2000.

giate championships, national and provincial games for disabled and senior athletes, and professional hockey and football training camps. The facilities constructed or improved to host these events in turn have helped raise the city's reputation as a "Tournament Capital" and thus attract countless smaller competitions.

Tourism has also benefited from significant investments in the region's transportation infrastructure — most notably, the Coquihalla Highway. Completed in 1986, the Coquihalla Highway reduced the travel time between Kamloops' and Vancouver's city centres from more than six to less than four hours. Several new or significantly renovated resorts have been constructed in response to this compression of travel time between the core and the periphery. Under new ownership since 1992, Sun Peaks Ski Resort, for example, experienced more than $300 million in new investment in this decade. Located 40 minutes north of Kamloops, this resort was attracting more than 200,000 skiers per season by the end of the 1990s (see Figure 3). Together with 7 hotels, 24 shops, and new private homes, chalets and townhouse complexes, Sun Peaks was estimated to be creating several hundred seasonal jobs and generating nearly $40 million in revenue per year (Wishart). Other planned or completed resorts include: the South Thompson Guest Ranch, Kamloops-on-the-Lake (formerly Six Mile Ranch), and a yet-to-be-named complex on the old Tranquille sanitarium property at the head of Kamloops Lake. The Kamloops-on-the-Lake (Six Mile Ranch) project generated considerable controversy because land was removed from the Agricultural Land Reserve (ALR). Plans for this proposed resort include a championship golf course, a 100-boat marina, an equestrian centre, a back-country recreation area and fly fishing complex, a golf resort lodge and conference centre, a village hotel, and, in what could be seen as an ironic tribute to the ALR and the region's staples history, a working cattle ranch, guest ranch lodge, and themed retail village. The Kamloops-centred region is increasingly being promoted as a lifestyle and recreation destination in Vancouver and in other North American metropolitan centres.[8]

### Reactions to the Postindustrial Economy

The stabilization of some of the region's staples industries and the concomitant growth of postindustrial service industries helped reverse the population loss Kamloops experienced in the early 1980s. By 1991, Kamloops' population had risen to 67,000 and, after a strong surge in the early 1990s, topped 76,000 in 1996 (see Figure 2). Population growth appears to have slowed since then, as province-wide economic

growth shrank.[9] Residential and commercial construction followed a similar pattern, although the latter, reflecting investments in the retail sector and quaternary businesses, has held up in more recent years. At present, Kamloops is the fifth-largest community in British Columbia (according to Census definitions) and the second-largest municipality in the province's interior.

The spatial pattern of residential growth during this period has been very uneven. Most of the growth has occurred in the southwest sector and in outlying suburban areas. Residential areas adjacent to the CBD and in the older suburbs (in North Kamloops and parts of Brocklehurst) have stagnated or lost population, despite the availability of vacant, infill sites in these areas. Only 50% of the city's population now resides in the original urban concentrations on the South and North Shores. A similar, but much more dramatic, directional shift has also taken place in commercial land use. Since the construction of the suburban Aberdeen Mall in 1978, all of the CBD's department stores and many of its major retailers and grocery outlets have moved into the southwest sector (see Figure 11). Commercial areas in North Kamloops, Westsyde and Valleyview have also declined. Recent fieldwork conducted by the authors revealed a 15% vacancy rate along Tranquille Road, North Kamloops' main commercial drive.

While reluctant to regulate commercial growth in the southwest on the grounds of being branded "business unfriendly," the city has taken steps to encourage development in the CBD and older neighbourhoods on the North Shore. The city's "Official Community Plan" promotes, for example, the "concentration of intensive commercial [buildings], major public facilities, and cultural and high density residential [developments]" in the CBD in order to create a "vibrant and recognizable centre of the community" (City of Kamloops *Kamplan 1997* 20). Large public projects completed in the downtown since 1986 include a 5,000 seat arena (Riverside Coliseum, since renamed Sport Mart Place), a new municipal library and art gallery, a planning and civic services building, new headquarters for the Royal Canadian Mounted Police, and ongoing beautification of the principal downtown shopping district — Victoria Street (Favrholdt *Kamloops* 75). A proposal was also put forward for a publicly assisted convention centre; the proposal was shelved, however, after hotels in the southwest sector complained loudly about unfair competition and a public referendum did not solicit majority support for the proposal. Planners have also drawn heavily on "livable city" concepts in their efforts to retain the character of the older, heritage neighbourhoods and to take best advantage of the remaining view and riverfront sites within or near the urban core (City of Kamloops *City Centre*). These efforts, complemented by the establishment of a twice-a-week farmer's market and street- or park-based cultural events, have met with a measure of success. The former Canadian National Railway Station and associated industrial land was redeveloped into multi-family housing, and marketed to empty nesters and single urban professionals. This complex, nostalgically named "The Station Plaza," includes a neighbourhood restaurant and lower-floor retail space. Several large seniors-oriented apartment and activity complexes have also been constructed recently, while established downtown neighbourhoods — popular with educated professionals and others who value their accessibility and character — have experienced considerable social and commercial upgrading (City of

Kamloops *Kamloops Tomorrow #2* 5-6; Stewart and Moore 5-10).[10] These developments, in combination with the loss of anchor retail tenants, are changing the personality of Kamloops' CBD. Once the centre of town, the CBD is gradually developing a lifestyle community to complement its traditional high-order business and commercial functions.

Initiatives on the north shore of Kamloops have focused on the revitalization of Tranquille Road. This road, once the main street of the separate municipality of North Kamloops, is now a struggling commercial strip populated by second-hand stores, automobile-oriented businesses, ethnic restaurants, and neighbourhood services. At the request of the local business community in the early 1980s and again in the mid 1990s, the city twice implemented strategies to capitalize on its "unrealized potential as a major pedestrian-oriented shopping street" (City of Kamloops *Tranquille Road*; City of Kamloops *North Shore* 7). Improvements included the removal of overhead wiring, the addition of trees, planters, bricked sidewalks, benches and ornamental lighting, and the encouragement — through guidelines and grants — of façade improvements. The objective was thus not to compete head on with high-volume, low-margin retailers, but to offer an alternative: a human-scaled, "funky" market street. Other recent initiatives and plans call for a "Smart Park" at the airport (high-technology businesses and light industries), a tourist-related hotel and marina facility near McArthur Island (a major sporting / tournament venue), a resort on the former Tranquille sanitarium site, a mental health facility, a mini-call centre, and a performing arts centre (NSBIA *North Shore*; NSBIA *Kamloops Airport*).

As in the CBD, there are important social

undercurrents to these postindustrial developments on the North Shore. In particular, there is a sense and a concern that the North Shore — once a solid blue-collar, yet middle-class, collection of neighbourhoods — is being left behind. This concern came to the fore in public reaction to a proposed low-income housing project. Many local residents and business owners were opposed to the project because the site selected was part of an area identified for a central market in the Tranquille revitalization plan. While city planners questioned the current feasibility of this element, residents felt that it was a critical ingredient in efforts to stimulate business and halt residential decline. If the revitalization plans were effectively set aside, locals reasoned, socio economic differences between the North Shore — now home to some of the city's poorest neighbourhoods — and the South Shore would only widen. Similar sentiments were subsequently expressed in public planning meetings (City of Kamloops *2001 Citizen*) and surveys. North Shore respondents to the city's "Citizen Satisfaction Survey" tended to rate quality of life indicators much lower than residents in other areas (City of Kamloops *2001 Citizen*). North Shore residents also had greater concerns about crime, police services, and basic infrastructure (street lighting and sidewalks). The recent relocation of the area's only department store (Zellers) to the city's southwest raised a similar outcry about uneven development. City council and planners are taking these concerns seriously. A design workshop involving local residents and business owners was held recently to generate a development plan for the market centre site (City of Kamloops *MacKenzie Island*).[11] Two additional workshops were organized for nearby lots on Tranquille Road. The Kamloops City Council has also asked planners to revisit the city's official community plan ahead of

schedule in order to address the broader issues as promptly as possible.

## Conclusion

The deep recession of the 1980s influenced more than just the way staples industries do business. It also had an impact on the province's staples mentality — the once-firm belief that the extraction and export of staples is the "natural" economy of British Columbia. In the Lower Mainland core, and in the periphery, there is now a general acknowledgment that staples industries, for a variety of economic and environmental reasons, will and should play a less significant role in British Columbia's economic future (Wood 193). The transition to a postindustrial service economy, thus, has been both welcomed and actively pursued by public officials and the business community in Kamloops and elsewhere. High-technology, retail, tourism, and public service jobs are not only needed to compensate for lost staples employment and to insulate the economy from cyclical fluctuations in commodity prices; they are the economic future.

While seen as necessary and inevitable, planners and labour market analysts are also apprehensive about the labour force transformation. Service jobs, particularly those in the retail, tourism, and communication sectors, pay relatively low wages. These sectors also rely more heavily on part-time and seasonal employment, and provide less generous (if any) benefit packages (City of Kamloops *Kamloops Tomorrow #1* 8). Together with the general "decrease in higher paying resource sector jobs," the growth of the service sector may result in a less affluent community, and, in turn, create long-term affordability, taxation and servicing issues for the city (City of Kamloops *North Shore* 6). The negative side of the postindustrial economy is also showing up in trends on the city's North Shore and in its CBD. The growth of postindustrial sectors has both diversified and stabilized the local economy. But it also appears to be undermining the traditional functions of these areas and magnifying the socioeconomic differences between neighbourhoods.

The range and character of social and economic changes in Kamloops indicates that the impact of postindustrial and post-Fordist forces in interior cities can differ markedly from those in Vancouver or small communities in the periphery. Unlike Vancouver, Kamloops has not developed significant employment in the high technology or business-service sectors. Extensive areas of gentrified housing, an isolated underclass, and "edge cities" are similarly absent in Kamloops. Yet, unlike in Powell River, Tumbler Ridge or Port Alberni, postindustrial and post-Fordist trends have helped stabilize and diversify Kamloops' economy. The city has also developed a more complex urban geography, one in which "big city" phenomena are starting to emerge. The Kamloops experience appears to fall somewhere between those of the Lower Mainland core and the traditional periphery, suggesting that responses to the opportunities and challenges posed by postindustrial economies are, at the very least, scale dependent.

The transition to a postindustrial economy has also affected Kamloops' status in British Columbia's urban hierarchy. The arrival of big-box retailers and the expansion of post-secondary and medical facilities have extended the city's hinterland, and, in tandem with the decline of staples industries, have altered its traditional relationship with the Vancouver-centred core. Kamloops' largest staples industries are still controlled from head offices in Vancouver. However, the control centres of most of its new services are located elsewhere. Convergys' head office is in Ohio, Wal-Mart's is in Arkansas, and

Costco's is in Washington State. The Kamloops airport is currently run by Vancouver Airport Services, a subsidiary of the Vancouver International Airport Authority. Nav Canada's geographical organization, however, ignores this fact; the mandate of its Kamloops operation is to provide, not receive, flight information services to the rest of the province. Thus, it may not simply be a case, as Davis suggests, of Vancouver "decoupling" from the periphery. As the nature of the periphery, and its relationships with other control centres evolve, the linkages between Vancouver and the rest of the province are weakening from both directions.

It is clear that the structure of Kamloops' workforce changed significantly during the last two decades, and that this change has altered the city's internal characteristics and external connections. Nonetheless, one must be careful not to overstate the case. At present, Kamloops still derives a relatively sizable amount of its basic income from staples industries. It also remains to be seen whether Kamloops can develop a high-wage and value-added high-technology sector. The current global downturn in this sector, and stiff competition from the more rapidly growing conurbation in the central Okanagan, has dampened short-term prospects. Yet, without more substantial, high-order postindustrial employment, Kamloops' ability to weather the scheduled closure of the Highland Valley copper mine, reduce leakage, and escape its traditional dependence on foreign markets, capital, and control centres is doubtful. As a relatively small city in a relatively remote and under-populated province, Kamloops will long be subject to the twists and turns of the global economy. The driving sectors of the local economy may have changed, but not the underlying economic and power relationships.

## Notes

1. Backward linkages are all of the necessary economic inputs that support resource extraction (such as the building of transportation systems); forward linkages are a measure of the value added to the staple through further processing; and final demand economic linkages are the total goods and services produced for the local, domestic market (Watkins 55; McGillivray 96).

2. Agglomeration economies are the economic advantages and savings that arise in industrial concentrations. They permit the sharing of specialized knowledge and equipment, large-scale purchasing and marketing, access to a common pool of skilled labour, and other mutual benefits, including shared public utilities and communication facilities. (Fellman et al. 328).

3. Economic activities can be divided into "basic" (or export-earning) activities and "non-basic" (or service) activities (Wood 182).

4. The authors of the study used a city-sized adjusted specialization index to measure the degree to which employment was concentrated in particular economic sectors. Places with an equal percentage in each sector received an index of 1. Kamloops' index value was 1.93. In comparison, Kelowna, Prince George and Nanaimo had index values of 2.05, 1.73, and 1.36, respectively. Values for smaller, resource-dependent communities tended to be much higher. Kitimat's index, for example, was 5.21, Trail's 3.35, and Powell River's 4.27. Vancouver (2.34) and Victoria (3.48) also registered higher degrees of sector specialization than that calculated for Kamloops (Li et al.).

5. The Highland Valley mine is only a 40-minute commute over the Coquihalla Highway. The town of Logan Lake is now part of the Kamloops census agglomeration (see Figure 3).

6. The term Fordism refers to: "the mass production of standardized goods, usually at a centralized assembly plant," as pioneered by Henry Ford in the automobile industry (Wallace 244). Post-Fordism reflects a move away from the mass production of standardized products towards "the fragmentation of the production process, whereby the phases of a given process are divided and assigned various locations in the most cost efficient manner" (Barnes 56 and McGillivray 99). The rise of information technology and improved telecommunications has led to the reshaping of the production (and consumption) process.

7. Category killers are national retail chains that feature low prices and a wide range of selection (makes and models) for a limited number of products. Future Shop, which specializes in home electronics and appliances, is an example. Power centres are shopping centres that have many big box, discount, and category killer stores. Unlike traditional malls, stores in a power centre are typically separated by parking areas and thus do not share walls or a common roof.

8. A full-page, colour advertisement appeared in *The Globe and Mail* on September 21, 2000, promoting "waterfront lots" at Stump Lake, near Kamloops. This advertisement reveals some significant aspects of the new regional economy of the Kamloops region: "We can provide what every high-flying ... high-tech whiz kid needs ... dot. calm." Complete with a panoramic photograph of Stump Lake and its pastoral surroundings in the Nicola Valley, the advertisement promotes the climate of the southern Interior, the region's "western ranch culture" and the area's relative accessibility to Vancouver — "only a 3-hour drive from Vancouver and featuring ... one of the best fly fishing lakes in the world and countless activities for the whole family."

9. The 2001 census lists Kamloops' population as 77,281. Local officials feel, however, that this figure is too low given the amount of residential home construction since 1996.

10. There is a concentration of The University College of the Cariboo faculty in downtown neighbourhoods, including the "West End," the oldest residential neighbourhood within the municipal limits of Kamloops.

11. The low-income housing project was built on an alternative site on the North Shore.

## Works Cited

Amin, Ash. *Post-Fordism*. Oxford: Blackwell, 1994.

Androkovich, Robert A., and James R. Seldon. "The Economic Impact of The University College of the Cariboo on the Region: 5 Years of Growth." Unpublished paper. Kamloops, BC, June 22, 1995.

Angel, David. *Restructuring for Innovation: The Remaking of the US Semiconductor Industry*. New York: Guilford, 1994.

Balf, Mary. *Kamloops: A History of the District up to 1914*. 3rd ed. Kamloops: Kamloops Museum Association, 1989.

Barman, Jean. *The West Beyond the West: A History of British Columbia.* Toronto: U of Toronto P, 1996.

Barnes, Trevor. "External shocks: Regional Implications of an Open Staple Economy." *Canada and the Global Economy: The Geography of Structural Change.* Ed. John N.H. Britton. Montreal: McGill-Queen's UP, 1996. 48-68.

———. *Logics of Dislocation.* New York: Guilford, 1996.

Barnes, Trevor, and Roger Hayter. "Economic Restructuring, Local Development and Resource Towns: Forest Communities in Coastal British Columbia." *Canadian Journal of Regional Studies* 17 (1994): 289-310.

Bell, Daniel. *The Coming of Post-Industrial Society: A Venture in Social Forecasting.* New York: Basic, 1973.

Belshaw, John, and David Mitchell. "The Economy since the Great War." *The Pacific Province: A History of British Columbia.* Ed. Hugh J.M. Johnston. Vancouver: Douglas & McIntyre, 1996. 313-342.

Black, John. "Kamloops, A City in the Southern Intermountain Region of British Columbia." Unpublished MA thesis. Kent, OH: Kent State University, 1965.

Bradbury, John. "British Columbia: Metropolis and Hinterland in Microcosm." *Heartland and Hinterland: A Geography of Canada.* Ed. Larry McCann. Scarborough, ON: Prentice, 1987. 400-441.

BC Stats. *After Much Economic Diversification, B.C. Exports are Still Mainly Resource Based.* Victoria: Ministry of Finance and Corporate Relations, Exports (B.C. Origin), November 2000.

———. *British Columbia's Changing Industrial Structure.* Victoria: Ministry of Finance and Corporate Relations, Business Indicators, November 1998.

———. *B.C. Local Area Economic Dependencies and Impact Ratios — 1996.* Victoria: Ministry of Finance and Corporate Relations, 1999.

———. *Export Emphasis Shifts to Manufactured Goods as Resource Commodities Falter.* Victoria: Ministry of Finance and Corporate Relations, Exports (B.C. Origin), March 1998.

Bryson, John, Peter Daniels, Nick Henry, and Jane Pollard, eds. *Knowledge, Space, Economy.* London: Routledge, 2000.

Castells, Manuel. *The Information Age: Economy, Society and Culture.* Malden, MA: Blackwell, 1996-97.

City of Kamloops. *KamPlan.* Kamloops, BC: Stanley Associates Engineering Ltd., 1974.

———. *Tranquille Road Commercial Plan: A Report on Development Opportunities.* Kamloops, BC, 1982.

City of Kamloops, Department of Development Services. *2001 Citizen Satisfaction Survey Final Report.* Kamloops, BC, 2001.

———. *City Centre Plan.* Kamloops, BC, 1994.

———. *Kamloops: A Demographic Profile.* Kamloops, BC, 1989.

———. *Kamloops Tomorrow: Planning for the Twenty-First Century, Background Newsletter #1, Population.* Kamloops, BC, 1995.

———. *Kamloops Tomorrow: Planning for the Twenty-First Century, Background Newsletter #2, Land Use.* Kamloops, BC, 1995.

———. *Kamloops Trends 2000.* Kamloops, BC, 2000.

———. *KamPlan 1997: A Community Plan for Kamloops.* Kamloops, BC, 1997.

———. *MacKenzie Island Design Charrette Summary Report.* Kamloops, BC, 2002.

———. *North Shore Revitalization: Strategy and Concept Plan.* Kamloops, BC, 1995.

Cominco *Annual Report.* Vancouver, BC, 1999.

Davis, H. Craig. "Is the Metropolitan Vancouver Economy Uncoupling from the Rest of the Province?" *BC Studies* 98 (1993): 3-19.

Davis, H. Craig, and Thomas A. Hutton. "The Two Economies of British Columbia." *BC Studies* 82 (1989): 3-15.

Denike, Ken G., and Roger Leigh. "Economic Geography 1960-70." *British Columbia.* Ed. J. Lewis Robinson. Toronto: U of Toronto P, 1972. 69-86.

Dicken, Peter. *Global Shift: The Internationalization of Economic Activity.* New York: Guilford, 1992.

Dubinsky, Lon, and W.F. Garrett-Petts. "'Working Well, Together': Arts-based Research and the Cultural Future of Small Cities." *AI and Society* 16 (2002): 332-349.

Elam, Mark. "Puzzling out the Post-Fordist Debate: Technology, Markets and Institutions." *Post-Fordism.* Ed. Ash Amin. Oxford: Blackwell, 1994. 43-70.

Favrholdt, Ken. "Domesticating the Drybelt: Agricultural Settlement in the Hills around Kamloops, 1860-1960." *Beyond the City Limits: Rural History in British Columbia.* Ed. Ruth W. Sandwell. Vancouver: U of British Columbia P, 1999. 102-119.

45

———. *Kamloops, Meeting of the Waters: An Illustrated History.* Burlington, ON.: Windsor Publications, 1989.

Fellmann, Jerome D., Arthur Getis, and Judith Getis. *Human Geography: Landscapes of Human Activities.* New York: McGraw, 2003.

Forward, Charles N. "Urban system." *British Columbia: Its Resources and People.* Ed. Charles N. Forward. Victoria, BC: U of Victoria Department of Geography, Western Geographical Series 22, 1987. 359-382.

Gilroy, William. *Xeriscaping: The Reluctant Emergence of a Residential Landscape in Kamloops.*Kamloops: UCC Research Report funded by the Royal Canadian Geographic Society, 2000.

Gordon, Sally, Stewart Rubin, John J. Chen, and Natasa Agathocleous. *Gauging Economic Diversity in Canadian Cities.* Toronto: Moody's Investor Services, 2000.

Harris, R. Cole. *The Resettlement of British Columbia: Essays on Colonialism and Geographical Change.* Vancouver: U of British Columbia P, 1997.

Harvey, David. *The Condition of Postmodernity.* Oxford: Blackwell, 1989.

Hay, Robert, and Ken Favrholdt. *Biodiversity of the Shuswap-South Thompson Region: A Cross Cultural Overview.* Report prepared for the Living Landscapes project. Victoria: Royal British Columbia Museum, 1996.

Hayter, Roger. *Flexible Crossroads: The Restructuring of British Columbia's Forest Economy.* Vancouver : U of British Columbia P, 2000.

———. *The Dynamics of Industrial Location: The Factory, the Firm, and the Production System.* New York: Wiley, 1997.

Hepworth, Mark E. *Geography of the Information Economy.* New York: Guilford, 1990.

Holmes, John. "Restructuring in a Continental Production System." *Canada and the Global Economy: The Geography of Structural Change.* Ed. John N.H. Britton. Montreal: McGill-Queen's UP, 1996. 230-254.

Hutton, T.A. "The Innisian Core-Periphery Revisited: Vancouver's Changing Relationships with British Columbia's Staple Economy." *BC Studies* 113 (1997): 69-100.

———."Vancouver as a Control Centre for British Columbia's Resource Hinterland: Aspects of Linkage and Divergence in a Provincial Staple Economy." *Troubles in the Rainforest: British Columbia's Forest Economy in Transition.* Ed. Trevor Barnes and Roger Hayter. Victoria, BC: Western Geographical Press, U of Victoria Department of Geography, Canadian Western Geographical Series 33, 1997. 233-262.

Innis, H. *The Fur Trade in Canada: An Introduction to Canadian Economic History.* Toronto: U of Toronto P, 1930.

Kamloops This Week. "Convergys Corporation Announces 600 Employee Call Center in Kamloops." *Kamloops This Week* 26 January 2000. 11 April 2001. <http://www.linxbc.com/Convergysnews.html>

Kuby, Michael, John Harner, and Patricia Gober. *Human Geography in Action.* New York: Wiley, 2001.

Kunin, Rosly, and Joachim Knauf. *Skill Shifts in Our Economy: A Decade in the Life of British Columbia.* Vancouver: Canada Employment and Immigration, Regional Economic Services Branch, 1992.

Li, Shiu-Yeu, Douglas Scorrar, and Michael H. Williams. "City Functions, Manufacturing Activity, and the Urban Hierarchy." *Readings in Canadian Geography.* Ed. R. Irving. Toronto: Holt, 1978. 89-101.

Mandel, Charles. "Silicon Vineyards." *ROB Magazine.* June 2000. 11 April 2001. <http://search.robmagazine.com/archive/2000ROBj une/html/ft_silicon.html.>

Massey, Doreen B, and John Allen. *Uneven Re-development: Cities and Regions in Transition.* London: Hodder and Stoughton, 1988.

McGillivray, Brett. *Geography of British Columbia: People and Landscapes in Transition.* Vancouver: U of British Columbia P, 2000.

McKinnon, Ian. *The British Columbia Economy and the Forest Industry.* One of a series of "Focus on our forests" discussion papers prepared for the BC Ministry of Forests. Victoria: Pacific Issues Partners, 1999.

McLean, Alistair. "History of the Cattle Industry in British Columbia." *Rangelands* 4 (1982): 130-34.

Moffat, Riley M. *Population History of Cities and Towns in Canada, Australia, and New Zealand: 1861-1996.* Lanham, MD: Scarecrow Press, 2001.

Momer, Bernard. "The Small Town that Grew and Grew and … A Look at Rapid Urban Growth and Social Issues in Kelowna, British Columbia, Canada." *Salzburger Geographische Arbeiten* 32 (1998): 65-80.

Morse, Jock. *Kamloops: The Inland Capital.* Kamloops: Kamloops Museum Association, 1957.

North Shore Business Improvement Association. *Kamloops Airport Area Land Use and Development Plan.* North Shore Business Improvement Association, Kamloops: Urban Systems, 2000.

———. *North Shore Development Opportunities Assessment.* North Shore Business Improvement Association, Kamloops: Urban Systems, 1999.

Parker, Paul. "Canada-Japanese Coal Trade: An Alternative Form of Staple Production." *The Canadian Geographer* 41 (1997): 248-67.

Richardson, Ranald, and J. Neill Marshall. "The Growth of Telephone Call Centres in Peripheral Areas of Britain: Evidence from Tyne and Wear." *Area* 28 (1996): 308-317.

Richardson, Ranald, Vicki Belt, and J. Neill Marshall. "Taking Calls to Newcastle: the Regional Implications of the Growth in Call Centres." *Regional Studies* 34 (2000): 357-369.

Robinson, J. Lewis. "Agriculture and Industry in a Growing Community." Paper presented to the *BC Divisional Conference of the Community Planning Association.* Kamloops, BC, October 1952.

Rollins, Rick. "Tourism." *British Columbia, the Pacific Province: Geographical Essays.* Ed. Collin J.B. Wood. Victoria, BC: Western Geographical Press, U of Victoria Department of Geography, Canadian Western Geographical Series 36, 2001. 215-228.

Rubenstein, James M. *The Changing US Auto Industry: A Geographical Analysis.* London: Routledge, 1992.

Science and Technology Council of the Okanagan. *Okanagan High-Tech Study.* Study prepared for Economic Development Commission, Regional District of Central Okanagan, Science and Technology Council of the Okanagan, Okanagan High Tech Council, Victoria: Calibre Strategic Services, 2001.

Scott, Allen J. *New Industrial Spaces.* London: Pion, 1988.

———. "The Technopoles of Southern California." *Environment and Planning A.* 22 (1990): 1575-1605.

Statistics Canada. *Census of Canada.* Ottawa: Government of Canada, 1981.

———. *Census of Canada.* Ottawa: Government of Canada, 1986.

———. *Census of Canada.* Ottawa: Government of Canada, 2001.

Stewart, Carla, and Tracy Moore. *Inner City Redevelopment in a Small City: Kamloops, British Columbia.* Kamloops, BC: UCC Research Report, funded by the Royal Canadian Geographic Society, 1997.

Technology Kamloops. *Towards a Connected Community: A Vision for a Community Fibre Network.* 11 October 2001. <http://www.city.kamloops.bc.ca/technology/cfn/cfn.html>

Venture Kamloops. *Kamloops Community Profile.* Kamloops, BC: Venture Kamloops, 2000.

Wallace, Iain. *A Geography of the Canadian Economy.* Don Mills, ON.: Oxford UP, 2002.

Watkins, Mel H. "A Staple Theory of Economic Growth." *Canadian Journal of Economics and Political Science* 29 (1963): 141-148.

Weir, Thomas R. *Ranching in the Southern Interior Plateau of British Columbia.* Ottawa: Geographical Branch, Mines and Technical Surveys, Memoir #4, 1964.

Wishart, Allan. "Sun Peaks: World Class Resort." *Kamloops This Week.* 25 March 2001.

Wood, Collin J.B. "Spatial Economy." *British Columbia, the Pacific Province: Geographical Essays.* Ed. Collin J.B. Wood. Victoria, BC: Western Geographical Press, U of Victoria Department of Geography, Canadian Western Geographical Series 36, 2001. 175-196.

Wynn, Graeme. "Walking the Tightrope of Compromise: Developing Arts Degree Programs in New Hybrid Institutions." Paper presented to the Canadian Studies Association Workshop on Higher Education in Canada and Israel. Jerusalem, 1998.

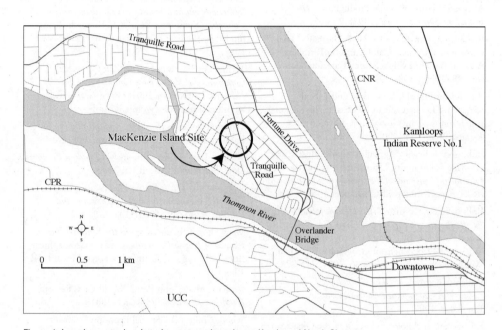

Figure 1. Location map showing charrette project site on Kamloops' North Shore[1]

# Culture and Community in Kamloops: Observations from the Small Cities Initiative

## Lon Dubinsky, Ross Nelson, and Julie Schooling

### Introduction

In February 2002, over three hundred people attended the opening of three new exhibitions at the Kamloops Art Gallery: a survey of works by nationally known painter Takao Tanabe; "Tapestry Gardens," a solo show by local artist Tricia Sellmer; and 40 small pieces by members of the Kamloops Water Media Artists. This combination embodied the gallery's commitment to showing historical and ·contemporary work and to programming aimed at community involvement. The number of visitors may seem small relative to a *vernissage* at a large institution, but it is significant for the gallery and for Kamloops, that is, for a city with a population of just over 80,000.

This engagement calls attention to cultural participation in a small city. Traditionally, and increasingly so in Canada, when we think of cities, we think big: Toronto, Montreal, or Vancouver. We might include Calgary, Winnipeg, or Ottawa, whose populations have swelled because of amalgamation. The small city, with a population between 50,000 and 100,000, often goes unnoticed — even by many who live there — as eyes fix on mega-cities in Canada and abroad, or on smaller places and rural areas at the other end of the continuum.

Kamloops has much to tell us about cultural life in the small city because it is currently the site of a multi-year and multifaceted research and community-based initiative called "The Cultural Future of Small Cities." What follows is an account of one planning project that consisted of an historical and economic study of Tranquille Road, the main thoroughfare in Kamloops' North Shore area, and a design charrette undertaken by the City of Kamloops that coincided with this research. A review of this project serves two purposes: (1) to demonstrate how planning research and community engagement are working in concert within the context of a larger initiative in and about Kamloops; and (2) to identify several aspects of participation when community development and cultural planning come together — aspects that may have implications for researchers, planners, arts and heritage staff, and citizens, especially those in cities of comparable size.

### Cultural Assets

First, as the Small Cities CURA proceeds and more local groups and organizations become involved, Kretzmann and McKnight's notion of asset-building community development continues to inform the initiative. For example, the Biography of Streets Project described below is contributing to the city's self-knowledge. The research and the design charrette that coincided with it have become part of an inclusive community planning process. From the outset, both have involved diverse participants and have recognized different views on what comprises a city's cultural assets and infrastructure.

### Cultural Expression

Second, because heritage is recognized as a key component of a city's assets and a determinant of what counts as its infrastructure, several research projects are documenting Kamloops' cultural past and present. More specifically, visual artists are participating in these investigations or in phases of other projects. In some cases, the artist works closely with a researcher and community partner, becoming in effect a co-researcher producing work integral to our study. In others, the artist is an observer who will make a new work or contribute an existing one in response to a specific research agenda. In all cases, the works will culminate in an exhibition at the art gallery and other venues. For example, the Representing Kamloops theme features a community mapping project that includes art-as-research (Garrett-Petts and Lawrence).

### Cultural Participation

Third, as the work of Hayden and others in public history demonstrates, the engagement of artists and/or citizens as researchers is not confined to smaller cities, but as the city of Kamloops illustrates, making and celebrating history in a small city allows the whole community to get involved, and in potentially diverse ways. This engagement is part of a larger phenomenon of participation in Kamloops, and, as indicated at the outset, one of the factors that led to the emergence of the Small Cities initiative. Participation in

general is also the focus of researchers such as Bennett Berger, who suggests exploring the relationship between the cultural (i.e., symbolic) choices that people make and the social locations in which they take place. This attention is also one way of asking what civic engagement really means and what it takes culturally to be an "intelligent community," to use Peter Katz's term for a city that is both livable and economically sustainable.

### The Culture of Participation

Finally, the small cities initiative itself is a microcosm of cultural participation in Kamloops. We are a diverse group of people including staff from arts organizations, university researchers and students, staff from a social agency, a forest extension partnership, a First Nations society, a business group and local government, elementary school children and teachers, and local residents. How we collaborate, but also conflict, is being documented and assessed in order to further understand the dynamics of participation that go into creating and sustaining cultural life in a small city. The very idea of what makes a community remains central to how we work as an entity and, in particular, to how the initiative is working as a community-university alliance.

### A Focus on Culture and Planning

If ever there was an issue and field that can be served by collaboration, it is urban planning. When conflict about land use increases and the demand for facilities and services accelerates as cities grow, the need to work differently in order to work well together becomes even more pressing. Indeed, as planning issues multiply, so do the participants who may be involved: municipal politicians and planning staff, developers, businesses and business associations, residents' organizations and other community groups, social agencies, and individual citizens. From the beginning, the Small Cities CURA recognized that these challenges and possibilities have a direct connection to culture, whether the focus is on supporting artists and arts organizations, on integrating a cultural component into a new development, or on what was identified as cultural participation and the culture of participation. With respect to participation, the City of Kamloops was therefore approached to be not only a funder of projects, and, in particular, a series of Small Cities forums, but as a full community research partner. The intention and the hope were and are that research and community activities will dovetail with the city's overall planning agenda and, more specifically, with its plans for the arts and culture.

Both objectives are beginning to see fruition in several coincidental and collaborative ways. The most substantive research work thus far is the Biography of a Street Project, which has taken place in the North Shore area of Kamloops, specifically the main thoroughfare Tranquille Road. This research is providing an historical and economic context and analysis for "KamPlan," the city's five-year development strategy currently in preparation. It is also a key reference point for a series of community consultations about the future of the North Shore, where cultural issues are now an integral part of the agenda. The research coincided with a design charrette, organized by the City of Kamloops, which involved two local groups, the North Shore Business Improvement Association (NSBIA) and the North Shore Residents Association (NSRA). What follows is the biography of the Biography of a Street Project and the account of the charrette, which, among other things, explored the possibility of artists' spaces as part of a mixed-use development in a previously contested parcel of land.

## Culture and Community on Tranquille Road

### Context

An economic and spatial history of Tranquille Road provides an understanding and appreciation of the events that led up to the charrette and describes the character of the proposed site and buildings. The history provides several points of entry for asking questions about the ownership and obligation of official plans, the construction of collective identity, the framing of debates, and the ties between our cultural and political economies. Kamloops is a city of 86,000 people, making it the fifth most populous urban area in British Columbia. Like the rest of the BC interior, the Kamloops economy traditionally relied on staples industries while transportation and services have also played an important role due to the city's central location. However, over the last 20 years, the economy has shifted. Staples industries and their associated linkages have declined while postindustrial industries have grown. Public services like education, health, and legal, are now the city's most vibrant economic sector.

The economic shift has a local geographic counterpart. Most of Kamloops' recent growth has occurred in the city's southwest, where the university, light industrial parks, new subdivisions, and retail space are concentrated. While the downtown is still the most densely settled part of the city, and contains most of Kamloops' high-order services and entertainment functions, its future as a retail centre is less certain. The last department store in the downtown moved to the southwest in the fall of 2001. The growth of the southwest has also hurt commercial areas in the city's north shore neighbourhoods, including North Kamloops, Brocklehurst, and Westsyde, areas that developed during the resource boom of the 1950s and 1960s. Fuelled by strong commodity prices and large

51

public sector investments, the city doubled in size from 1951 to 1961 and then doubled again by 1971. The city grew another 50% by 1981. The North Shore's flat, low-lying areas absorbed much of this growth, as residential neighbourhoods replaced apple orchards and tomato fields (MacKinnon and Nelson).

Tranquille Road developed as the North Shore's major arterial-commercial strip during this growth phase. The commercial stretch of Tranquille begins at the bridge connecting Kamloops' north and south shores, runs west and then north for two kilometres, terminating in a commercial centre. Many older residents fondly remember the street as the downtown of North Kamloops. It featured a range of retail, service, institutional, and industrial land uses. However, like many postwar strips, it was not a beautiful or pedestrian-friendly environment. Tranquille Road was dominated by the automobile, automobile-oriented services and rough-and-ready cinder-block architecture. By the late 1970s, it was beginning to show its age and signs of decline (Nelson et al).

At the same time, Kamloops' first indoor shopping mall (Thompson Park Mall) and major department stores (The Bay and Woodwards) were located downtown. Provincial government offices, the courthouse, and the regional hospital were also located on the South Shore. In contrast, a large development site on Tranquille Road hosted a drive-in movie theatre until the mid-1970s. while the construction of Fortune Drive as a four-lane arterial diverted traffic away from the Tranquille Road commercial area.

Revitalization plans

Commercial strips were never a favourite with planners, and those employed by the City of Kamloops were not exceptions. The

1974 "KamPlan" — the city's first official community plan — recommended that, "No further strip commercial developments should be permitted" in the city for infrastructure, cost and aesthetic reasons. It also recommended that Tranquille Road, specifically, should not be "widened for the sake of traffic movement" but should be "considered a special area for which the city might initiate some design concepts in the near future." Over the next 25 years, numerous studies have been conducted and strategies implemented to improve the appearance and vitality of Tranquille Road. These studies have addressed a wide range of issues, including parking, festivals, street banners, and hotel developments (Stanley Associates; NSBIA).

The two most comprehensive and important plans were conducted in 1982 and 1995 (City of Kamloops, *Tranquille Road*; City of Kamloops, *North Shore*). These plans were developed at the request of the local business association and make up part of the city's official community planning documents. The primary objective of the revitalization plans was to transform Tranquille Road into an attractive, vibrant, pedestrian-oriented, market street. To accomplish this, the plans recommended human scale developments, minimal building setbacks, distinctive façades, natural materials and earth tones, the removal of overhead wiring, and the addition of sidewalks, textured crosswalks, ornamental lighting, plantings, and street furniture. More flexible zoning regulations were also established in order to permit a greater variety and density of uses. The estimated costs of the plans totalled $3 million and were shared by local businesses and all levels of government.

Despite the improvements made by the 1982 plan, shopping surveys conducted during the 1990s suggest that Tranquille Road had the least pedestrian traffic of any commercial area in the city (Brent Baker

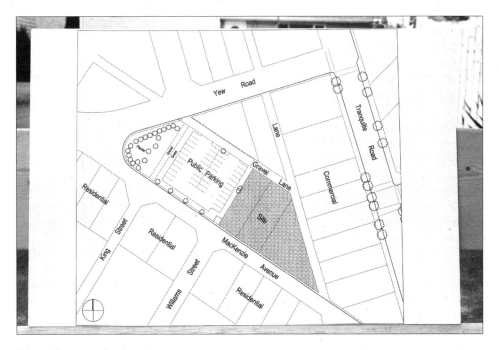

Figure 2. Base map of project site.

Consulting). The 1995 revitalization plan tried to address this shortcoming by creating more entry points, improving pedestrian crossings, and adding more benches, trees, and plantings. It also tried to establish nodes that would serve as focal points and thereby break the linear strip into more manageable chunks. Two key nodes were identified: a waterfront park / plaza near the south end of the street and a "market common" area at the strip's midway point. The "market common" area was envisioned as the "hub" of the street; it would contain "additional commercial, high density residential, and public open space." This block also had several other potential focal points. The triangular block between Tranquille Road, Yew Street, and MacKenzie Avenue was underdeveloped yet large enough to contain several new buildings. A portion of the block, as well as adja-

cent properties were owned by the city. In addition, the building massing, frontage and architecture along Tranquille best fit the guidelines advocated by the 1982 and 1995 plans. Existing restaurants, art shops, and even a converted heritage home added to the block's flavour.

There is no doubt that these plans were successful in improving the aesthetic qualities of Tranquille Road. In particular, the removal of overhead wiring and the addition of decorative lampposts, benches, and trees calmed and softened the street. Owners of more than two-dozen buildings, moreover, tapped the revitalization façade program to repaint, add awnings and patios, and alter storefronts and rooflines. The plans have been less successful, however, in stimulating commerce and thus in addressing the challenges posed by the city's burgeoning southwest sector. The percentage of vacant storefronts has more than doubled over the last decade. Empty lots and buildings have sat for years without an offer. Proposed developments have fallen through and the number of adult-video stores, pawnshops, and second-hand stores has increased. The reasons for the economic decline of Tranquille Road are complex. Alterations to the road network, uneven local development, shifts in the provincial economy, and trends in the retail sector have played a role. All of these forces are implicated in the most recent attempt to revitalize the street and the neighbourhoods around it.

### The Genesis of the Charrette

In the spring of 2000, the City of Kamloops received a development proposal from the John Howard Society for a site in the heart of the market common. The Victory Inn project, as initially proposed, was a 35-unit social housing complex for low-income single people. Like many cities, large or small, Kamloops has a shortage of affordable accommodations. The neighbourhoods around the Tranquille market street are among the poorest and roughest in Kamloops. The teen pregnancy rate in North Kamloops is comparable to those in depressed, Black neighbourhoods in large American cities, while the low birth-weight rate is twice the provincial average (Lu et al; Nelson). Antipoverty groups, city planners, and the city's social planning council, therefore, actively supported the project. On the other hand, many local residents and business owners strongly opposed the project. One hundred and fifty people turned out for a meeting to organize against the project: a 50-name petition was collected; over 40 letters were printed in local newspapers; and 2,000 copies of a newsletter were distributed throughout the area. Opposition was so vocal that the issue was picked up by regional media and discussed in the provincial legislature.

Opposition to the project grew out of fears about the project's clientele and the appropriateness of the site. The John Howard Society is primarily known for its work with parolees and the criminal justice system. Several years earlier, the society had lost a loud and protracted battle to rezone property for a halfway house on the North Shore (Deutschmann). While there were no provisions for halfway houses in Kamloops' zoning regulations, some residents were concerned that the Victory Inn would essentially function as one. Other residents argued that the context of the site was inappropriate for its targeted clientele. Located within several hundred metres of the site were liquor and adult-video stores, a gun shop, a bar and strip club, and drug houses. There were also the more mundane but standard concerns about excessive traffic, imposing structures, and inadequate parking.

Advocates of the project argued that there were several similar and well-integrated facilities in the neighbourhood already and that the site met the criteria for publicly assisted low-income housing projects (for example, grocery stores and public transportation within walking distance). Opponents' concerns, they suggested, stemmed from negative stereotyping and "Not-In-My-Backyard" attitudes (Deutschmann). City planners similarly pointed out that the social and economic background of proposed residents could not by law be considered in land-use decisions. Since the proposed development was an acceptable use under the current zoning regulations, the project's feasibility could only be decided according to technical zoning requirements such as adequate onsite parking.

While there were few legal hurdles to surmount, the project became a very sensitive political issue at both the provincial and municipal levels. The provincial New Democratic Party government of the day was the project's principal source of funds. However, the government was also on record that funding depended on public support for the project. The real viability of the Tranquille site thus depended on city council and its reading of public opinion. In mid June of 2000, a final council hearing on the proposed development was held. Opponents focused on the status and future of the neighbourhood. The site in question, they pointed out, was part of the market common area proposed in the 1995 revitalization plan. Adjacent shop owners argued that the project did not adhere to the original plan and, given its clientele, might effectively prohibit its implementation. While city planners questioned the current feasibility of this element of the 1995 plan, locals felt that it was critical for stimulating business and halting residential decline. If the revitalization plans were effectively set aside, locals reasoned, socioeconomic differences between the North Shore and South Kamloops would only widen. They also argued that the area was already saturated with social services and that this concentration contributed to the North Shore's negative perception in the eyes of many middle-class Kamloopsians. From this perspective, the debate was not just about the status of a single project, but rather the direction of growth in the city.

Kamloops is a city of neighbourhoods. This fact is a product of geography: three rivers, dramatic changes in elevation, and hazard lands (unstable silt terraces) split the city into distinct zones and in some cases isolated communities. The historical sequence of development has also contributed to the city's residential mosaic. The strongest distinction is between neighbourhoods on the north and south shores of the Thompson River. Legally separate municipalities until 1967, the North Shore has always been the poorer cousin. North Shore neighbourhoods developed after a commercial and business

centre had become well established on the South Shore. They also grew in a less organized and regulated manner and attracted immigrants, working-class, and lower-income populations because of their stock of more affordable housing. Over the years, the perceptual status and realities of the North Shore's differences have been intensified by shifts in the local economy and the uneven developments they have engendered.

How heavily this geographical and historical context played in the minds of councilors is unknown. Council passed, by a narrow margin, a motion asking the society to find an alternative location for the Victory Inn. A committee composed of the project's advocates, planners, politicians, as well as local residents was subsequently struck to select a new site. By the fall of 2000, a decision had been made and, within the year, construction began on a property approximately two kilometres distant from the original site.

### MacKenzie Avenue Design Charrette

The controversy around the Victory Inn project raised a question: What form of development *would* be desirable on the MacKenzie Avenue site? The City of Kamloops recognized design charrettes as opportunities to bring diverse interests into a participative process with the aim of defining a shared vision. In the case of the original Victory Inn site, which became known as MacKenzie Island through the charrette process, the NSBIA and the NSRA were strongly committed to creating such a vision. The city relied on "bottom up" planning, inviting public input to drive the process. This is in contrast to traditional planning initiatives, where plans conceived at the "top" are presented to the public for review, usually in a way that leaves citizens feeling like this step was a token gesture. As for the charrette process, it has a history of success in Kamloops: CN Station Plaza, with architect

Figure 3. Photograph showing existing conditions on project site at the southeast corner.

Stanley King, was originally conceived through a charrette and was built less than three years later in a form that's remarkably true to the original concept.

Initiation

In an effort to move forward collectively, representatives from the business community, the NSRA and the Small Cities CURA were invited to participate in a full-day session on November 17, 2001. A tour of the proposed MacKenzie Island site prompted discussion about balancing vehicular and pedestrian use, being sensitive to the scale of the surrounding neighbourhood, and taking advantage of views to the site to create a landmark feature. The original Victory Inn site consisted of only three lots, but the group decided early in the day to consider the entire triangular block in developing a vision. This is a striking example of the way in which design char-

rettes can have a life of their own, taking facilitators and participants alike in unexpected directions. As Kamloops' Community Planning Manager Andrew Tucker observed after the process, "Sometimes it feels like the process gets hijacked as visions may not reflect fiscal realities. This was not the case in the Mackenzie Island charrette, which truly represented the participants' aspirations to improve the image of their neighbourhood through words and graphics" (Tucker).

The charrette participants also suggested painting murals on the blank walls facing the project site — an idea, successfully implemented in other locations in Kamloops, which opens the door to a wide range of artistic and cultural expression. There was also vocal support for public sculpture, an element lacking in Kamloops. The group reacted strongly to vehicular domination of the site, resulting in later proposals of traffic-calming measures and a central pedestrian courtyard. While each of these ideas can be viewed as design components, they also directly express values held by the group or individuals within it. For example, this neighbourhood values human interactions highly, and rejects the priority given to vehicles for the sake of convenience. At the same time, the need to support local businesses through convenient access and parking was acknowledged; based on the group's values, however, the plan shows parking concentrated at one edge of the site and underground, rather than in a central, dominating location.

Idea Generation

To get the discussion started, Mona Murray, president of Sheridan Property Management, gave her perspective on the real estate market in Kamloops and on the North Shore in particular. She encouraged the group to accept some realities, such as the limited viability of retail use on the site but supported several ideas generated by the group, including:

- A heritage feel to reflect the significant history of the North Shore
- An eclectic mix in terms of building style and potential uses
- Residential uses catering to seniors and students
- Supportive live/work arrangements to attract artists and new businesses, and subsequently their patrons
- Mixed residential and commercial uses, such as doctors' or dentists' offices
- Landmark potential related to views down MacKenzie Avenue

Facilitator Julie Schooling used "precedent photos" illustrating public art, mixed-use, and higher density development forms to get the creative juices flowing. The use of photos from urban developments elsewhere allowed

participants to think about potential development scenarios and to look at those scenarios as being more than a repetition of previous development patterns. This creative exploration was tempered by Murray's economic analysis. To create a vision of what the development might actually look like, participants examined images of existing developments to help incorporate elements they liked. Favourable elements included:

- Animation, character, earth materials, and attention to detail as suggested by photos of European shop windows and a sculpture in an Ottawa public square
- Classy heritage look to set a tone for redevelopment in the neighbourhood as exemplified by a row of brick brownstones and a respectful renovation of a multi-unit Kamloops residence

Charrette participants noted that many North Shore residents and businesses have a strong sense of pride, which contributed to their rejection of the housing project that seemed to stereotype the neighbourhood as socially troubled. There was also a respect for existing residents which resulted in the group's idea of making a sensitive transition from existing single-storey homes along MacKenzie Avenue, to proposed two-storey brownstones, and then to taller mixed-use buildings. Other ideas included:

- Pedestrian access to generous public space to attract life to the site
- Human-scale, distinctive, and detailed architecture
- Supportive site design, including ramped access, benches and lighting
- Traffic calming, including closing MacKenzie Avenue and preventing short-cutting through the back lane

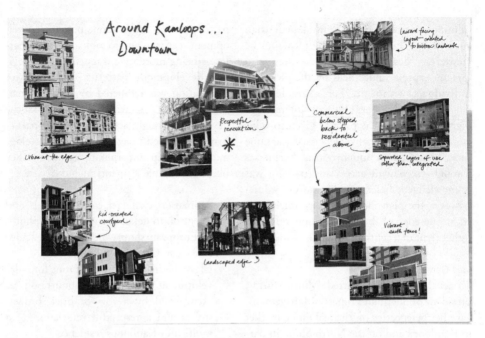

Figure 4. Panel of "Precedent Images" showing residential and mixed-use developments in Kamloops.

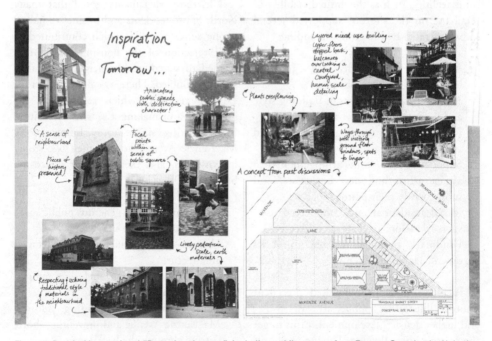

Figure 5. Panel of international "Precedent Images", including public spaces from Eastern Canada, the United States, and Europe.

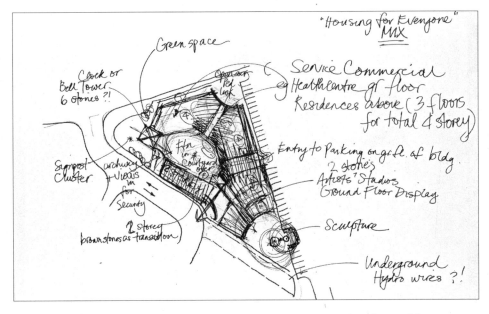

Figure 6. Rough concept plan developed during the charrette exercise based on input from participants.

Representing the Group's Vision

With just over two hours left in the afternoon, it was time to shape the plan. The clarity of the ideas captured on flipcharts throughout the morning made it relatively easy to translate them into a rough plan and two perspective drawings. One of the strengths of the charrette process is that it allows participants who are verbally strong to contribute a lot during the discussion phase, while visual thinkers support and stimulate ideas as they are drawn. The rough plan sketched during the charrette was re-drawn for the report to provide accuracy while preserving the intent of the group's ideas. The participants agreed upon the following elements:

- Central courtyard with water or sculptural feature, overlooked by all buildings and accessible from all directions

- A landmark clock tower (or bell tower), accessible to the public
- Live/work studios or shops, potentially art shops, galleries, cafes, bookstores
- Brownstone homes, two storeys with gardens bordering on the courtyard
- Apartments above ground-floor service commercial, potentially a health centre
- "Housing for Everyone," created by a healthy mix of dwelling types and sizes

Once spatial relationships were clarified in the plan view, the participants guided the artist's rendering of two perspective views. As these drawings took shape, a sense of wonder came over the group, or, as Andrew Tucker noted: "And then a miracle happened." Tucker pointed out that there is always a moment in the charrette process when participants see what they have been talking about drawn before their eyes. "That's exactly it!"

59

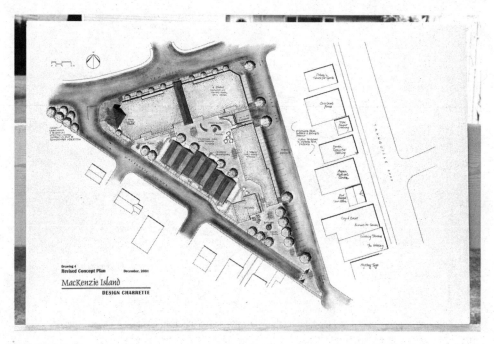

Figure 7. Finished concept plan, refined and rendered following the charrette (full-panel view).

they exclaim. Along with their amazement came an immediate sense of ownership of the drawings, demonstrated by the group's naming of the project, "MacKenzie Island."

### Achievements

The group unanimously agreed that the vision they had created was a compelling one. The energy generated through the event has created momentum — the group now feels that a message can go out with its visionary plan. As Andrew Tucker puts it, "We're open to sensitive development — respect our ideas, and you'll get our full support." The achievement felt by all the participants at the end of that day has remained. There is a strong sense of having contributed to making a difference and of being heard by those who guide development in the community. Indeed, as city

staff, researchers, residents, and business owners shared their views, common ground also emerged in a way that minimized social, cultural, and economic differences.

### Looking Ahead

The downside to a charrette process is the raising of expectations that may take years to realize. The CN Plaza project mentioned previously occurred in a more buoyant real estate market than did MacKenzie Island. Despite a shared vision and community support, the development industry remains reluctant to invest in MacKenzie Island. The challenge now is one of implementation, which includes finding a developer and acquiring the land necessary for realizing the vision. This will not be an easy task. The price has already risen on one lot that has been for sale

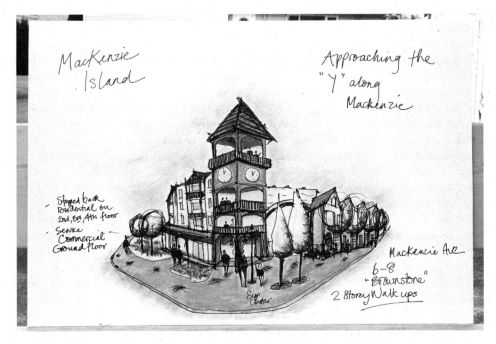

MacKenzie Island

Approaching the "Y" along MacKenzie

- Stepped back Residential on 2nd, 3rd, 4th floor
- Service Commercial Ground floor

MacKenzie Ave 6-8 "Brownstone" 2 Storey Walk ups

Sign Cluster

Figure 8. Perspective drawing of charrette participants' vision (viewed from the west corner of the site).

for many years — financial speculation in response to the community enthusiasm for the development.

Yet the participants remain unfazed, and several even participated in a second charrette on the North Shore. As a result of this charrette, land currently occupied by a tire company was proposed as the potential site for a performing arts centre, something long contemplated and desired by the city and many cultural organizations. This development too is a long way from being realized, and there are potentially several competing sites, so it is less likely to happen than the MacKenzie Island project. Nevertheless, both charrettes are significant as far as the cultural future of Kamloops is concerned because they gave vision and voice to issues and options that were not previously explored in the North

Shore. These were not cases of imposing cultural possibilities on a community; rather they emerged from a complex history and a consultative process that recognized desirable and appropriate opportunities for the sites in question. In the meantime, the NSBIA is beginning to explore other cultural options, including turning vacant properties into spaces for artists.

## Implications

What are some implications of the community planning that occurred in the North Shore for the city of Kamloops, for the Small Cities CURA, and for research and study where cultural and planning considerations intersect? First, and as noted in the introduction, the identification of a community's assets, both existent and potential, must be broad-based and include various individuals, groups, associations, services, facilities, and organizations. This may sound easy enough, if not obvious, yet must be, as Kretzmann and McNight put it, "by necessity internally focused and relationship-driven" (9). In stressing these components, the authors point out that they are not minimizing the impact or contribution of external forces: "The focus is intended simply to stress the primacy of local definition, investment, creativity, hope and control" and "that asset-based development is about building and rebuilding relationships between and among local residents, associations and institutions" (9).

Recognizing these realities and possibilities in the context of the North Shore, the involvement of the NSBIA is especially instructive. When biographical research began on Tranquille Road, the association was not only a source of information; it was immediately recognized as an asset in the community. As the research progressed, the association realized that the study was very useful in providing an historical, economic, and cultural context for its work of encouraging business development on the North Shore. At the same time, its executive director, Peter Mutrie, and several of its members participated in the charrette, thereby contributing to the building or rebuilding of relationships among researchers, business people, local residents, city planners, and designers. While the NSBIA was not an initial partner of the small cities initiative, it has, in effect, now become one, owing to the confluence of interests and the mutual support that has emerged. In fact, as indicated above, preliminary discussions have begun about finding and using spaces on the North Shore for various activities, including the artist-based research, which has become an integral part of the initiative.

Second, further mention must be made of the design charrette as a form of community participation. As Patrick Condon and others demonstrate, during the past ten to fifteen years, charrettes have become increasingly popular and effective as a means for moving along the planning process, by encouraging dialogue and formulation about a specific development. Small projects, such as the MacKenzie Island site in Kamloops, take place over a single day, while large developments may run over a weekend or for an entire week. Whatever the size, location, or timeframe, most charrettes are meant to be "visioning" exercises, or at least one component of such a process. As such they have become part of a trend and repertoire increasingly prevalent in all aspects of city planning, ones that profess a commitment to collaboration and citizen participation.

In addition to the specific work on the North Shore, the charrette process — with its definition liberally extended to mean a participatory or collaborative creative exercise — has since figured in the small cities initiative as a whole. In August 2002, for example, all researchers, student assistants, and community partners met to explore themes common to their research projects, including the biography of streets. Those present were randomly assigned to one of four groups, and each engaged in the modified charrette process as a means of depicting the emergent considerations of home, place and space, mapping and representation. The exercise gave participants an opportunity to explore collaboratively a theme for which they had affinity and a vested interest, but not necessarily direct involvement. What resulted were four very distinctive visual displays that yielded further and common understanding about the cultural realities and challenges of Kamloops. This convergence has by no means flattened research activity to the extent that all efforts now resemble a two-dimensional canvas, to use another visual metaphor. Rather, and as de Sousa Briggs suggests, we were involved in "performative" activities that tried to articulate and document intersections of culture and community, while fulfilling our aim of working collaboratively and reflecting on it. We were engaged in what was earlier identified as "the culture of participation," with the charrette process helping to provide a composite of work accomplished so far in the small cities initiative. It also suggested to researchers and community partners where they may want to go next as far as working individually or as a collective — and this includes the North Shore contingent.

The City of Kamloops will no doubt continue to use the concept of the charrette for community planning while the small cities initiative may further employ it as a form of charting and assessing its own development. Consensus may be a desired objective, but undoubtedly and understandably there will be differences, just as there were in the North Shore where this cultural journey began.

## Acknowledgments

A version of this paper was presented at the colloquium "Cultural Development in Canada's Cities," Canadian Cultural Research Network, Toronto, Ontario, May 31-June 1, 2002. The authors would like to thank Andrew Tucker, Community Planning Manager, City of Kamloops for his contributions and suggestions. Tucker's detailed notes have been interwoven into the chapter, making him, in effect, a fourth author. At the time of writing, there has been no further development on MacKenzie Island.

## Note

1. All images in this chapter are used courtesy of the City of Kamloops Planning Department.

## Works Cited

Berger, Bennett. *An Essay on Culture: Symbolic Structure and Social Structure.* Berkeley: U of California P, 1995.

Brent Baker Consulting. *Pedestrian Intercepts (Kamloops): Consumer Origins and Destinations.* Kamloops, July 1997.

City of Kamloops. *KamPlan.* Stanley Associates Engineering Ltd., Kamloops, B.C., 1974.

———. *Tranquille Road Commercial Plan: A Report On Development Opportunities.* Kamloops, BC, 1982.

City of Kamloops, Department of Development Services. *KamPlan 1997: A Community Plan For Kamloops.* Kamloops, BC, 1997.

———. *MacKenzie Island Design Charrette Summary Report.* Kamloops, BC, 2002. 16 August 2004. <http://www.city.kamloops.bc.ca/planning/developments/Mackenzie/index.html>

———. *North Shore Revitalization: Strategy and Concept Plan.* Kamloops, BC, 1995.

Condon, Patrick M., ed. *Sustainable Urban Landscapes: The Surrey Design Charrette.* Vancouver: U of British Columbia P, 1995.

Cultural Future of Small Cities. University College of the Cariboo. 20 July 2004 <www.cariboo.bc.ca/smallcities>

De Souza Briggs, Xavier. "Doing Democracy Up-Close: Culture, Power, and Communication in Community Planning. *Working Papers*, Politics Research Group, Kennedy School of Government, 1998. 17.

Deutschsmann, Linda Bell. "The Risk Society in My Back Yard." *The Small Cities Book: On the Cultural Future of Small Cities.* Ed. W.F. Garrett-Petts. Vancouver: New Star Books, 2004. 338-348.

Hayden, Dolores. *The Power of Place: Urban Landscapes as Public History.* Cambridge: MIT Press, 1996.

Helling, Amy. "Collaborative Visioning: Proceed with Caution! Results From Evaluating Atlanta's Vision 2020 Project. *Journal of the American Planning Association*, 64:3. 335-49.

Katz, Peter. "The 70 Percent Place." *Government Technology.* (May 2000): 8-9, 45-47.

Kretzmann, John P., and John L. McKnight. *Building Communities From The Inside Out: A Path Toward Finding and Mobilizing A Community's Assets.* Chicago: Acta Publications, 1993.

Lu, James, Ross Nelson, Helen Parkyn, and Shelley O'Grady. *Teen Pregnancy, Thompson Health Region, A Report of the Medical Health Officer to the Thompson Regional Health Board.* September 1997.

Massey, Doreen. "Places and Their Pasts." *History Workshop Journal* 39 (1995): 182-92.

——. *Space, Place and Gender.* Minneapolis: Minnesota UP, 1994.

Nelson, Ross. "Low Birthweights: Spatial and Socioeconomic Patterns in Kamloops," *The Western Geographer,* 8/9 (1998/99): 31-59.

Nelson, Ross, C. Nickel, Alyssa Lowen, Karen Black, Keir Hunt, and Clive Lovett. "Tranquille Road Planning Priorities Survey." Report prepared for the City of Kamloops, Development Services and the North Shore Business Improvement Association, Kamloops, BC, June 2002

North Shore Business Improvement Association. *North Shore Development Opportunities Assessment.* NSBIA, Kamloops: Urban Systems, 1999.

Shipley, Robert, and Ross Newkirk. "Vision and Visioning in Planning: What Do These Terms Really Mean? *Environment and Planning B: Planning and Design.* 573-91.

Stanley Associates Engineering. *City of Kamloops North Shore Commercial and Parking Study.* Kamloops, BC, 1977.

Tucker, Andrew. Personal Interview. 9 March 2004.

# The Culture of Participation

## Lon Dubinsky

### Introduction

Severe weather was not the only thing that plagued many cities in Canada during the winter of 2004. Several were also beset with budget crises, and the arts and heritage were predictably on the chopping block. City administration in Ottawa initially proposed (although city council later rejected) closing all the museums it owned and terminating funding for several others it had inherited in a municipal merger. Regina was preparing to close the Dunlop Art Gallery, a cultural mainstay that had been a part of the Regina Public Library system for over fifty years. Other arts organizations were also vulnerable, with symphonies, for example, facing grave financial woes in Kelowna, Vancouver, Winnipeg, Saskatoon, and Toronto. In Kamloops, however, the circumstances were significantly different. Working from the Cultural Strategic Plan commissioned in 2003, city council set aside $150,000 for a new full-time manager for culture and related administrative costs, while maintaining its substantial support for arts and heritage organizations.

Why is the situation different in Kamloops? Is there something particular about it as a small city? If so, what are the implications for other cities of comparable size, and even larger ones, such as Ottawa and Regina? This chapter attempts to answer these questions in three ways. First, it traces the history of the arts and heritage in Kamloops by looking at the evolution of the city's leading cultural organizations and at mechanisms of support, including municipal support and structure. Second, it examines the key issues of leadership and competition tied to the evolution of activity and to the city's cultural present and future. Third, it situates various findings and issues within the context of debates about the dynamics of urban life, or lack thereof, that have been raised, most notably in recent years by Richard Florida and Robert Putnam.

In his influential work *The Rise of the Creative Class*, Florida maintains that a city's success is tied to attracting highly skilled and educated people, such as high-technology entrepreneurs, and to having amenities and services that cater to and/or are operated by other creatively driven groups, which Florida identifies as the Bohemian class (192-96). In contrast, Putnam sees a major decline in community affiliations, in traditional forms of social capital, such as memberships in voluntary organizations and neighbourhood activities, with the result being a marked decrease in civic involvement. According to Putnam, people, including members of the creative class, may be engaged in all manner of activities, cultural or otherwise, but significantly less engaged in community organizations. As he puts it in his now-famous dictum, people are "bowling alone."

From Richard Florida's perspective, Kamloops, and possibly other small cities of comparable size, presents an interesting case. While it may lack a sufficient creative class, Kamloops has a range and a degree of arts and heritage activities that are consistent with the needs and interests of the creative class. As this chapter will demonstrate, the kind of social capital that Putnam suggests is in rapid decline is, in fact, what is responsible for Kamloops' vital cultural life. What becomes evident as a distinctive feature of arts and heritage in Kamloops is a high degree of citizen involvement relative to both the size and scale of the city. This cultural participation is also consistent with involvement in other sectors of the community, constituting what is best described as a "culture of participation."

Before turning to the evolution of the major organizations and to other factors, several conceptual and methodological issues require attention. As noted in the introduction to this book, most research and writing on cities, and across academic disciplines, is decidedly "metrocentric." The situation is even more pronounced when it comes to sector-specific considerations, such as examining the development, composition, and impact of arts and heritage, perpetuating the belief that culture is somehow associated with the big city life except, perhaps, in the case of small cities that are tourist destinations and/or small communities that have retained their rural traditions. The methodological task is to avoid any superimposition and take advantage of studies that focus on large cities

and metropolitan areas, whose perspectives and criteria are also appropriate for smaller cities where local conditions differ. A recent work by Arthur Brooks and Roland Kushner, for example, attempts to quantify what makes a city an "arts capital." Their study, which provides something of a model, questions the difficulties in measuring culture. Referring not to city size but to the extent of cultural activity in any given place, they note the challenges of undertaking a "systematic, quantitative study of the *magnitude* of arts and culture" (12-13, their italics), and ask: "Do we measure the quantity of the arts produced, or the quantity consumed? Perhaps quantity means less than some measure of excellence, access, content diversity or reputation. Perhaps the most important measure of arts magnitude is the health of the sector" (12-13). Addressing the issue of magnitude, Brooks and Kushner also note that any study is complicated by the use of aggregates as a justification not only for existing arts organizations and activities, but as a rationale for more support, although amounts may not necessarily provide an accurate composite of the sector. Faced with this dilemma, and to provide criteria for describing a city's "cultural environment" that is not merely reduced to the number of organizations, the authors incorporate five questions to guide their consideration of aggregates: (1) How well does the city provide opportunities for its citizens and visitors? (2) How financially healthy are a city's art institutions, on average? (3) What is the relative vitality of the city's philanthropy in the arts? (4) What can we say about the quality of the arts in the city? (5) How strong is the city's infrastructure; can it sustain future growth?

Focusing on major American metropolitan areas, they attempt to correlate several rankings of cities, derived from economic profiles and from polling data, with the revenues and numbers of their non-profit arts organizations. Accordingly, the examination of cultural activity that follows here incorporates the five questions of the Brooks and Kushner study. It also examines several policy considerations, such as recommendations from the Cultural Strategic Plan noted at the outset. The policy considerations are complemented by several qualitative observations in an attempt to capture some of the everyday, participatory aspects of cultural life, including what Virginia Dominguez describes as the "messy" side of involvement, such as individual and organizational differences over governance, funding, and a vision of what arts and heritage engagement should be. These interactions are a constituent part of civic engagement and are often contingent on the forms of social capital that Putnam identifies, such as community affiliations and trust relationships that exist within and beyond the arts and heritage sector. Within this context, I, as participant/observer, provide some observations and analysis. [1]

As a research associate at the Kamloops Art Gallery, I am not a disinterested spectator. On the other hand, as someone who has come to Kamloops for a specific period of time to try to understand why the arts and heritage flourish in a small city, I possess, or at least should possess, sufficient requisite distance to provide some claims and conclusions. Yet objectivity is not always easy. One's perceptions and one's actual participation in the everyday can often converge as one attempts to understand the ties and tales that give meaning and form to community as both an idea and as a reality. As Lucy Lippard explains: "I often find myself conflating place and community. Although they are not the same thing, they coexist. A peopled place is not always a community, but regardless of the bonds formed with it, or not, a common history is being lived out. Like the places they

inhabit, communities are bumpily layered and mixed, exposing hybrid stories that cannot be seen in linear fashion" (24).

Having introduced several conceptual and methodological issues, including participation as both a method and an object of study, the historical account of the arts and heritage now proceeds. Appropriately, it begins with a personal observation that highlights an instance of everyday participation.

## History of the Arts and Heritage in Kamloops

Like most other western Canadian cities large and small, Kamloops is little more than a hundred years old. Yet, for a relatively young place, it has been particularly conscious of its heritage. Its downtown is not a model heritage district, but if you stroll along Victoria Street, the main thoroughfare, and look closely at various buildings, you will see plaques that indicate the year of construction and also give information about their ownership and other historical facts. These official designations are not only recognition of the city's built history but also of the people who made it.

We find further evidence of history's local value inside some of the buildings. On the corner of Victoria and 4th Avenue sits the Plaza Heritage Hotel, built in 1927 in the classic Spanish Moorish style popular at the time. Inside, the walls are covered with photographs and texts about various individuals and families who contributed to the city's economic, social, and cultural development, including politicians and business people, as one would expect, but also a music teacher, an entomologist, and several celebrated mothers. This photographic record may seem quaint by some standards, but it is an authentic record, made available through the efforts of the hotel management.

This dedication to heritage is characteris-

Figure 1. Offices of the Western Canada Theatre. Photo by Kim Clarke.

tic of cultural activity that occurs — and has occurred for a considerable length of time — in Kamloops. As I'll demonstrate, various arts and cultural organizations attend to their mandates and interests, but they never seem very far removed from the community in which they reside. There is an engagement with arts and heritage that stretches beyond the expected, and the enthusiasm for the local and the vernacular, as expressed by the management of the Plaza Heritage Hotel, is but one illustration. Consistent with this individualized case of participation are collective endeavours that have resulted in the formation of a city museum, a theatre company, a symphony, an art gallery, as well as many other cultural groups and organizations.

The Kamloops Museum & Archives began in 1936 as the Thompson Valley District Museum and Historical Association. By 1939, it and the city library had a permanent home — a large house provided through the generosity of Mrs. J.S. Burris, a daughter of one of Kamloops' first families. The group was renamed the Kamloops Museum Association, and it was a strictly volunteer effort. By the mid 1940s there was concern about the safety of the wooden structure, especially given the artefacts and archives it had amassed. By 1956, a new building, which the museum still occupies, was constructed.

The library moved to another location in 1978, and the vacated space was occupied by the newly formed Kamloops Art Gallery (KAG). In 1998, when the KAG moved to new quarters, the museum became the sole occupant. Since that time there have been extensive renovations, and with additional space the museum has been able to expand its exhibitions and programs. It is funded almost entirely by the city, with current funding just under $500,000. Although staffed with city employees, the Kamloops Museum Association continues to advise the director and work on the museum's behalf.

While the museum has a history of over sixty years, the other major organizations — Western Canada Theatre (WCT), the Kamloops Symphony Orchestra, and the KAG — emerged between the late 1960s and late 1970s. The WCT began with initial support from the Local Initiatives Program of the federal government and through the efforts of Tom Kerr, who became a nationally recognized theatre director. The local school district was also instrumental, and drama teachers, such as Lanni McInnis, who is currently the theatre's associate director, became involved.

Figure 2. Jean-Michel LeGal in *Unity (1918)*, by Kevin Kerr. Western Canada Theatre, 2003. Photo by Kim Clarke.

Tom Kerr remained until 1976; he was succeeded by Frank Glasson and Michael Dobbin, and, in 1983, David Ross, the current director, took over. The first five years saw lots of activity and recognition, and by the mid-1970s WCT had received its first grant from the Canada Council and was on its way to becoming a professional theatre company. In 1978, WCT began staging performances in the Sagebrush Theatre, a newly constructed facility adjacent to one of the city's high schools. In recent years, WCT has received a fee to manage the Sagebrush in addition to the annual operating grant that it receives from the city.

Up until the late 1990s, the company also sponsored several kinds of performing arts events, but more recently it has concentrated on plays, including its own productions and related theatrical works. It now presents about seven plays annually, including two that are staged at the Pavilion Theatre, a small space in the same building as its administrative offices and workshop areas. The repertoire is diverse, from commissioned works to plays by young Canadian playwrights like Kevin Kerr (*Unity 1918*), who was born and raised in Kamloops, to more classic and established works and revues. As in its early years, a strong link still exists between education and theatre. The community connection has been continuous throughout the company's history, with yearly attendance remarkably consistent (on average 45,000), while the number of current subscribers is over 2,500. Western Canada Theatre receives support from various levels of government. The City of Kamloops currently provides $132,000 yearly for operating support, the Canada Council

Figure 3. Music Director Bruce Dunn and the Kamloops Symphony Orchestra, Riverside Park, Kamloops, 1991-92 season. Photo by Kim Clarke.

$131,000, and the British Columbia Arts Council $82,700. One of the most solid indicators of the theatre company's development and success is emulation: Theatre North West in Prince George, B.C. has taken WCT's lead in terms of what it stages, its relationship to its community, and how it manages its operations (MacInnis and Rothman).

The origins and the development of the Kamloops Symphony Orchestra and the KAG parallel that of WCT. In fact, it is no coincidence that all three came of age during the 1970s. By that time, the so-called baby boom generation was into its late twenties and early thirties and settling down, and, in Kamloops at least, it was a ready-made audience that went hand-in-hand with the long-time arts interests and volunteer efforts of

several citizens.

The Kamloops Symphony Orchestra formed in much the same way. After years of travelling to Kelowna to hear the Okanagan Symphony, several local residents, including James Dewar, Mary Ann Milobar, Dan Seymour, and Art Hooper, recognized that Kamloops was ready for and capable of having its own orchestra. By 1976, the orchestra had been established, and its initial objectives were basic and straightforward, namely to promote and foster classical music in Kamloops. Its first conductor was James Verity, whose enthusiasm carried with it an ideological agenda when he pledged, "to fight rock and roll music" (Bennett 3).

By 1983, the symphony board committed to engaging and paying ten musicians, and it also became increasingly committed to presenting programs and events for children and young people. Today, the professional core of musicians is 25, supported by about 25 amateur players. In addition, a Symphony Chamber Orchestra plays several concerts in the Calvary Temple. The symphony also has a thriving music school that offers school concerts and instruction to adults and youth. Its consistent professionalism has resulted in ongoing support from the Canada Council for the Arts and the BC Arts Council, $22,000 and $29,000 respectively in 2004. The symphony's range of activities and diverse performances has also translated into consistent support from the City of Kamloops (presently $49,500) and from corporate and individual donors, which together with earned revenue bring the annual budget to about $500,000. With nearly 500 subscribers, the season's 12-13 concerts get near-capacity crowds, and the symphony is in the black, making it one of the few with this distinction in Canada.

The Kamloops Art Gallery was established in 1978. Local artists were given encouragement by an "outreach program" of the Vancouver School of Art, now the Emily Carr College of Art and Design, which Nini Baird, now Chair of the BC Arts Council, was engaged to develop. As Baird recalls: "Instead of imposing a program on the province, we decided to consult with people throughout the province to determine how the program would best meet local needs and aspirations. The Cariboo College region was identified as one of four pilot regions" (3).

In early 1978, Baird met with the arts community, and, as she notes, the headline for the account of this consultation in the *Kamloops Daily News* was "We want a gallery." Baird indicated that there were discussions about the need for a central location, and she cautioned the group not to approach the Kamloops City Council for support with-

out "a clear idea of the kind of gallery" it wanted (Baird 3). A councillor agreed, but also urged people to "strike while the iron was hot" because the council seemed supportive of the arts and planned to finalize its budget at the end of January. Several concerned citizens led by Julia Mitra, President of the Arts Council of Kamloops, moved quickly, and a year later the inaugural exhibition of the gallery opened at a downtown location, in the basement of the museum.

Sylvia Verity was hired as the first curator/manager but left soon after when her husband, who was the symphony's conductor, took a position elsewhere. She was succeeded by Nora Berkhout, a board member who was curator/manager from 1979-82. Gary Essar took the position for one year, and he was succeeded by Donna McAlear. During her tenure, the gallery became more professional in its exhibition and program offerings. Renovations were completed, and the gallery also sought advice about its governance and its future direction from other regionally based galleries. All of the changes and hard work resulted in the initial awarding of both federal and provincial grants, which in turn made the gallery a more professional organization. Yet, as McAlear points out, this shift could not have been accomplished without extensive community support. She notes, "I recall the generosity of the many volunteers who left their mark on the gallery's forward-moving achievements. Community volunteers will always be an essential core of public galleries, no matter what professional changes the institution is experiencing" (3-4). In 1987, Jann L.M. Bailey became the director. She continued to develop the professional aspects of the gallery while maintaining a commitment to showing local work and to making art accessible through educational programs and community activities.

The idea of moving out of the basement

of the Kamloops Museum was never far from anyone's mind. In fact, it had been a dream as early as 1982. In 1987, the idea was put to a referendum vote, but, despite high hopes, it lost. The defeat did not deter the gallery's director, board, and staff from continuing to push for a new gallery while also strengthening the collections, exhibitions, and programs. In 1998, the dream was finally realized, and the gallery moved into its present home in the Thompson-Nicola Regional District civic building. The city, through a strata agreement with the Thompson-Nicola Regional District, bought the gallery space, while city funding, federal government infrastructure support, plus a capital campaign that raised one million dollars, made the gallery a reality. For the past five years, the gallery has continued to maintain its local, regional, and national commitments and reputation and, in doing so, now manages a budget of approximately $1.4 million. This budget includes a current operating grant of $275,000 and maintenance support from the City of Kamloops, Canada Council support — which at $140,000, is one of the highest grants in the country — and current support from the BC Arts Council for $70,000. The remainder of funds comes from earned revenue, other government programs, and corporate and individual donations, including donations of art and in-kind contributions.

Figure 4. Interior of the Kamloops Art Gallery. Photo by Kim Clarke.

Recalling Brooks's and Kushner's questions posed at the beginning of this chapter, the history of the major cultural organizations demonstrates that they have become financially stable institutions, although this is generally not the rule in the arts and cultural sector. While the museum historically has been funded almost entirely by the city, the gallery, symphony, and theatre company have developed a balanced approach to their operations, which is reflected in their various programs and in their diverse sources of support. All four organizations also provide a range of cultural opportunities to Kamloops' citizens, both young and old, and as both consumers and volunteers. In addition, benefits to visitors are becoming more recognizable in Kamloops as a key to further economic development by arts and heritage organizations, the city, and the Thompson-Nicola Regional District.[2]

To answer the third question, Kamloops does not have the magnitude that exists in large cities by way of foundations or extensive corporate-giving programs, but once again individual volunteerism relative to the city's population surely compensates.[3] Quality, the subject of Brooks's and Kushner's fourth question, can be seen in the professional evolution of all four organizations and in their specific programs, be it the KAG's exhibitions, which have received national recognition, or WCT's world premiere of *Ernestine Shuswap Gets Her Trout*. Finally, there is the question of infrastructure. As indicated earlier, the gallery moved into its award-winning space in 1998; the museum is completing renovations; and the Sagebrush Theatre, where the symphony and theatre company perform, has a new and expanded lobby. Yet, these latter organizations, as well as amateur groups, have requirements for more space and/or improved facilities. The city's recent Cultural Strategic Plan recognized these needs, and I will address them later in the chapter.

Infrastructure notwithstanding — and it is more of an issue than an impediment — the answers to the Brooks and Kushner questions suggest that the magnitude of cultural activity is considerable in Kamloops *relative* to the population of the city and the availability and use of resources. Moreover, other cultural organizations and activities must be taken into account to appreciate the full spectrum of participation, for the so-called major arts and heritage organizations do not exist in a vacuum. The University College of the Cariboo (UCC) increasingly contributes to the cultural life of the city, and since the university is also one of the city's largest employers, in a local economy that is becoming more service driven, students, faculty and staff are also an increasing component of the producers, consumers, and volunteers that contribute to arts and heritage activity. Consider as well the Kamloops Indian Band (KIB) — directly across the Thompson River — and 16 other bands of the Shuswap Nation in the region. The Secwepemc Cultural Education Society located on KIB land plays an especially important role in cultural activity and was instrumental in the development of WCT's production of *Ernestine Shuswap Gets Her Trout*. The Kamloopa Pow-Wow draws

individuals and bands from across North America each summer. The art gallery also works closely with the First Nations community, as evidenced by its record of exhibitions and works in its permanent collection, while the symphony has also commissioned Aboriginal works.

In addition to the four major organizations, the Cultural Strategic Plan identified 30 other non-profit arts and heritage organizations, which in a city of 80,000 translates into one organization for approximately every 2,300 people. (Again, according to Brooks and Kushner, activities are not only measured in aggregates but also in the scope and kinds of activity.) The following four examples are exemplary, though by no means the only, instances that further demonstrate diversity in content and in community participation and investment.

The Community Arts Council of Kamloops encourages the production and exhibition of work by local artists and has been active for at least 30 years. Every March, the Kamloops Cowboy Festival is four days of poetry readings, music, and other cultural events, with a total attendance of over 4,500 people from across North America, including at least 12 American states and 7 provinces. A core group of 5 volunteers plan and organize the festival throughout the year and 45 additional people assist with the actual event.

The convergence of heritage and education is also significant as there is a strong contingent of schoolteachers, principals, and volunteers who, for the last decade, have been leaders in the Heritage Fair program of the Historica Foundation, which encourages children and youth to research and create displays about Canadian history. Kamloops, in fact, held the National Fair in 2001, which was successful enough to merit two pages of coverage in *Maclean's*. As with other cultural organizations and events, the volunteer effort

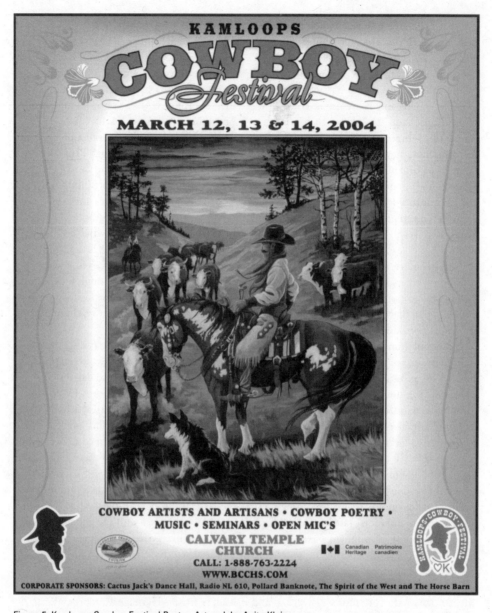

Figure 5. Kamloops Cowboy Festival Poster. Artwork by Anita Klein.

is substantial relative to the community's size.

The Kamloops Film Society, throughout the year, screens films not likely to be shown in commercial venues or subject to limited runs or distribution. It now uses the resources of the Film Circuit, a distribution arm of the

Toronto Film Festival, but it was consistently and successfully doing for almost 30 years what this recently developed circuit now does for many small communities across Canada. A highlight of the year is the Society's film festival, held every March. Filmmaker Atom Egoyan, who made his film *The Sweet Hereafter* in the region, was a guest of the festival in 1998. The enthusiastic reception he received is described in an entry to a diary he kept of his trip to the Academy Awards that included a stop-off in Kamloops:

> I am here for the opening night of the Kamloops International Film Festival (featuring nine films) and the excitement at the Paramount Theatre is extraordinary. No one can believe I'm here. Why would a double Oscar nominee be in this small B.C. town weeks before the most glamourous event in the world? To thank the district, that's why. This is the area where the film was set (in a fictitious town called Sam Dent) and where most of the exteriors were shot. After I introduce the film to this insanely pumped-up crowd, I go over to see the local hockey team, the Blazers, beat a U.S. team from Spokane 4-3. It is easy to forget how exciting a hockey game in a town like this can be. The fans — from three-year-olds to people who hadn't missed a game in 40 years — go absolutely nuts. In places like Kamloops you can still feel what Canada is all about. (Egoyan 62)

As Egoyan confirms, the participatory spirit that characterizes cultural activity is also abundant in the recreational arena. The turnout for the film and for the game cannot be regarded solely as discrete forms of local involvement: both are instances of venturing out in the community rather than remaining at home to see mediated versions of culture or sport contests. Moreover, the Blazers are only one side of a substantial commitment to sports and sporting events that allows Kamloops to promote itself now as the "Tournament Capital of Canada." Competitions abound. Some are regional; others are national and include, for example, the annual Kamloops International Bantam Hockey Tournament and the Canada Curling Cup. These events have their equivalents in local recreational activities, including various sports leagues for children, youth and adults, and all are instances, once again, of substantial social capital.

To further its objectives as the Tournament Capital, the city held a referendum in November 2003. Residents gave the city approval to borrow up to $37.6 million dollars "to design and construct expanded or improved tournament capital facilities" (City of Kamloops). While the facilities proposed are designed to attract more competitions, they will also benefit local citizens. One facility is slated for McArthur Island Park, in the city's north shore, an area already used for various recreational activities; the other at UCC, adjacent to an Aquatic Centre, which was built in 1993 when Kamloops hosted the Canada Summer Games. These games also strongly confirmed the city's ability to marshal resources and to host an event that required extensive volunteering and local organization.

Cultural participation in Kamloops, then, whether consumptive or voluntary, or in the activities of major organizations or smaller entities, is significant.

## Municipal Support and Structure

Having traced the evolution of arts and heritage development and established its larger context, I want to consider the specific role of municipal support. What has been the city's financial record over time, and where is the city headed? Does the Cultural Strategic Plan contain a vision and a set of policy and pro-

| City | City Population | City Structure | Regional Structure (if applicable) | Total Arts and Heritage Grants (2001) | Arts & Heritage Grants: Per-Capita Measure |
|------|-----------------|----------------|-----------------------------------|----------------------------------------|---------------------------------------------|
| Toronto | 2,542,844 (2000) | Amalgamation of 6 former municipalities | N/A | $13,363,700 (arts and heritage) | $5.26 (arts and heritage) |
| Montréal | 1,029,828 (2000) before amalgamation | City of Montréal exists within Montréal Urban Community | Montréal Urban Community consists of 28 municipalities | $11,653,000 (arts and heritage) | $11.32 (arts and heritage) |
| Calgary | 876,519 (2001) | City of Calgary | N/A | $5,748,000 (arts and heritage) | $6.56 (arts and heritage) |
| Ottawa | 791,100 (2001) | Amalgamation of 12 former municipalities | N/A | $3,077,503 (arts and heritage) | $3.89 (arts and heritage) |
| Winnipeg | 631,700 (2001) City of Winnipeg only | Winnipeg only within Winnipeg Metro | Winnipeg Metro consists of 12 municipalities | $2,705,885 (arts and heritage) | $4.28 (arts and heritage) |
| Vancouver | 565,905 (2000) City of Vancouver only | Vancouver within Greater Vancouver Regional District | GVRD consists of 18 municipalities | $6,589,526 (arts and heritage) | $11.64 (arts and heritage) |
| Halifax | 384 619 (1999) | Amalgamation of 4 former municipalities | N/A | $ 439, 245 (arts and heritage) | $1.14 (arts and heritage) |

Table 1. Cultural Grants (Arts and Heritage) in Major Canadian Cities.[5]

gram directions? How does the arts and heritage community regard proposed future actions?

Significant support for cultural organizations and activities began in the late 1980s, and especially during the tenure of Mayor John Dormer. By the late 1990s funding had risen to about $1 million annually and included operating grants for the major arts organizations, the museum, the community arts council, various festivals, and a small grants program for the creation of works. By 2003, the amount of yearly support for these expenditures had increased to approximately $1.2 million.[4] The figure is small relative to the expenditures of a major city, but in per capita terms it translates into approximately $15, putting Kamloops near the top, percentage-wise in Canada (see Table 1).

The city's financial commitment also runs counter to a trend prevalent in many communities across British Columbia. As recent-

ly reported, federal government support for the arts in British Columbia is proportionally the lowest of all the provinces and has been so for several years (Birnie 1-2). Megan Williams, Executive Director of the Canadian Conference of the Arts, attributes this ranking to low provincial funding, noting a correlation between funding by the two levels of government, where provinces with the highest rates of support receive higher federal contributions (qtd. in Birnie 1-2). The trend, unfortunately, continues in many provinces at the municipal level. Yet, in Kamloops' case, the city compensates to some degree for the lack of provincial support, and, in this regard, it is similar to Vancouver and Victoria. Victoria is absent from the table but, according to a recent study, its per capita spending in 2002 was $19.59.[6]

However, municipal support in Kamloops for arts and heritage is not without its bumps.

The recent experience of the KAG is illustrative. The account that follows is not intended to be a platform for the gallery's particular circumstances; rather, it highlights another form of participation, in this case negotiations about what should be supported culturally, for how much, under what conditions, and to what extent the "messy" side of cultural politics is revealed (to recall Dominguez). Policy issues also emerge that pertain to the governance of arts and heritage, including references to the Cultural Strategic Plan. As well, and as noted at the outset, the following account is an instance in which I, as author, am necessarily a participant/observer, given my affiliation with the gallery. Here my intent is to provide several qualitative observations that complement the historical and quantitative analyses offered thus far.

When the KAG moved into its new quarters in 1998 it had a five-year lease agreement with the city that included annual support for operations and building maintenance. The agreement came due in August 2003, and in January 2004 the gallery appeared before a meeting of city council to make a presentation about its activities. Included was a request that the new agreement include a reinstatement of $50,000 per year that it had initially received in addition to its base operating and maintenance grants, and an increase of $25,000 for new program development.

Negotiations ensued between the gallery management and city management staff from its Department of Recreation Services, which is responsible for arts and culture. Before long, the perceptions and circumstances surrounding the discussions became as significant as the amount desired. The negotiations and the information provided became great fodder for the local media.[7] Press reports of the gallery's budgetary situation were interspersed with opinions and clarifications as

the "actors" — including the gallery's director, and the chair of its Board of Trustees, city management and individual city councillors — stated and restated their positions about the request. The extent of the coverage not only illustrated the interest by the local media in the arts and heritage; it also confirmed the high degree of cultural activity and in the process served to encourage or reinforce participation. To illustrate, from the first of January until the first week of April 2004, there were 41 entries — or one every two days — devoted to just the gallery's programs and activities or to a broader arts subject for which it had some interest or relationship (Kamloops Art Gallery).

The scramble was not unlike the situation in other cities where arts organizations face municipal budget crunches, but what was especially characteristic of Kamloops is the closeness of the encounter: it is a small city imbued with significant traditional social capital. The web of community ties is obviously considerable, with individuals maintaining several overlapping affiliations and trust relationships that traverse government, business, the non-profit sector, including arts and heritage, as well as their private lives. These connections also exist in larger cities, but the arena is not as confined or, to put it another way, participation is not as consistently up close and personal. Moreover, the situation suggested that the city was going through a sea change with respect to its relationships with arts organizations and the arts community as a whole. This apparent shift is buttressed by city council's approval in principle of the Cultural Strategic Plan and what it portends for future strategies.

At issue are clearly matters of policy as the wrangling over the specific financial request sounded an alarm about the extent to which the city should or could manage the affairs of the gallery (or any other non-profit society

77

for that matter) on the basis of its role as a principal funder. In previous years, requests were also made in the form of a presentation to the council and through discussions with city management. Often, there were differences; there were compromises; and there were resolutions, all of which were facilitated by strong, long-standing ties and trust relationships that matter in the life of a small city. However, relations are shifting and becoming more formalized, although not yet through a strict application procedure or some other bureaucratic mechanism. It is as if, for now, there has been a skip from a rather open-ended process to a protracted situation until a new structure and a new set of relationships and expectations fall into place.

No doubt city administration and council regard the Cultural Strategic Plan as a blueprint for future procedures and plans. Moreover, the plan has a section on governance, which lays out three overall options: (1) an arm's-length commission or council, which would review and provide support to organizations and individuals and would be equipped with a professional staff; (2) city government delivery, in which all services, programs and organizations would be run by the municipality; and (3) a "public-community partnership model," in which planning, coordination, and policy development would be managed by the city and in which non-profit arts and heritage organizations would deliver the activities and services (Janzen & Associates 72-75).

The plan opts for the third model, noting that it is already successfully working in Kamloops given the operations and activities of the major arts organizations and various community groups (Janzen & Associates 75). City staff also point to the consultations undertaken about the plan as evidence that the community is both informed and heeded. However, many of the plan's main recom-

mendations, such as the building of a multi-purpose arts and heritage centre, have already met with doubt or outright opposition. The symphony strongly favours a new designated performing arts centre that can accommodate its many activities, while the theatre company believes that existing locations, such as its Pavilion space, can be enlarged and upgraded. Others, including individual artists and several community groups, wonder about the extent to which the proposed centre can serve all their diverse needs.

These are expressions of citizens and organizations in a city that may be small in population, but in terms of its cultural milieu may have outgrown what is being proposed. The most appropriate comparisons here are the bedroom communities of Maple Ridge and Richmond. Both have such multi-purpose centres and are larger in population than Kamloops, yet neither have the same kind of autonomy, scale, and degree of cultural activity. The centres also suffice because of the close proximity of these two cities to Vancouver, which offers many cultural events and venues. It would seem that the current situation in Kamloops would be of interest to other cities of similar scale and population that intend to increase their commitment to arts and culture.

The availability of funds and the desire for capital projects are not the only driving forces; control is also a crucial determinant for cultural support and development, and it is especially pronounced relative to the size of a city, if familiarity has been the norm. An issue, therefore, now facing Kamloops, and no doubt other cities, is what kind of governance and planning can best ensure a city's cultural future and provide a vision, particularly when the city is expected to grow. Will the city assume more responsibility not only by providing financial support and initiating capital projects, but also by prescribing specific directions for the arts and heritage community? As noted, the Cultural Strategic Plan recommends maintaining a public/community governance model, but will it actually translate into partnerships and collaborations?

These questions are more than rhetorical; they refer once again to issues of policy and policy making, and ultimately to participation, if citizens are to remain engaged in shaping the cultural present and future of Kamloops. These questions also apply to the supervision of other sectors, but they have particular resonance for the arts and heritage in Kamloops, given the well-documented, comparatively rich history of cultural participation. I'm not implying that there should be no accountability, fiscal or otherwise, or that artists and arts and heritage organizations represent a special case and that a climate of entitlement should prevail. Rather, I want to underscore the presence of existing strengths, demonstrated by the evolution of the major arts organizations and by the level and kinds of community participation. To state it another way, a cultural plan or policy can be a helpful and effective tool and a rationale for moving ahead what a municipal government requires, but it can also be an instance where culture "is something that is evoked rather than something that is," to use a characterization that is appropriate to many policy documents (Dominguez 23).

## Leadership and Competition

Leadership and competition are two pertinent issues in the examination of cultural participation and the culture of participation in small cities. First, consider leadership. A recent study of policies and funding for culture in 26 Canadian cities claims that there are three necessary pillars of support: consistent and substantial municipal funding, local leadership, and a commitment by business

(Baeker and Cardinal). As I have already noted, funding by the City of Kamloops is certainly significant and proportionally well above the national average. By contrast, business support is waning — not for lack of interest, but because of a decline in the number of companies and/or company operations. The support of Weyerhaeuser, owner of the city's pulp mill, is a case in point. In the late 1990s it contributed $350,000 to the art gallery's building campaign, but since then much of Weyerhaeuser's management operations have been centralized in Vancouver. While the company remains a key component of the city's industrial base and continues to support many local organizations, including those in the cultural sector, its actual corporate presence is considerably less. Many local businesses continue to provide support through sponsorships, donations and in-kind contributions, but it is harder and harder to find new support, owing again not to resistance and indifference but to economic uncertainty.

Leadership has been strongest and most consistent in the arts and heritage sector itself and this applies to people working in the sector and to volunteers, including many from the business community. For one thing, the contribution of the heads of the major arts organizations in years has been quite remarkable. Bruce Dunn and Kathy Humphreys have each served fourteen years as, respectively, music director and manager of the symphony. Jann L.M. Bailey has been director of the Kamloops Art Gallery for more than seventeen years, and David Ross is currently celebrating his twentieth year as artistic director of WCT. Lori Marchand has been the theatre's administrative director for only four years but she has long-standing connections to the community. Elisabeth Duckworth has served the Kamloops Museum for over twenty years while others, such as Julia Mitra, have long-term relationships with various organizations, including the Community Arts Council of Kamloops. The volunteer side is equally significant, evidenced for example in the account of the symphony's development, during which several board members of the theatre company gave over twenty years of service.

Whereas Putnam's notion of social capital has accounted for many patterns of cultural activity in Kamloops thus far, including the importance of leadership, Florida's idea of the creative class and what attracts them to a community is also now relevant. For one thing, Florida prizes innovation as a stimulant to economic development but sees it primarily in the form of high-technology employment; he also stresses the importance of cultural amenities and services to attract the various constituents of the creative class. Yet, for him, the efforts required are to be found not in old affiliations but in new ones. He states: "Places with dense ties and high levels of traditional social capital provide advantages to insiders and thus promote stability, whereas places with looser networks and weaker ties are open to newcomers and thus promote novel combinations of resources and ideas" (273).

As the evolution and diversity of the arts and heritage organizations once again demonstrates, stability is a key factor of success, as evidenced by the pattern of long-standing leadership, Yet leadership has not placed the reins on innovation, on what Florida calls the novel combination of resources and ideas, be it the work of particular individuals or arts groups or the commitment to increasing recreational activities. Substantial investments of time over many years are also necessary for development; a sustainable environment is perhaps better achieved on a smaller scale in a small area, where social capital is abundant and, by

extension, where fuller community participation is more realizable and recognizable. The result, to recall Brooks and Kushner, is a magnitude of cultural activity that is significant given the population of Kamloops but at present is not yet faced with the dilemma of overcapacity.

However, there are challenges. One that pertains to the arts and heritage sector is future governance. Another is the inevitable challenge of succession, which the four major cultural organizations will have to face eventually. Moreover, while Kamloops may offer significant opportunities and possibilities for future arts administrators, artists and educators, it will have to compete on a national scale with larger cities and metropolitan areas. Despite all of its virtues and amenities, including its cultural strengths, the perception of Kamloops as a small city may be a handicap.

Competition is also not confined to the job market, because like leadership it is tied in many ways to the city's cultural present and future. Perception is also very much at the heart of what are regarded as competitive forces, internally and externally. First, and as indicated, cultural participation is part of a wider culture of participation in Kamloops that is especially evident in sports and recreation. There are two ways of interpreting this relationship. It can be considered a virtue and a source of potential for both the development of the arts and heritage and for the city as a whole. Or it can been seen as competitive in a disabling sense, with financial and organizational support for culture paling beside the investments in sports and recreation, such as the recent decision to develop or upgrade facilities. The concern is not so much that cultural consumption, production or volunteering will decrease, but that the prominence of sports and recreation will dwarf it, and that Kamloops will be increasingly represented and perceived as a city, indeed a community and a place, known for sports and recreation. Call this the consequences of branding, but it raises issues regarding the future of participation as far as residents and visitors are concerned, and which will no doubt go beyond the specific commitment and concerns of the arts and heritage sector.

Outside competition is primarily found two hours south, in Kelowna and the entire Okanagan region. There has been a historical rivalry between the two cities and regions; more recently the stakes, at least from Kamloops' perspective, have become bigger and more serious given how fast Kelowna and its surrounding communities have grown. The main development is increasing centralization of resources and services — in the area of health care, for example — with the result that Kelowna is the *de facto* centre of the British Columbia southern interior. The reallocation or transfer of services is by no means particular to Kelowna; British Columbia's government, and other provincial governments for that matter, are rationalizing services through various kinds of mergers and regional centralization. Other contributing factors play a role, including Kelowna's current status as a preferred destination for retirees and its agricultural richness, especially its wine industry.

Nevertheless, Kamloops makes a case for competition as an enabling factor. Most notable is the development of the city as a site for sports and recreational activities for both residents and visitors. While the "tournament program" may not be a direct response to the rapid developments of Kelowna and the Okanagan region, it certainly does distinguish Kamloops and does so by building on community assets and support. Kamloops may also have a competitive edge as a more liveable community precisely because Kelowna's fast, but not necessarily smart,

growth may be resulting in as many problems as enhancements. For example, it is estimated that the Okanagan region has a population of over 300,000 including Kelowna, which is now over 125,000, making it more a midsized city with the concomitant challenges that come with a rapid population increase, such as sprawl, traffic congestion and rising housing prices.

The arts and heritage also present a particular case in point. For the past ten years Kelowna has invested heavily in facilities located in a cultural district near its main lake and adjacent to a large resort hotel and casino. Yet the arts organizations themselves are not especially stable: a theatre company and the Okanagan Symphony have had financial woes, and while the Kelowna Art Gallery has made notable strides, this is only a recent development. The city and the surrounding region also strongly encourage tourism with the promotion of what is termed the Okanagan Cultural Corridor. By comparison, Kamloops arts and heritage organizations are distinguished by stability in many respects and by the magnitude of activity relative to its population.

## The Culture of Participation: A Summing Up

This account of cultural activity in Kamloops reveals a substantial amount of long-standing commitments and connectedness, an involvement in the arts and heritage community rooted in what has been termed a culture of participation stretching across sectors, age groups, and neighbourhoods. This situation is by no means something easily achieved, given the interplay of factors: municipal structure and leadership and the close proximity of people, organizations, and events may strike some as something of a fish bowl experience. Yet it is the very lack of connection that many studies, especially Putnam's, suggest is missing in urban life. Consider, for example, a recent study of Silicon Valley, perhaps one of the most affluent places in the world and seemingly incomparable to Kamloops or cities of similar size or relative geographic isolation.[8] Called the *Creative Community Index*, the study attempts, through an elaborate framework, to understand how the arts produce tangible and economic benefits and in doing so contribute to the creative capacities of individuals and groups. It identifies four phenomena as instrumental: (1) *cultural levers*, such as leadership, investment and policies; (2) *cultural assets*, such as venues and facilities; (3) *cultural participation*, which includes variables such as actual attendance; and (4) *cultural outcomes*, which for this region are creativity, local contributions and connectedness. The noticeable lack of the latter was confirmed by the "Social Capital Benchmark Survey,"[8] in which Silicon Valley ranked the lowest on an indexed measure of participation and membership in associations and similar kinds of groups, such as sports leagues, neighborhood associations and service clubs (*Creative Community Index* 5, 13).

I want to point out as well that the study by Brooks and Kushner, which provided initial conceptual and methodological guidance to this chapter, includes San Jose, the largest city in the Silicon Valley region, in their sample and the findings are especially consistent. In the general art rankings of cities they used, San Jose was relatively high with respect to the level of audience activity. But, as is evident from the Kamloops experience, attending events is only one component of cultural participation. Arts organizations may attract lots of paying customers, but the presence of these customers is no guarantee of community connectedness, if we apply the findings of the Social Capital Benchmark Survey. Brooks and Kushner also found that the number of

arts organizations was decidedly low relative to the size of the population, as was the amount spent per inhabitant on the arts — measures that would seem to be further consistent with the lack of overall participation.

I suspect that Florida and Putnam would not be surprised by any of these findings, but they would base their responses on very different perspectives. Florida would point to the presence in Silicon Valley of a substantial "creative class" of highly skilled and educated people who greatly contribute to the wealth of places, and whose "participation" in activities or use of resources, cultural or otherwise, is not predicated on old forms of social capital, such as trust relations, but on loose or weak social ties. By contrast, Putnam would claim that the lack of traditional social capital is, in effect, responsible for the lack or decline of community and the lack of connectedness found in the region. Moreover, and as evidenced by the discussions in his Saguaro Seminar, he may contend that arts and heritage involvement has the potential to assist in building community precisely because it requires the participation of people as producers, consumers and volunteers. As well, one cannot assume, as Florida does, that traditional social capital only provides "advantages to insiders" (3), for if a university or some other major service employer and knowledge maker is in a given community, there is the potential for the co-existing, if not overlapping, of various kinds of traditional social capital and new or looser networks. Kamloops confirms Putnam's analysis and even his remedy to the extent that social capital seems to be thriving rather than dwindling.

Let me end with a concluding personal observation. In October 2003, I spoke at a morning meeting of a Rotary Club, which in Putnam's world is an exemplary form of social capital, and which includes several club members who are also cultural stalwarts. As the meeting was coming to an end, it was proudly announced that a fifth club was to be established in another part of Kamloops.[9] For Florida, this achievement, in a city of 80,000, is probably nothing more than the stuff of nostalgia, and blindness to the rapid and intense social, political and economic changes felt locally and globally. He may well be right. But in the specific case of arts and heritage, if the small city, with Kamloops as case study, has anything conclusive to say, it is that the futures of culture and community are inextricably linked if the real desire is for an urban life that is truly participatory.

## Acknowledgments

I would like to thank Stephanie Rothman, my research assistant, for gathering and assembling information about arts and heritage organizations, and Jann L.M. Bailey, Nancy Duxbury, Kathy Humphreys, Trish Keegan, Lanni MacInnis, Lori Marchand, and Mike Puhallo for their time and knowledge. I would also like to acknowledge the editorial comments of four anonymous reviewers.

## Notes

1. Participant observation as a qualitative methodology has a rich history in the social sciences. For an indication of various approaches see, for example, D.L. Jorgenson, James Spradley and Lon Dubinsky.

2. This includes, for example, tourism marketing, much of which is undertaken by Venture Kamloops, which promotes through various publications, trade show presentations and other forms of advertising, the city's various amenities, services and resources in sports, recreation and culture.

3. For a further confirmation of the scope of voluntary activity in the heritage community in Kamloops and the Thompson-Nicola region, see the summary of the focus group conducted in Kamloops by Catherine C. Cole and Lon Dubinsky in March 2003, for a study of volunteerism by Catherine C. Cole and Associates commissioned by the Department of Canadian Heritage.

4. Source: Rec\Arts\Budget 1997-2003, City of Kamloops. The yearly amount does not include support of approximately $235,000 in the form of lease or service agreements, such as the funds received by the gallery for maintenance costs and fees and a fee to Western Canada Theatre to manage the Sagebrush Theatre space. During 2003, as well, an additional $1.6 million dollars was set aside for capital expenditures projects.

5. See Carla Ball. The amounts indicated do not include support from lease and service agreements, capital expenditures and are confined to expenditures such as operating grants to arts organizations, community arts initiatives and other program activities.

6. See Anne Russo and Tracy Seddon, p.39. This amount only refers to operating grants and does not include support arising from service and lease agreements or capital expenditures. It also must be noted that the amount applies to Victoria proper within the Capital Regional District, yet the city accounts for only approximately 25% of the population in the region, whereas per capita support by other municipalities is negligible. By comparison, Kamloops has a population equalling Victoria's, and the support by other communities in the Thompson-Nicola Regional District is equally negligible.

7. For a sampling of press coverage see Robert Koopmans, Cam Fortems and Darshan Lindsay.

8. *Creative Community Index: Measuring Progress Toward A Vibrant Silicon Valley*, 5. The social benchmark study was particularly cited by this report because it provided recent data that attempted to compare forms of social and cultural capital in many cities.

9. Weekly meeting of the Daybreak Rotary Club, Coast Canadian Inn, October 10, 2003.

## Works Cited

Baeker, Greg, and Donna Cardinal. *Municipal Cultural Planning Project*. 16 August 2004. <www.culturalplanning.ca/MCPP>

Ball, Carla. *Cultural Grants (Arts and Heritage) in Major Canadian Cities*. Halifax Regional Municipality, Culture & Heritage Unit, August 2002

Baird, Nini. "The Birth of the Kamloops Art Gallery." *Kamloops Art Gallery Newsletter*. November/December 2002/January 2003, Vol. 15, No. 5.

Bennett, Sherry. "Kamloops Symphony Orchestra — A 'Class'ical Act." Unpublished paper, Canadian Studies Course, The University College of the Cariboo, 1998.

Birnie, Peter. "B.C. Still Last in Arts Funding from Ottawa." *Vancouver Sun*. 14 January 2004. Section C, 1-2.

Brooks, Arthur C., and Roland J. Kushner. "What Makes an Arts Capital? Quantifying a City's Cultural Environment." *International Journal of Arts Management*. 5.1 (Fall 2002): 12-23.

City of Kamloops. *Arts and Recreation Budget*. Rec\Arts\Budget 1997-2003.

*Creative Community Index: Measuring Progress Toward A Vibrant Silicon Valley*. Silicon Valley: Cultural Initiatives, 2002.

Dominguez, Virginia. "Invoking Culture: The Messy Side of Cultural Politics." *South Atlantic Quarterly*, Vol. 91, No.1, Winter (1992): 19-42.

Dubinsky, Lon. "Musing About Small Cities in an Intercultural World." Lecture delivered at the Reinwardt Academy, Amsterdam School of the Arts, Amsterdam, Netherlands, June, 2003.

Dubinsky, Lon, and W.F. Garrett-Petts. "'Working Well, Together': Arts-based Research and the Cultural Future of Small Cities." *AI & Society*, Vol. 16, No. 4. November (2002): 332-349.

Egoyan, Atom. "Atom's Oscar Diary." *MacLean's*, April 6 (1998): 61-64.

Florida, Richard. *The Rise of the Creative Class*. New York: Basic, 2003.

Fortems, Cam. "City Manager Wants Council to Rein in Gallery, Arts Groups." *The Daily News*. 21 January 2004. A5.

Janzen & Associates. *Kamloops Cultural Strategic Plan*. Commissioned by the City of Kamloops, December, 2003

Jorgenson, D.L. *Participant Observation: A Methodology of Human Studies*. Thousand Oaks, CA: Sage, 1989.

Kamloops Art Gallery. Collected *The Daily News* and *Kamloops This Week* press clippings, January — April 2004. Unpublished collection.

Koopmans, Robert. "Art Gallery Denied Extra Funding as Council Trims List." *The Daily News*. 11 February 2004. A5.

——. "Art Gallery Requests $50,000 Grant to Keep Programs Going for Another Year." *The Daily News*. 7 January 2004. A2.

——. "Gallery Fears Program Cuts Will Appeal to Councilors." *The Daily News* 12 February 2004. A4.

Lindsay, Darshan. "Band-aids Not Wanted for Arts." *Kamloops This Week* 21 January 2004. 7.

——. "Local Gallery Well Funded by the City." *Kamloops This Week* 5 March 2004. 5.

Lippard, Lucy. *The Lure of the Local*. New York: New Press, 1997.

McAlear, Donna. *Kamloops Art Gallery Newsletter* Vol. 16, No. 2. June/July/August (2003): 3-4.

McInnis, Lanni, and Stephanie Rothman. Personal Interview. 26 February 2004.

"New Budget Information Adds Weight to Gallery's Request." *The Daily News* 24 February 2004. A4.

Putnam, Robert. *Bowling Alone*. New York: Simon, 2000.

Russo, Anne, and Tracy Seddon. *Inventory of Local Government Investment in The Arts Capital Regional District*. Prepared for the Capital Regional District Arts Committee, Victoria, B.C.: October, 2002.

*Saguaro Seminar: Civic Engagement in America*. 16 August 2004.
<www.ksg.Harvard.edu/saguaro/mtg7.html>

Spradley, James. *Participant Observation*. New York: Thomson International Publishing, 1997.

# A Cultural Hinterland?
# Searching for the Creative Class
# in the Small Canadian City

## Ross Nelson

## Introduction

Over the last decade, Kamloops' civic administrators and business community have re-oriented their efforts to attract new investments and jobs and to retain those already established. In the past, the city has concentrated on opportunities closely related to the city's traditional economic base: resource industries, transportation and distribution facilities, and regional retail functions. However, the region's economy is currently experiencing significant structural change. Education, government services, tourism, and cultural functions are now the city's most dynamic sectors (MacKinnon and Nelson). This economic shift has encouraged civic officials to invest in new infrastructure, to supplement their traditional pitch with an appeal based upon an "outstanding quality of life set in a spectacular landscape" (ThompsonJobs.com).

A recent decision to invest $37.6 million into sporting facilities suggests evidence of the city's commitment to infrastructure. Approved in a recent referendum, the goals of the planned expenditures are (1) to "make Kamloops a Quality of Life center" by enhancing its recreational capacity, and (2) to stimulate "new economic development and

growth" through its Tournament Capital of Canada program. Other completed initiatives include the establishment of Kenna Cartwright Nature Park in 1996, which, at almost 800 hectares, is the largest municipal park in British Columbia, the construction of interconnected walking and biking trails along the banks of the North and South Thompson Rivers, the formulation of a strategic plan to co-ordinate arts and heritage organizations in the city (Janzen & Associates), and the elevation of the local and regional presence of University College of the Cariboo (UCC). The city actively supported, for example, a recently realized public campaign to graduate UCC to full university status. City officials and UCC also collaborated on plans to establish a technology park as well as a retail-office-student services corridor on the edge of campus (City of Kamloops and University College of the Cariboo). The broad vision behind these efforts is, in the words of the Chair of UCC's Board of Governors, to create a "university city" within the city (Olynyk).

Kamloops is not alone in its attempts to re-orient its economy. Culture, in the form of the arts, history, architecture, education, recreation, and life-on-the-street — the sense of a place that arises from the unique intersection of a built environment and a local population — have become hot commodities generally. Contrary to the prevailing theory that we are becoming a society of individuals who "bowl alone" (Putnam), cocoon in home theatres, and inhabit virtual worlds of cyber junkies, our study of Kamloops and small cities generally supports Richard Florida's contention that "place and community are more critical factors than ever before" (219). He also argues that tax incentives, industrial parks, and relaxed regulations — the standbys of traditional regional economic development schemes — are outdated and insufficient. The key ingredients for attracting high-tech firms, business and professional services, and health care are the so-called intangibles: lifestyle, diversity, social networks, authenticity, and identity. From this perspective, the character or quality of a place becomes its most saleable feature; it is a key ingredient in the competition to lure the "creative people who generate innovations, develop technology-intensive industries and power economic growth" in the modern world (Gertler et al. ii).

The goal of this chapter is to use Kamloops and other small cities in Canada as a lens for exploring the themes raised by Florida and others. In particular, the chapter reports the results of a class research project I developed during the winter term of 2004. I begin by describing the pedagogical basis of the project and its place within the Cultural Future of Small Cities research agenda. This large, federally funded project aims to elucidate the character and role of culture, broadly defined, in cities with less than 150,000 people. The paper then reviews the connection between culture, societal changes, and regional economic development, paying particular attention to the theoretical place of small cities within debates about the creative

class, specifically, and the qualities of postmodern culture and postindustrial society, generally. Two studies conducted by students form the empirical heart of the paper. One of the studies replicates an earlier assessment of the creative class in large Canadian cities by Gertler et al. The other study is a more selective assessment of the cultural capital of small Canadian cities that are home to postsecondary institutions. The chapter concludes with an assessment of both the study's pedagogical merits and the character of small city culture — as a product and as an element of a place — within Kamloops' economic future.

## Strategies for Integrating Student Research into the Classroom

The empirical section of this chapter is based on research conducted by senior undergraduate students in my Geography of Tourism course at the UCC. This course forms a regular part of the curriculum, but its content was re-oriented to address themes of interest to the larger CURA project. In particular, the course was built around ideas that explore the role of culture in tourism and the impact of tourism on the culture of urban and rural spaces. Lectures and seminar discussions considered how the emphasis on lifestyle, leisure, and recreation in contemporary society has elevated the status of tourist experiences, and how the cultural ascendancy of tourist spaces within postindustrial society has reshaped the built and symbolic environment. Along the way, all of the students, some 35 in number, were required to write and present critical reviews of four articles. The purpose of the reviews was two-fold: to introduce students to the theoretical and empirical literature on cultural tourism, and to practise writing strategies for summarizing complex material. Initial reviews concentrated on seminal works by Dean MacCannell, Lucy Lippard, Erik

Cohen, and John Urry. Students were subsequently asked to assess empirical studies that addressed the issues at hand within the context of small cities and rural areas. Some examples include Mitchell's and Dahms's assessments of changes in Niagara-on-the-Lake and St. Jacobs, Ontario; Paradis's work on Galena, Illinois, and Roswell, New Mexico; studies of the connections between First Nations' tourism, culture, and rural areas (Zeppel; Notzke); and analyses of the role and impact of cultural institutions on tourism in small cities (Mitchell; Jamieson; Bascom; Bunting). I concluded the course with examples of my own reviews on Marxist interpretations of cultural tourism.

Students subsequently used this theoretical backdrop to situate group research projects on cultural tourism. Several projects summarized material in existing studies of cultural tourism (e.g., reports produced by cities actively pursuing the creative class) or examined how data assembled by cultural agencies (e.g., Canada Museums Association) or governments (Government of Canada) informed our research agenda. Other projects adapted the methods and data sources of existing studies to fit the scale and context of the Cultural Future of Small Cities project. Key examples here, and the subject of subsequent sections, include an assessment of the creative class in small Canadian cities and an evaluation of the culture of "university" towns across Canada.

Although these studies do not address tourism directly, they are concerned with a critical dimension of tourism — the consumption of place — that runs through contemporary society. Members of Florida's creative class are very similar to Dean MacCannell's tourists: both are motivated by a perceived loss of authenticity in everyday life and thus by a "developing interest in the 'real life' of others" (91). They share, in other words, a common "fetish" with "urban public street life, rural village life, and traditional domestic relations" — a fetish that is played out in the act of postmodern tourism and the creation of lifestyle communities.

From the outset, the Community-University Research Alliances (CURA) research team has sought pedagogically sound ways to integrate meaningful research experiences into its undergraduate curriculum. Unlike the province's major universities, the UCC does not offer graduate degrees in the mainstream arts and science programs.[1] Researchers consequently draw upon the skills and resources of an undergraduate program. In addition to re-orienting regular course material to address our research themes, CURA faculty have also employed students as research assistants, tapped into UCC's student research scholarship program, and offered directed research and service-learning courses to individual students or small groups.

The Biography of a Building and 1901 Population Profile are examples of two other research projects that have run within regular courses. The former ran within a Historical Geography of Canada after Confederation course. In it, students used records housed by the Kamloops Museum and Archives to build heritage profiles of residential dwellings. Students traced construction and renovation details, property subdivisions, ownership, tax assessments, and values. They also used the archive's cross-referenced files to search for photographs of the buildings and bibliographic information about people who lived in them. In a similar fashion, students in the Historical Geography of Urbanization course have collaborated with the Kamloops Museum and Archives to create a statistical database of the city in 1901. Each student was responsible for digitizing several sheets of the 1901 federal census and the city's tax files for the same year. Students also helped create a digital map of properties in 1901 by marrying scanned archival maps with the city planning department's Geographic Information System files, digital data sets and maps used by city planners. Students used the end products in research projects on the demography and geography of ethnic groups, the status of women, the social and business networks of prominent citizens and landowners, and the occupational profile of the city. The Biography of a Building and the 1901 Population Profile projects are linked to the CURA's Neighbourhoods 2000 Project. The goal of the neighbourhoods theme is to document the evolution of Kamloops' cultural landscape and thereby provide a background for understanding planning issues currently before the city.

UCC's service-learning courses were created to foster interaction between the community and the university generally, and among the Cultural Future of Small Cities partners, students, and research faculty specifically. With a maximum enrolment of five third- or fourth-year students, service learning provides a shell course, granting students credit for participation in community or work-based projects. Projects are proposed and approved on a "one time only" basis, supervised by a community partner and a faculty member, and graded either pass or fail. Examples of CURA-related service-learning projects include the documentation of historical land use and the planning initiatives in a north shore neighbourhood (undertaken with city planners) and a study of how differences in cultural values and communication styles lead to conflict in debates over land use (with the Forest Research Extension Partnership). The latter project culminated in the creation of a 22-minute video now used in provincial and international workshops designed to foster more efficient communica-

tion by narrowing the rhetorical divide between forest sector stakeholders (Baker et al.).

CURA faculty have also developed special topics courses to address central themes of the project. "Art and Culture in the Small City" and "Reading and Writing the Small City" are two examples. The former looks at how arts organizations are implicated in community development and, in particular, in the creation of the cultural capital that some believe is critical to the health of contemporary cities. The latter explores how contemporary rhetorical theory informs descriptive and creative writing about small cities. The collective goal of these efforts is not just to further the objectives of the research program; it is hoped that the inclusion of research within the classroom will deepen students' educational experiences in ways that are often not available within undergraduate curricula and that it will help build the research culture on a campus that was a two-year transfer institution only fifteen years ago.

## The Theoretical Context
Florida, the Creative Class,
and the Search for Culture

Richard Florida's *The Rise of the Creative Class* has certainly struck a chord with urban studies professionals, and others. Published in 2002, the book quickly became an award-winning best seller in North America. It has also attracted an international audience. Florida currently rubs shoulders with the likes of J.K. Rowling, Bill Bryson, and Michael Moore on top twenty lists in Denmark, the Netherlands, and Finland. Florida is also highly sought after on the lecture circuit — requests for his five-figure engagements are handled through an agent — and fronts a team of consultants that helps "regions and organizations to become more creative places" (Florida "Speaking/Media") Recently, he has relocated from Pittsburgh, where he was the H. John Heinz III Professor of Regional Economic Development at Carnegie Mellon University, to George Mason University in Washington, DC, in order to address a wider audience (Copeland). Florida's ideas have also attracted the interest of academics. More detailed assessments of the trends outlined in the *Creative Class* can be found in journals such as *Economic Geography*, the *Journal of Economic Geography*, and the *Annals*, the flagship publication of the Association of American Geographers.

The subject of Florida's book is difficult to define precisely. Like the bourgeoisie or proletariat, members of the so-called creative class share economic, social, and cultural traits. However, the creative class is thought to be more multi-faceted and loosely connected than its historical predecessors; as a group, says Florida, they "defy classification based on race, ethnicity, gender, sexual preference or appearance" (79). Florida does allow, nevertheless, that the creative class can be broken into two broad employment categories. The "Super Creative Core" includes people who generate new ideas, knowledge, and products. This group includes innovators in business and science (engineers, computer scientists, and analysts), the arts and entertainment (writers, actors, musicians, and architects), as well as politics and affiliated occupations (opinion-makers, newspaper editors, and social and cultural icons). Surrounding this core, we find creative professionals: lawyers, bankers, managers, physicians, and high-tech workers not included in the first group. People engaged in these occupations are creative problem solvers — their primary mandate is to test, refine, and apply existing knowledge to problems that arise in the normal course of workplace activities

(69). Because of the emphasis on knowledge in these occupations, members of the creative class tend to be highly educated (i.e., possessing university degrees); they also typically earn higher wages and are more geographically mobile than people working in other sectors of the economy.

Florida estimates that the creative class constitutes approximately 30% of the work force in the United States, 40% of whom are members of the super-creative core, making it the second largest segment of the labour force. People employed in traditional working-class occupations (manufacturing, transportation, maintenance, and construction) used to hold this status; however, this sector's share of employment has steadily declined since the 1950s. Only one in four people now make their living in this sector. Traditional services (e.g., personal services, retail, food preparation, repair, clerical, janitorial, and security occupations) currently constitute the largest sector, representing approximately 43% of the labour force. Florida's data suggests, however, that the relative importance of this sector has begun to decline, especially in light of the rapid growth being experienced by the creative class. People employed in extractive industries (agriculture, mining, forestry) account for the remaining 2% of the work force (72-77). In Canada, the relative order is similar, although the percentage employed in extractive industries is slightly higher, and the working class slightly lower.

Florida argues that the significance of the creative class far exceeds its numbers. The creative class is made up of trendsetters. They are reshaping not only the economy, but also the character of the workplace and face of cities. Drawing on the work of Peter Drucker, Florida argues that knowledge workers are more akin to volunteers: they are less motivated by money than by the experience of work. They expect to enjoy work and to dress casually, and to participate in administrative decisions. They are willing to work long hours, but want flexible schedules, and, perhaps above all, they want to work in a creative environment — in a place with high ceilings, bold colours, lots of light, and places to hang out. In short, in a place that feels like home (116-162). Given this orientation to work, the creative class, according to Florida, is strongly influenced by lifestyle considerations when looking for work. Florida believes that the creative class — especially its younger representatives — is drawn to cities with diverse populations, a vibrant nightlife, street-level culture, opportunities for outdoor recreation, and a unique and authentic atmosphere. Amenities and experiences are what matter most; or, in other words, the creative class wants to work where it recreates. If correct, Florida's interpretation suggests that traditional locational criteria such as low-cost labour, transportation linkages, or resource endowments are less critical for explaining the geography of the knowledge economy. By implication, tax subsidies, serviced industrial parks, and training allowances are not enough, perhaps even inconsequential. The creative class itself is the motor of the new economy. To lure the creative class, city officials must invest in the "livability" of their communities.

While not an advocate of bricks and mortar strategies, Florida does single out universities as essential building blocks in the new economy. He argues that the "presence of a major research university is ... more important than the canals, railroads and freeway systems of past epochs." Universities are "a huge potential source of competitive advantage" because they are "amazingly effective talent attracters," and because talent in turn generates spin-off companies and attracts new business (291-292). As intellectual, cultural, and economic hubs, universities offer both the research infrastructure and highly skilled labour pools required by high-technology firms. They also attract a diverse population and foster the "progressive" and dynamic environments that the creative class finds appealing (292).

Measuring the Creative Class

Florida's arguments offer a synthesis of a wide range of ideas put forward in urban planning, sociology, economics, and business studies over the last 40 years. He draws heavily on classics such as Jane Jacobs' *Life and Death of Great American Cities,* Daniel Bell's *The Coming of Post-industrial Society,* and William Whyte's *The Organization Man,* as well as recent but widely debated works by Putnam (*Bowling Alone*), Brooks (*Bobos in Paradise*), and Ray and Anderson (*The Cultural Creatives*). The *Creative Class* is, however, more than a survey or theoretical account; it also functions as a manual for detecting and attracting knowledge workers. In particular, the book provides a set of constructs for measuring the creativity of a community; it provides a road map to the winners and losers in the new economy. While few concrete planning or marketing strategies are detailed, brief case studies and personal anecdotes hint at possibilities. The popular success of the *Creative Class* is due primarily to these practical elements.

According to Florida's surveys, interviews, and focus groups, the creative class has three general clusters of values: individuality, meritocracy, and diversity and openness. The last of these is the most critical — it is "a fundamental marker" of the creative class (79). The emphasis on diversity reflects both the makeup of members in the creative class and their taste and tolerance for diversity. Three of Florida's six indices focus on this dimension. The Melting Pot index (percent of the population that is foreign-born) assesses the ethnic diversity of a region; the Gay index (the proportion of gay people in a region compared to the nation as a whole) social diversity; and the Bohemian index (the relative presence of artistically creative people) assesses cultural diversity. The other indices are more traditional economic measures. The High-Tech (output generated by high-tech industries as a percent of the economy), Innovation (patents per capita), and Talent (the proportion of people with a bachelor's degree) indices assess the tangible presence of knowledge industries in an area. Florida uses these measures individually and collectively in the form of a composite "Creativity Index."

Florida and his collaborators have had to drop or modify some of the indices to study the creative class in Canada. In a report prepared for the Ontario Ministry of Enterprise, Innovation and Creativity, four indices are used: Talent, Bohemian, Mosaic (equivalent to the Melting Pot), and Tech-Pole (Gertler et al.). The first three are very similar to those used for the United States. The fourth is roughly equivalent to the High-Tech index, but uses employment rather than economic output to assess the regional importance of the high-tech industry. The Gay and Innovation indices were not included due to inadequate data.

Florida's applications of these indices confirm his broad arguments. Top-ranked cities are typically well-known centres of the computer industry. San Francisco, Austin, Boston, San Diego, Seattle, Raleigh-Durham, Houston are respectively the top seven "creative" cities in the United States; while Montreal, Toronto, Ottawa-Hull, Vancouver, and Calgary are the top five Tech-Poles in Canada. At the bottom we find smaller, regional centres, especially those dependent on resource or heavy manufacturing industries: in the United States, Bloomington (Indiana), Lynchburg (Virginia),

Lubbock (Texas) are representative — in Canada, Chicoutimi-Jonquiere, Windsor, and Sudbury. Florida's research has also found strong connections between the indices. In the United States, the Gay index proved to be the best predictor of the concentration of high-tech industry. The statistical correlation (r) between these measures has steadily increased over time and now exceeds 0.55 for the 268 cities he examined, and over 0.70 for cities with a population over 1 million (255-257).[2] The strongest predictor in Canada was the Bohemian index (r=0.74). In both countries the Melting Pot / Mosaic indices were the weakest, despite the fact that each country's largest cities are the favoured destinations of international migrants.

The Creative Class and
the Prospects of Small Cities

In hindsight, the *Creative Class* provided an excellent pedagogical tool. Students recognized links between Florida's ideas and those they already knew or were concurrently learning. There are strong parallels between, for example, the creative class and what the urban geographer David Ley calls the "new middle class," and between Florida's geography of the new economy and Sassen's discussion of how the globalization of finance and producer services is causing a system of world cities to arise. Students were especially cognizant of differences between Florida's cultural assessment of the creative class and those of Marxist or conservative critics. Many felt that the *Creative Class* neither adequately examines the narcissistic and hedonistic tendencies of the creative class, nor explores how these tendencies are embedded in the capitalist system. Some cynics even suggested that the book is too eager to please planners and politicians, and, in the process, glosses over the creative class's negative dimensions and impacts, for example, displacement caused by gentrification and the commodification of place. Others were suspicious of the methodology and variables used. Several argued, for example, that the measures chosen only indirectly assess the creative class and the amenities they seek. The Melting Pot / Mosaic index, for example, assumes a direct correlation between the prevalence of foreigners and the number of ethnic restaurants, international bookstores, and movie festivals in a community. Discussions around this topic generated lists of alternative variables and methodologies. The decision to duplicate the strategy used by a commercial firm for evaluating college towns was a direct outcome of these debates.

The most common and undoubtedly the most passionate criticism raised concerned geographic scale. Students argued that the *Creative Class* is inattentive to the prospects of smaller cities, and, when addressed, too dismissive. Florida considers many small communities to be "hopeless" cases. In particular, he suggests that small communities, especially those tainted with the residue of resource extraction or noxious industries, cannot go head-to-head in the global competition to attract postindustrial firms: they lack the diversity and cultural capital necessary to attract the creative class. According to Florida, "the hopeless places are the Enid, Oklahomas, the Youngstown, Ohios, the small places with huge working-class backgrounds, or places that are service-class centers that aren't tourist destinations. They're all at the bottom of my lists. They're the places that are just being completely left behind. So size really is an advantage. If you're big, you can offer a lot of options and do a lot of things" (qtd. in Dreher).

Florida's position is understandable. Metropolitan cities — by virtue of their size and diversity — are the primary destinations for immigrants, artists, marginalized popula-

tions, and capital. As a result, population growth in recent years has been concentrated in large cities. For example, Canada's four largest cities accounted for 62% of the nation's growth between 1996 and 2001, while cities with 300,000 or more people captured 92% of the total (Simmons and Bourne). In contrast, many smaller cities have struggled. According to Simmons's and Bourne's analysis, the average growth rate for regions outside the commuter zone of metropolitan areas was -0.4% over this period. Places particularly hard hit are typically located in the country's resource periphery. This situation is not, furthermore, a short-term trend. Some of the forest, mining, and fishing towns of northern Ontario, Quebec, and British Columbia are smaller now than they were 30 years ago. The population of Powell River in 2001, for example, was 1.5% less than in 1971, Prince Rupert 3.1% less, and Port Alberni 7.5% less. Even more dramatic examples are found on the prairies. Here, a combination of factors has led to the virtual abandonment of many small communities. Escalating freight rates for grain, mechanized agricultural practices, and weak commodity prices have contributed to the demise of family-run farms, and with them, the need for local grain elevators, schools, banks, general stores, and recreational facilities (Boyens). As in other western societies, small communities in remote, resource-dependent regions have lost more than they have gained from the high-tech, globalized, information economy (Epp and Whitson).

## College Towns, Counterurbanization, and the Small City

While many small cities have recently struggled, others have held their own, or even prospered. Notable examples are college towns in the United States. College towns are small cities and towns under 150,000 where universities are the largest employer and the dominant cultural influence. College towns are unconventional and cosmopolitan centres of creativity and diversity: they "are home to unusual numbers of people who listen to National Public Radio, read Marx, vote Green, ride bicycles, or belong to a food co-op" (Gumprecht 5). Srebnick even argues that many American universities play this advantage to the hilt, selling their campuses to prospective students as academic "theme parks" (171), as places where students can purchase the "total experience" (174). College towns also attract workers and retired populations that value the "spark that comes … from young blood … [and the] jazz clubs, literary events, book stores, and cafes" and yet want outdoor recreational opportunities, safety, and lower living costs (ePodunk). Thus, college towns offer the best of both worlds: the diversity and worldliness of big cities with the community and charm of small towns. Communities that offer this combination of amenities, like Richard Florida's cultural centres, have recorded among the highest population growth rates in recent decades (Smutny). A statistical study of population and employment growth in the Mountain West region, for example, found that rates of in-migration are strongly influenced by the presence of post-secondary institutions (Booth).

Florida's emphasis on centres of high-tech also ignores the fact that many small communities, especially those in the shadows of metropolitan areas and those in well-endowed amenity locales, have experienced substantial population growth in recent decades. In British Columbia, the fastest growing areas over the last decade were the Squamish-Lillooet (population increased 37.8%) and Central Okanagan (34.5%) regional districts. Growth in the first region was driven by the transformation of Whistler from a local ski

hill into a year-round, international resort and lifestyle community for the affluent. The Central Okanagan has also benefited from its tourist-friendly climate and amenities, as well as its new role as one of Canada's five "high-tech boom towns" (*Kelowna Daily Courier*) Local economic development statistics suggest that Kelowna's high-tech sector grew 15% annually in the late 1990s. The region is trying to build on this success, promoting the "Silicon Vineyard" to "new ventures and growing companies looking for a lower cost, higher quality community" (Central Okanagan Economic Development Commission). Other areas that approached or exceeded the growth rate of Greater Vancouver (25.9%) include the Fraser Valley (29.5%), Sunshine Coast (25.0%), Nanaimo (27.1%), Cowichan Valley (20.8%), and North Okanagan (20.8%) regional districts. Affordable housing is probably the principal driving force in only one of these regions (Fraser Valley). In the others, the distance and cost of commuting to Vancouver or Victoria suggests that amenity and lifestyle factors are equally critical.

British Columbia's growth patterns are not unique. Above-average growth rates in non-metropolitan areas have been documented in many industrialized countries since the 1970s, reversing the "century-long migration towards high density core regions" (Vining and Pallone 339). In Canada, the migration to and subsequent transformation of small towns and rural areas within Toronto's urban field — a region of dispersed settlements beyond its municipal boundaries but with which it has regular economic and social contact — have been well documented (Coppack et al.; Wilkinson and Murray; Dahms; Mitchell, Atkinson and Clark; Dahms and McComb). Elora, St. Jacobs, Collingwood, and Niagara-on-the-Lake are notable examples of this trend. The economic base of all of these communities has shifted from agriculture or industry to tourism and service functions associated with their role as bedroom communities for long-distance commuters. A sizable literature has also developed on the mountainous west of the United States — collectively Montana, Idaho, Wyoming, Colorado, Utah, Nevada, New Mexico, and Arizona. This region has recently experienced among the highest growth rates, more than doubling its population since 1970 (Power). Furthermore, data compiled by Shumway and Davis indicate that with the exception of an out-flow during the first half of the 1980s, migration has been the driving factor behind population growth, and that growth rates have been high in both urbanized and rural counties. Since 1985, population and employment growth was stronger in the region's non-metro counties (those not within metropolitan statistical areas) than in the United States as a whole, and three times greater than their counterparts in other regions (Cromartie and Wardwell; Beyers).

From the Local to the Global:
Currents of Change

It is relatively easy to document the growth trajectories of small cities through census figures and business statistics. It is much more difficult, however, to explain the causes of growth or decline. In our highly interconnected and mobile societies, the economic and demographic vitality of a community is dependent not only on the health of local resources and developments, but also on the contexts within which they exist. In fact, many geographers argue that the globalization of markets has created "an ever-tightening mesh of networks which strengthens the interdependencies between different parts of the globe and, in so doing, helps to undermine the ability of nation-states [and cities]

to manage their own economic activities" (Allen 60-61). The pursuit of the creative class is a case in point: civic officials recognize that the fortunes of their communities are bound up with trends beyond their boundaries.

I have arranged the complex of economic, social, technological, and cultural factors shaping small cities into a five-armed star, with each arm corresponding to a contextual force (see Figure 1). The metaphorical reason for choosing this shape should be obvious: these are the forces that are energizing the growth of selected small cities. The star shape also suggests that while distinct, these forces are intimately interconnected, each dependent on and responsive to the others. Starting at the apex, and proceeding in a counter-clockwise fashion, the contextual forces are: (1) the rise and dominance of the new middle class; (2) the rapid growth of employment in the quaternary sector; (3) the evolution of new business and manufacturing strategies; (4) the development of new communication technologies and the extension of existing transportation linkages; and (5) the flowering of a cultural outlook that values "real" community and places. The first and second arms together form the focus of Florida's thesis and thus have already been described in some detail. In brief, I would argue that the creative class's social orientations, educational backgrounds, and career paths contribute to the possibilities of growth in small cities. The creative class is more geographically mobile than its predecessors; its members are, in other words, less rooted in place; they are more prepared and willing to relocate to new environments.

The third arm of the star is an economic context related to the creative class through the application of its knowledge base, but which has influenced a broader spectrum of small cities in recent decades. Post-Fordism,

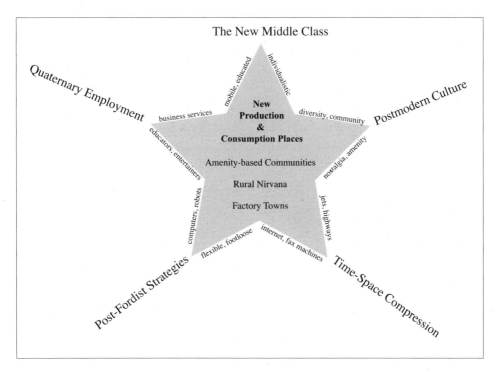

The New Middle Class

*mobile, educated*

*individualistic*

*Quaternary Employment*

business services

**New Production & Consumption Places**

diversity, community

*Postmodern Culture*

*educators, entertainers*

Amenity-based Communities

*nostalgia, amenity*

*computers, robots*

Rural Nirvana

Factory Towns

*jets, highways*

*flexible, footloose*

*internet, fax machines*

*Post-Fordist Strategies*

*Time-Space Compression*

Figure 1. The forces generating growth in small cities in postindustrial societies.

as described elsewhere in this volume, is an academic term that describes a phase of economic production. This phase, whose origins are conventionally associated with the economic upheavals of the 1970s, differs from the preceding phase in several ways that are critical for small cities. In very simple terms, Fordist manufacturing production systems typically sought to maximize profits by building factories as large as possible. Bigger factories meant more opportunities for breaking the manufacturing process into a series of logical steps, with each machine worker performing a limited number of tasks. The cost-savings generated by the specialization of labour and capital are known as economies of scale. Systems based on economies of scale and large cities went hand-in-hand. Large

factories attracted large pools of labour, which in turn generated demands for local services and goods, which attracted more investment and labour, which in turn created larger markets for factory output.

In the post-Fordist phase, economies of scale play a less significant role. Many industrial companies now try to reduce costs, for example, through just-in-time delivery and production systems. This strategy saves money by minimizing inventories and thus interest, depreciation, handling, and storage costs. Manufacturers have also capitalized on computers and robots to drive costs down and increase their ability to adjust to a rapidly changing marketplace. Smaller "lean and mean" operations have in turn reduced the strategic importance of industrial location.

Post-Fordist firms are considered footloose — they are more flexible in selecting a location, and more ready to pick up and go as business and regulatory environments change. In the United States, small cities in the Sun Belt are key destinations, although communities located in the agricultural lands that surround traditional manufacturing centres have also grown (Mills; Hart). Low labour and land costs, and less stringent environmental regulations, are the principal attraction. In Canada, the impact of economic restructuring on population growth is less dramatic. There are, nonetheless, examples in the hinterland around Toronto and in the prairies (Dahms and McComb; Broadway).

The ideas behind time-space compression, the fourth arm of the star, are very similar to those captured in McLuhan's notion of the global village. Originally coined by the geographer David Harvey, time-space compression suggests that the world is becoming a smaller and more interconnected place due to advances in modern communications and transportation. E-mail, fax machines, websites, cell phones, and satellite transceivers have altered the connections between residence and the workplace. People who telecommute can now live and work "virtually" anywhere. The construction of high-speed, limited-access freeways have expanded the urban fields of metropolitan centres across North America. These developments have enabled the creative class to migrate to small cities, towns, and rural areas while retaining physical connections to the centres of employment and entertainment (creative activity).

In combination, the new physical and electronic connections have created new settlement forms that Pierce Lewis calls galactic cities (a collection of communities, often, but not necessarily, arranged around a central metropole). Lewis argues that individual communities constitute a singular entity if they are linked by a transportation network and share a commercial, economic, and leisure infrastructure. However, the role of small cities and rural areas in this mix is limited. In the galactic city, Lewis quotes Robert Riley, "the new non-urban landscape is being shaped largely by people to whom the rural landscape is nothing more or nothing less than an alternative residential location. Whether they be commuters, retirees, or desktop publishers earning a living from their den, to them the rural landscape is not a productive system or a way of life, but a locational amenity" (59). The regions centred around Philadelphia, Boston, Toronto, and Washington, DC are galactic cities. The Georgia Strait urban complex — including Whistler, Chilliwack, Courtenay, Nanaimo, Duncan, Victoria, White Rock, the Greater Vancouver Regional District, and perhaps even Kelowna, Kamloops, and Penticton — is a local example.

Time-space compression has also stimulated the demand for small city environments from the opposite perspective. According to Harvey, time-space compression has created an instantaneous and placeless world, a world in which "it is hard to tell exactly what space we are in when it comes to assessing causes and effects, meanings or values" (298). Time-space compression, in other words, is a homogenizing process that has upped the scarcity value of uniqueness and difference. In an interconnected world traversed by people in search of diversity, a unique identity is a difficult, yet precious, quality to possess — thus the fifth arm of the star.

Small cities, towns, and rural areas benefit from this reaction because they are reserves of community and culture long since lost in the expansive and bland suburbs of major metropolitan areas (Dahms and McComb; Coppack; Halfacree). At least, that is the imagery conveyed nightly in TV shows such as the *Gilmore Girls* and *Ed,* and physically manifest in main-street makeovers and festival market places. The ideal small city is a place of architectural charm, historical ambiance, scenic beauty, recreational opportunities, and spontaneous outbursts of civil society. Coppack suggests that debates over accuracy of these stereotypes are immaterial. Instead, he argues that the idyllic imagery is real insofar as it motivates people to visit or relocate to small communities.[3] The small city is an "experiential" and "economic commodity" — a collection of amenities that people consume to satisfy their psychological desire to be connected in place and time (43). Economists have tried to measure the value of this postmodern, cultural outlook by assessing the income immigrants forego in order to live in amenity-rich communities. Power and Barrett, for example, argue that lower wage levels in small cities in the mountainous states of the American west are equivalent to "entry fees" (113). As is the case with Florida's creative class, Power and Barrett argue that many migrants to this rapidly growing area voluntarily pay these fees because they are motivated more by lifestyle than wage income.

## In Search of Vibrant, Small Canadian Cities

When designing new courses, one of the basic challenges faced by university instructors is finding a logical route through the ideas one wants to explore. This challenge is present in all courses, but is perhaps steepest in advanced courses that try to critically engage students in the debates of academically diverse fields such as tourism and urban studies. Selected readings may address a common theme, yet there are usually a multitude of ideas, contexts, and examples running through them. If one gives in to temptation

and follows several of these threads, there is a danger that the central theme can be lost, leaving students dazed and confused as to what it all means. The danger of conceptual confusion is even greater when marrying a theoretical theme with a research agenda. Courses have finite time frames. Students are more flexible, but still have limited capacities for absorbing material, practising skills, and understanding the links between them. In other words, it is not possible to explore all the dimensions of a research project within the parameters of a thirteen-week, undergraduate schedule.

Given the potential pitfalls, the decision to focus our Geography of Tourism course around the *Creative Class* proved to be fortuitous. Intended for a general audience, Florida's book provided a highly readable and fun introduction to the course material. The book provided a touchstone, a point to which we continually returned as we worked our way through the supplementary literature. The controversial positions staked out in the *Creative Class* also stimulated students to examine and define their own perspectives. Baited by Florida's comments about the relative prospects of small cities, and after an initial reading of Gertler's study of the creative class in Canada, students quickly decided that a reassessment was in order. Ideally, the proposed study would have simply extended Gertler's rankings to include smaller urban areas. However, given time and data limitations, I recommended that the sample should be limited to cities Gertler and his colleagues did not include. I also suggested that a sample of small cities might tease out differences that would be lost if large cities dominated the ranks. These suggestions led to a debate about the relevance of Florida's indices for small cities. Some wanted the measures to be consistent; however, others argued that the indices have a "big city bias," that they do not address the qualities of, and forces behind, the growth of smaller centres. These discussions generated, in turn, new research topics. Students wanted to examine alternative ranking strategies, especially ones that addressed small cities from the outset. Others were asked to explore cultural data sets that could be used to construct our own classification system, while some proposed parallel investigations of existing studies using the data sets in some capacity. While not all of the projects bore fruit, the class ultimately led the CURA research faculty to consider the broader possibilities of creating an "official" small cities index. The goal of this ongoing project is to create a link between the CURA's various arms.

### The Creative Class and the Small City

Two students were asked to establish a benchmark study of small Canadian cities by replicating Gertler's analysis. The study examined all cities with a population between 10,000 and 150,000.[4] In total, 122 cities were included — Barrie, Ontario, was the largest (148,480) and Kitimat, British Columbia, the smallest (10,285). Care was taken to replicate Gertler et al.'s four indices as closely as possible, with variables available in the most recent census (2001). Nevertheless, some adjustments were made to take advantage of readily available census variables and to accommodate the 2001 Census of Canada's release schedule. As in the Gertler study, the Mosaic index — a measure of the diversity and, by extension, the "tolerance" of a community — was simply the percentage of a community that was foreign-born in 2001. The students' Talent index also paralleled Gertler et al.'s — the proportion of the population that holds a bachelor's degree or higher — although our base population differs slightly.[5] The reader should also be aware that data for this index was taken from the 1996 census because 2001 educational attainment variables were unavailable at the time. Like Gertler, the students also used location quotients to assign a community's Bohemian index.[6] (The Bohemian index is a measure of employment in artistic professions [e.g., writers, musicians, interior designers, actors, and photographers]). The students also used a location quotient to generate Tech indices. These indices used information in Statistics Canada's *Canada Business Patterns* file to assess the significance of employment in high-technology industries in a community. Due to recent changes in the classification of employment (by industry), the jobs included in this index differ slightly from Gertler et al.'s.

Cities were ranked against each index, and a composite index was generated by summing the ranks for each city. The composite index provides an assessment of a community's overall status in terms of the creative class. No attempt was made to assess the appropriate weight of the indices.[7] The composite index must be considered, consequently, a relatively crude tool. The students did analyze the relationships between the indices using simple regression techniques (as per Gertler et al.). These assessments were conducted for the entire sample and for cities in British Columbia. In light of the diversity and distance between labour markets in Canada, the students felt that patterns might be clearer, if not stronger, within a regional context.

The ranks for the top 25 cities are shown in Table 1. Guelph had the top score, followed by Kingston, Whitehorse, Kelowna, and Nanaimo. Kamloops ranked 21st, just behind Thunder Bay and one ahead of North Bay. In general, cities with larger populations ranked higher than smaller cities. All of the cities ranked among the last 25 have populations of less than 30,000. In contrast, only three cities among the top 25 were this small, while 10 have populations greater than 100,000. Only two cities (Chatham-Kent and Cape Breton) with more than 100,000 were not ranked in the top 25.

Not surprisingly, many of the higher ranked communities are home to major post-secondary institutions. Whitehorse, Yellow-knife, and Stratford, are exceptions to these trends. The first two probably benefit from their roles as government and service centres, while the third is a major arts centre located within Toronto's urban field. Larger cities that did not make the top 25 tend to be agricultural communities (Chilliwack, Chatham-Kent, Saint-Hyacinthe, Medicine Hat, Leamington) or classic resource towns (Prince George) and processing centres (Drummondville, Sault Ste. Marie, Cape Breton).

While there appears to be a logical pattern to the ranking of so-called creative cities, it should be pointed out, nevertheless, that there is considerable variation among the indices. Only two cities — Guelph and Kingston — appear in the top 25 on all four indices, and only eight others on three of the indices (Fredericton, Lethbridge, Moncton, Peterborough, Trois-Rivières, Saint John, Sarnia, and Barrie). This result reflects relatively weak relationships among the indices. In particular, the correlations between the Mosaic index and the other three were extremely weak ($r^2$ values between 1 and 10%). These results are weaker than, but generally concur with, Gertler et al.'s — suggesting that the proportion of foreign-born population is not a good measure of diversity and tolerance in Canada. It may also indicate that ethnic diversity may not be as strong a draw for the creative class in countries where multi-culturalism is officially sanctioned and encouraged to a greater degree than in the United States (Goldberg and Mercer). The

relationships among the other indices were all in the expected direction, but still not great. The strongest correlation is between the Talent and Tech indexes ($r^2$ = 26.3%), followed by the Tech and Bohemian ($r^2$ = 25.6%) and the Talent and Bohemian ($r^2$ = 18.2%). Comparative values for metropolitan cities were much higher (respectively 59%, 74%, and 65%) (Gertler et al.). Correlations for the BC sample of small cities were better except for those involving the Mosaic index (all less than 4%). The BC results were: Talent-Tech (49.6%), Tech-Bohemian (39.6%), and Talent-Bohemian (31.6%).

Overall, the students' findings indicate that the same basic relationships among education, quaternary sector employment, and cultural occupations (in the arts) exist across small cities as they do in the country's larger centres. The study also appears to corroborate the importance of size, and thus the agglomerative pull of business and institutional clusters: larger cities can attract more educated and creative class migrants because they are more economically diverse and more likely to have a critical mass of arts organizations, government offices, and post-secondary institutions. In other words, many small cities, especially the smallest of the small, appear to lack the economic and cultural resources thought necessary to attract the creative class. It is worth re-emphasizing, nevertheless, that several smaller cities — including ones in the far north and the Maritimes — ranked high, and that the indices used are only crude measures of the cultural and economic vitality of a community. If the Mosaic index is dropped from the composite index on the grounds that it is not strongly associated with talent or technology, and is biased towards the country's major immigrant destinations (i.e., Canada's metropolises), the frequency and rank of smaller cities generally improve (see

| City | Province | Population | Component indexes | | | | Composite | | |
|------|----------|-----------|--------|--------|------|----------|-------|------|----------------|
| | | | Mosaic | Talent | Tech | Bohemian | Total | Rank | Less Mosaic |
| Guelph | ON | 117,344 | 4 | 2 | 1 | 24 | 31 | 1 | 3 |
| Kingston | ON | 146,838 | 21 | 4 | 3 | 18 | 46 | 2 | 2 |
| Whitehorse | YK | 21,405 | 30 | 5 | 29 | 3 | 67 | 3 | 6 |
| Kelowna | BC | 147,739 | 13 | 45 | 2 | 9 | 69 | 4 | 13 |
| Nanaimo | BC | 85,664 | 8 | 29 | 7 | 29 | 73 | 5 | 15 |
| Barrie | ON | 148,480 | 26 | 23 | 4 | 21 | 74 | 6 | 10 |
| Fredericton | NB | 81,346 | 62 | 1 | 5 | 7 | 75 | 7 | 1 |
| Courtenay | BC | 47,051 | 17 | 31 | 26 | 1 | 75 | 7 | 14 |
| Peterborough | ON | 102,423 | 43 | 12 | 10 | 16 | 81 | 9 | 7 |
| Yellowknife | NWT | 16,541 | 35 | 3 | 30 | 20 | 88 | 10 | 12 |
| Lethbridge | AB | 67,374 | 23 | 8 | 17 | 57 | 105 | 11 | 16 |
| Sarnia | ON | 88,331 | 18 | 21 | 15 | 52 | 106 | 12 | 19 |
| Abbotsford | BC | 147,370 | 2 | 64 | 11 | 34 | 111 | 13 | 28 |
| Moncton | NB | 117,727 | 85 | 9 | 8 | 11 | 113 | 14 | 4 |
| Saint John | NB | 122,678 | 77 | 17 | 13 | 15 | 122 | 15 | 8 |
| Stratford | ON | 29,676 | 29 | 34 | 55 | 4 | 122 | 15 | 22 |
| Charlottetown | PEI | 58,358 | 76 | 6 | 36 | 5 | 123 | 17 | 9 |
| Trois-Rivières | QC | 137,507 | 102 | 14 | 9 | 6 | 131 | 18 | 5 |
| Red Deer | AB | 67,707 | 44 | 32 | 6 | 49 | 131 | 18 | 18 |
| Thunder Bay | ON | 121,986 | 31 | 13 | 16 | 72 | 132 | 20 | 23 |
| Kamloops | BC | 86,491 | 36 | 50 | 14 | 42 | 142 | 21 | 26 |
| North Bay | ON | 63,681 | 66 | 18 | 25 | 40 | 149 | 22 | 17 |
| Vernon | BC | 51,530 | 19 | 74 | 27 | 32 | 152 | 23 | 35 |
| Owen Sound | ON | 31,583 | 54 | 37 | 53 | 14 | 158 | 24 | 25 |
| Belleville | ON | 87,395 | 45 | 67 | 20 | 26 | 158 | 24 | 29 |
| Rimouski | QC | 47,688 | 116 | 7 | 32 | 13 | 168 | 28 | 11 |

Table 1. Selected creative class rankings.

Table 1). Clearly, better assessments of community are necessary before stronger conclusions can be drawn.

University Culture and Small Cities
A case can be easily made that universities play an important economic role in Canada. Meyer and Hecht contend, for instance, that like their counterparts in the United States, Canadian universities are important growth engines, generating "a higher level of income, employment, and general prosperity" within local economies (263). In their study, Meyer and Hecht compare a variety of cities with a university against those without. Using median income, average house values, employment rates, the secondary and quaternary labour forces, and population growth as

measures of economic well-being, the study found significant differences on four out of the six indicators. Other researchers argue that Canada has few real university towns. Srebnick even suggests that most Canadian universities lack a cultural heart, that "there is no genuine 'college life' … since the majority of students are commuters" (180). It is true that most of Canada's major universities — with the exception of those in the Maritimes — are located in the country's metropolitan centres. It is also true that the sporting and alumni dimensions are nowhere near as developed in Canada as in the United States. And, it is also true that the small-town, liberal arts college phenomenon is much less common in this country. Still, it does not follow that cultural linkages are non-existent. Even at UCC, one of Canada's many peaks-and-points campuses, sporting events, public lectures, staged events, community research projects, international students, and joint planning efforts have built bridges with the community.[8]

Regardless of the broad cultural status of Canadian university environments, students in the class were understandably very interested in how Kamloops stacks up as a place to go to school. As a result, and cognizant of the students' criticisms of Florida's indices, I asked two students to investigate the strategy that a company called ePodunk had developed for ranking college towns in the United States. ePodunk is a research firm that specializes in providing information about smaller communities in the United States. It has created several lists ranking communities according to their historic qualities, walkability (proportion of a workforce that walks to work), sense of community (the depth of residents' roots and home-town feel), and college atmosphere. Focusing on the latter, students collected information for 25 Canadian cities with populations between 10,000 and 160,000 and with a four-year degree granting post-secondary institution. The students' objective was not to rate the institutions in these cities, but rather to determine if there were any relationship between a community's cultural richness and the relative size of its student population.

Following ePodunk's general strategy, the students created two "eh!Podunk" indices (that is, ePodunk with a Canadian inflection): cultural vibrancy and economic vitality. The Vibrancy index measured the "cultural life" of a community. In particular, they used the *Canadian Business Patterns* publication to determine the number of entertainment venues (bars, restaurants, night clubs), recreational facilities, book and music stores, arts organizations (symphony orchestras, theatre companies, museums, heritage sites), and information services (libraries, radio stations, newspapers) present in each city. They also assessed communities in terms of the value of grants that local arts organizations had received over the past three years.[9] Counts and grants were standardized by population, ranked by business category, and summed.

Five measures of a community's economic vitality were included in the second index: population growth between 1996 and 2001, median age, percent of owner-occupied housing, median personal income, and the rate of unemployment. Data for the economic variables was acquired from the 2001 census. Like indicators in the Vibrancy index, economic measures were independently ranked and then summed. The cultural vibrancy and economic vitality indices were, in turn, ranked and summed to create an overall index. Relationships between these indices, their constituent indicators, and a community's student-to-population ratio were subsequently assessed using non-parametric correlation tests.[10]

The final economic, cultural vitality, and composite ranks are shown in Table 2. Top-ranked was Fredericton — the capital of New

| City | Province | Population | Institution | Students per 1000 Residents | Component Ranks | | |
|------|----------|------------|-------------|----------------------------|------------------|------------------|------------------|
| | | | | | Economic | Cultural Vibrancy | Composite Rank |
| Fredericton | NB | 81,346 | UNB/ St. Thomas | 145.2 | 4.0 | 3.0 | 1.0 |
| Brandon | MB | 41,037 | Brandon | 75.4 | 8.0 | 4.0 | 2.0 |
| Kamloops | BC | 86,491 | UC Cariboo | 66.1 | 5.0 | 5.0 | 3.0 |
| Guelph | ON | 117,344 | Guelph | 135.9 | 1.0 | 18.0 | 4.0 |
| Lethbridge | AB | 67,374 | Lethbridge | 107.4 | 3.0 | 15.0 | 5.0 |
| Charlottetown | PEI | 58,358 | UPEI | 61.2 | 19.0 | 2.0 | 6.0 |
| Peterborough | ON | 102,423 | Trent | 54.2 | 13.0 | 6.0 | 7.0 |
| Moncton | NB | 117,727 | Moncton | 50.2 | 10.0 | 7.0 | 8.0 |
| Rimouski | QC | 47,688 | Québec | 92.9 | 21.0 | 1.0 | 9.0 |
| Camrose | AB | 14,854 | Augustana | 61.2 | 6.0 | 14.0 | 10.5 |
| Kelowna | BC | 147,739 | Okanagan UC | 34.0 | 12.0 | 9.0 | 10.5 |
| Nanaimo | BC | 85,664 | Malaspina UC | 54.1 | 14.0 | 8.0 | 12.0 |
| North Bay | ON | 63,681 | Nipissing | 64.4 | 11.0 | 16.0 | 13.0 |
| Sherbrooke | QC | 153,811 | Sherbrooke | 103.8 | 18.0 | 10.0 | 14.0 |
| Kingston | ON | 146,838 | Queen's | 124.1 | 15.0 | 17.0 | 15.0 |
| Corner Brook | NFLD | 25,747 | Sir Wilfred Grenfell | 46.6 | 23.0 | 12.5 | 16.0 |
| Chicoutimi | Q | 154,938 | Québec | 38.6 | 24.0 | 12.5 | 17.0 |
| Abbotsford | BC | 147,370 | UC Fraser Valley | 38.7 | 2.0 | 25.0 | 18.0 |
| Prince George | BC | 85,035 | UNBC | 38.3 | 7.0 | 24.0 | 19.5 |
| Trois-Rivières | QC | 137,507 | Québec | 68.4 | 25.0 | 11.0 | 19.5 |
| Thunder Bay | ON | 121,986 | Lakehead | 50.3 | 9.0 | 22.5 | 20.5 |
| Sault Ste Marie | ON | 78,908 | Algoma | 11.0 | 17.0 | 19.0 | 22.0 |
| Sudbury | ON | 155,601 | Laurentian | 43.6 | 16.0 | 21.0 | 23.0 |
| Saint John | NB | 122,678 | UNB | 22.8 | 20.0 | 20.0 | 24.0 |
| Cape Breton | NS | 109,330 | UC Cape Breton | 31.5 | 22.0 | 22.5 | 25.0 |

Table 2. Ranks for small cities with universities.

Brunswick — followed by Brandon, Kamloops, Guelph, and Lethbridge. Kelowna — Kamloops' neighbour and rival — ranked 10th, while Nanaimo (12th), Abbotsford (18th), and Prince George (19th) rounded out the BC entries. Moncton (8th) and Rimouski (9th) were the top-ranked cities with French-language institutions. Like the small cities Creative Class index, the variety of communities (and institutions) at the top of the scale indicates that no area of the country (nor institutional age or focus) has a monopoly on university culture. However, in contrast to the Creative Class index, the composite university rank and population were inversely related — smaller cities tended to rank higher — although the strength of the relationship was not dramatic.[11] Perhaps even more notable are relationships with the student density ratio. Communities with higher

| Indices | Population | Student Ratio |
|---|---|---|
| Economic Index | -0.17 | 0.34 |
| Population Change | -0.02 | 0.45* |
| Owner-occupied housing | -0.20 | -0.32 |
| Median age | -0.04 | 0.29 |
| Median income | -0.05 | 0.01 |
| Unemployment rate | -0.07 | 0.57* |
| | | |
| Vibrancy Index | -0.35 | 0.47* |
| Books and Music | -0.44* | 0.41* |
| Information companies | -0.32 | 0.57* |
| Arts and culture | -0.15 | 0.57* |
| Entertainment businesses | -0.41* | 0.06 |
| Recreation facilities | -0.17 | -0.01 |
| Restaurants and pubs | -0.09 | 0.34 |
| Endowments for the arts | -0.03 | 0.66* |
| | | |
| Composite Index | -0.43* | 0.69* |

\* significant at p = 0.05

Table 3. University index correlations.

student ratios tended to rank higher on the economic ($r^2$ = 11%), cultural vibrancy ($r^2$ = 23%), and thus the composite index ($r^2$ = 48%). This connection was particularly strong for the information and arts components of the Vibrancy index (see Table 3), underscoring the positive link between bohemians and talent identified in the other study.

While sample differences make it difficult to directly compare the results of the studies, the top-ranked cities are fairly similar. If only cities in common are considered, four of the top ten in the university list are among the top ten on the creative list (Fredericton, Guelph, Peterborough, and Kelowna). The number increases to seven if the Mosaic index is dropped from the comparison (Fredericton, Guelph, Charlottetown, Peterborough, Moncton, Rimouski, and Kelowna). Brandon, Kamloops, and Camrose were notable additions to the university top ten, while Kingston, Trois

Rivières, and Saint John dropped down the list. These changes may in part reflect the size of the cities and thus the relative presence of post-secondary institutions within smaller communities. The populations of the three that fell exceed those that rose. Still, Kingston's low ranking is surprising given its relatively high student ratio and its second-place standing on the composite creative class indices. Kingston is, furthermore, one of only two cities that Gumprecht identifies as Canadian college towns.[12] It failed to make the top ten due to low housing, income, entertainment, and recreation scores. These index components have the weakest association with the student ratio and thus may inaccurately reflect Kingston's true status. On the other hand, Brandon and Kamloops scored well on the Vibrancy index despite ranking low against the Bohemian index (respectively 81st and 42nd). The fact that both cities have well-developed arts communities suggests, in line with Brooks and

103

Kushner's advice, that "policy-makers and administrators [should] use the largest possible number of measures" (21). Clearly, the task of defining, measuring, and ranking concepts such as community and culture is a challenging one.

The economic and vibrancy indices were weakly correlated. Abbotsford, for example, ranked 2nd on the Economic index but 25th on the Vibrancy; Rimouski's scores were similarly inverted, ranking 21st on the economic and 1st on the Vibrancy index. On the surface, this result seems to contradict Meyer and Hecht's findings that Canadian universities function as economic growth poles, as well as Florida's and others' arguments about the link between cultural amenities and economic growth. The students were careful to stress in their analysis that the connection is complicated in Canada by high wages in the staples industries, low living costs in smaller cities, and weaker linkages between universities and their urban contexts. Unfortunately, many post-secondary institutions in Canada, especially those in the West, were built on the outskirts of cities — the shortsighted assumption being that cheap land and scenic vistas outweigh the economic (and cultural) synergies an institution can generate in a more intimate urban location. They also pointed out that the economic value of universities might have been clearer if communities without four-year degree granting institutions had been included in the sample.

## Conclusion: The Prospects and Problems of Small Cities

The future of small cities is not as universally bleak as Richard Florida's vision of a creative place suggests. Many of the smaller communities located within the urban field of metropolitan areas have benefited from new forms of commuting, flexible work schedules, evolving economic systems, and affordable housing. Small cities in more remote but amenity-rich landscapes, especially those ones with a well-developed sense of community and safety, distinctive heritage architecture, and strong cultural institutions, have held their own. The vitality and viability of these smaller centres is clearly evident in the sustained migration of lifestyle seekers from metropolitan centres over the last 30 years, and in the profusion of guides that cater to their interests.[13] In this day and age, places — be they small or large — still matter.

Ranked lists are a fun way to adjudicate the pull of competing communities. Rankings appeal to our pride of place, to the intuitive values that we hold about the communities we live in — or would like to live in. At the same time, it is important to acknowledge that rankings should be interpreted cautiously. Ranking methodologies, no matter how sophisticated, are blunt instruments for summarizing the multiple dimensions of modern cities. We should also note that there is something ironic, or perhaps symbolic, in our attempts to boil down the essence of a place to a single number. Nostalgia, community, and ambiance are quintessential postmodern values, but they are apparently subservient to the numerate logic that drives the information economy. Rankings are very sensitive, as the students came to realize, to both the categories and the statistical procedures employed. Our composite Creative Class and University indices, for example, are only weakly related. Kingston ranked 2nd on the Creative Class scale, but 15th on the University index; Kelowna dropped 6 positions, as did Nanaimo, while Abbotsford fell 5. Rimouski, on the other hand ranked 19 places higher on the University index, Kamloops 18, and Fredericton 6. The inconsistencies are due to differences in the scope of the studies and to the built-in biases and sensitivities of the indices used. The students preferred the University index by a wide margin — an understandable result given both Kamloops' standing and the inclusion of bars, restaurants, and nightlife in the mix. However, the authors of the index were less confident. Their report carefully explains that nightlife rankings, for example, are based solely on counts of establishments. No effort was made to evaluate the quantity (the size of dance floors or number of beer taps?) or quality of nightlife, nor its connection to campus (the number of students as patrons?).

We used the limitations of the ranking strategies as pedagogical segues into theoretical discussions. We started with a simple question — "Can small cities like Kamloops compete for the creative class?" — but quickly moved into a broader literature on the character of contemporary economies, cultures, and societies. In particular, the students' projects made them very aware of how politically charged the creative class, amenity landscapes, and culture can be. Local development officials covet the creative class for its economic benefits. However, with the assistance of social scientists such as Dean MacCannell, Tom Paradis, Sonya Salamon, Clare Mitchell, and Jon Goss, students also explored how the intrusion of wealthy, amenity-driven outsiders can disrupt social networks and alter the cultural fabric of a community. Some critics go further, arguing that creative-class-oriented development strategies turn local activities and landscapes into "commodities that can be bought, sold, or invested in unsentimentally" (Salamon 8). This darker perspective caused some students to question the purpose of the ranking exercise and the "be creative or die" philosophy that underscores Florida's message.

From a research perspective, the students' projects supported our working premise that small cities are a rich and distinctive subject for study. Several of the sampled cities share key attributes with Florida's creative capitals; Kingston, Fredricton, Kelowna, and Guelph are notable examples. While the magnitude of the creative class in these communities is not on par with Toronto, Montreal, Ottawa, and Vancouver, all deserve further attention given their high-technology, education, and, to a more varied degree, cultural rankings. One could even argue that the students' analyses underestimated the importance of these cities, given the big-city bias of the Mosaic index. Subsequent studies should experiment with alternative yardsticks, ones that are better suited for assessing the kinds of cultural and lifestyle resources that can drive growth in smaller centres. In fact, it is not clear why one would expect critical measures to be scale independent since the dynamic flow of people, ideas, and capital between centres large and small is a product of the different economic and lifestyle opportunities they present (or appear to present).

The research produced by the students indicates that the experiences of small cities are far from uniform. Select communities are obviously well positioned. Others have stagnated, while many in Canada's resource periphery have decayed. Differences in location and scale, economic and cultural resources, and ethnic and social diversities are critical. As a result, the trends that are reshaping our economy and society — globalization, digital communication technology, and an aging population — resonate in place-specific ways. These divergent starting points and outcomes, along with the strategies small cities adopt in their efforts to compete, are obvious starting points for future research.

### Acknowledgments

This paper owes a significant debt to discussions generated by UCC students. In particular, I am indebted to first-rate research conducted by four students: Alma Klarich and Krista Simpson collaborated on a project entitled "The Creative Class: An Analysis of Small Canadian Cities," while Alison Krimmer and Clive Lovett contributed "Brains, Bars, Bohemians: A Ranking of College Towns." These papers — submitted in partial fulfillment of the course requirements — are the heart of the empirical section.

## Notes

1. The provincial government announced on March 19, 2004 that the UCC would become a university in April, 2005. Graduate programs in the traditional arts and sciences are not, however, part of the new institution's mandate in the near future.

2. Correlation results are often expressed as r or $r^2$. A correlation's r-value is positive if the indices are positively related; that is, as the values of one index increase, the values of the other index also increase. The opposite is true for negative correlations: as the values of one index increase, the values of the other index decrease. The strength of a correlation is indicated by absolute value of r. Weak correlations will have absolute r-values close to 0. Perfect correlations have absolute r-values of 1. The expression $r^2$ (i.e., r times r) indicates how well indices are correlated in percentage terms. A $r^2$ value of 0.36 (i.e., r = 0.6) indicates that 36% of the variation in one index is explained by the variation in the other index.

3. This explanation for population growth in small cities and rural areas is commonly referred to as the deconcentration hypothesis.

4. Populations were based on 2001 census agglomeration and census metropolitan figures where applicable.

5. Their population base was defined as people over the age of 18, whereas the students' was over 15.

6. A location quotient assesses the concentration of a quality in a community with respect to its concentration in a larger context (all the cities, in this case).

7. The usual caveat with rank indices applies here as well: depending on the magnitude of original data, the ranking procedure can potentially understate or overstate the differences between cities.

8. Many post-secondary institutions in Canada have been built on scenic but hard-to-access sites on the edge of communities. Simon Fraser University, the University of British Columbia, and the new University of Northern British Columbia are good examples. UCC's campus sits on a bench high overlooking the Thompson River. Light industry, warehouses, government offices, and big-box retailers dominate most of the developed land adjacent. However, as mentioned in the introductory paragraphs, UCC and city officials are currently collaborating on plans to develop more student-centred functions on and off campus.

9. This indicator was derived from information compiled by the Canadian Council for the Arts.

10. Data sets that are composed of ranked (ordinal) values are not, by definition, normally distributed; that is, they do not describe a bell curve when graphed to show the frequency of values. As a result, parametric statistical tests — which require normally distributed data — cannot be used. Non-parametric statistical tests do not make this requirement.

11. The $r^2$ value was 18.1%.

12. The other city is Waterloo, Ontario. Grumbrecht also identifies Wolfville, Nova Scotia, and Sackville, New Brunswick, as college-oriented communities. None of these communities met our population thresholds (Kitchener-Waterloo CMA is too large and the others too small) and thus were not included in this study.

13. Aside from broadly based issues like *Places Rated Almanac*, there are now guides to *The 100 Best Small Art Towns in America* (enticing readers with *Creative Communities, Fresh Air*, and *Affordable Living*), *America's Most Charming Towns & Villages*, *Small Town Escapes*, and *The Great Towns of Northern California*, as well as ones that will help you *Choose a College Town for Retirement*, and *Mak[e] Your Move to One of America's Best Small Towns*.

## Works Cited

Allen, John. "Crossing Borders: Footloose Multinationals." *A Shrinking World?: Global Unevenness and Inequality*. Ed. John Allen and Chris Hamnett. Oxford: Oxford UP, 1995. 55-102.

Baker, D.J., et al. *Understanding Conflict in the Forest: The Words Behind the Message. Cultural Future of Small Cities Research Program*. Kamloops, BC, Canada, 2002.

Bascom, J. "'Energizing' Rural Space: The Representation of Countryside Culture as an Economic Development Strategy." *Journal of Cultural Geography* 19 (2001): 53-73.

Bell, Daniel. *The Coming of Post-Industrial Society: A Venture in Social Forecasting.* NY: Basic, 1973.

Beyers, William. "Employment Growth in the Rural West from 1985 to 1995 Outpaced the Nation." *Rural Development Perspectives* 14.2 (1999): 38-43.

Booth, Douglas. "Spatial Patterns in the Economic Development of the Mountain West." *Growth and Change* 30 (1999): 384-405.

Boyens, Ingeborg. *Another Season's Promise: Hope and Despair in Canada's Farm Country.* Toronto: Penguin, 2001.

Broadway, Michael. "Planning for Change in Small Towns or Trying to Avoid the Slaughterhouse Blues." *Journal of Rural Studies* 16.1 (2000): 37-47.

Brooks, A., and R. Kushner. "What Makes an Art Capital? Quantifying a City's Cultural Environment." *International Journal of Arts Management* 5.1 (2002): 12-22.

Brooks, David. *Bobos in Paradise: The New Upper Class and How They Got There.* New York: Simon & Schuster, 2000.

Brown, Larry T. *America's Most Charming Towns & Villages.* 5th ed. Cold Spring Harbor, NY: Open Road, 2003.

Bunting, Trudy and Mitchell, Clare. "Artists in Rural Locales: Market Access, Landscape Appeal, and Economic Exigency." *The Canadian Geographer* 45 (2001): 268-84.

Central Okanagan Economic Development Commission. *High Tech.* 1999. 26 November 2002. <http://www.edccord.com/hightech/hightech.htm>

City of Kamloops, and University College of the Cariboo. *McGill Corridor / Southgate Project Concept Plan.* Kamloops: True Consulting Group, 2001.

Cohen, Erik. "Authenticity and Commoditization in Tourism." *Annals of Tourism Research* 15 (1988): 371-86.

Copeland, David. "CMU's 'creative' thinker makes creative move" *Pittsburgh Tribune-Review* 2004. 28 April 2004. <http://www.pittsburghlive.com/x/search/s_184360.html>

Coppack, Philip M. "The Role of Amenity." *Essays on Canadian Urban Form 3: The Urban Field.* Ed.

Philip M. Coppack, Lorne H. Russwurm and Christopher Bryan. Waterloo: Department of Geography, University of Waterloo, 1988.

Coppack, Philip M., Lorne H. Russwurm, and Christopher R. Bryant. *Essays on Canadian Urban Form 3: The Urban Field.* Geography Publication Series. Vol. 30. Waterloo: Department of Geography, University of Waterloo, 1988.

Crampton, Norman. *Making Your Move to One of America's Best Small Towns.* New York: M. Evans, 2002.

Cromartie, John, and John. Wardwell. "Migrants Settling Far and Wide in the Rural West." *Rural Development Perspectives* 14.2 (1999): 2-8.

Dahms, Fred A. "St. Jacobs, Ontario: From Declining Village to Thriving Tourist Community." *Ontario Geographer* 36 (1991): 1-13.

Dahms, Fred, and Janine McComb. "'Counterurbanization', Interaction and Functional Change in a Rural Amenity Area - a Canadian Example." *Journal of Rural Studies* 15.2 (1999): 129-46.

Dreher, Chris. *Be Creative or Die.* 2002. 23 February 2003. <http://www.alternet.org/story.html?StoryID=13325>

ePodunk. *Epodunk: The Power of Place.* 2002. 3 April 2003. <http://www.epodunk.com>

Epp, Roger, and David Whitson, eds. *Writing Off the Rural West: Globalization, Governments, and the Transformation of Rural Economies.* Edmonton: U of Alberta P, 2001.

Florida, Richard. "Bohemia and Economic Geography." *Journal of Economic Geography* 2.1 (2002): 55-71.

———. "The Economic Geography of Talent." *Annals of the Association of American Geographers* 92.4 (2002): 743-55.

———. "Regional Creative Destruction: Production Organization, Globalization, and the Economic Transformation of the Industrial Midwest." *Economic Geography* 72.2 (1995): 315-35.

Florida, Richard L. *The Rise of the Creative Class: And How It's Transforming Work, Leisure, Community and Everyday Life.* New York: Basic Books, 2002.

Richard Florida Creativity Group. "Speaking/Media" *CreativeClass.org* 2003. 28 April 2004. <http://www.creativeclass.org/taking.shtml>

Gertler, Meric S., et al. *Competing on Creativity: Placing Ontario's Cities in North American Context.* Toronto: Ontario Ministry of Enterprise, Opportunity and Innovation and the Institute for Competitiveness and Prosperity, 2002.

Goldberg, Michael A., and John Mercer. *The Myth of the North American City : Continentalism Challenged.* Vancouver: U of British Columbia P, 1985.

Goss, Jon. "Disquiet on the Waterfront: Nostalgia and Utopia in the Festival Marketplace." *Urban Geography* 17.3 (1996): 221-47.

Gumprecht, Blake. *The American College Town.* New York: Routledge, [forthcoming].

Halfacree, Keith. "Contrasting Roles for the Post-Productivist Countryside: A Post-Modern Perspective on Counterurbanisation." *Contested Countryside Cultures: Otherness, Marginalisation and Rurality.* Ed. Paul Cloke and Jo Little. London: Routledge, 1997.

Hart, John Fraser. "Small Towns and Manufacturing." *Geographical Review* 78.3 (1988): 272-87.

Harvey, David. *The Condition of Postmodernity : An Enquiry into the Origins of Cultural Change.* Cambridge MA: Blackwell, 1990.

Jacobs, Jane. *The Death and Life of Great American Cities.* New York: Vintage Books, 1961.

Jamieson, Walter. "An Ecomuseum for the Crowsnest Pass: Using Cultural Resources as a Tool for Community & Local Economic Development." *Plan Canada* 29 (1989): 14-23.

Janzen & Associates. *Kamloops Cultural Strategic Plan.* Kamloops, 2003.

Ley, David. *The New Middle Class and the Remaking of the Central City.* Oxford Geographical and Environmental Studies. Oxford ; New York: Oxford UP, 1996.

Lippard, Lucy R. *On the Beaten Track: Tourism, Art and Place.* New York: New Press, 1999.

Lubow, Joseph M. *Choose a College Town for Retirement: Retirement Discoveries for Every Budget.* Choose Retirement Series. 1st ed. Old Saybrook, CT.: Globe Pequot Press, 1999.

MacCannell, Dean. *The Tourist: A New Theory of the Leisure Class.* New York: Schocken Books, 1976.

MacKinnon, Robert, and Ross Nelson. "Postindustrial Adjustments in a Staples Economy: Urban and Economic Change in Kamloops, 1961-2002." *Western Geography*, [forthcoming].

Meyer, Stephen, and Alfred Hecht. "University Growth Poles in Canada: An Empirical Assessment." *Canadian Journal of Regional Science* 19.3 (1996): 263-82.

Mills, Edwin S. "The Location of Economic Activity in Rural and Nonmetropolitan United States." *The Changing American Countryside: Rural People and Places.* Ed. Emery N. Castle. Lawrence: UP of Kansas, 1995. 103-33.

Mitchell, Clare. "Cultural Centres in the Canadian Urban System." *The Operational Geographer* 9 (1992): 13-17.

Mitchell, Clare, Greg Atkinson, and Andrew Clark. "The Creative Destruction of Niagara-on-the-Lake." *The Canadian Geographer* 45 (2001): 285-99.

National Geographic Society (U.S.). *Guide to Small Town Escapes.* Washington, D.C.: National Geographic, 2000.

Notzke, Claudia "Indigenous Tourism Development in the Arctic." *Annals of Tourism Research* 26 (1999): 55-77.

Olynyk, Ronald. "An Open Letter to the British Columbia Progress Board from the University College of the Cariboo Board of Governors." Kamloops, 2003.

Paradis, Thomas. "Conceptualizing Small Towns as Urban Places." *Urban Geography* 21 (2000): 61-82.

——. "Main Street Transformed: Community Sense of Place for Nonmetropolitan Tourism Business Districts." *Urban Geography* 21.7 (2000): 609-39.

——. "The Political Economy of Theme Development in Small Urban Places: The Case of Roswell, New Mexico." *Tourism Geographies* 4 (2002): 22-43.

Power, Thomas. *Lost Landscapes and Failed Economies: The Search for a Value of Place.* Washington, DC: Island Press, 1996.

Power, Thomas, and Richard Barrett. *Post-Cowboy Economics: Pay and Prosperity in the New American West.* Washington, DC: Island Press, 2001.

Putnam, Robert D. *Bowling Alone: The Collapse and Revival of American Community.* New York: Simon & Schuster, 2000.

Ray, Paul, and Sherry Anderson. *The Cultural Creatives: How 50 Million People Are Changing the World.* New York: Harmony, 2000.

Salamon, Sonya. *Newcomers to Old Towns: Suburbanization of the Heartland.* Chicago: U of Chicago P, 2003.

Sassen, Saskia. *The Global City: New York, London, Tokyo*. Princeton, NJ.: Princeton UP, 1991.

Savageau, David. *Places Rated Almanac*, New York: Wiley, 1999.

Shumway, Mathew, and James Davis. "Nonmetropolitan Population Change in the Mountain West: 1970-1995." *Rural Sociology* 61 (1996): 513-29.

Simmons, James, and Larry Bourne. *The Canadian Urban System, 1971-2001: Responses to a Changing World*. Toronto: University of Toronto, Centre for Urban and Community Studies, 2003.

Smutny, Gayla "Patterns of Growth and Change: Depicting the Impacts of Restructuring in Idaho." *Professional Geographer* 54 (2002): 438-53.

Srebrnick, Henry. "Football, Frats and Fun Vs. Commuters, Cold and Carping: The Social and Psychological Context of Higher Education in Canada and the United States." *Canada and the United States: Differences That Count*. Ed. David M. Thomas. Peterborough, ON: Broadview, 2000. 165-91.

ThompsonJobs.com. "City of Kamloops: Tournament Capital of Canada" *Thompson Jobs — City of Kamloops* 2004. 28 April 2004. <http://www.thompsonjobs.com/employers/city-ofkamloops>

Urbanska, Wanda, and Frank Levering. *Moving to a Small Town: A Guidebook for Moving from Urban to Rural America*. New York: Simon & Schuster, 1996.

Urry, John. *The Tourist Gaze. Theory, Culture & Society*. 2nd ed. London: Thousand Oaks: Sage, 2002.

Villani, John. *The 100 Best Small Art Towns in America: Discover Creative Communities, Fresh Air, and Affordable Living*. 3rd ed. Santa Fe, NM.: John Muir, 1998.

Vining, Daniel R., and Robert Pallone. "Migration between Core and Peripheral Regions: A Description and Tentative Explanation of the Patterns in 22 Countries." *Geoforum* 13.4 (1982): 339-410.

Vokac, David. *The Great Towns of Northern California: The Guide to the Best Getaways for a Vacation or a Lifetime*. 1st ed. San Diego: West Press, 2003.

Whyte, William Hollingsworth. *The Organization Man*. New York: Doubleday, 1957.

Wilkinson, Paul F., and Alex L. Murray. "Centre and Periphery: The Impacts of the Leisure Industry on a Small Town (Collingwood, Ontario)." *Society and Leisure* 14.1 (1991): 235-60.

Zeppel, Heather. "Cultural Tourism at the Cowichan Native Village, British Columbia." *Journal of Travel Research* 41 (2002): 92-100.

Figure 1. Heritage consultant leading culture and education meeting. Photo by Helen MacDonald-Carlson.

# Art at Work: Culture-Based Learning and the Economic Development of Canadian Small Cities

## John A. Bratton and W.F. Garrett-Petts

### Introduction

The argument for a strong arts and cultural community has been well documented as a strategy for economic development in large cities. Studies suggest that "the arts" have a significant role in terms of encouraging employment growth, facilitating downtown regeneration and attracting tourists (Arora et al.; Brooks and Kushner; Florida "Economic Geography" "The Rise"; Frey; Hughes). A thriving culture industry also has psychological impacts on community members, helping construct and affirm the "image and feel of a place" (Wynne). As noted in the introduction to this book, if not by definition, then certainly by default, "culture" is associated with big city life: big cities are equated commonly with "big culture"; small cities with something less. How, then, can small cities compete when, as Jason Azmier, a Senior Policy Analyst for the Canada West Foundation, asserts, in Canada it is the "large cities" that are generally regarded as "not only population hubs, but also economic hubs that drive a province's or region's competitiveness" (2)?

In the so-called new economy, the portability of network-oriented information and communication technologies (ICTs) makes it possible for investors and knowledge workers to select their work locations, in an endlessly variable geometry of value searching and settlement (Braman; Castells). This portable infrastructure has especially serious implications for the economic development of small cities. Knowledge-based investors and professionals are extraordinarily inclusive of what they value in the networks of business and community interaction, including, as Florida and others argue, the existence of a critical mass of cultural activity in a community.

What then constitutes the critical mass of cultural activity necessary to attract and sustain a community of knowledge-based investors and professionals? More specifically, what special circumstances affect arts and culture development in small cities? Are arts and culture defined and enacted differently in small city settings? And how can the creative capital of small cities measure up to that of their larger neighbours? These are some of the questions referenced indirectly by the Western Cities Project (Canada West Foundation), the Culture of Cities Project (detailed studies of urban experience in Montreal, Toronto, Berlin, and Dublin), and the United States' Arts and Culture

Indicators in Community Building Project — and currently under direct investigation by the Cultural Future of Small Cities research program based in Kamloops, British Columbia.

This chapter builds upon these studies by focusing on what we have identified as several key indicators of a healthy small city culture: (1) opportunities for direct and indirect participation in local arts and culture; (2) a generative mix of high art and vernacular cultural expression; and (3) an effective rhetoric of arts and culture advocacy. In particular, working with the City of Kamloops and an arts and heritage consultant hired to prepare a new Cultural Strategic Plan, the Small Cities CURA contributed to "Strategy E" of the plan, a section on culture and education, which reads: "*The Kamloops Cultural Strategic Plan* reveals the strong and inextricable link between culture and education and clearly shows their contribution to life-long learning and the building of a 'learning community'" (Janzen).[1]

This recipe for building a learning community marks an important public acknowledgement of a potential role for the arts in linking education to community development. That said, we are aware that while such indicators may point to a culture of participation, they are not always correlated with positive economic development. According to the existing literature on large urban centres, the opportunity to establish strong community ties may actually deter some people from moving to small communities and thus inhibit growth: deep community involvement is said to be commonly rejected or avoided by itinerant knowledge-sector workers and members of the so-called creative class, who characteristically prize personal flexibility and opportunity over community responsibility and commitment.

We see this negative association as a partial misreading of the evidence drawn from small cities — as an interpretation better suited to the big city setting. We argue, instead, that small city settings put special emphasis upon these indicators — and, further, that they create a complex but important role for work-based lifelong learning related to the development of cultural capacity. Traditionally, art and culture tend to be seen as distanced from any significant association with work and recreation; "artistic" products of work and play are regarded as forms of craft, hobby, or local personal expression — not "art." Small city settings narrow this divide between art and work: social proximity affects political realities, including access to exhibition and performance spaces, funding, media attention, and active participation in decision making. We see in the small city setting (and especially in the Kamloops Cultural Strategic Plan) an openness to explore the complementary relationship between the arts and sustainable innovation (the potential for arts to invigorate innovators) in the workplace (Galbraith; Harris; Tushman and Nadler). However, we are aware that there is a need for us to demonstrate what might be called a dialectical link between individual participation in the arts, informal learning, and workplace innovation. With this task in mind, we have begun to examine the range of activities that link art to learning and innovation.

In what follows we shall explore (1) the range of learning spaces at work and in the community; (2) best practices that promote learning either *in* arts and culture or *through* arts and culture; (3) the structures, institutional and otherwise, that influence human agency and the links between lifelong learning wherever it is found (within and beyond the workplace); and (4) the kinds of innovation, of creativity, that shape the future of small cities. We shall outline a fairly recent body of knowledge known as "cultural-historical activity theory" and apply it to an example of art making in order to answer the question: How does art help learning in the workplace and the community? The purpose is to illustrate the complex interdependency of creativity, informal learning, and innovation. From this perspective we speculate on the role of art as a pedagogical tool for adult learning, sustainable innovation, and community development; and, further, we outline the conditions necessary for making creativity visible as a stimulus for workplace learning and the creation of creative capital.

**Learning at Work and Through the Arts**

In our view, the existence of a critical cluster of artists and cultural activity in a small city not only acts as a magnet for attracting investment in knowledge-based ventures and for recruiting and retaining knowledge workers, but it also increases the capacity for sustained engagement in work-based informal learning and innovation. It is the latter benefit that we feel has been overlooked in the research literature. We see a need to reposition discussion of creativity, moving from the notion of *creativity as a commodity* to be imported to *creativity as a local asset* to be developed.

As notions of knowledge-work, core competencies, and innovation have entered the contemporary management lexicon: there has been a growing interest in learning in organizations (Billett; Boud and Garrick; Bratton et al.; Foley). Within contemporary formulations of human resource management (HRM) strategy, it is suggested that an organization's investment in training and learning acts as a powerful signal of its intentions to develop its "human assets," which can help develop commitment to the organization rather than simply compliance. And current management thinking advocates the

pursuit of worker flexibility through reflexive learning extensively as a lever to sustainable competitive advantage: the ability to learn "faster" than competitors (Dixon). Similarly, Thomas Kochan and Lee Dyer advise those companies adopting a "mutual commitment" strategy to gain competitive advantage to make the necessary investment in their workforce and adopt the concept of *lifelong learning* (our emphasis, 336). This belief, therefore, in the efficacy of continuous reflexive learning is linked to a broader discourse on human resource management (HRM) practices that attempts to facilitate work-related learning in order to gain worker commitment and facilitate organizational change (Bratton et al.).

A variant of this argument posits learning as a key "lever" that can increase "sustainable innovative" capacity within the workplace (Tushman and Nadler). Innovation requires a full integration of creative thinking, managing, and implementing (Kitagawa 4). Sustainable innovation, it is contended, enables organizations to improve the quality of the service or product, enter new markets, react to competitive encroachment, leverage new technology, and revitalize mature businesses. However, organizations have problems innovating (Dougherty). The persistence of these problems has led to greater emphasis being placed on learning processes as a vehicle to achieve sustainable innovation and on knowledge workers — those people who are the innovators, the problem definers, and the problem solvers (Haughey). Innovative workplaces are said to be highly effective at learning, self-critical, and committed to continuous improvement. According to Jay R. Galbraith, innovation requires that an organization's structure, rewards, processes, and people are combined in a specific way to create an innovating workplace, "one that is designed to do something for the first time" (156). Of particular relevance to our inquiry is Galbraith's argument that certain "key processes" and "people practices" increase the creative agency and the organization's ability to innovate. One key process involves "getting ideas" when there are "match-ups" between idea generators and sponsors. Building exchange networks, creating a common physical space, and organizing events for matching purposes can improve the process of getting ideas. The variations of such events are endless, but this line of inquiry is predicated on the belief that art, artists, and cultural events in a small city can improve the odds of "match-ups" between idea generators and sponsors.

The second design feature relevant to this research involves people practices. The assumption made by Galbraith is that prospective innovators possess certain psychological attributes, including irreverence for the status quo — a propensity to achieve and to take risks. Idea generators "often come from outcast groups or are newcomers to the company; they are less satisfied with the way things are and have less to lose if there's a change" (176). The main argument is that people who have the psychological attributes of successful innovators are not only more likely to be attracted to a location where there is a vibrant art and cultural community, but that exposure to the arts provides an impetus for innovation. The point to be emphasized here is that the arts have the potential for developing reflexive and innovative labour processes. With the perceived need to attract and retain "knowledgeable" workers, with relearning and innovative capacities that are now considered necessary for sustainable competitive advantage, organizational structures will need to change (Clegg and Gray) and develop new learning strategies (Argyris). Our central premise, however, is straightforward: the arts provide fertile conditions for

developing and validating new "crazy" ideas or "out-of-the-box" thinking; in other words, the arts foster innovation.

Research on the arts-innovation connection is an underdeveloped area. However, a number of case studies provide *prima facie* evidence that artists embedded in the workplace are associated with positive performance outcomes. In a U.S. establishment, Craig Harris's account of Xerox's "artist-in-residence program" documented the benefits of pairing artists with scientists in a high-tech environment. The assumption was that Xerox would "benefit in some unspecified way by integrating artists into the research environment and encouraging artists and scientists to work together collaboratively" (23). Similarly, Lola Rasminsky reported on business leaders who have "discovered" that hiring an artist accelerates innovative thinking processes and, moreover, is good for the corporate "bottom line." For example, North American companies have hired musicians who help attune a project team to "disharmonies and to voices not being heard" (A13). Rasminsky emphasizes the importance of appropriating not just the specificities of artists' experience and expertise, but also their perceived psychological attributes: "The most successful enterprises harbour and support creative thinkers, people skilled at breaking the rules ... artists do take more risks and are less afraid of chaos than the rest of us. As a result, they can shape order out of seemingly chaotic situations" (A13).

As a strategy for sustainable competitiveness, the arts-innovation model inherently celebrates the innovative potential of artistic deviance; it also emphasizes the critical importance of harnessing workers' knowledge and creativity through a range of workplace practices aimed at increasing the value added of human capital: such practices as team working, empowerment, cognitive apprenticeships and informal learning.

We should note, however, that the learning-advantage model has its detractors. A body of scholarly literature exists which takes a critical approach to the emerging field of learning at work. This alternative perspective focuses attention on how power relations, organizational politics, conflicts of interest, gender, race, and ethnicity shape learning at work. Within this school, writers emphasize how "cultural control" can be reinforced through learning (Legge) and how formal learning of "competencies" can render work more "visible" in order to be more manageable (Townley). And John Coopey challenges popular management writers such as Peter Senge, who in *The Fifth Discipline* asserts that learning theory assumes a managerial perspective, that inherent tensions in the employment relationship are largely ignored, that power is omnipresent, and that political activity within the workplace is likely to impede learning. Coopey goes on to argue that the likely effect of new learning regimes is to strengthen the power of senior management. By adopting a "learning strategy," therefore, it is argued that managers hope to unfreeze traditional attitudes and work practices and foster innovative thinking and new ways of doing. Neglecting these wider socio-economic dynamics, tensions, and contested aspects of learning might mean that learning practices become a tool to impose higher work quotas and increase managerial control in the workplace (Forrester; Spencer "Changing Questions"; Thompson and McHugh).

## The Activity System of the Artist-Innovator

While innovation is often associated with ingenious individuals diligently working to create a new product or process, most workplace innovations are built upon the cumula-

tive effect of existing knowledge and practices undertaken by *groups* of individuals. If we use only creative individuals as the lens for understanding innovation, then we get a very restrictive view of the innovation process. We can obtain a more inclusive view of the innovation phenomenon by adding another complementary lens: the context. A central proposition advanced in the chapter is that cultural-historical activity theory helps us to work towards a more inclusive approach to studying workplace learning and innovation by focusing on complex relations among individuals and groups, learning and innovation, workplace and community. Activity theory emphasizes that any particular human activity is socially constituted, and that differences of interests, power, and possibilities for action are ever-present. As Jean Lave puts it:

> Any particular action is socially constituted, given meaning by its location in society, historically generated systems of activity. Meaning is not created through individual intentions; it is mutually constituted in relations between activity systems and persons acting, and has a relational character. Context may be seen as the historically constituted concrete relations within and between situations. (18)

Cultural-historical activity theory evolved from the work of two Russian psychologists, Lev Vygotsky and Alexei Leont'ev, in the early Soviet era. Vygotsky believed that an individual couldn't be understood as divorced from her or his social structure — defined as the enduring and patterned social interaction governed by norms — and that society couldn't be understood without considering the human agencies that use and produce artefacts. This idea of cultural mediation of actions came to be conceptualized by the triadic relationship of subject, object, and mediating artefact (see Figure 2).

In the model, the *subject* refers to the individual(s) — for example, designer and artist — whose agency is selected as the point of analysis. The *object* refers to the "raw materials" (e.g., product, process, or problem) at which the activity is directed and which is transformed into outcomes by using mediating *artefacts* (social language, tools, materials, and technologies).

Alexei Leont'ev's account of the difference between individual action and *collective* agency provided the basis for further expansion of activity theory. The Vygotsky-Leont'ev cell of activity theory is seen to represent just the "tip of the iceberg." A more complex reformulated model shows individual and group agency to be grounded in a complex interlocking social system of community, division of labour, and rules (see Figure 3). The *community* refers to multiple individuals and groups who share the same general object. The *division of labour* refers to both the horizontal division of functional tasks between members of the community and the vertical concomitant division of power and status. The *rules* are comprised of social norms and explicit and implicit regulations. The *object*-oriented outcomes are characterized by ambiguity, sensemaking, and potential for innovative change. This enlarged triangular configuration is a heterogeneous entity, composed of multiple voices; it is dynamic and didactic in nature. People, the model argues, not only use instruments; they also continuously renew and transform them. They follow rules, but they also reshape and reformulate them. They experience contradictions and conflict, but they also practise accommodation and cooperation (Engeström, "Developmental Studies"). Furthermore, while the model attempts to contain the roots of *past* traditions and modes, its *future* trajectory is embedded in the social relations and actions of the *present*. Yrjö Engeström ("Developmental Studies") proposes a cultural-historical activity theory that incorporates five central principles: First, a collective, artefact-mediated and object-oriented human activity system; second, a community of practice of multiple voices, traditions, and interests; third, historicity, that is, learning which is shaped and becomes transformed over periods of time; fourth, contradictions and social tensions in the capitalist labour process drive change; and fifth, an understanding that expansive transformations in an activity system are accomplished through contradictions when "the object and

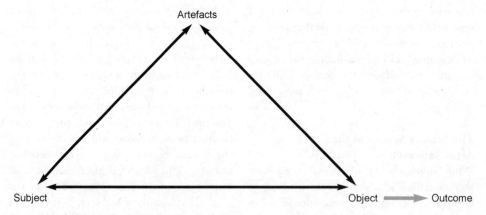

Figure 2. Vygotsky's triadic model of mediated actions.

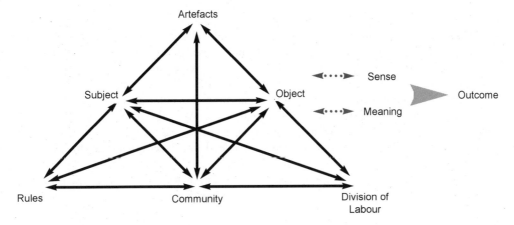

Figure 3. Engeström's complex model of human agency (Engeström "Learning by Expanding").

motive of the activity are re-conceptualized to embrace a radically wider horizon of possibilities than in the previous mode of activity" (Engeström "Expansive Learning" 137).

How can we use this conceptual tool to study the mechanisms of learning and innovating with and through the arts? Learning and innovating using this theoretical framework can be understood as a process of reciprocal transformation between an individual's (workers/artists, managers, and users) or group's image of the object operating within a community of practice, rules, and mediated by interlocking levels of power. Drawing on the work of Charles Keller and Janet Keller, sculpturing, for example, can be seen as an activity system. The sculptor brings knowledge to bear on problem solving in the creation of an artwork. Relevant knowledge includes the internal image of the object and the sculptor's conceptualization of the creative sequence. From a cultural-historical activity theory perspective, neither the individual sculptor nor the external context is solely responsible for the creative outcome. Every artist or innovator's work incorporates the knowledge accumulated by his or her community and society in the course of its history.

The interdependency and the connections between individual creativity and community, division of labour, and rules is clearly evident. We are artists, blacksmiths, carpenters, designers, engineers, sculptors, writers, or whatever. But each of us performs our specialized actions using artefacts invented and developed by others, and by applying knowledge and practices accumulated and transmitted to us by others. The sculptor, for example, uses tools invented and produced by others and is informed with knowledge learned from others. Creativity and innovation in the workplace or the community in the strictest sense cannot, therefore, spring from the individual alone; it is a collective phenomenon.

Several writers have highlighted another aspect of human agency, the power/politics associated with learning and innovation in the workplace (Blackler and McDonald; Coopey; Rasminsky). These authors are critical of workplace-learning studies that neglect power and politics in work organizations, and that fail to ask the question of whose interests are being served. Although learning and creative thinking may be seen as necessary for sustainable competitive advantage, some may also view it as a potentially subversive force. Innovation depends on motivated individuals and groups who are prepared to experiment, to take risks, and to challenge the status quo. Yet, in many organizations, senior managers and administrators are reluctant to encourage learning and creative thinking. If they feel that their power is threatened, they will probably behave defensively, restricting learning and creativity (Coopey). The issues of power and politics are also tied up with sense-making, for those in dominant positions, either in work organizations, communities, or professions, can define, construct, and reconstruct meaning through discourse (Nonaka; Weick). This form of constructivist argument suggests, for example, that what constitutes a case of avant-garde art depends upon a few — those who assert the legitimate authority to pronounce upon artistic meaning, and have the resources to disseminate their interpretation — sense-making for the many. Activity theory helps us to understand the ambiguities of organizational life. It draws attention to the contradictions and potential conflicts in the innovative process arising from differences in employer and employee interests, the unfolding experience, and the application of the knowledge. A fundamental premise of our approach is that an understanding of innovation must include an analysis locating the application of the creative thinking or practice in the sociocultural context in which it has developed and proceeds.

## The Phenomenon of Creative Clusters

It is difficult, especially when looking at the innovation process through a cultural-historical activity theory lens as we have attempted to do, to avoid the conclusion that creative activity in and through the arts is contingent upon both a vibrant cluster of creative people and a receptive community. Creative activity is also at least partially dependent upon the community's receptiveness to the notion that learning and innovating take place through the arts. We'd like to consider one further aspect of the argument that says artistic clusters lead to prosperity and thus the need for attracting and accommodating the creative class. At the heart of Richard Florida's much-celebrated book *Rise of the Creative Class* is a curious contradiction, one based on his understanding of creativity. On the one hand, early in his book, he posits a wonderfully broad, even egalitarian, notion of creativity: "Spurred on by the creative ethos," he says, "we blend work and lifestyle to construct our identities as creative people.... [Today] one person may be simultaneously a writer, researcher, consultant, cyclist, rock climber, electronic/world music/acid jazz lover, amateur gourmet cook, wine enthusiast or micro-brewer" (13). Creativity, thus defined, is something inherent (or latent) in all of us. On the other hand, Florida spends most of his study making the case for a special class of people — artists, computer programmers, architects, doctors, professors, lawyers, entertainers, media specialists, designers, and so on — who are more "creative" than other workers. He insists that economic health and development hinge on whether any given city fosters a social environment attractive to such people. The creative class is, for Florida, a mobile commodity, an endlessly portable social group with relatively loose ties to the immediate community. Indeed, Florida argues that those cities that fail to attract the new creative class will decline and wither.

Florida's conclusions cast the creative person as "other," as someone set apart from the ordinary, and, significantly, as someone with relatively little interest in the kind of close-knit affiliations we tend to associate with small city living. Those in the creative class seek a vibrant social life, diversity, tolerance, and a range of social and professional opportunities; they also tend to abstain from civic responsibility, viewing community ties as "tying down" their creative impulses. Traditional indicators of social capital — volunteerism, church affiliation, neighbourhood involvement, rich personal interactions and networks — no longer hold: they are portrayed as factors likely to repel the creative class.

To his credit, Florida reports dismay at the new economic imperative he finds himself describing; but he argues that it is impossible to "bring back the kind of community we used to have." He hopes his research might lead the way to a "new model," where people can lead "real lives in real places" (281) — but he ends up in a rhetorical cul-de-sac, where innovation and growth can only be achieved by compromising traditional measures of social capital (Putnam).

While we don't question the celebration of creativity as a force for community development, we wonder why Florida's initial premise — that creativity is inherent in all of us — gets lost along the way. Why not seek to stimulate and make visible the creativity already present in the community? It is our contention that, given the creative class's reported aversion to traditional social values, small cities — which by nature of their scale discourage anonymity and encourage civic participation — may not have any other choice but to draw out creativity from within.

### The Case of Artists and Workers

The initiative for this research stems from two ongoing research programs: the Cultural Future of Small Cities program, which focuses on Kamloops, a city of 80,000 in the southern interior of British Columbia, and the Working Class Learning Strategies project (WCLS), which focuses on a cross-section of unionized workers in southern Ontario, Canada (Livingstone and Sawchuk). Last year, participants in these two separate projects began to consider working together on an international collaborative research project under the Initiatives on the New Economy (INE) program. This led to a consideration of two case studies — Hamilton, Ontario and Kamloops, British Columbia — interested in creating agency and innovation in the workplace through the arts. We detail here our preliminary observations on art and work in Kamloops.

The Cultural Future of Small Cities program of research is supported by a Community-University Research Alliances (CURA) grant from the Social Sciences and Humanities Research Council of Canada (SSHRC) and has nine partners: the Kamloops Gallery (KAG) as lead organization, The University College of the Cariboo (UCC), City of Kamloops, Forest Research Extension Partnership, Kamloops Museum & Archives, John Howard Society, Secwepemc Cultural Education Society, Stuart Wood School, and Western Canada Theatre. The focal point for this interdisciplinary research has been exploring the cultural challenges and possibilities that face small cities in a world increasingly dominated by large urban centres, suburban sprawl, and economic globalization. The overall research program is self-referential as it explores the structures, institutional and otherwise, and resources, such as social capital, that shape the cultural fabric and future of small cities. The KAG's role as lead organization has given increased emphasis to questions of visual representation and display. One consequence for the program has been an interest in involving artists as co-researchers. The expressed goal: to facilitate dialogue and enhance the learning experiences for both the university researchers and the community partners:

> Artistic practice — and the presence of working artists — offers the possibility of well-crafted critique, playful destabilization and an identifiable "third view," one not tied directly to either the university or the community partners. As an aspiring learning community, we continue to pursue our initial purpose, but we have also turned to art and artists to help refine our terms of reference, to help redefine our working relations. (Dubinsky and Garrett-Petts 347)

The Small Cities CURA is now in the midst of working out forms and models of collaboration involving artists, academic researchers, and community organizations — including how artists are to be chosen for each project, the role artists might play, and the financial considerations. To date, four artists have been engaged to work with four community-based research teams. Each is following one of three inquiry models:

> (1) *Affinity*: where the artist is encouraged to match existing work with issues under exploration by a particular research group.
> (2) *Response*: where the artist is encouraged to create new work responding directly to the particular research group's project.
> (3) *Integrated*: where the artist works with a particular research group, becoming in effect a co-researcher by committing skills, insights and art production to the research findings. (Dubinsky and Garrett-Petts 344)

We see these inquiry models, drawn from local experience, as possible templates for introducing artistic practices into the workplace generally. The models can also help to address the question: "If people learn and

innovate through art and by participating in ongoing artistic activity, how does this come about?" Accordingly, we wanted to know whether the community would see value in — and welcome — one or more of these models.

The data were collected by means of semi-structured interviews conducted in the first three months of 2003. All the interviews were scheduled for one hour, but in most cases lasted up to two hours. All the interviews were tape-recorded. The content of this paper is based upon a small group of people employed in the community as, respectively, the director of a centre for innovation, a professional artist, an office manager, two trade union leaders, and an arts and heritage consultant. The in-depth interviews provided us with rich insights into the issues surrounding creative agency in a small city's labour processes.

All the respondents expressed enthusiasm for the notion of learning through the arts, although, not surprisingly, each emphasized different aspects of the human capital argument. The director of an innovation centre, for example, described a more traditional link between artists and innovation and entrepreneurship:

> There is a real need for design, there is no doubt about that, and the furniture industry, especially the high-end market, relies on that for a very large degree. And there is a high-end market for furniture. So the Kootenay School of the Arts has a very strong furniture design group, and that plays out nicely into the [local] furniture industry.

The director tended to see art as strictly functional, as an element in the production process and not really conforming to any one of the three models. He indicated that a more pronounced role for "artists-in-residence" might be seen as an unwelcome, even disrup-

Figure 4. Employment collages. Photo by Susan Dueck.

tive, challenge to everyday practice.

In contrast, the perception that artists are "greater risk takers," are "less afraid of chaos," and could promote more creative thinking in the workplace was expressed by the professional artist this way:

> *Many artists work back and forth between a process of risk-taking and chaos and some kind of more ordered activity. If you take an exhibition in a gallery, for example, the activity of getting the exhibition into the gallery has to come about through some ordered process of packaging the work, of framing it, working with the curator to come up with scheduled time lines. There is a whole pile of ordered activities that must of necessity lead up to an exhibition. Yet in the studio, the production of the work, depending on the artist, may have been a chaotic procedure. It's one thing to highlight that artists are, by and large, good at organizing themselves, particularly if they are professional artists exhibiting in galleries, although I*

> *don't wish to exclude others by saying that. I think they are people good at moving back and forth between realms of chaos and risk-taking and figuring out how to shape something into a more concrete objective.*

The artist made clear distinctions, throughout the interview, between professional and amateur practices, while remaining interested in all three models. He recognized the value of encouraging general artistic appreciation and involvement, but he was careful to advocate that learning be tied to high art criteria. The artist may provoke creative thinking, but the artist is not a neutral agent — not someone without a stake in the creative outcomes.

The office manager of an employment agency and the two union representatives acknowledged the potential of learning through the arts, but all three expressed scepticism about the employer's possible reactions

Figure 5. Employment collage, detail. Photo by Susan Dueck.

and motives. The office manager was in the process of producing a video documenting her centre's work with the unemployed:

> R1: *I am a manager now, but also work as a member of a fairly tight team and we all help each other, artists that we are, but it's always great when someone comes in, like you did this morning and just says, "Did you ever think of going to a business person and asking that question?" Just to have an outside perspective, because we kind of get set in our ways, as much as we like to think we are not set in our ways and we are open to all kinds of learning. When you work in one environment, in one field and with the same people, you do assume roles and ways of doing things that I think need to be shaken up every once in awhile ... And our documentary-making effort shook us up in a major way.... We tapped into a lot of people ... I think artists see things differently. People don't think they are artists. People who are trapped in certain life work roles and responsibilities and*

*commitments ... I think artists could change the way people think. Absolutely.*

Despite her enthusiasm for incorporating art, the office manager felt restrained in discussing and promoting an existing arts-based learning program her team had already initiated — a program that had positive results and obvious potential for expansion. One of the more difficult tasks for someone disadvantaged and unemployed is to visualize an employment future. Working with such at-risk clients, the manager found that asking them to create collages — to cut and paste magazine images of people at work — helped both client and counsellor (1) identify past work experience and (2) envision a place for future employment. When asked whether bringing in a working artist would enhance this training program, the manager responded affirmatively, but cautioned that she'd be unwise to report on the program to her government funding organization, Human Resources Development Canada (HRDC): she anticipated that her team's innovative approach would be seen as a deviation from the *approved* delivery of employment counselling.

Here the affinity approach would enable an artist to model — and take responsibility for — the collage program. The ideal relationship, she said, would be the integrated model, where artists could be accessed as direct resources by both clients and counsellors.

The two union representatives also voiced great interest in the possible links between art and learning, but they said their membership would be suspicious if the employer initiated any arts program:

R2: *No question there is a link. … So for them to buy-in there would have to be balance and checks there. … But having said that, I believe there is a big role for the arts. Obviously, my understanding before today was very limited but hearing you two put the questions on what arts really is, there is no question that it can be of benefit in the workplace.*

R3: *I suppose so. But there would be a danger of any new kind of concept like that coming into the workplace. In that, if it was initiated by the employer, I think the workers would be looking, "What's the hook here? Where is this going? Is this another productivity scheme? Is this a mind game?"*

The union representatives nonetheless saw immediate value in the response model (especially in employing art as a vehicle for promoting workplace literacy and safety). More generally, they thought that the mere presence of art — photography, painting, music, and theatre — would make work a happier, more "tolerant," place. One of the representatives speculated that the affinity model

might, if introduced, inspire workers to celebrate, even exhibit, their own art at work.

Within work organizations, the quality of this informal learning experience may depend upon how the organization is structured and how work is designed (Bratton "Gaps"), or how individuals engage, interact, and construct knowledge from these paid work situations (Billett). Workers also learn that there are things they can do to prevent unwanted consequences. For example, working at the pace set by the work team, sometimes referred to as "norms," can prevent being ostracized by other members of the group. In a related manner, workers can learn not to learn because of perceived negative outcomes. For example, individually or collectively, workers may be reluctant to embrace learning and self-development because the resultant changes might either undermine the collective interests of the learners or challenge the workplace expectations of the employer (Bratton "Why Workers"). As the two trade union representatives told us:

R2: *It's going to depend how this is presented to the work floor because over the last 15 years, especially the last 10 years, there has been quite a thinking change in the way management manages. … And that union and non-union has to be very careful on how they buy into certain topics because a lot of the time certain buy-ins are only to downgrade or lessen the membership for the dollar. So people are very cautious about buying into that analogy (the arts-learning link) and I think if anything at all was coming forward in the arts covering that to the workplace, you would have to be awfully careful that it's presented in the right light — and, yes, it [better working conditions] can [make us] more productive — but as soon as [conditions are] more productive, what the employer does is whack the membership down.*

123

R3: *The role of the union is key in any informal learning. The union has to show some direction and leadership, and change how we do things. So, if the membership is not going to be sceptical, they have to see that the union is part of it. … If it's a legitimate kind of literacy/arts thing coming into the workplace, I think it's critical that the union has to be part of it.… It doesn't detract from the collective agreement.… The union is there to speak up.… There is always this scepticism of "Where is management taking us?"*

Not surprisingly, the arts and heritage consultant enthusiastically embraced the concept of linking art and work. She rehearsed how businesses regularly integrate the arts as "part of their corporate identity" by variously displaying artworks in offices, supporting artistic events, or creating opportunities for their employees to volunteer in the arts. Next, she described in detail an affinity model, where an Alberta iron works company had employed a sculptor as a temporary artist-in-residence:

*And what you had was these guys churning out equipment to get oil out of the ground, and then you had this artist doing a sculpture related to the iron works. And the artist said he learned a lot from the welders, etcetera. He said at first he was this freak that was brought in — and what was interesting was how this relationship developed between the industrial and the creative.… What the welder does every day is really art itself. Welding is an art.… So I think partnerships can begin where there's a strong link with the product produced, where (the artist) uses the materials that the company uses and creates something different.*

She offered the following comments on our project:

*The unexplored area right now is … artists actually on the workplace floor. That's a whole new*

concept, whether they are there to essentially serve in an artists-in-residence program or some other way. Now that's leading edge.… I think that "arts in the workplace," boy, that has legs, but it's got a long way to go. It's not anywhere near there yet — and I think it's terrific and very revolutionary and exactly where we should be going.

While each person interviewed responded positively to the potential role of "art in the workplace" as a bridge to new learning, each also identified a set of pre-existing attitudes and workplace relations that they believed would influence how art and artists might be received.

**Conclusion**

The findings reported in this chapter are limited to a small sample of data collected in a small city setting. On this basis, we have sought to demonstrate the potential for incorporating artistic practices and even artists as vehicles for enhanced workplace learning and innovation. What we can say with confidence is that, in the small city setting, there's ample interest and support to initiate further projects designed to understand "art at work" and to develop organizational cultures of innovation, that is, connecting small city art and culture to creative thinking in the workplace. Such projects would require a holistic approach to learning and a good fit between the workers, the workplace, and the *affinity*, *response*, and/or *integrated* models chosen. That said, our findings suggest that any project linking learning and creative agency will need to address: (1) the relationships between local practices that contextualize the ways people act together, both in and across contexts; (2) the inherent tensions in employment relations, especially union-management relations; (3) the anticipated scepticism or fear surrounding new approaches or ideas; and (4) the biases and agendas of the artists themselves. The quality of the learning experience and, with it, the concomitant potential for developing reflexive labour processes will necessarily depend upon how the organization and the work is designed, on the workplace climate, and on the art's overall relevance to all parties (including the artists). What we have identified is a local willingness to participate in a variety of arts-centred learning projects. This willingness speaks to a tacit understanding regarding (1) the value of art and creativity, and (2) the inherent desire of workers to acknowledge, share, validate, and, where possible, integrate their own creative capital.

## Acknowledgment

Our thanks to Diane Janzen of Janzen & Associates for her collaboration in the preparation of this study. Janzen was under contract by the City of Kamloops to conduct a comprehensive economic, cultural, and social survey of the arts and heritage community.

## Note

1. The plan goes on to say, "The statistics and the participation of more than 1 in 3 Kamloops residents in some kind of arts educational activity is evidence of the strength in this area. 24,447 of all Kamloops residents were shown to participate in some kind of arts and heritage activity put on by a Kamloops arts and heritage organization, whether it be a school heritage tour, formal music or lessons; a lecture, workshop, art or dance class. And while…. Only a minority of organizations … have identified themselves as having as a primary activity 'arts education,' 71% of arts and heritage organizations in Kamloops provided some kind of arts or heritage educational experience. In addition, The University College of the Cariboo and the Kamloops School District are vital players in the arts and heritage education. Recommendations were presented and related to encouraging arts and heritage in the schools, promoting greater partnerships with UCC, promoting research and publication into Kamloops arts and heritage issues, and creating greater linkages between the educational and arts and heritage sectors" (Janzen).

## Works Cited

Argyris, Chris "Teaching Smart People How to Learn." *Harvard Business Review* 69.3 (1999): 99-109.

Arts and Culture Indicators in Community Building Project. 7 July 2004. <http://www.urban.org/nnip/acip.html>

Arora, Ashish, Richard Florida, Gary Gates, and Mark Kamlet. *Human Capital, Quality of Place, and Location.* Pittsburgh: Carnegie Mellon UP, 2000.

Azmier, Jason J. *Culture and Economic Competitiveness: An Emerging Role for the Arts in Canada.* A Western Cities Project Discussion Paper. Calgary, AB: Canada West Foundation, March, 2002: 1-11.

Billett, Stephen. *Learning in the Workplace: Strategies for Effective Practice.* Crows Nest, AUS: Allen & Unwin, 2001.

Blackler Frank, and S. McDonald. "Power, Mastery and Organizational Learning." *Organization Studies* 37:6 (2000): 833-851.

Boud, David, and John Garrick, eds. *Understanding Learning at Work.* London: Routledge, 1999.

Braman, Sandra "Art in the Information Economy." *Canadian Journal of Communication.* 21 (1996): 179-196.

Bratton, John A. "Gaps in the Workplace Learning Paradigm: Labour Flexibility and Job Design." 1st International Conference on Researching Work and Learning. University of Leeds, England, 1999.

———. "Why Workers are Reluctant Learners: the Case of the Canadian Pulp and Paper Industry." *Journal of Workplace Learning,* 13:7/8 (2001): 333–343.

Bratton, John A., and Peter Sawchuk. Editorial. *Journal of Workplace Learning* 13:7/8 (2001): 269-273.

Brooks, Arthur C., and Roland J. Kushner. "What Makes an Arts Capital? Quantifying a City's Cultural Environment." *International Journal of Arts Management* 5:1 (2002): 12-23.

Castells, Manuel "Information Technology and Global Capitalism." *On the Edge: Living with Global Capitalism.* Ed. Will Hutton and Anthony Giddens. London: Jonathan Cape, 2000. 52-74.

Clegg, Stewart, and John Gray. "Metaphors of Globalization." *Postmodernism Management and Organizational Theory.* Ed. David Boje, Robert Gephart, Jr., and Tojo Thatchenkery. Thousand Oaks, CA: Sage, 1996.

Coffield, Frank. *Learning at Work.* Bristol, UK: Policy Press, 1998.

Coopey, John "Crucial Gaps in the Learning Organization." *How Organizations Learn.* Ed. Ken Starkey. London: International Thomson Business Press, 1996.

Culture of Cities Project. 7 July 2004. <http://www.yorku.ca/culture_of_cities/>

Cultural Future of Small Cities Community-University Research Alliances. 7 July 2004. <http://www.cariboo.bc.ca/smallcities/>

Department for Education and Employment. *The Learning Age: A Renaissance for a New Britain.* London: Stationery Office, 1998.

Dixon, Nancy. "Organizational Learning: A Review of the Literature with Implications for HRD Professionals." *Human Resource Development Quarterly* 3:1 (1992): 29-49.

Dougherty, Deborah "Organizing for Innovation." *Managing Organizations* Ed. Stewart Clegg, Cynthia Hardy, & Walter Nord. London: Sage, 1999. 174-189.

Dubinsky, Lon, and W.F. Garrett-Petts. Working Well, Together: Arts-Based Research and the Cultural Future of Small Cities. *AI & Society* 16:4 (2002): 332-49.

Engeström, Yrjö. "Developmental Studies of Work as a Testbench of Activity Theory: The Case of Primary Care Medical Practice." *Understanding Practice: Perspectives on activity and context.* Ed. Seth Chaiklin and Jean Lave. New York: Cambridge UP, 1996. 64-103.

——. "Expansive Learning at Work: Towards an Activity Theoretical Reconceptualization." *Journal of Education and Work* 14:1 (2001): 133-156.

——. *Learning by Expanding: an Activity-Theoretical Approach to Development Research.* Helsinki: Orienta-Konsultit, 1987.

——. *Training for Change: New Approaches to Instruction and Learning.* Geneva: International Labour Organization, 1994.

Fitzenz, Jac. *The ROI of Human Capital.* New York: AMACOM, 2000.

Florida, Richard. *The Economic Geography of Talent.* Pittsburgh: Carnegie Mellon UP, 2001.

——. *The Rise of the Creative Class. And How It's Transforming Work, Leisure, Community and Everyday Life.* New York: Basic, 2002.

Foley, Griff. *Strategic Learning: Understanding & Facilitating Organizational Change.* Sydney: Centre for Popular Education, 2001.

Forrester, Keith, John Payne, and Kevin Ward. *Workplace Learning: Perspectives on Education, Training and Work.* Aldershot, UK: Avebury, 1995.

Frey, Bruno S. *Arts and Economics,* Berlin: Springer-Verlag, 2000.

Galbraith, Jay R. "Designing the innovative organization." *How Organizations Learn.* Ed. Ken Starkey. London: International Thomson Business Press, 1996. 156-181.

Harris, Craig, ed. *Art and Innovation: The Xerox PARC Artist-in-Residence Program.* Cambridge, MA: MIT Press, 1999.

Hart, Mechkhild. *Work and Educating for Life: Feminist and International Perspectives on Adult Education.* London: Routledge, 1992.

Haughey, Margaret. "A Global Society Needs Flexible Learning." *Flexible Learning, Human Resource and Organizational Development.* Ed. V. Jakupec and J. Garrick. London: Routledge, 2000.

Hughes, Howard. *Arts, Entertainment and Tourism.* Oxford: Butterworth-Heinemann, 2000.

Janzen, Diane. *Kamloops Cultural Strategic Plan—Summary.* Report presented to the City of Kamloops, the Kamloops Arts Commission and the Kamloops Heritage Commission. Kamloops, 2003. N. pag.

Keller, Charles, and Janet Dixon Keller. "Thinking and Acting with Iron." *Understanding Practice: Perspectives on Activity and Context.* Ed. S. Chaiklin and J. Lave. New York: Cambridge UP, 1996. 125-143.

Kitagawa, Kurtis. *Building and Sustaining a Culture of Innovation / Entrepreneurialism in Canada for Competitiveness and Growth.* Conference Board of Canada: Ottawa, 2001. 1-11.

Kochan, Thomas, and Lee Dyer. "HRM: an American View." *Human Resource Management: A Critical Text.* Ed. John Storey. London: Routledge, 1995.

Lave, Jean "The Practice of Learning." *Understanding Practice: Perspectives on Activity and Context.* Ed. Seth Chaiklin and Jean Lave. New York: Cambridge UP, 1996. 3-32.

Legge, Karen. *Human Resource Management: Rhetoric and Realities.* Basingstoke: Macmillan, 1995.

Leont'ev, Alexei. *Problems of the Development of the Mind.* Moscow: Progress Publishers, 1981.

Livingstone, David W. "Expanding Notions of Work and Learning: Profiles of Latent Power." *Sociocultural Perspectives on Learning through Work.* Ed. Tara Fenwick. San Francisco: Jossey-Bass, 2001. 19-30.

Livingstone, David W., and Peter Sawchuk. "Beyond Cultural Capital Theory: Hidden Dimensions of Working Class Learning." *The Review of Education/Pedagogy/Cultural Studies* 22:2 (2001): 121-146.

Nonaka, Ikujiro. "A Dynamic Theory of Organizational Knowledge Creation." *Organization Science* 5:1 (1994): 14-37.

Putnam, Robert D. *Bowling Alone: The Collapse and Revival of American Community.* New York: Simon, 2000.

Rasminsky, Lola. "Hire an Artist, it's Good for Business." *The Globe and Mail* 14 July 2001: A13.

——. "Taming Creativity." *The Globe and Mail* 24 Dec. 2003: B17.

Sawchuk, Peter. *Adult Learning and Technology in Working-Class Life.* New York: Cambridge UP, 2003.

Schultz, Theodore W. *Investing in People: The Economics of Population Quality.* Berkeley, CA: U of California P, 1981.

Senge, Peter. *The Fifth Discipline.* New York: Doubleday, 1990.

Spencer, Bruce. "Changing Questions of Workplace Learning Researchers." *Sociocultural Perspectives on Learning Through Work.* Ed. Tara Fenwick. San Francisco, CA: Jossey-Bass, 2001. 31-40.

——. *The Purpose of Adult Education,* Toronto: Thompson Educational Publishing, 1998.

Thompson, Paul, and David McHugh. *Work Organizations (Third Edition).* Basingstoke: Pagrave, 2002.

Townley, Barbara. *Reframing Human Resource Management.* London: Sage, 1994.

Tushman, Michael. and David Nadler. "Organizing for innovation." *How Organizations Learn.* Ed. Ken Starkey. London: International Thomson Business Press, 1996. 135-155.

Vygotsky, Lev. *Mind in Society: the Development of Higher Psychological Processes.* Cambridge: Harvard UP, 1978.

Weick, Karl. *Sensemaking in Organizations.* Thousand Oaks, CA: Sage, 1995.

Wynne, Derek. *The Culture Industry.* Aldershot, UK: Avebury, 1992.

# Part II

# Cultural Narratives
# and Representations

# From *Into the Fold*

## Jacqueline Turner

Chase chases memories say sand
between toes to start plus a lake, a red
pier and a desire to swimslither cold
(blue water, blue sky) skin prickles
expands again red (that feeling) hair
turning burns blonder still

[insert photo here]


ache edges depth vast and waits wind
winds too cold of a shout offshore
without future lakes in mind

[yearning, fingers, fear]


lake this mountain train track fresh
sulphide fliesfurious (intention always
reveals itself) lost blue against

[ankles, angst]


one hair turn turning

small


Chase chases memories
same as same
water up a nose
flintstone lunchbox breaks
tongue rips cold metal
swings taken again
scratch:  snack stolen
purple banana bike seat
red tablets:
how to brush your teeth
jumping the high stair
backs broken crack

Chase chases memories

blank big stop 'run til you puke'
headache breaks easily against cracks

whirling inside 'all you can do' too big
for skin scrapes refuse bones ache burst

blue slaps big boulders water falls
behind desire for just one just one more

yearn yellow of a white car drives
'around and around'

lake lascivious wraps thighs cool bluegreen
almost alone again

Shuswap lakes me log cabin lemon
legs stretched deck fresh and big air breezes
slink on a too hot hafta go in baby's heard
againlanguish up

wave to Dad delivering the mail

rocky beach water sooo warm you wanna
sudden deep dives cool but not so
scrape against rock again and air

keep an eye on B in inflatable penguin

vast grass up the hill: rocks and feet heavy
arms failing penguin falls blows back down
B even redder than before kicks head back
tired slides stubborn sleep aside

gazebo Dad built for the wedding
(like he said he would)
plastic swimming pool plastic slide
bare toes hair curls still
really big tomatoes
aqua boat + purple skis
bathing suits on the freezer
long, long drives


Shuswap lakes me on the last day of school
boats a two-four with N and S
J and her bikini weren't allowed to go

N knew he'd work on a golf course S
probably didn't know he'd try to kill himself
later seems like the right word water glinting

got going real fast and we'd stop suddenly
and jump in pee in the lake in the clearest
body of water in Canada fluid the water we
knew our skin

S's little sister starts crying drank too much
she wants to go later on the lawn by the beach
she tells me she was pregnant once believes i
won't tell anyone and i don't until now

waves turn foamy white blue cold to my car
water falls against rock on the ride home
contemplate a nap and what's for supper
walkman drowns out the broken stereo

Kamloops calls pulp mill
fresh says don't stay too
long but "Sahali" offers
something desert dry drive
and drive

stuck in the back singing
'who were you talking to'
unseatbelted bends and
bends alone again  river
moves "cell by cell into
a realm unreal" and trains

picture w/ Santa –
she looks like a boy!
yeah
almost asked:
can we stop for a hamburger
too afraid felt
inside the chest
we passed it
banging the window
why what

Call Kamloops "your friend's in the
hospital" psyche ward
again but only organic
brown duster busted
joint in the Plaza parking lot
bright light promises/threatens
hot legs on saturday night
slip between river and lake
fresh black cold
yellowline as

# The City Small and Smaller

## Aritha van Herk

The city is beauty
unbreakable and amorous as eyelids,
in the streets, pressed with fierce departures,
submerged landings,
I am innocent as thresholds
and smashed night birds, lovesick,
as empty elevators

—"I" From thirsty, by Dionne Brand

In a chill and translucent February, I awoke on a night lanterned by a moon so lucent that nothing would do but that I must get up and wander the huddled and sleeping house. Barefoot, I stood at the back window that overlooks the open schoolyard behind my yard. This restlessness must come with middle age, ideas and ghosts arriving unexpectedly, knocking so loudly that ordinary sleep is interrupted. I do not know how often the denizens of cities stand at their windows at the wolf hour of three, dreaming themselves a field or a forest. We didn't practise such insomnias when I was growing up in the country. There we knew what lived outside the window. The poplars sighed behind the house, the slough rocked glacé and cat-tailed, the barns stood solid and humped with authority, the animals within making animal noises. We farming people lived in the outdoor world enough not to wonder at its secret life too much. The night was a welcome enwrapment, respite.

But on that winter's night in a suburb of a city just large enough to be vehement about itself, that city Calgary, Alberta, I felt myself to be a small organism in the midst of a larger, humming trace of space, and yet alone, the sole wakeful proprietor of this somnolent beehive of humans. The houses across the coulee, crouched in darkness, slept, only one window — a crying baby? a late-night assignment? — a light. And in the park, sere as an alpine desert, the bare open schoolyard/park so powerfully illuminated by the moon, someone as wakeful as I was walked his dogs.

Someone must have been walking his dogs because two dogs ran and gambolled and played, stopped to sniff the air, rolled on their backs in the snow. I watched them with the curiosity of a human seldom able to take the time to watch dogs, envying their nocturnal freedom, their patient owner. An owner who was nowhere to be seen. He must have let the dogs out to run, knowing that at that hour no one would care that they were leashless, that he would not have to track them with his municipally ordained plastic bags and clean up after their defecations.

It was mild enough that I grabbed a jacket and stepped out onto the balcony, sniffing, like the dogs, the almost impending ginger tang of spring. And the dogs trotted and paced one another, drifted like wraiths across the expanse, as curious as ghosts and as carelessly oblivious to the blank and drowsy houses regarding their invisible passage. At what seemed a pre-arranged signal, perhaps the nightly freight train that I could hear grinding up the tracks beside the Bow valley, they sat down on their haunches and howled in unison.

They were not domestic dogs but coyotes, a pair of loping, tail-flicking and utterly unencumbered coyotes, enjoying the moon, hunting for mice, occupying my field with the insatiable impudence that coyotes make virtuous. The coyote in winter, the coyote in the city, the coyote as invader, snoop and rogue, was reconnoitring a schoolyard that would be crossed by the tangled paths of elementary children in less than five hours. Whose parents would have a surly suburban fit if they imagined that two coyotes were hiding out in the bush-copses that edged up the coulees surrounding the schoolyard, owners who would howl at city hall if they had any inkling that their little Fluffy could be snatched by marauding predators. Coyotes will do that, cheerfully run smaller dogs to ground, circling and enticing, inviting them to join the pack. Or happily kill them. Urban roughnecks.

Everyone in Calgary recites the presence of the coyotes who live on Nose Hill, that splendid park decrying the bare beauty of the prairie, a huge acreage in the northwest quadrant of the city. "Keep your dogs on a leash," say the Nose Hill signs. "Coyotes in the vicinity." But here, far below the shoulder of that protected space, in the four-block radius of a combined schoolyard/ball dia-

mond/tobogganing hill, right between the leaning frames of the houses that now stagger over every dip and indent, coyotes are insolence. Calgary — that monstrous tentacular organism of box houses lining over-planned suburban sprawl, muscle and groin and determined filament of light and casement, prefabrication and substructure above hot tubes of sewage circulating below the plastic-piped arteries of water and gas, all overlain by cement and sod and asphalt — is secretly owned by coyotes, laughing, cheeky coyotes, medicine wolves, jackals, hyenas, mongrels. At play in the night.

Sometimes the city is beauty.

They still appear, infrequently but bolder than ever. I see them on my nocturnal vigils and even in the day, oblivious to the dangers of municipal jails and pest eradicators, the legislated fears of urban occupation. They lope the park because my neighbours, with their vulnerable cats and toddlers, do not know they are coyotes, have perhaps never seen a coyote, an Alberta coyote as cheerfully insouciant as our cowboys and our cars. Calgary may be a large city, but large cities house an agglomerate of oblivion, dumb with absence. Only those of us who grew up knowing coyotes, who heard them night after night, howling in the clumps of trees that pepper the parkland, can heed their insolence, recognize that they are signs and signatories, registers of speech, a physical visitation of the city as impostor.

◢     ◢     ◢     ◢

The beautiful city, singing its own shattered habitudes, resides now in an uneasy but anointed place, a place of poetry and prurience, pity and woe encoded in its gritty mythologies. Our cities no longer locate themselves according to nature's gifts (Venice because of the sea's gift of salt and Copenhagen because of the sea's gift of herring) (Jacobs 55), but as service providers, the sum of human and natural gifts in transition, exchange. They have become sporadic, loud with exhaust, anxious as bloody bandages, mouths full of pins and determined to measure and publish size, distance, density cartography, average house price, population, prosperity, vacancy rate. Statistics bristle, thick as flies. And the confluence of two rivers where a hopeful settler hammered together the boards of a shack, the long inlet of the ocean providing safe harbour, have become secondary to the sweat and tremble of a city on the brink of its own elocution, stuttering and deaf.

Urbanization is as viral as money, as ambiguous as neighbourliness, and as epidemic as anonymity. Cities are markers of civilization, but they are also acts of defiance and disappearance, cultural instrumentality running high, dissonant with their own competing tropes and colours. At their greatest pitch of colour and noise, they can be absurdly beautiful — Times Square in frozen flashes. At their most squalid intensity, they can also be more frightening than death itself. They offer humans opportunity and despair, chance and failure. They gift to every inhabitant the ability to disappear.

As I write this, I have just returned from Paris, that most arrogant of all arrogant cities, begun as Lutétia around 2000 BC, conquered by Julius Caesar, pillaged and sacked by Rome, bishoped by St. Denis, taken over in progression by the Franks, the Merovingians, the Carolingians, a commercial and religious centre sacred to the memory of St. Geneviève, until the Left Bank gave birth to the Sorbonne and Notre Dame began to gargoyle its buttresses, home to civil unrest, feuds, the plague, and the heart's desire of Jeanne d'Arc (who got for her trouble a severe cindering), spoil of the Renaissance, home to the Louvre and the stone quays of the Seine and the St.

Bartholomew's Day massacre and *palais* after *palais*, *jardin* after *jardin* leading to Jacobins and guillotines, Napoleon and Haussmann, the Tour Eiffel, the *petit bourgeoisie*, Stein and Joyce and Hemingway and Cole Porter and Mata Hari and Jimmy Morrison, and, oh god, Paris made me homesick for a city with just a little less memory, a city without that particularly arrogant angle of repose that demands undiminished attention to every stone block and every balconied corner.

I craved that comforting oxymoron, the small city. A centre off the beaten track, subsidiary to the self-importance of "city" without a modifier, those "worldly" cities that rest on the laurels of history and romance. I knew I was experiencing a Canadian abnegation, cultural cringe. We hide, here in Canada, in cities small enough to disappear. The secret of cities is their ability to disappear their citizens, but smaller than large Canadian cities practise a graceful disappearance of their own. Geographers research cartographical programs that will "unclutter" maps by erasing the small cities and exaggerating the large; airlines that now fly only to hubs abandon small cities to bus lines and cars; commerce huddles around a flat-roofed mall instead of a peak-roofed, red-painted railway station.

The small city speaks to its own intimate murmur, its habits precise as a local vernacular. In the small city, signage is unnecessary, programmed space unheard of, and friction factors minimal. Small cities deny the rub of manipulation, the false hype of busyness. In the small city, we can escape the gigantic, take refuge in a space less miniature than harmonious. If you will forgive me Bakhtin's "experimental fantasticality" (Bakhtin 95) to take on, for a moment, a Menippean perspective, I will cite Charon's view of the busy, hyperbolically citified world when Mercury enabled him to see it from a huge distance, a perspective removed and from above. "He

137

saw a vast multitude and a promiscuous, their habitations like molehills, the men as emmets. ... Some were brawling, some fighting, riding, running, *solicite ambientes, callide litigantes* (earnestly suing or cunningly disputing), for toys and trifles. ... In conclusion, he condemned them all for madmen, fools, idiots, asses" (Burton 47). Such "largeness" or giantism can only contribute to demonstrations of otherness, outsiderhood, and alienation. The small city refuses such a terrible microscopy, and insists on habitation, a neighbourhood, family, a living, and thus occupies a perspective not removed but immediate. As Henri Lefebvre points out, "these representations of space can be understood only as correspondences to a space of representation, a social space within which and through which ideological formations will be produced. But, those lofty ideologies announce a pluralism too entangled in its own excess to visit the origins of longing, homesickness, a chair that can be pulled up to a table" (Stewart 80-81).

Size has become the gauge of everything. Gargantua, the giant of the Middle Ages, renames Lutétia by drenching the citizens with his tremendous micturitive activity (that's pissing to those of us from small cities), drowning more than 260,000 people. Those who escape proclaim, *"We've been drenched par ris,"* "We've been drenched by piss." And there you are, a large city is invented, sewers and electricity and telephone wires, the hanging gardens of fire escape steps, the notional gesture of trees fenced by wire, the extravagance of bread too expensive to buy. The coyotes are laughing. This is the trickster's moment of origin, and gestures towards the division between large and local.

I am tempted to digress on the monstrous embellishments of the gigantic, the paradox of monument, and the arguments of sizism. My more vociferous arguments with my big

bilabialled male friends have to do with the valourization of the large — the big book, the big sculpture, the big brandish. I will not resort to the inverse carnivalizations of such insecurities, but I will quote one of my male students, who in a recent presentation showed a videotape of one of his male friends behaving largely, and who declared for the camera that his drunk and disorderly phases of giganticism were necessary to compensate for his being, and I quote, "hung like a fruit bat." Which I can only assume relates to miniaturism and its own discourses of absence. But I digress, as former denizens of a small city are permitted to do.

Aristotle declares that "a picture, or any other composite object, if it is to be beautiful, must not only have its parts properly arranged, but be of an appropriate size; for beauty depends on size and structure" (Aristotle 27). This aesthetic presumes that the affect of a place is relevant to its memory, quality, consciousness, and individuality. The public or exterior performance of a city cannot be divorced from the private and intimate components of that same place. Surfeit is surfeit, and while carnivalization and hyperbole can lay claim to their own particular braggadocio in small cities as well as large, the sheer multiple excess and repetitiousness of the large city denies an access to that intimate laughter. You have to know that Spoolmak spells Kamloops backwards to participate in that city's carnivalization, to understand why Kamloops practises the deliberate and carnivalesque inversion of driving snowmobiles across the Thompson River in the summer. The small city lives its culture publicly, argues against the big-box architecture of disinfectant, the pseudo-intimacies of Wal-Mart and Safeway. In the small city "the body [still serves] as our primary mode of understanding and perceiving scale" (Stewart 101). And this is the body that remembers and forgets; this is the body that experiences outrageous desire and that forms habits; this is the body that occupies space, that maps and mopes and monologues; this is the body that wants to visit a certain coffee shop and walk down a particular street; this is the body that watches coyotes with specific attention. Specific attention.

◢    ◢    ◢    ◢

The small city is an extension of home and homesickness, their powerful seductions resonant beyond time. My measurement of small cities is etched by my childhood-induced nostalgia for the Rose City — Camrose, Alberta — an agricultural service centre that stretched between a clapboard railway station and the Battle River valley of the central Alberta parkland, a small city that forever marked my imagination with its auction mart and creamery, library, and dime store. Camrose was and is a small small city, a rural community more than an urban centre, although the public information hastens to assure visitors that it is located within an hour's travelling distance of a major urban centre (Edmonton, Alberta). Still, Camrose is large enough to supply all "major services" as well as a mixture of cultural and sporting activities. With a carefully tabulated population of 15,669, Camrose nevertheless insists that it covers a trading area of 104,000 and boasts a diversified economy based on agriculture, industry, and retail business. In contemporary terms, it markets its desirable "lifestyle," but in fact the city of Camrose is an act of optimism balanced on the other side of slow decline. It served more as a service centre in the sixties when I was growing up, when a trip to Edmonton was lengthy and difficult enough to be unusual. And so Camrose was city, the city supplying the surrounding farmers and small businesses with goods and necessaries. In my memory it still carries a configuration of longing. At one end

of main street was Woolworths and at the other Saan and Safeway. In between were clothing stores, Five to a Dollar, Kresge's, two barbershops, one jewellery store, and a jostle of people that made this street seem "city" to me, a farm kid, a farm kid whose eyes got larger and rounder every time I got away from my parkland farm.

Camrose, earlier known as Sparling. My most repeated question as a child was a refrain that I am sure drove my parents to distraction. "Are we going to Camrose? Are we going to Camrose? Are we going to Camrose?" Camrose was a metaphor for my restlessness, for my desire to witness chaos and excitement.

Camrose meant more than Camrose. Going to Camrose meant going to an urban centre — I think they call it an agri-service centre now — full of stores, action, longing, suggestion, that I didn't get to see much of in the rural Battle River area or in the village of Edberg, sleepy with its own dust, its post office, its two elevators and three stores and yawning dogs who knew all about coyotes. Going to Camrose meant going to the auction mart where, between cigarettes, men rolled out long ticker tape of indecipherable words, going going gone, whobiddaforty-five. Every item demanded a bid for forty-five dollars or cents, and it is only now that I know about onomatopoeia and iambic pentameter that I understand why the numbers rolled so pleasurably and repeatedly off the tongue of the auctioneer. The auctioneer's glamour was enhanced by a cowboy hat above and a bolo tie below, framing a mouth that sold everything from old cream cans to ancient sauerkraut crocks to livestock, from weaner pigs to yearling calves to an occasional piebald pony with a dusty tail, superannuated but not quite ready for the cannery, still a few years of child's canter and oat-tins left. And after the auction, the treat-taste of a stale white bun around a hot dog, the bite of virulently yellow mustard, and the blue-haired waitress at the coffee bar, still there probably, splashing coffee into green cups and tucking her pencil into her beehive hair. Trucks rattling stock racks rolled away, and late Saturday afternoons dozed into their own dust. The auction mart gathered clusters of farmers and what they needed to sell, to buy, to trade in a timeless time before stock markets would send collective shudders through all of us and when RRSPs were just letters of the alphabet.

Camrose meant Woolworths, that emporium of Melmac dishes and mascara — I loved the black powder in the small red sliding Maybelline boxes, powder that you rubbed with water in order to make a paste, the brush as diminutive as eyelashes themselves, make up a reduced gesture. And material and dressmaking patterns and thread — I knew how to sew then: I could compose a dress by buying a piece of cloth and laying a tissue-paper pattern down on it (even making alterations) and cutting that cloth and sewing those pieces together into a garment that I would actually wear. I had learned this from my home economics teacher, Mrs. Radomski, a practical skill that could be engaged, resulting in clothing, which I didn't have much of, and which my parents didn't have a lot of extra money for. I cannot forget my own delight and pragmatism, the lengths of cloth that I bought at Woolworths, pink and blue but never green, the pants and dresses that grew under my fingers and the Singer treadle sewing machine that my mother kept in a corner of our large farm kitchen, a sewing machine so smooth and so solid that I never have liked electrics that snarl and race and seldom achieve the same solid, even stitching. That sewing machine is the physical reason why I drive a standard transmission; it entranced the body, the foot moving

the pedal at the same time as one hand guided the material and the other notched the flywheel. Not that I sew anymore. I wouldn't know where to begin. It is a skill for those who live in small cities.

And in the Camrose Woolworths, the lunch counter made the best hamburgers and fries, old-fashioned milkshakes in a green Beecham machine, the booths squirming with horny teenagers. I never necked in the coffee shop there, but I fainted once. I'd been to the dentist who gave me too much freezing — that Camrose dentist absolutely the roughest and least sympathetic of drillers in Alberta — and I fainted dead away on the linoleum floor. I opened my eyes to a circle of farmwomen hovering over me, their round faces a message of home-baked buns and turkey dinners and concern. They were the furies and saints of the small city, emissaries and giant matriarchs, whose very lives cast long shadows.

◢　◢　◢　◢

The centre of the small city is the library. In Camrose, the old library lived in a white-pillared building that hovered at the beginning of Main Street, a hallowed collection more sacred than church. At first we were relegated to the children's library in the basement — and the picture books had pictures and pictures and pictures, and I stared and read and stared and read until my eyes danced out of my head and I developed permanent myopia. I was allowed to take out six books, but I'd read them all in the back seat of the car even before we got home to the farm, 23 miles due south of Camrose, making myself carsick but unable to stop, words and pictures and pictures and words and reading, reading, reading, so that the small city made me a bookworm and myopic, instilled in me the narrative of reading as escape and return, books more important than bread. I confess, that is still the case. I would rather read a book than go out to dinner. There were no choices in that small city but books, words shoving open doors to a journey to the world's cities, a journey that began between the clefts of the Battle River, which was, I knew in my bones, beautiful beyond words. Words seduced me, made my mouth water, but they were words that were at home in a small city, and my seduction was the fault of the library, its stately stairs, its oiled floors, the creak when you walked behind a shelf, the smell of wet wool in the winter. I could hardly wait to get out of the children's library, upstairs into that hushed precinct of adult words, the librarian with her grey Marcelled hair severe, sitting behind a desk with the date stamp that I remember echoed the thump of a heart. I read my way through that library, from one book to another without stopping, and she encouraged me by saying nothing at all. The rest of the world suggested that I ought to do something practical, paint my father's barn or take teacher training or learn to skate, and I received several suggestions that included marriage. I was able to wear a disguise and perform very practically, driving the harrow in circles around my father's summer fallow field, picking saskatoons, and even washing dishes and becoming a reasonable baker of food-colouring-speckled angel food cakes. But those skills were not enough. I confessed to the woman with the grey marcelled hair, the chief librarian, sober and daunting, of the Camrose County Library, shyly and in a lowered voice, knowing my desire was shameful, that I wanted to be a poet. I imagined that this desire would convey me instantly and without fail, to a big city.

The librarian did not laugh. She did not even crack a smile. She looked at me and nodded and told me to keep reading, to pass Grade Twelve and prepare for university. It was very good advice, and she offered it with a signal gravity that I have never again encountered, a gravity that I later wished my slipshod university professors had echoed even faintly. I inhaled the aroma of those ancient wooden shelves, those oiled floors, I dawdled and delayed in that small city county library, sometimes on winter afternoons for hours. I wanted to live there, under its high mullioned windows, breathing in the dust of words. Only the small city offers such pauses, such intricate destinations for dreams.

The small city as destination performs a different act of connection than those cities requiring arrivals at echoing airports, craven taxi rides and barbiturate hotels. Going to Camrose embodied ritual and remedy, the ceremony of errand. I went to Byers Flour Mills for Sunny Boy Cereal, to the Fair Grounds for the Camrose Fair, where the school children's art hung in rows and rows of ducks and sunsets, to the CIBC bank to update my savings passbook, a dollar at a time. I went to the Jaywalker's Jamboree and rode a Ferris wheel. I went to the Smith clinic and puzzled at the intricacies of Venetian blinds and terrifying nurses. I went to St. Mary's Hospital when I was sick as a preschool child, where I loved the toys and the miniature tables and chairs, but hated the doctor who put his hands around my neck and tried to choke me to death. And I was terrified of the nuns, their swishing skirts and cloistered faces. I think I had strep throat. I lived to forget what illness I suffered. But I was so homesick that I got sicker from homesickness than from the sick I was and only recovered when I got to go home. The small city then was a place to visit and to retreat from.

But it does not retreat from memory. I remember the cars cruising up and down the street, mufflers like horns. I remember going to the house of our aging neighbours, six brothers and sisters who had sold their farm and moved into town. I remember the building of the Safeway store at the end of the street and the garage where my father bought a new green Pontiac. I remember the Five to a Dollar store, and Mirror Lake and the Lutheran church, and the creamery with its amazing ice cream and butter, although I never went to Camrose Lutheran College (then it was not yet called Augustana University College) or the Composite High School where boys learned automotives and girls went to beauty school. Going to Camrose was a treat, an expedition, an adventure, a day away, a reward, the centre on the edge of the outside world. It became the pilgrimage of rural to urban, that small city in the heart of the Battle River country. And if you want to be a poet, a small city is a good place to start. I became a novelist, a big city denizen, and I am homesick still for the landscapes of small cities, their unnecessary maps, their memory a text of community, their exchanges about weather and harvests economical and eloquent. What language does a place teach? How does it infiltrate the blood of articulation? And why, when time erodes the jangle of stimulation, does the small city hover, its main street the stage set for a drama comprising taste and smell, touch and awakening?

▲ ▲ ▲ ▲

My urban coyotes explain perfectly the pleasures of loneliness, the memory map of possibility. The small city recites yearning and regret together, and I become a coyote visiting Camrose. There, many of the stores that swelled with unattainable sweaters or typewriters or glass bowls have been converted to a refuge for second-hand despair. Some have been elevated to "Antiques," the flower-clustered china and wooden highboys of farm front rooms holding uneasy court with one another. I ramble through them wolfishly, tempted by a wooden school desk, its inkwell

intact, tucked between two dressers with swag-mirrors foxed with age, the faces that they reflected still hidden under the glass. We part the curtain of time that divides us from what we have forgotten tentatively, swallow the *chien mechant* of what memory might confront us, the inescapable artefacts of smallness solid and measurable.

The *unheimlich,* the unhomely, only exacerbates the memory map aroused by unmarked graves, misprisions of location, leftover signs for places long settled into dust. Huddles of human habitation do pray for companionship. Honest opinion longs for gossip. We all traverse our streets looking for one bright moment of inspiration, that perfect glance of light, that brief and concentrated drama of meeting, that tender maze of geography and accident.

Claude Leví-Strauss declares that the city "is both natural object and a thing to be cultivated, individual and group; something lived and something dreamed; it is *the* human invention, *par excellence*" (Leví-Strauss 127). He thought of the city as a concentration, a collective gesture of complicity or perhaps hope. Together this gathering of humans would compose a narrative. But the holistic ideal of the urban story is no longer a viable practice in large cities; only in small cities can some vibrant localism carry out a mutual declaration, a community chronicle. If, as Fernand Braudel suggests, "a city is a city wherever it is" (Braudel 481-483), then a small city is more where than there, more a cross-genre of protean annual and memoir, journal and history than the municipal plan of the larger city. That "set of lies agreed upon" that Napoleon condemned to history is in a small city a tapestry embellished and encrusted with multiples. The "whereness" of location is perhaps the model slippage for the small city, its marginality enabling it to supercede the "thereness" of the larger city, where flatulent occupation can resist its own multiple memories by virtue of the sheer "prodigiousness" of accumulated and incremental archaeologies. The small city generates a different corpus of locality, willing itself to be liminal, ecstatic with locality. Unwilling to resist its home vernacular, not eager to take on the polish and prose of the artificial aesthetic of the metropolis determined to be bigger than itself, the small city occupies a discourse that is replete with proportionality, modesty. Small and smaller bespeaks a confidence that the bustling elbows of the citified city dare not contemplate. The small city does not require the intensities of criminality or cogency, banks or insurance offices, agencies or consultants. The small city builds itself carefully, a brick at a time, with a nod to the weather and the water and the highway that leads in and out of town. In chain to the dominatrix centres, small cities perform still as agents of themselves, not needing to attract big conventions, sibling rivalry, superstructures of sport. Small cities grow next to a riverbank, a well, a farm fence. They seldom hire architects to create a grand design but invent themselves by living, that pragmatic dream of occupying the necessary moment rather than dynasty-founding and foundering.

The shape of the small city. A barrel of flour, a pair of shoes. A bridge and a beer parlour. Let us engage in small mythologies, the steeple no higher than necessary in case of lightning, the split level an effective division of stairs. A plow will plow, a pillow will plump, and in a small city, the birds are noisy and the stars are not quite obliterated. Nor are the coyotes required to haunt their own stealth.

## Works Cited

Aristotle. *On the Art of Fiction: "The Poetics."* Trans. L. J. Potts, Cambridge: Cambridge UP, 1968.

Bakhtin, M. M. *Problems of Dostoevsky's Poetics.* Trans. R.W. Rostel. Ann Arbor, MI: Ardis, 1973.

Braudel, Fernand. *The Structures of Everyday Life: Civilization & Capitalism 15th-18th Century.* Trans. Sian Reynolds. Berkeley, CA: U of California P, 1992.

Burton, Robert. *The Anatomy of Melancholy.* New York: Random, 1977.

Jacobs, Jane. *The Nature of Economies.* Toronto: Random, 2000.

Lefebvre, Henri. *La Production de l'espace.* Paris: Editions anthropos, 1974.

Levi-Strauss, Claude. *Tristes Tropiques.* Paris: Plon, 1955.

Stewart, Susan. *On Longing.* Durham, NC: Duke UP, 1993.

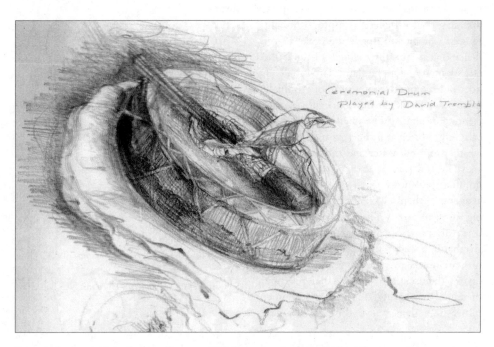

Figure 1. *Ceremonial Drum,* by Laura Hargrave, 2003. Reproduced courtesy of the artist.

# Vernacular Landscapes: Sense of Self and Place in the Small City

David MacLennan, Donald Lawrence,
W.F. Garrett-Petts, and Bonnie Yourk

*All the great narratives of world literature contain maps, maps that we can read…. Yet these maps remain implicit. The first maps that were introduced explicitly into a text, appearing in extenso under their visual aspect rather than their textual one, were probably those that corresponded to allegorical narratives, such as the carte du tender, the "map of tender love," which appeared around 1660 as an illustration in Mademoiselle de Scudéry's Clélie. Another such map decorated Bunyan's Pilgrim's Progress.*
— Claude Gandelman

Since 2002, our research group (consisting of a sociologist, a language researcher, a visual artist, and a student research assistant) has been conducting a community mapping project called "Representing Kamloops": part travelling art exhibition, part social science research, the mapping project has brought us into contact with multiple communities within the city. We have been inviting the residents of Kamloops to "help us create a story map of Kamloops," a collection of personal images and narratives that, with the aid of an artist-researcher, we are in the process of shaping and exhibiting as a public artwork — a sculptural map with the stories embedded.

The concept for the "sculptural map" arose during discussions at the outset of the project, when we began plans for a large sculptural construction to be exhibited at the Kamloops Art Gallery and housed thereafter in the Kamloops Museum and Archives. We recognized early that the shape of the final exhibit would have to emerge from the research — that before gathering the community's story maps, it would be premature to attempt conception of the exhibit's final form. We decided nonetheless that a smaller, more tentative, less "sculptural" map would be useful for fieldwork, for eliciting stories from interested participants. Constructed by two research assistants in the summer of 2001, the map consists of a topographical representation of the Kamloops landscape pieced together from multiple layers of cardboard and cast in two solid foam sections. Each cast half was placed within a folding, case-like structure that, when unfolded, displays the whole topographic map. In this manner the sculptural map provides a kind of prototype situated between its general, science-oriented look and the less certain detailing of the topography that comes from the choice of foam rather than some other casting material. Our objective was to create something not only useful for the mapping of readily definable data, but also something aesthetically inviting and intriguing for the community.

We begin by asking participants to tell their personal stories of place — to first draw

145

a map (a visual representation of "their Kamloops") and then to tell us orally the story of their maps. As philosopher-critic Claude Gandelman notes, maps are often implicit in the narratives we share. When internalized maps are made explicit, they present important prompts for narrative exploration. The respondents are diverse: they speak to us from different positions in physical and social space. Using maps, images, and narratives, they offer their accounts of valued places, both private and public. What is emerging from our process is a different kind of map. It is too early to tell whether our map will lead to new ways of envisioning community, but we believe it may be a step in this direction.

What follows, then, is a study of the located or emplaced self. Our basic premise is that important features of the self are not enclosed within an introspective private self; instead, the sense of who I am and what I care about is a lived experience grounded in the routines and spatial patterns of everyday life. Knowledge of self and knowledge of place, we maintain, develop together. Who I am will influence my experiences in a particular location. Perceptions of place will be shaped by the values, goals, and interests that together define my selfhood.

This phenomenological approach to self and place provides a theoretical perspective for the study: its methodological implications are discussed below with reference to the idea of the vernacular.[1] Also important to the study are the ideas on "the homeless mind" developed in the 1970s by Peter Berger and his colleagues. Berger framed his thesis in the classical tradition of social theory. Like his predecessors, he wondered about the impact on human consciousness of the large-scale social changes associated with modernization, industrialization, urbanization, and secularization. Central to the homeless mind

analysis — and to our inquiry — is an attempt to explore the relationship between large-scale social changes and changes to human consciousness and selfhood. It is informed by the premise that the complex inner lives of human beings — what they experience, care about and hope for — are influenced by changes in the surrounding environment.

This said, we do not expect all our respondents to relate their experiences to large-scale social changes. While some may experience feelings of nostalgia and loss, others will focus primarily on the present. But the grand themes of modernization and progress will not be entirely absent from respondents' accounts. While we do not expect to find explicit critiques of modernization, we do expect that respondents will devote particular attention to the pleasures of small city living.

Indeed, it seems reasonable to expect that certain negative aspects of modernization — social exclusion and the homeless mind experience — will be felt less acutely among residents of the small city. Put differently, we expect that the small city will offer its inhabitants opportunities to socialize, express themselves and encounter nature in satisfying ways. All this, combined with ease of movement, will serve to distinguish the small city from larger urban environments.

We do not hold a naively romantic view regarding the virtues of the small city. The small city is not totally insulated from the negative aspects of modernization. Nor is the small city able to offer the broad range of cultural amenities common to larger urban centres — and this may be an important concern for some residents. Moreover, the small cities of the once resource-rich hinterlands of Canada are particularly vulnerable to the negative impacts of economic change. There are, then, certain drawbacks to small city living. Most significant to our inquiry, however, is the possibility of cross-neighbourhood variations in the small city experience. While not as differentiated as big cities, cities like Kamloops are not homogeneous. Characteristics of neighbourhoods will vary in relation to such factors as ethnicity, income, and occupational status. We thus intend to explore the small city experience, but we are also interested in charting its cross-neighbourhood variations.[2]

## Method of Inquiry

The data for the map are gathered in group settings involving 10 to 20 people. We try to choose a venue which is central to community life in a particular neighbourhood. We begin with a standard verbal description of our research and illustrate the description with a travelling exhibit of maps and drawings produced by previous participants in the study. Each member of the group is invited to draw his or her own personal map of Kamloops. We ask that this map include places or landmarks that have special meaning to the respondent. The maps are typically produced in a group setting. Afterwards, each respondent works with an interviewer, often in a semi-private setting. We ask the respondents to tell us about the maps or drawings they have produced. What happened here and why is this place or landmark particularly meaningful? What are the stories associated with this place? Finally, we ask the participants to respond to a prototype of the sculptural map of Kamloops, asking them to comment on the sculpture — to compare their drawings with the three-dimensional representation.[3]

Issues like the quality of life and the cultural health of communities are important to this inquiry. But we start from the premise that objective indicators of the quality of life are not simply reflected in subjective experiences of place. The smaller worlds of self,

family and neighbourhood may be highly idiosyncratic, where individuals create community or experience estrangement in unpredictable ways. Likewise, the story maps[4] — the "data" of our study–are not a prescribed genre; rather, they present a more open invitation to articulate what has been recently identified as a "vernacular theory" — in this case, a vernacular theory of self, place, and community. Informed by the work of Thomas McLaughlin in *Street Smarts and Critical Theory: Listening to the Vernacular*, we see story maps and the oral histories the maps generate as important vehicles for theorizing the small city from the ground up, giving voice to, as McLaughlin puts it, "a critical language grounded in local concerns, not the language spoken by academic knowledge-elites" (6). The theoretical work of our informants arises from the environments they inhabit, the personal attachments they form, and the circumstances they confront.

In introducing the idea of the vernacular in this context, we should stress that vernacular theory is distinct from conventional forms of theory. Vernacular theory is to practical (or embodied) knowledge as conventional theory is to academic or formal knowledge. Sociologist Margaret Archer distinguishes "practical knowledge" from purely linguistic ways of knowing. She maintains practical knowledge "comes in chunks or stocks rather than in linear sequences such as sentences, that it is stored by being embodied in the seat of our pants rather than in the declarative memory, and that it may be accessed by all of our senses, not just by one part." If, as Archer argues, "practical knowledge authentically discloses part of reality which is beyond the limits of language" (160-61), then, as researchers interested in eliciting authentic disclosure from the Kamloops community, we needed some way to tap into non-linguistic knowledge. Story mapping is

Figure 2. Story mapping at the Chief Louis Centre. Photo by Helen MacDonald-Carlson.

one way to augment our linguistic understanding of personal experience. Moving from image to narration allows our informants to "know" their subjects differently, to explore and validate that which cannot be fully expressed in words. Vernacular theory is situated in this intermediate space where image, embodied knowledge, and discursive knowledge overlap.

In terms of story mapping — our approach to data collection — the process of moving from drawing to talking tends to provoke a narrative of the mind in action, one moving back and forth between the hard core of visual detail (lodged in objects of memory, intuition, and practice) and the possibilities for reflection offered by linguistic expression and sharing. The personal narrative documented thus becomes a progressive transformation of initial feelings, a process where discovery occurs through a kind of conversation among the different ways of knowing.

Our study also seeks to recognize and highlight different modes of representation — in particular, the contrast between the ver-

nacular landscapes represented in the story maps and the landscapes of conventional or scientific geographies. The standpoints of scientific geographies are points in space. Consequently, while scientific maps reflect the specific purposes of those who produce them, they do not reveal — nor are they intended to reveal — personal emotions and understandings. In contrast, the vernacular landscapes of the story maps reveal the qualities of the person who produces them as much as they reveal the objective qualities of the spaces that person inhabits. Indeed, respondents' maps generally represent attempts to negotiate personal space within the familiar visual forms of maps and other pictures: this negotiation manifests itself in an intriguing blend of vernacular and symbolic representational styles.

## Expressing the Vernacular

A detailed analysis from a sampling of specific story maps provides further illustration of these points. All the maps in this chapter were collected at a story-mapping session

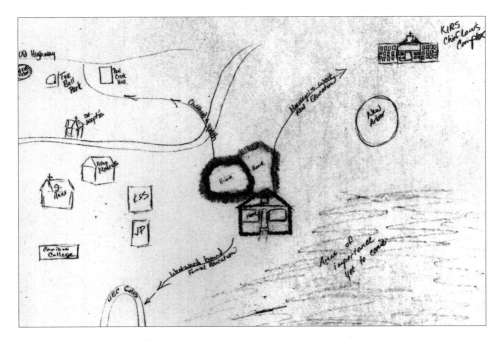

Figure 3. Story map by Janice Michel.

held at the Chief Louis Centre, located on the reserve lands of the Kamloops Indian Band (see Figure 2). The maps draw upon local knowledge and lean more towards vernacular expression than the more detached viewpoint that characterizes conventional maps and scientific geographies. In varying degrees, many of the maps do exhibit some crossover between those modes of vernacular and scientific inquiry (and, of course, any such absolute distinction is neither tenable nor desirable — local knowledge and the work of the amateur has often guided scientific investigation and vice versa). Here, however, we seek to probe the manner in which vernacular response to place is articulated through these story maps. We begin with two maps in particular, ones by Janice Michel and Charlotte Manuel (see Figures 3 and 4).

Michel's map is highly structured with respect to its overall geometry. It situates the three homes that she has had in Kamloops in the centre of the drawing — their importance further highlighted by coloured outlining, which stands in contrast to the simpler use of pencil throughout the rest of the map. Such a mixing of the personal and the symbolic is carried throughout. The upper-left quadrant represents Michel's "Childhood and Youth" — a journey that winds its way through buildings and other landmarks along the "Old Highway" and up into the surrounding hills of the Paul Lake area. The lower-left quadrant is the site of a "Westward bound" journey towards "formal education" and the "UBC Gates" — each presented as an iconic landmark significantly more generic (and thus symbolic) than the buildings along the Old Highway. Most detailed in its rendering is the former Kamloops Residential School — now the site of the Chief Louis complex, Michel's work, and also the sites of her mar-

149

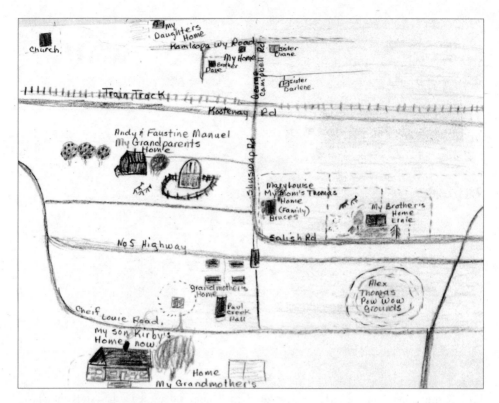

Figure 4. Story map by Charlotte Manuel.

riage and "Real Education." The lower-right quadrant is ill-defined, a cursory area of rough shading that is inscribed as "Areas of importance yet to come." For Michel, the geography of the varied landscapes of her experience have been brought together in a geometric composition that moves back and forth between vernacular rendering and symbolic representation.

In contrast to the range of vernacular and symbolic representation apparent in Michel's map, Charlotte Manuel's drawing exists more clearly in the vernacular realm. Local knowledge is highlighted here. The site of her map — depicting numerous buildings, outbuildings, corrals, trees, animals, roads, and railway tracks — provides an inventory of her most important landmarks in a part of the Kamloops landscape that roughly corresponds to the area shown in the upper-left quadrant of Michel's story map. The Old Highway region of Michel's map is complicated in Manuel's by the addition of numerous other roads — most of them named, and most with one or more of the buildings (or other personal landmarks) alongside. Each of the buildings is individuated in some manner, by detail and by colouring, and also by details of the surrounding landscape. These details include various types of trees — not entirely realistic in their representation but distinguishable nevertheless by being depicted as evergreens or as deciduous trees with or without fruit. Such a recollecting and representing of specific detail speaks to a manner of working from local knowledge — of working in the vernacular mode.

Though Charlotte Manuel's map constitutes a vernacular inquiry in this sense, we note that choices of scale have been made, that her "son Kirby's home" is in fact several times larger in the drawing than the church. If this were a conventional landscape view rather than something more "map-like," the church would be in the distant background, with her son's home in the immediate foreground. Ambiguity therefore complicates our reading of the map: there's no clear indication in the drawing itself whether such a change in scale between the two buildings suggests that Manuel wants to give the house greater symbolic importance or that she is simply attempting a realistic representation of perspective, with the more distant objects diminished in size. Such ambiguity speaks to the manner in which the respondents' drawings generally represent an attempt to negotiate a personal space within the familiar visual forms of maps and other pictures. Vernacular theories are constructed where personal representational strategies compete with or otherwise intersect the symbolic — where the private meets the public.

Manuel's revised map, replete with an extensive narrative text, provides a ready illustration of how story mapping implies — and, in this case, leads to — a more fully developed theory of the world. Manuel expresses this as a theory of family and land and "passing on" (see Figure 5). As a vernacular theoretical statement, Manuel's revision clarifies how family relations help shape her perception of the land; it provides a kind of gloss on the representational strategy of her story map. Her story stretches from early days with her own grandparents to the present and her various grandchildren. As she explains further in her interview, both the

time frame — which spans generations — and the sheer number of persons involved contribute to the complexity of the account: "I have lots of brothers and sisters, like those are only eight ... there's sixteen of us ... fifteen younger ones and me, so I got lots of family." It is clear from her account that kinship and property are closely linked. Property is not a commodity to be sold on the market to the highest bidder. Property makes it possible to sustain the extended family over time: "history of family and land is an acknowledgement of our existence to our life passed on to our relatives." At first glance, the densely textured story of property and social relations seems contained within a kilometre or so of the urban reserve lands. However, it soon becomes evident that it extends well beyond the borders of what many non-Aboriginals would consider the reserve. The narrative is "spread out" in time and space: it reaches up the valley and onto a plateau in the mountains behind the reserve.

## The Small City Difference: A First Nations Perspective

The vernacular reflects the highly personal and idiosyncratic world each of us inhabits. The story maps highlight the fact that each person has a unique way of being in the world. But the story maps also share common features. Because each person inhabits both personal and social worlds, the maps offer insights into sociological themes — themes which complement and help further explain the respondents' vernacular/symbolic representational strategies. We are introduced to a range of experiences associated with the small city difference.

One hallmark of modernization is the tendency to "carve up" the world into discrete social spheres: religion and spirituality retreat to specialized domains; art belongs in one world, science another. According to the

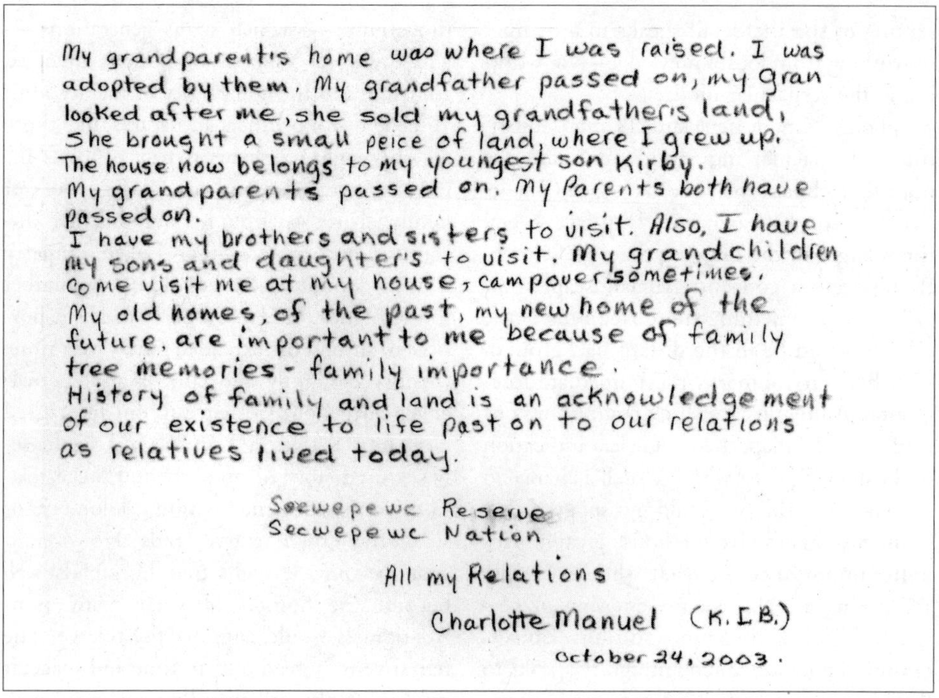

> My grandparents home was where I was raised. I was adopted by them. My grandfather passed on, my gran looked after me, she sold my grandfather's land, She brought a small peice of land, where I grew up. The house now belongs to my youngest son Kirby. My grandparents passed on. My Parents both have passed on.
>
> I have my brothers and sisters to visit. Also, I have my sons and daughter's to visit. My grandchildren come visit me at my house, campover sometimes.
>
> My old homes, of the past, my new home of the future, are important to me because of family tree memories - family importance.
>
> History of family and land is an acknowledgement of our existence to life past on to our relations as relatives lived today.
>
> Secwepewc Reserve
> Secwepewc Nation
>
> All my Relations
>
> Charlotte Manuel (K.I.B.)
>
> October 24, 2003.

Figure 5. Revised story mapping by Charlotte Manuel.

authors of the *Homeless Mind*, this kind of differentiation of the social world is often experienced in negative terms, with everyday life seeming to lack a meaningful centre. One of the most important issues here concerns the experience of nature: the residents of modern urban environments are cut off from the natural world. Nature — where it is preserved — is compartmentalized and domesticated. For some, this experience of nature may be quite satisfying. For others, it is a poor substitute for nature in its "rawer" forms.

One of the virtues of the small city — and of more rural environments generally — is the potential for a closer relationship to nature. An appreciation of the natural world and its proximity to the inhabited world was clearly evident in our first mapping session

(see Figure 7). Both the proximity to nature, and its tendency to "spill over" into the neighbourhood, were highlighted by our respondents. This positive view of nature may be a theme common to both Aboriginal and non-Aboriginal residents of small cities, a view they share with many residents of rural and semi-rural environments — but, as noted above, to appreciate vernacular theories of the world around us we must recognize and account for the mix of the public (inherited and imported ideologies, community values, and symbols) and the private (how these ideologies, values, and symbols are accommodated through lived experience).

The views of nature expressed by a nine-year-old boy who accompanied his parents to the mapping session are particularly interesting. It would be difficult to conceive of a

Figure 6. Revised story map by Charlotte Manuel.

visual imagination more richly populated with wild animals. But these are not the wild animals of storybooks. At least some of the animals of this boy's imagination — moose, fish — are sources of food for his family. One animal, a moose, stands out for the boy because of the amount of room it occupies in the family's freezer (see Figure 8).

Some respondents expressed an appreciation of multiple relations among nature, kinship, and the passage of time. There is a feeling among some that their parents had a closer and more complex relation to nature. For example, when one participant was invited to view the sculptural map, she remarked: "When I see something like this I always think of my dad, because his ties are really

land based, and he's been a farmer all his life, a hunter all his life, and so when I see something like that without the buildings, where it's almost in a state where there wouldn't have been a lot of buildings ... I always think about my dad ... whereas myself, I find I'm more building oriented." She describes her dad's relation to nature in more detail: "[My dad] would look at that and say, 'Oh I remember this place, this is where I camped ... This is where I got all the deer, this is ... the best place to go for moose, this is the best fishing area.'" She, however, no longer sees the land this way. She is aware that a certain source of meaning has been lost. That said, she also points to other sources of meaning in her life. She is hopeful about the future, a

153

Figure 7. Story-mapping interview. Photo by Helen MacDonald-Carlson.

future that for her is closely tied to her education and that of her children.

In another interview, an older respondent speaks of the mountainous terrain surrounding the reserve. When invited to compare her story map with the sculptural map displayed in the interview setting, she mentions her participation in a family-based logging operation: "We all logged up in here ..." While she grew up on the reserve, her early years on the mountain remained significant. Moreover, she takes full advantage of the "bird's-eye" perspective offered by the sculptural map to express what amounts to a pre-reserve sense of place. When asked if she knew this place well, she responded: "Not as good as my mother knew it. She rode these mountains. My mother rode all these mountains here on both sides of the river.... She enjoyed riding all over the area, all that whole area. She knew the mountains. She knew the land." Here we encounter a sense of place that is not circumscribed by the reserve and the grids of settler society. While the respondent does not express an overt political message in her comments, she expresses feelings of both loss and historical injustice, something more than mere nostalgia.

For some respondents, personal relations to nature have changed with the passage of time. They experience some sense of loss as a consequence. For many, however, nature continues to figure significantly in their sense of self and place. One respondent, who lives in a mountainous area near the reserve, thinks of her home as a refuge from the city: seeing a deer in the morning adds to the peaceful atmosphere of the natural setting. For one respondent, natural symbols have a special, almost spiritual value: the horses she keeps in her yard represent her father, who has passed away.

The relationship between nature and Aboriginal spirituality is complex. In the

Figure 8. Story map by Montana Gottfriedson.

prayers spoken at the beginning of the session, an elder offers thanks to the Creator for "the goodness of life" and for "strength to live our life in a good way." She also asks for protection for "our families." Nature or "Mother Earth" receives special attention in the prayer:

I thank you for Mother Earth and all that comes from Mother Earth ... I ask you ... Creator to watch over and protect Mother Earth. To help her, rid her of her disturbances, that create ... these problems on Mother Earth, such as flooding, fires ... But help us, also, protect Mother Earth in a good way.

Yet another respondent describes the rela-

tion between nature and spirituality. The respondent is asked to situate his story map in time: are the map and its stories oriented to past, present, or future? Referring to a ritual conducted with crystals, the respondent speaks of "hope for the future" and of the significance of the river: "the big thing is the river itself. It's the key to our survival here, and if we don't look after the river, we're gonna be in deep trouble." Later in the interview, the respondent elaborates, referring again to the ritual with crystals: "we worked with what needs to be done. And so what we did was, we tried to look after the water.... And so the water would look after us."

For many respondents, then, nature is an

Figure 9. Story map by Skye Gottfriedson.

important aspect of self and place. Nature has a calming effect. It is a link to the past, a source of food and healing, and a key part of the struggle for a better future. Staying close to nature, cultivating one's relation to nature, protecting nature — these are all worthwhile activities, and a place where these activities are part of everyday life is a good place.

## The Role of Family and Kinship Networks in Defining Space

Another key aspect of modernization is what sociologists call the "nuclearization" of the family (see Canak and Swanson). As modern individuals respond to the demands of a changing economy and embrace the dream of social (and frequently geographic) mobility, the family shrinks. Relations to kin weaken and new relationships — friendships and work acquaintances — become more important. Of course, this trend toward nuclearization is not universal. It varies in relation to factors like rurality, class, and ethnicity. One of the aspects which stands out in our interviews — and Charlotte Manuel's "All my Relations" statement is emblematic of this — is just how important the extended family continues to be in the respondents' sense of self and place.

Family is central to the stories and maps of

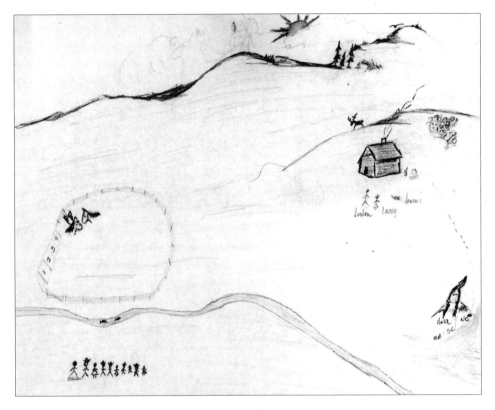

Figure 10. Story map by Robin Gottfriedson.

two younger respondents as well (see Figures 9 and 10). The first of these two younger respondents uses her parents' house as the central reference point on her map: "I just basically drew ... the whole property around my mom and dad's house, and ... what's all involved with it because that's where I grew up." She includes her car, her cat, and her boyfriend on the map, but indicates that her grandfather (who has passed away), her uncle, and her father are important people in her life. "Me and my dad work on this field ... we do irrigation pumps and that, so it's like quality time with my dad." As the interview progresses, it becomes clear that the centre of her map (her parents' house) is not on the urban reserve lands. The map's centre is located near a lake in the mountains behind Kamloops. While she lives on the urban reserve lands and views her attendance at the local university as integral to her future, her roots are in this rural setting: "It's way quieter up there. And my mom and dad have lots of land, so we have lots of stuff to do ... where I live now, I have just a little house, it's like a yard and that's it ... I usually go home [laughs] if I want to do anything."

The second of the two younger respondents speaks of immediate family: a son, a daughter, a cat and "a very special person in my life" who is at present living elsewhere. But other members of her family, many of

Figure 11. Residential School, by David Tremblay, 2003. Watercolour, acrylic and graphic on paper (31 x 45 cm). Reproduced courtesy of the artist.

whom have passed away, are also present in her map: "These are the spirits of my mother and father who are Native. I always see them, think of them watching over me, always part of me…. This is my brother Bob, who is important to me, he passed on, his … nickname was Grizzly and so I incorporated his Grizzly spirit in the clouds along with the wolf and my parents." She talks as well of other members of her family — brothers, sisters, and their offspring — noting she did not draw herself: "Self-importance is not important to me."

For these respondents, extended family is a defining influence in their sense of self and place. This exception to the general modern trend toward nuclearization is not entirely unexpected. However, what is perhaps most striking is the way the place occupied by the family does not fit neatly into the observable boundaries of the reserve. Individual respondents may currently reside in urban reserve subdivisions and grids, but the important places in their lives are located on plateaus and valleys in the mountains beyond the small city reserve.

## The Relation Between Aboriginal and Non-Aboriginal Spaces and Institutions

"The social world," as Bourdieu puts it, "is accumulated history" (46). We knew when we embarked on this research that the history of Aboriginal/non-Aboriginal relations would influence our respondents' sense of self and place. But we could not anticipate how the past would be reflected in the present. Nor did we deliberately highlight in the interviews issues like social exclusion and marginalization. The basic patterns are most evident in the maps. While there are some exceptions, most respondents did not include in their maps the places and institutions of non-Aboriginal Kamloops. The important places for the respondents were located on urban reserve land and in the plateaus and valleys above the reserve. While there is plenty of light industry and some recreational facilities on urban reserve land, these predominantly non-Aboriginal spaces do not appear on the maps of our respondents. Representations of the building that housed the former residential school are also generally absent (see Figure 11).

Cole Harris's characterization of the reserve system as the "primal line on the map of British Columbia" seems to be reflected in the lived experience of our respondents (xviii). But the view of Aboriginal space as a world entirely separate — another version of the "two solitudes" phenomenon — does not capture the whole story. The key exception, as noted above, is the system of formal education. Despite the crimes committed by the residential schools in Canada, and despite the ongoing difficulties experienced by Aboriginal students in the schools (Milloy; Schissel and Wotherspoon), formal education figures significantly in our respondents' worldviews. In many instances, schools are mentioned in interviews or included in maps. While the schools are often on the outer edges of the maps, they are not portrayed in a negative way. Many respondents view the schools as an important part of their lives and as stepping stones to a better future for themselves and their children — part of, as Janice Michel's map so eloquently captured it, the "Westward bound" journey.

More generally, though, such exceptions should not lead us to overlook the general pattern of "separable worlds" — that is, while the story maps are characterized by complex negotiations between the public and the private, between shared heritage and personal history, the multiple symbolic and vernacular intersections of Aboriginal and non-Aboriginal experience are not fully resolved; the kind of visual ambiguity we noted with the maps manifests itself in the interviews as a form of verbal elision or equivocation. What's not said becomes important. For example, appropriate relations between Aboriginal and non-Aboriginal worlds are not fully explored by the respondents. When they are addressed, the images and thoughts evoked are often troubling.

Aboriginal and non-Aboriginal Kamloops

are linked by several bridges, one a railway crossing not designed for pedestrian traffic (see Figures 12 and 13). One respondent, David Manuel, included this railway bridge on his original "rough" map, but the bridge is missing from his more polished version:

Interviewer: Is there any particular reason … why you have the railway tracks but not the railway bridges?

Manuel: I did that because I didn't have time or I didn't feel like I could do the bridge in a good way … there's a lot of stuff that happened on the bridge closest to the city. I wish the bridge wasn't there, to tell you the truth.

Interviewer: And on your map it's not.

Manuel: It's not … because reality is a lot of our band members have died on the bridge … they got run over by the train or they fell in the river when they were crossing…. [O]ne of the elders told me that fourteen people in our community have died along the bridge. So I wish that those bridges weren't there because the people have lost their lives there.

Interviewer: That's the general dilemma, of course, of the relationship between the cultures, right? You spoke earlier about the railway being something that's … helped to build the community.

Manuel: Yeah, it's opened it up.

Interviewer: It's "opened it up" — that was your phrase. Yet here [pointing to the railway lines] is the aspect of it that's been a detriment to your community.

Manuel: Yeah, in a really big way, yeah.

Signalled by the visual mapping, and elaborated upon in the interview, the goal of representing lived experience "in a good way" remains problematic. Respondents struggle, often successfully, to find meaning and coherence in their everyday lives. But unresolved points of ambiguity and tension remain.

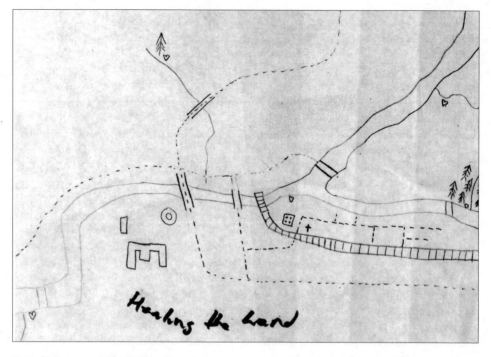

Figure 12. Story map by David Manuel.

## Conclusion

Our research on sense of self and place in Kamloops is in its early phases and raises more questions than it answers. We believe, however, that the story-mapping method has great potential. It offers a means of gathering, validating, and indexing vernacular theories of place; it offers a means of self-discovery to respondents. When pressure to conform to researchers' categories is reduced, respondents find new ways to recognize themselves in the places they inhabit. The result is a fresh perspective on what makes life in particular places meaningful and satisfying. Also evident, as the account of the bridge suggests, are images of the ambiguous and troubling aspects of place. As we conduct story-mapping sessions in different neighbourhoods, we expect to find both variations and common themes in the small city experience. The information we collect will lead to new understandings — especially new vernacular theories — of what community means to individuals and to the residents of particular neighbourhoods.

## Acknowledgment

We are grateful to our research assistant David Tremblay and to Vicki Manuel for organizing, hosting, and introducing the Chief Louis Centre session.

## Notes

1. A classic statement of this phenomenological view is Merleau-Ponty's *Phenomenology of Perception*.

2. Elisabeth Duckworth's study of Kamloops neighbourhoods is instructive here, for, as she notes of Kamloops' North and South Shores, "It is true that a wide river flows between the two neighbourhoods

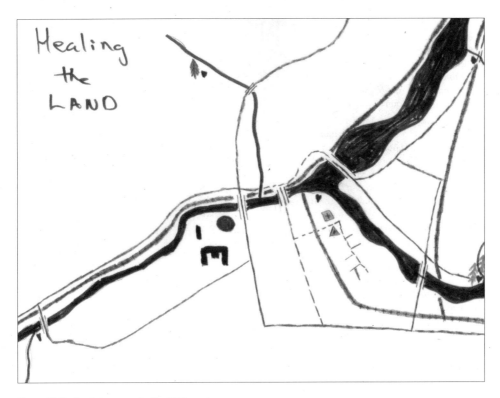

Figure 13. Revised story map by David Manuel.

and that a four-lane bridge connects them. But it is neither the river that divides North from South Shore Kamloops nor the bridge that binds them: it is history." She goes on to say that "Kamloops' two oldest neighbourhoods share a common time line, but their founding histories have driven a noticeable wedge between the two that still exists today...." In 1912, when BC Fruitlands looked to Eastern Europe for hardworking, cheap labour,

> The population of the North Shore suddenly and rapidly swelled with a new multicultural cross-section of people. Herein lies the root of the division between the North and South Shores, and the development of two such unique neighbours. On the south shore were the British elite. They were established in the valley first, were richer, had a developed town site, lived in fine homes, spoke the governing language.... The new north shore immigrants spoke the wrong language, spoke broken accented English, had foreign customs and clothing, and for the most part were poor and uneducated.... The split is still evident today, although most people have long forgotten why the feeling of inferiority clinging to the North Shore ever came into being. Although people of all races and backgrounds live everywhere in Kamloops, and the two communities voted to amalgamate in 1967, the stigma persists for the North Shore — an enigmatic frustration. (15-17)

3. The research group has come to recognize the opportunities that can emerge from — as well as what can be learned from — the varied disciplinary perspectives of the three primary researchers. Such opportunities for collaborative exploration and refinement of ideas are, however, continually challenged when the limitations and parameters of any singular disciplinary perspective come to light. In particular, the methodologically sound basis that shapes working methods in the social sciences is sometimes at odds with the experimental, let's-try-this attitude that often characterizes research in the

visual arts. Collectively, we endeavour to look for shared thematic and theoretical links even when such approaches seem at first quite disparate. The challenge for our research group is to resolve, or come to terms with, the manner in which the rigour of academic study may be worked together with less certain modes of inquiry and representation.

4. Early in our study we used the terms "story map" and "memory map" interchangeably. At first, "memory map" was our preferred term, with its precedent in the memory mapping of artists like Marlene Creates and Ernie Kroeger. Over time, and with much debate, we moved to the more neutral "story map," a term that allows for the inclusion of memories but does not privilege the past as a site for constructing and representing stories of place. We think of story mapping as a protocol for eliciting visual/verbal narratives. Other terms used for variations on this procedure, especially by researchers in the social sciences, include "mental mapping" (Crouch; Gould and White; Lynch; Soya); "cognitive mapping" (Downs and Stea; Huff; Jameson; Kitchin and Freundschuh); and "deep mapping" (Least Heat-Moon).

## Works Cited

Archer, Margaret S. *Being Human: The Problem of Agency*. Cambridge: Cambridge UP, 2000.

Berger, Peter, Brigitte Berger and Hansfried Kelner. *The Homeless Mind: Modernization and Consciousness*. New York: Knopf, 1974.

Bourdieu, Pierre. "The Forms of Capital." *Education: Culture, Economy and Society*. Ed. A.H. Halsey, Hugh Lauder, Phillip Brown and Amy Stuart Wells. New York: Oxford UP, 1997. 46-58.

Canak, William, and Laura Swanson. *Modern Mexico*. New York: McGraw-Hill, 1998.

Crouch, David. "The Street in the Making of Popular Geographical Knowledge." *Images of the Street: Planning, Identity, and Control in Public Space*. Ed. Nicholas Fyfe. New York: Routledge, 1998. 160-75.

Downs, Roger, and David Stea, "Cognitive Maps and Spatial Behavior: Process and Products." *Image and Environments*. Ed. Roger Downs and David Stea. Chicago: Aldine Publishing, 1973. 8-26.

Duckworth, Elisabeth. "Divided We Stand: Kamloops' North and South Shores." *Patchwork City: A Sampler of Articles on Kamloops' Distinctive Neighbourhoods*. Ed. Yvonne Phillips. Kamloops: Kamloops Museum and Archives, 2002. 15-17.

Gandelman, Claude. *Reading Pictures, Viewing Texts*. Bloomington, IN: Indiana UP, 1991.

Gould, Peter, and Rodney White. *Mental Maps*. 2nd Ed. Boston: Allen and Unwin, 1986.

Harris, R. Cole. *Making Native Space: Colonialism, Resistance, and Reserves in British Columbia*. Vancouver: UBC Press, 2002.

Huff, A.S. *Mapping Strategic Thought*. Chichester, UK: Wiley, 1990.

Ignace, Marianne, and George Ignace. "Tagging, Rapping and the Voices of the Ancestors: Expressing Aboriginal Identity Between the Small City and the Rez." *The Small Cities Book: On the Cultural Future of Small Cities*. Ed. W.F. Garrett-Petts. Vancouver: New Star Books, 2004. 303-318.

Jameson, Fredric. "Cognitive Mapping." *Marxism and the Interpretation of Culture*. Ed. Cary Nelson and Lawrence Grossberg. Urbana: U of Illinois P, 1988. 347-60.

Kitchin, Rob, and Scott Freundschuh, eds. *Cognitive Mapping: Past, Present, and Future*. New York: Routledge, 2000.

Least Heat-Moon, William. *PrairyErth (A Deep Map)*. Boston: Houghton, 1991.

Lynch, Kevin. *The Image of the City*. Cambridge: MIT P, 1960.

McLaughlin, Thomas. *Street Smarts and Critical Theory: Listening to the Vernacular*. Madison: U of Wisconsin P, 1996.

Merleau-Ponty, Maurice. *Phenomenology of Perception*. London: Routledge, 2003.

Milloy, John Sheridan. *A National Crime: the Canadian Government and the Residential School System, 1879-1986*. Winnipeg: U of Manitoba P, 1999.

Schissel, Bernard, and Terry Wotherspoon. *The Legacy of School for Aboriginal People: Education, Oppression, and Emancipation*. Don Mills, ON: Oxford UP, 2003.

Soya, Edward. *Postmodern Geographies: The Reassertion of Space in Critical Social Theory*. New York: Verso, 1989.

——. *Thirdspace: Journeys to Los Angeles and Other Real-and-Imagined Places*. Malden, MA: Blackwell, 1996.

# Appendix 1

# Representing Kamloops
# A Photographic Record

## A Story Mapping Public Art Project

Creating the sculptural model:

Student researcher Linda Goddard
working on the model.

The sculptural map in process.

Story mapping in the classroom:

Artist-as-researcher, Donald Lawrence, explaining story
mapping to a third-year writing class.

Student research assistant Erin
Moen documenting the class'
story mapping activities.

Setting up the exhibition:

Student research assistant Bonnie Yourk preparing one of the UCC exhibitions.

Arranging the sculptural model.

Mapping and interviewing:

Working with two story map participants (UCC, Student Street Exhibition).

David MacLennan conducting a post-mapping interview.

A visual sequence depicting the entire story mapping process:

Explaining the project.

Signing the consent form.

Drawing and completing the map in 10 – 20 minutes.

Post-mapping interview, asking the participant to tell the story of her map in 5 – 15 minutes.

Exhibitions in a variety of public spaces, including the Aberdeen Mall and Riverside Park (during the Canada Day celebrations):

Faculty researcher Will Garrett-Petts explaining the story mapping project to a group of Heritage Fair participants, Riverside Park, Canada Day celebrations.

# Vernacular Landscapes II:
# Relocating the Homeless Mind

## W.F. Garrett-Petts and Donald Lawrence

"Each city receives its form from the desert it opposes."

Italo Calvino, *Invisible Cities*

"Place history is most often recorded in maps. People from oral traditions carry detailed maps in their heads over years; the rest of us depend on outside sources."

Lucy Lippard, *The Lure of the Local*

"The map is the greatest temptation. And perhaps the map is the ultimate genre that we'll all engage. The new map, the old map. After all, if you aren't interested in geography, you can't live in Canada."

Aritha van Herk, in conversation with Dawne McCance, *Mosaic*

This chapter began as a provisional curatorial statement distributed to artists selected for a gallery exhibition of community story mapping. We asked the participants to respond informally or via individual artist's statements. These comments and statements facilitated a kind of dialogue, helping guide and refine both the exhibition and the present essay. Like the works in the exhibition, the artists' statements resituated and challenged our understanding of the small city, grounding it in local experience. The artists' statements were collected and displayed in a binder as part of the exhibition. In addition, during the second week of the exhibition we held a public symposium: Michel Campeau, Robert Kroetsch, and Eileen Leier led us in discussion about issues of home, homelessness, memory, mapping, visual representation, and the small city. The following week, a working seminar, led by Dawne McCance,

helped us all explore theories of "memory, architecture, and the archive." Finally, in the course of our research into the region's glacial scours and terraces, we benefited from discussions with geologist Ken Klein. We thus conceived of *The Homeless Mind* as both a conventional exhibition and a form of collaborative research *through* art, where artistic practice (including curatorial practice) becomes a vehicle for producing and representing new knowledge.

### This Part of the Country: Exhibiting the Small City

Over the last 25 years or so, cities have become the familiar focus of museum exhibition. Major shows organized at the Pompidou Centre in Paris, and the recent Century City exhibition held at the Tate Modern in London, celebrate the metropolis as the centre of art and culture, as the home for the development of the *avant-garde* and modernism. The city has always been a place of extreme possibilities: it magnifies human ambitions, encourages dreams, but it also heightens fears and nurtures insecurities.

According to Peter Berger's Homeless Mind thesis, by the mid-1970s, the big city had become for many a place of alienation, ironic association, and transience, where individuals learned to define themselves, not in relation to the immediate community, but through identification with imagined or distant spaces, with imported rituals, fashions, ideals. The question "Where are you from?" replaced "Where do you live?"

Unlike the major urban centres, smaller cities, especially in the West, seldom find themselves the subject of either artistic representation or sociological investigation. As Guy Vanderhaeghe notes, for most of the 20th century, "the western Canadian city scarcely made an appearance in fiction [,] and when it did, the representation was usually an uneasy compromise between what had to be said because characterization and plot demanded it, and the desire not to divulge where you were really talking about." Vanderhaeghe attributes this ellipsis of the small city to a crisis in creative confidence. Writers "had doubts about the material they found to hand. Could it really be the stuff of art?" (127-28). The small town, made distinctive variously through its idiosyncrasy or anonymity, might not invite literary comparison to larger centres, but the small city does. If not by definition, then certainly by default, "high culture" is associated with big city life: big cities are equated with big culture, big opportunities, big social problems and big stories; small cities with something else. It is that "something else," the place of the small city in the Canadian imaginary, that *The Homeless Mind* exhibition explores.

Something of the Homeless Mind exists in small places too — that is, Kamloops is large enough to lose oneself, one's sense of belonging; but the city itself seems still too young, too unencumbered by history, tradition, and scale "to have become a fallen place."[1] The challenge for artists seeking to represent small cities may not be one of homelessness but what geographer Edward Ralph calls "placelessness," an "underlying attitude that does not acknowledge the significance in [local] places"(143). The local too often remains undefined because of a shared "refusal to assert the validity of a place and a voice." As Vanderhaeghe argues: "For artists on the margins, autonomy [identity] can only be bought at the price of vigilant self-awareness" (129).

Difficult to define as either rural or urban, cities like Kamloops occupy an uncertain position, situated somewhere between the local and the cosmopolitan. Their social and physical space shares something in common with the suburban "edge cities,"[2] areas that also blur boundaries between town and country. Kamloops is no sprawling, diffuse conglomeration of office towers, malls, and freeway interchanges, but, by virtue of its proximity and contrast to Vancouver, the small city inevitably sees itself, at least in part, as a city on the margin, on the edge. The comparison remains an uneasy one, though: unlike true "edge cities," say, Abbotsford or Coquitlam, Kamloops is geographically separate, has its own pioneer history, and boasts a recognizable downtown core. Indeed, Kamloops itself spreads out into a number of amalgamated communities — including Dallas, Barnhartvale, Westsyde, and Rayleigh — communities on the edge of the city.

What, then, are the implications for the small city? Elizabeth Wilson maintains in "The Rhetoric of Urban Space" that all cities are becoming increasingly "multi-centred"; the challenge in an age of so-called post-urban space is to develop a new sense of urbanism, "one that includes the periphery rather than delegitimating it" (155).

Wilson encourages us to recover the periphery on the edges of our cities; even more provocatively, she wants us to celebrate "peripheral" spaces within the city, spaces that seemingly "escape" the city plan. "It was always the interstices of the city, the forgotten bits between, the corners of the city that somehow escaped, that constituted its charm, forgotten squares, canals, deserted houses — private, secret angles of the vast public space." Wilson is not thinking of small cities when describing her search for "the lost charm of the periphery" (160), but small cities also have their own centres and edges, their own "forgotten squares" and "secret angles."

As part of our study of vernacular landscapes (see MacLennan et al.), we turned to the city's artists, inviting them to contribute works for a formal exhibition. Significantly, like the First Nations participants described in the previous chapter, the contributing artists mapped their stories of the city at the margins of the urban landscape — often in surrounding neighbourhoods or satellite communities, in hidden places discovered through walking or hiking, places that remind us of home, those half-remembered *sub*urban topographies first shaped in childhood. "I grew up in a creative, loving family at the nexus of art and nature in the rural suburbs of Los Angeles," says Leslie Bolin.[3] Now living in the Heffley Creek area, which she describes as "half an hour northeast of Kamloops," Bolin positions herself in *Thompson Woodlands* on the "fringe of the mainstream" — but such proximity to the city has become a precarious position, for the mainstream remains ever-threatening. She sees logging, commercial recreation, and a growing rural population as soon displacing her pastoral pleasures. Nonetheless, her work embraces the impermanence of the moment. Mapping such a personal landscape inscribes gestures of memory, and, inevitably, invokes narratives of home. But these gestures do not imply some nostalgic rehabilitation of the rural idyll; rather, they point towards what we see as a new urban vision.

As noted, the *Homeless Mind* exhibition began as an inquiry into the personal representation of place in a small city setting. We went out into the community, asking people to construct "story maps" detailing their attachment to Kamloops landmarks, both public and private. We asked people to first draw a map of "their city," and then tell us its story. Some of these community maps were included in the exhibition, but the majority of the contributions are more considered artworks, images, and texts that extend our understanding of mapping, memory, narrative, and place. What became clear as we gathered the works is the profound intertwining of place and self: sense of place anchors the sense of self, offers a way of disclosing the self, giving shape to "where I'm from" and "what I care about *here*." The maps are not all celebratory, the narratives are not all fully resolved or settled, but collectively they speak to the possibility of finding community — often multiple communities — on the borders or edges of the urban and the rural that define the small city.

## Lines of Sight: Reading the Landscape

In a city the size of Kamloops, there is no single line delineating town from country. When driving or walking, lines of sight are commonly drawn away from road or pathway and towards the upland features of the Thompson and South Thompson River valleys, shaped during two primary periods of continental glaciation 250,000 and 10,000 years ago. Many lakes in this area — Monte

Lake, Kamloops Lake, Shuswap Lake, Lac Le Jeune — remain as traces of glacial action, formed as stagnant and dead ice melted and receded towards a central dome to the north of Kamloops. Active tongues of ice worked their way up and down the valley walls, carving out such features as the canyon of Peterson Creek and, through run off, depositing the terraced gravel delta that descends from Knutsford into the valley below (Fulton, *Deglaciation* 25; Fulton, *Glacial* 6). In the language of glaciologists, "ice form lines" are used to delineate these areas that lie on the margins of glacial action.

While the migration of glaciers is commonly marked by the paths of terminal and recessional moraines, deposits left behind by receding glaciers, such features are sporadic on the surface topography of the Kamloops region, where the record has been obscured by icemelts and layers of soil. Thus the shape of the receding ice-margin becomes a matter of interpretation, of inference: geologists engage in their own form of memory mapping, constructing "synchronous lines," conjectural lines drawn across time to join and explain "those ice-marginal meltwater channels and other features inferred to have formed at the ice-front at a specific [period]" (Fulton, *Glacial* 9). The city's geological history, inscribed as a kind of physical memory, announces itself, becomes part of the artist's "vigilant self-awareness" and an insistent counterpart to the urban geometry of streets, highways, fences, rail lines, telephone wires, neighbourhoods, and buildings. In Kamloops, looking down takes effort.

### Secret Angles, Edges, and Forgotten Squares: Walking the City

Motion is central to the story of the city, to discovering its centres and edges, defining its character. Jane Augustine's study of cities in literature finds that "the city as character is present when the human characters, especially the protagonists, are travelling, in transit, rootless, not fixed in a domestic environment." (74). Augustine's reference to "rootlessness" reminds us of the Homeless Mind, of the mind in transit. What is true for the way we read images of the city in literature has implications for the way we read and represent actual cities — that is, we need to be conscious of how narrative is tied to personal movement and travelling. It is the comings and goings of the city, the arrivals, and departures, which give it energy, drama. Motion, though, is more than automobile traffic and gridlock; as Robert Kroetsch observes in his story-mapping poem written for the exhibition, "In this part of the country, sagebrush is a version of dance. / You must / Enter in slowly. / This is where train robbers learn their moves." Here, motion is a matter of "entering in slowly."

Laura Hargrave enters Kamloops through walks along the riverbank. Both a contributing artist and an artist-researcher working with us on the community mapping project, she found in the course of her participation that, for many in the community, "the act of physically traversing the land was in some way tied to the lasting quality of the memory." *River Walk Journal Project* takes its cue from the community and identifies the river as the focal point for a series of walks and field sketches.

For the exhibition she constructed four small, wall-mounted shelves, each with a shallow lip, displaying sand and one or two objects collected while walking: dried leaves, a stick, a piece of rusted metal, tree bark, a broken cup, a fuel filter, a part of a tennis ball. On the wall above the shelves are the river sketches, now more fully developed with watercolour pencils. A written text, extracted from her field journal, is inscribed on birch bark and other collected items.

Hargrave delights in the material, noting how the "birch bark and writing can be wound around other objects, relating indirectly to the intertwining of experience."

The process of walking, collecting, and reflecting allows Hargrave "to intensify [her] involvement with the land." Finding focus and story involves recollection, memory: "The collecting of objects along the way provides me with another sense of the river, forcing my attention downward. The process of choice is involved here. That and the physicality of the object help in gaining a lasting memory of the moment." As she gathers her materials, the city sits above her, personified. "A silent audience," she calls it. By looking down, Hargrave gains a new perspective. She writes in her journal of a river buoy swivelling in the current, its "silent solitary dance"; of "some river worn sticks which had only remnants of the bark left, leaving irregular horizontal stripes"; of Peterson Creek emptying into the South Thompson, where "swiftly moving water had eroded patterns into the clayish sand," depositing "debris here and there — waste of the plastic variety stranded before reaching the river." These remnants, waste, and signs of erosion are neither metaphors for decay nor a pretext for environmental critique. Hargrave's response is more personal: she is interested in capturing what she calls each scene's "gestural immediacy," the moment in motion.

Walking and collecting inform other works in the exhibition. Sandra Scheller's *A Walk in My Shoes* is perhaps the most overt example, inviting the viewer on a "self-guided tour" of personal memories, with the maps provided on ten wooden panels, each identifying a presumably personally significant geographical location. (These locations range from such communities in the BC interior as Lillooet and Quesnel to larger urban and suburban centres in western Canada and Bolivia.) Here again memories are represented in fragments, a mixed media collage — personal artefacts collected in canvas shoe bags and placed adjacent to the maps. A Nike running shoe is associated with Kamloops, the words "nature" and "camping" collaged on the map.

Krista Simpson's *The Whole Kit 'n' Kaboodle: an Exploration of ...* presented as a rough-hewn, corrugated cardboard journal, replete with snapshots, maps, and diary reflections torn and pasted onto its pages, describes numerous walks in and around the Sahali Mall. Here Simpson feels observed, judged, awkward, and on edge — as if passersby are inappropriately aware of her secrets. The central moment occurs, ironically, at the mall's periphery: it is a threshold moment, when, holding a door open for a stranger, she exchanges pleasantries and the anonymous man tells her, jokingly, "Someday people will sing songs about you." The comment seems excessive, not quite of a piece with the situation, out of place; she receives it as an unexpected gesture of confidence and acceptance, one that startles her into a confrontation with her public self. A passing comment makes her feel quite suddenly, inexplicably, at home.

On first impression, Maria Tarasoff's work seems more closely aligned to notions of stasis than motion. *Biogeoclimatic Zone: Ponderosa Pine-Bunchgrass (Py)* presents the fixed, ordered, urban structure of a grid. Yet the individual sheets of paper, handmade from recycled materials, have an independence, a freedom from the grid, coming, in part, from each signifying a material recollection of a walk along a BC Hydro right-of-way, from Tarasoff's process of collecting, of gathering. The accumulations of wheat grass and pine needles on one sheet, or seeds on another, echo the randomness of what Robert Fulton describes as the glacial "till or other

171

unconsolidated debris" (*Deglaciation* 24) that typifies the surface landscape of the Thompson River valley. Like Hargrave, Scheller, and Simpson, Tarasoff reconstructs memory through remnants; she consolidates the debris as four squares of paper. In doing so, she recognizes mapping as a physical narrative and a possible anodyne to homelessness. She writes in her poetic artist's statement: "Mapping: lines / Innate drive to name, categorize, and lock in our environment. / Boundaries are / comforting, grids give structure to limitlessness." In the end, though, the viewer senses that she resists delimiting her landscape (or herself) into tight squares of meaning. Instead, Tarasoff embraces the "limitlessness" of her subject, taking it for granted that the remnants she's gathered and temporarily fixed into place will decompose, creating new debris. Even in the controlled conditions of an exhibition space, the fragile nature of her medium reveals itself: pieces of pinecone and the occasional needle fall to the gallery floor.

Elaine Sedgman's sculptural map offers us another grid, another set of lines, and another walk. Walking the quarter sections of ranch land that surround her home allows her to ruminate, to find a place for herself and her art in the local histories of her neighbours. Like Tarasoff's papermaking, Sedgman's sculpture embodies little of the angst that characterizes the Homeless Mind. She says of her work, "My memory map of the Haughton Brothers [two ranchers from the outlying community of Knutsford] is not one of alienation and homelessness, but rather a celebration of a family that has memories but has moved on with their lives within this community." Though the sculpture replicates precisely the geographic shape of the Haughton ranch, when viewed from above, the quarter sections serendipitously suggest the figure of a horizontal cowboy

boot. Each quarter section is represented by a single panel of canvas or metal, with each image painted or screen-printed on its surface, the entire form elevated off the floor by a low dais that follows the shape of the map's contour. Sedgman saturates this landscape in borrowed text, photographs overlaid with paint and maps, filling with narrative the interstices, the evenly spaced lines that divide up the land. She grounds her sense of place in colour, texture, shape, in remembered word and image. There is an atmosphere of assumed intimacy here, a narrative referencing people and events more given than new.

## Migration Narratives:
## Entering the City Slowly

Evangelitsa Pappas's *1963: A Self Portrait*, a print made through a combination of collography and serigraphy, has in the centre a serigraphic, silk-screened component, showing a photograph of her younger self. She looks back from Kamloops to Sydney, Australia, to a world represented by a child in a frilly dress, by a landscape of green bows and lush ferns. A fossil-like record of this greenery exists in the surrounding field, where under the weight of a press a single impression is made from a matrix that includes the ferns — along with ribbons, lace, and fabric of a doll's or perhaps a child's frock. The print contains the snapshot, acting as a frame, giving structure to her memories; but an overlaid grid pattern imposes a more ominous sense of control, of pressure. "The grid," she says, "represents a form of control and stereotyping often faced by children of immigrants." The comment is cryptic, muted, as if the form of representation restricts further personal exploration. Pappas's work alludes to more than it shows — to unresolved questions of identity, travel, change, and the mapping of personal memories.

Where Pappas's print tries to explore identity by looking back to the past, the shock of the new characterizes a cluster of first-contact stories, works that complicate our understanding of migration and the city. Early settlers came by canoe or by trail; Shima Iuchi arrived from Japan by plane and by bus. *Her First Journal — 'What's there over the ocean'* records in mock-documentary manner her dismay in arriving at the Greyhound terminal only to discover the brown desert of a Kamloops summer. Back home in Japan, she dreamed of Canada as a place of snow and trees, of white winters and green summers.

"Upon arrival," she says, "the landscape was a disappointment. I thought to myself, I've never seen such a brown place." She would phone friends in Japan who refused to believe "Canada had a desert." Five years later, Kamloops feels "more like home." *Her First Journal* attempts to represent Iuchi's initial competing reactions, using realist conventions as a backdrop for a fantasy vision: a playful innocence projected onto the Kamloops scene in the form of a penguin, a doll-like construction made of clay. This vision plays off the documentary form of the travel journal, with maps and landscape photographs, cyanotypes,[4] that seemingly record her travels from Japan to Canada and to Kamloops. The four faux journals are archived within a carefully constructed, glass-fronted display case that folds inwards to become its own travelling case. Inside, the images and stories of penguins and whales frolicking in the Thompson valley speak to Iuchi's immigrant experience: they are no more startling, she seems to say, than her initial surprise at finding desert-like conditions in Canada. Their "bizarreness was not comically made," she insists; the journals are, rather, "an earnest consideration of memories from my journey."

This careful balancing between fantasy and craft is countered by the more serendipi-

tous occurrence of *Traces*, Iuchi's other work in the exhibition. Here a sheet of carbon paper delicately pinned to the gallery wall moves in response to the motion of the gallery viewers. It presents a palimpsest, a layering, of five inscribed maps that range in scale from the broad expanse of the Pacific Ocean to the urban core of Kamloops. This palimpsest is accidental, a memory left on the carbon paper in the process of creating a larger panoramic map, one later sandblasted into the surface of five glass panels for a larger body of work entitled *Transient's Voice*. (Interestingly, the exhibition invitation for *Transient's Voice* provides a further record of her cross-Canada travels, one in which a listing of cities, towns, and islands on the left margin functions as a kind of residual memory map or prose poem.)

Like Iuchi, Dana Novak-Ludvig uses the cyanotype process, tapping into what she considers to be its inherent dream-like qualities. In *The Boat from Bohemia,* Parts I and II, the negatives for these cyanotypes are made with a pinhole camera,[5] her practice of gathering the images thereby existing on the margins of conventional photographic practice, in an aleatory dream-like realm accentuated by the inherent chance of the medium. Novak-Ludvig's story is also one of migration from one country to another: from Czechoslovakia to Canada, and from the hardships of her former country to the outlying and placid setting of Lac Le Jeune.

The story unfolds in two parts, each comprising four overtly theatrical cyanotypes set within individual mats, and with a personal narrative written in calligraphic script extending across the four mats of each set. Part I tells of the journey from Czechoslovakia; like Iuchi's out-of-place penguin, a crude model clipper ship appears incongruously in each image: alongside a map, against a forest backdrop, on the bow of a kayak, and, finally, resting atop the artist's head, its white sails curiously blending into the reflections of the far shore of Lac Le Jeune. In Part II, "The Boat from Bohemia" is frozen within the winter landscape, and the artist, as the work's calligraphy details, remains "frozen in a dream." As someone new to the community and the culture, Novak-Ludvig found refuge in the rural setting of Lac Le Jeune. During the creation of this work, though, she felt herself in the dream state of transition; and following the work's completion, she now feels the confidence to move from the periphery to the city. "I'm able to wake from the dream," she says, "and move, cautiously, to the city."

Michel Campeau's photographs present an alternative sensibility to that of Iuchi and Novak-Ludvig. In contrast to the short tonal range of the pinhole and cyanotype processes, which yield little definition in the highlights and shadows, Campeau's silver prints present a full tonal range rich with detail in its extremes — and they exhibit a further subtlety of detail that comes from his choice of a medium-format camera. Such photographic modality is appropriate for the range of emotion that Campeau's photographs allow. The photographs, collectively arranged for the exhibition in a grid-like but not exactly rectilinear grouping, suggest gestures of introspection, some coming from his environs in Montreal and others as a response to areas in and around Kamloops.

In particular, Campeau has been drawn to sparse landscapes that feature the remains or discards of industry. The heavy machinery of mining at a lot in Savona, an abandoned car on the banks of the Thompson River, a heap of drywall at the Mission Flats landfill, a rock pile somewhere in or near Montreal: these compositions present a restrained theatricality, one open to the dramatic lighting of the midday sun, but resisting the overt staging

evident in such works as those by Dana Novak-Ludvig.[6]

In Kamloops for just the first few months of the year, Campeau has come upon these marginal landscapes through discussions with people he has only recently met. When he first arrived from Montreal, he began asking locals about places to photograph. "What is it shameful to photograph?" he inquired — not because he wanted to document community values or attitudes, but because he sought a suitable location to project his own inner state. "Being in Kamloops," he says, "I instinctively knew that I didn't want to document people and the city in the manner of standard documentary conventions." In his photographs, often neglected, sometimes provisional places answer the artist's search for a landscape complementary to the one already inscribed on his own body; in his work, he seeks to saturate the landscape with his own presence. Each photograph is a self-portrait.

### *Das Unheimlich*: Unsettling the City

Tonia Funk's *Amnesiac* was one of the first works selected for the exhibition. At first we responded more intuitively than critically, drawn to what we took to be the work's apparent simplicity. The central image's lack of definition — the result of stain painting, where acrylic paint or ink is literally soaked into an unstretched, untreated canvas — suggested the realm of memory, of an idea more emerging than fully resolved. Stylistically, *Amnesiac* seemed to be situated somewhere between the conventions of early landscape painting and mapping. There remains, however, something strangely unsettling about the work: it demands a dual perspective, a kind of double vision, for, to take in the landscape, the viewer must look across and down at the same time. We look across the hills and down on the lakes — one sitting implausibly on top of a mountain in the top-right quadrant of the canvas. Yet somehow, in this part of the country, the perspective *Amnesiac* proposes seems of a piece with local experience: a saturated canvas for a saturated landscape.

Other works in the exhibition seem similarly designed to unsettle. Linda Goddard's study of "home" gives notions of dislocation and migration a psychological inflection. *Homescapes of Desire* is without nostalgia. Instead, Goddard seeks to represent what she calls the *unheimlich* (literally, the "unhomely"), that which unsettles the viewer, making us uneasy in the presence of ostensibly familiar images.[7] The series of five canvas panels is exhibited horizontally, creating a readable line tracing her family's movement across western Canada — from Winnipeg, to Dufferin County, to two homes in North Vancouver. The series ends in 1921 and thus creates an unfinished, open-ended narrative: the story of her own home in Kamloops is missing, implied, like a "synchronous line," only by association.

The "house," as Goddard describes it, invites commonplace associations: house as "refuge, shelter, and resting place"; but in *Homescapes* she interpolates several competing representational strategies, competing stories, each designed to unsettle the grid of conventional response: each panel incorporates a photograph of a house superimposed over old maps, descriptive passages, postcards, and letters. Helvetica lettering (a passage from Margaret Atwood's *Journals of Susanna Moodie*) and a grid are overlaid, overcrowding the canvas and threatening to explode the frame. Goddard's medium saturates the eye with visual information; as she says of her work (in words that might be applied equally to Funk's *Amnesiac*), "The romantic and emotional is juxtaposed with the rational. ... The surface is glossy and shifting, alternatively absorbing and reflecting

light, conversely hiding and illuminating what is seen and what is beneath the surface."

Aspects of this same moodiness and unease are captured forcefully in David Tremblay's painting of the former Kamloops Indian Residential School. On the surface, this work exhibits a deliberate naïveté current among many contemporary First Nations artists — work where apparent innocence implies complex political intent. This rhetorical mix is disarming. The building, once a place of discipline and displacement, here resembles a storybook gingerbread house. The painting's more decorative elements, gilt-like embellishments that exist as gestural brushstrokes on the roof and as small medallions situated around the building, are countered by the overtly political implication of the work's title, *K.I.R.S.*, a vernacular derivation of the building's former official name. People in Kamloops know the school as a place where Aboriginal children were punished for using their local language and for dancing. Dawne McCance sees the work as "a wound," the deeper crimson of the building's architecture appearing almost like a scab.[8] Once understood in such terms, the gilt medallions — some existing against the more transparent washes of the russet sky and others as darker forms within the otherwise light-coloured and perhaps optimistic green of the ground — bring to mind the smallpox and other epidemics that coincided with the early period of the residential schools. Despite the richness of such potentially political allusions, though, the overall tone of Tremblay's painting argues against any such fixed reading. The work creates an uncanny space for both the imaginary and the polemical.

Robert Kroetsch's memory mapping poem, *This Part of the Country*, gives further voice to the *unheimlich*, especially to the problem of finding a sense of place and voice when feeling temporarily unsettled. The poetic line does not come easily here. Kroetsch describes his journey to Kamloops, where he's about to take up a position as, ambiguously, "visiting writer-in-residence." Feeling more like a visitor than a resident, he tells of driving the Yellowhead from Winnipeg, of a moment when, stopping for coffee in the town of Barriere, he listens in on a conversation taking place at the next table: "An older man was telling his companion about the logging in the area. 'In this part of the country,' he told her, not once but three times, 'we ... ' And he went on to explain how they used to log in the North Thompson valley" (qtd. from Kroetsch's "Artist's Statement").

The passing phrase comes as an unexpected gift, a focusing line for a poet attempting to write himself into a new community. The phrase gives him "focus, place, a track into memory, the possibility of arrival.... At last," he says, "I was able to drive into the city." The past is something that, through careful listening, can be tracked, can help him map both destination and point of departure. Kroetsch finds himself unsettled, feeling temporarily dislocated and, ironically, listening in on the words of someone who is evidently very much at home. Significantly, what the local holds onto is a "part of the country"; he finds pride of ownership and meaning in a fragment, in that part of the land he has evidently entered slowly and now knows well.

During the gallery symposium, in conversation with the other artists, Kroetsch reflected on the exhibition as a whole, seeing it as a celebration of the fragmentary, as moving us "from ruins to runes," where works excavate past attachments, the materials of the past, and resituate them in the present tense of lived experience. Echoing the aspirations of a character from one of his novels (Gus Liebhaber, a reporter and typesetter who has

learned how to "set the story, slightly in advance of the event"), Kroetsch speaks of his own writing in these terms, as an attempt to "remember the future."[9] Memory refuses to stay buried, for, as Michel Campeau's photographs also reveal, beauty lives and narrative abounds in the most unlikely of places — especially on the periphery of everyday experience, in garbage dumps, smokestacks, abandoned vehicles; in industrial follies, in roadside diners, and in an overheard phrase.

Memory informs present actions and charts future possibilities. The contributing artists in *The Homeless Mind* exhibition teach us that memory is spatial, topographical, offering the *topos* or place for future invention. Coming to terms with the small city, with "this part of the country," requires a recursive engagement with landscape and story — a piecing together (literally, a "remembering") and relocating life's edges, angles, and lines.

**Notes**

1. This evocative phrase belongs to Michael Heller, who, in his essay "The Cosmopolis of Poetics: Urban World, Uncertain Poetry," argues that the 19th-century American city had not yet fallen "barren, inert, decreative," that it remained open to "utopian possibility." In accord with Berger's Homeless Mind thesis, Heller sees the dystopian anguish of the city taking hold in the late 19th and early 20th centuries: "Certainly part of that anguish is a human rootlessness desiring and not finding roots, the absence of the city version, to paraphrase William Carlos Williams, of a 'peasant tradition' to give place character" (90).

2. Journalist Joel Garreau coined the term "edge city" to describe the "vast new urban job centers" created "in places that only thirty years before had been residential suburbs or even corn stubble" (xx) — small "cities" sprouting up on the margins of the North American metropolis. In brief, Garreau offers a five-part definition of the edge city: a place with "five million square feet or more of leasable office space"; "600,000 square feet or more of leasable retail space"; "more jobs than bedrooms"; the shared perception by its population that it is "one place, ...

that it 'has it all,' from jobs, to shopping, to entertainment"; and that it was "nothing like [a] 'city' as recently as thirty years ago" (6-7).

3. Unless otherwise indicated, all quotations are from either artists' statements exhibited in *The Homeless Mind* or from personal interviews conducted with the artists between February and March, 2003.

4. A cyanotype is an early form of photographic printmaking, dating from the 1840s and used by some contemporary artists in a manner essentially unchanged since that time.

5. A pinhole camera (commonly as simple as a cardboard box) admits light through a small opening rather than through the more complex configuration of lenses, shutters, and (more recently) microchips, which are common to photographic technology.

6. Most of the photographs were taken when the sun was high in the winter sky, the light catching the edges of form, accentuating the overall angular topography of his subjects.

7. The concept of the uncanny or *das Unheimlich* is usually traced back to Freud's 1919 essay "The Uncanny" ("*Das Unheimliche*"), though Goddard's usage owes more to the work of Anthony Vidler's *The Architectural Uncanny: Essays in the Modern Unhomely*. Vidler popularized the literal translation of *Unheimlich* as "unhomely."

8. Kroetsch cites McCance's reading in his contribution to the "Homeless Mind Symposium," a public forum featuring the participating artists and held during the exhibition.

9. From *What the Crow Said,* cited by Kroetsch during the "Homeless Mind Symposium."

## Works Cited

Augustine, Jane. "From Topos to Anthropoid: The City as Character in Twentieth-Century Texts." *City Images: Perspectives from Literature, Philosophy, and Film*. Ed. Mary Ann Caws. New York: Gordon and Breach, 1991. 73-86.

Berger, Peter, Brigitte Berger, and Hansfried Kellner. *The Homeless Mind: Modernization and Consciousness*. New York: Knopf, 1974.

Calvino, Italo. *Invisible Cities*. Trans. William Weaver. New York: Harcourt, 1974.

Freud, Sigmund. "The Uncanny." [1919] *The Complete Psychological Works of Sigmund Freud*. Vol. 17. Trans. James Strachy. London: Hogarth P, 1964. 217-56.

Fulton, Robert J. *Deglaciation Studies in Kamloops Region, An Area of Moderate Relief, British Columbia*. Ottawa: Geological Survey of Canada, Department of Energy, Mines and Resources. Bulletin no. 154, 1967.

———. *Glacial Lake History, Southern Interior Plateau, British Columbia*. Ottawa: Geological Survey of Canada, Department of Energy, Mines and Resources. Paper 69-37, 1969.

Garreau, Joel. *Edge City: Life on the New Frontier*. New York: Doubleday, 1991.

Heller, Michael. "The Cosmopolis of Poetics: Urban World, Uncertain Poetry." *City Images: Perspectives from Literature, Philosophy, and Film*. Ed. Mary Ann Caws. New York: Gordon and Breach, 1991. 87-96.

Kroetsch, Robert. *What the Crow Said*. Don Mills, ON: General, 1978.

Lippard, Lucy. *The Lure of the Local: Senses of Place in a Multicentered Society*. New York: New Press, 1997.

MacLennan, David, Donald Lawrence, W.F. Garrett-Petts, and Bonnie Yourk. "Vernacular Landscapes: Sense of Self and Place in the Small City." *The Small Cities Book*. Ed. W.F. Garrett-Petts. Vancouver: New Star Books, 2004. 145-162.

McCance, Dawne. "Crossings: an Interview with Aritha van Herk." *Mosaic* 36:1 (March 2003): 1-19.

———. "Memory, Architecture, Archive: a Kamloops Wunderblock." A paper presented at the Small Cities CURA Working Seminar, The University College of the Cariboo, Kamloops, B.C., March 18, 2003.

Ralph, Edward. *Place and Placelessness*. London: Pion, 1976.

Vanderhaeghe, Guy. "'Brand Name' vs. 'No-Name': A Half-Century of the Representation of Western Canadian Cities in Fiction." *The Urban Prairie*. Ed. Dan Ring. Saskatoon: Mendel Art Gallery, 1993. 111-29.

Vidler, Anthony. *The Architectural Uncanny: Essays in the Modern Unhomely*. Cambridge, Mass: MIT P, 1992.

Wilson, Elizabeth. "The Rhetoric of Urban Space." *New Left Review* 209 (1995): 146-160.

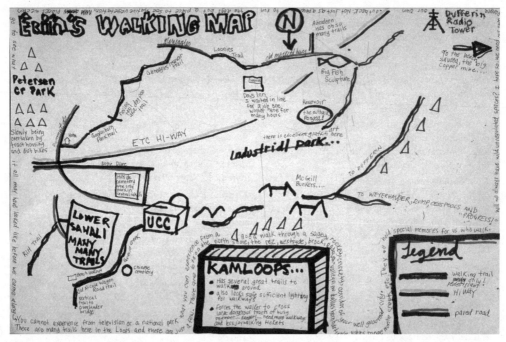

Erin de Zwart

Eileen Leier

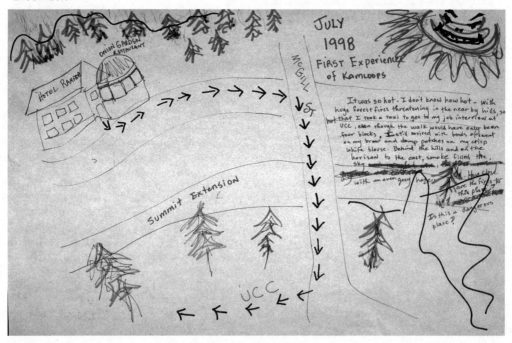

# Homeless Mind Exhibition

All dimensions on this and the following pages in centimeters.
Height, followed by width, followed by depth.

## On memory maps

*"Dasein ist nicht zuhause"*: (human) existence is not at-home, says Heidegger, not "housed." Instead, we track through the openness of existence, leaving traces of our passing on the various sites where we have sojourned. These traces are a memory, which we re-member in re-tracing them, in consciously mapping our journey. To retrace, to draw the map of journeying, is to convert traces into writing, into poetry. "Poetically humans dwell on the earth" (Hölderlin). We dwell by tracing and retracing, existing and remembering, converting our uncanny or unhomely *(unheimlich)* existence into dwelling.

*Memory Maps, 2001*
A selection of memory maps from the
*Representing Kamloops* project
Each map: 29 x 42 cm

Bruce Baugh

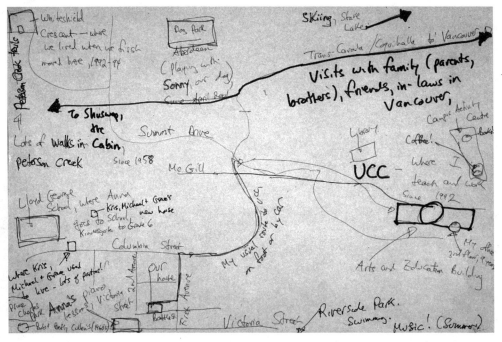

# Leslie Bolin

My clay forms are map-like, and the trans-
formative firing process I chose to work
with yields results reflecting my theme. The
combination of a thick application of non-
fritting slip with a thin overcoat of glaze is
ultimately removed following a process of
extreme heat and rapid cooling in a smoul-
dering environment. The resulting patterns
are random and uncontrollable, yet produce a draftsman-like quality.

*Thompson Woodlands*
2003
Clay and mixed media
31 x 20.5 x 8 cm

# Michel Campeau

My photographs are a spontaneous response to the physicality of the surroundings, an immediate reaction to inner feelings and thoughts that run from the enigmas of my origins …

*The Skeptical Photographer*
2003
Silver prints (working prints)
Each print: 18.5 x 22.5 cm

# Tonia Funk

I chose Monte Lake, British Columbia, as
my setting, being born there, raised
and once again returning for a map of my
amnesia. I found it difficult to piece
together—other than using the landscape.
The lakes, creeks and hills were the only
intimate crossover, the only way in.

*Amnesiac*
2000
Acrylic on canvas
174 x 166 cm

# Linda Goddard

My works in the last few years have explored themes of dislocation and alienation, and how we go about maintaining a sense of self within conditions of estrangement. The artworks look at architecture and surrounding systems of organization as ways that maintain the status quo. Each work has a sense of *unheimlich* or uncanny, an unsettling effect of something not quite right.

*Homescapes of Desire*
2001
Mixed media on canvas panels
Each panel: 56 x 56 x 5 cm

# Laura Hargrave

This is an ongoing project, consisting of a growing number of field sketches from a variety of places along the river, a collection of items of interest from along the shoreline, and a written account of my experiences on each walk. I prefer a small format for the drawings, as both time and portability are factors in the colder weather. I continue to develop the drawings from memory while back in the studio, instead of relying on photographs, and will sometimes go back to check on proportions afterwards.

*River Walk Project*
2002 (ongoing)
Mixed media works
Each with individual dimensions
Largest: 39 x 42 x 13 cm

# Shima Iuchi

When I came to Canada, I had no idea what Kamloops looked like, but I imagined, with the stereotypes of my Japanese culture, Kamloops as a town with much greenery. Therefore, I marvelled at the small brownish city in Canada.

*Traces*
2002
(a chance memory map from *Calls of Clans*)
Maps on carbon paper
45 x 65 cm

*Her First Journal — 'What's there over the ocean'*
2002
Cyanotype journals in folding case
25.5 x 147.5 x 7.5 cm

# Robert Kroetsch

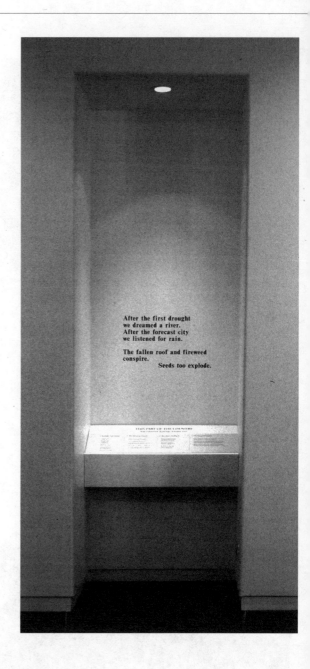

Kamloops is a place where prose and poetry speak to each other, give each other sustenance and inspiration, at once collide and invigorate. The forked rivers become a place of fusion and opening. The differing voices give weight to each other's concerns. This is where the individual and community collaborate. The silence speaks; the speaking allows both travel and arrival, becoming and being. The poem escapes the poet, becomes vital memory.

*This Part of the Country*
2003
Poem/installation
Installation space: 300 x 93 x 76 cm

# Dana Novak-Ludvig

Perhaps the *"homeless mind"* is an *inevitable part of adulthood* — experiencing both feelings of loss, and the mental (or) physical search for a place in mind where we feel *nurtured* and safe, o*pen to changes.*

*The Boat from Bohemia II* (detail)
2002

*The Boat from Bohemia I*
2003
Cyanotypes from pinhole negatives
Each cyanotype 24 x 27 cm
on panels with texts: each 137 x 77 cm

# Evangelitsa Pappas

The grid is used as a way of symbolically mapping out my childhood. It represents a form of control and stereotyping often faced by children of immigrants.

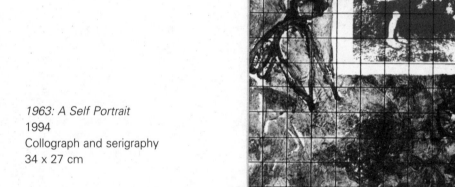

*1963: A Self Portrait*
1994
Collograph and serigraphy
34 x 27 cm

# Sandra Scheller

For me the question "Where are you from?" has been more difficult to answer than "Where do you live?" In search of an answer, I have retraced my steps through the varied landscapes of my life, arriving here in the small city of Kamloops with some questions still unanswered.

*A Walk in My Shoes*
2002
Mixed media collages with bags and associated artefacts
Each panel: 30.5 x 24.5 cm

# Elaine Sedgman

I am interested in the relationship between maps, landscape, and memory and the physical geography of memory. Maps become a means of storytelling and myth making. Mapping becomes a way of telling personal stories, whether they are my own or those of others.

*Haughton Brothers*
2001
Mixed media construction with
photography and silkscreen
21 x 432 x 326 cm

# Krista Simpson

Rather than allowing myself to draw memory maps freely, I was overly concerned with producing accurate representations of space. I was aware that I was limiting further exploration of my moment by placing boundaries on my creative freedom. I had to make a conscious effort to draw these maps with my memory and not my knowledge of geography.

*The Whole Kit 'n' Kaboodle:*
*an exploration of ....,*
2002
Documentation journal: corrugated cardboard, photography, maps, reflections
Book open: 16 x 88 x 27 cm

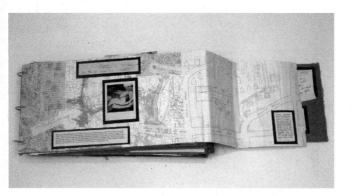

# Maria Tarasoff

Recycled paper holds fragments. Should I say I chose each item specifically? Only these, no other? They are the perfect representation of my memory? A limiting lie.

*Biogeoclimactic Zone: Ponderosa Pine-Bunchgrass (Py)*
2003
Handmade paper and landscape fragments
Overall 74 x76 cm,
each sheet 36 x 37 cm

# David Tremblay

I sat in on a class in 1990 at the University of British Columbia on Native Issues. Shirley Sterling lectured on the effects of the residential schools. The thing that hit me the hardest was the image Shirley painted of how children are normally taught to parent by being parented, but at the residential schools the one adult sometimes would supervise a hundred children.

*K.I.R.S.*
2003
Watercolour, acrylic, and graphite on paper
31 x 45 cm

# River Walk Journal

## Laura Hargrave

### Artist's Statement

The *River Walk Journal* and subsequent art-work was started as a response to the Small Cities CURA project entitled "Representing Kamloops." Upon joining the group as an artist/researcher, I reviewed transcripts of the story-mapping interviews. I became aware that many of the personal memories of the region were made while people were walking. It seemed that the act of physically traversing the land was in some way tied to the lasting quality of the memory. As well, I noticed that the river was mentioned frequently as an integral element in the perception of Kamloops. In some of the stories, it acted as a focal point, being described strongly in the recollection of an event. I began to look at the merging rivers (North and South Thompson) as an important feature, pondering its effect upon our identities. In such a dry land, we are drawn to the river for leisure activities in the summer months, but I wondered if it ran deeper into our sensibilities, deeper than the memory of an event, but into our sense of placement within the land.

For me, the need to walk the shoreline is directly related to my experiences of living close to a beach in Victoria, B.C. Although it differs vastly from the ocean, the river's similarities spark an interest. I tend to seek out the river for both leisure and comfort and consider it a reassuring presence. In doing so, I begin to build memories around this region, overlaying them upon past coastal memories.

As a response to the oral histories, I have done a series of river walks along shorelines in the Kamloops area, directly observing river activity. For one and a half years and 65 walks, I have observed, recorded, and collected from a variety of places along the shore-line. To maintain the momentum of the walks, I have created an artist's journal with both written and visual reminders of the day. When possible, I travel with art supplies and record my surroundings on the spot. I also collect found objects along the way, which provide me with another sense of the river, forcing my attention downwards as I search, choose, and save "artefacts" from the area. This process of choosing and the physicality of the object help me gain a lasting memory of the moment. Each walk unfolds differently from all the rest, each is a unique blend of sensation and activity.

The extended nature of the project has given me the opportunity to view the environmental, societal, and industrial aspects of the river that normally might go unnoticed. Over the course of the walks, I have experienced strong seasonal changes in water level, seen much evidence of wildlife activity, and observed how the river is used by industry, business, and by the community. It has been the focus of human pleasure and human tragedy. It has attracted me with its beauty and repelled me with its power. The walking research has acted as a basis for other artworks, which have spun off from the journal, the latest of which involve large drawings and castings of the collected items.

Willow tree area
at Airport Beach

My chances of drawing outside were
marred by the cold wind. I think it's
-10 today, or close to it.
I drove to the willow tree, in the hopes
of drawing it from another viewpoint, but
quickly realized it would be too cold.
I drew instead, from the inside of the van
and this narrowed my possibilities.
Perhaps it was because of limited
vantage point that I came to center
upon the cluster of small sheds. Two
narrow doors with rusted handles
caught my attention.

Pulp mill + Steam

March 16/03
Jack Gregson Trail Beach
South Thompson River

We walked first w.
then east along the shore
past our starting point and as
as the Maple that lies across the b

Last week it wo
and sunny. Th
We heard a
from acr

The water was still low - we cou
walk up to the red buoy; it was
in the water, about 2 feet away.
The smell of rotten salmon ling
around the carcasses her
there.

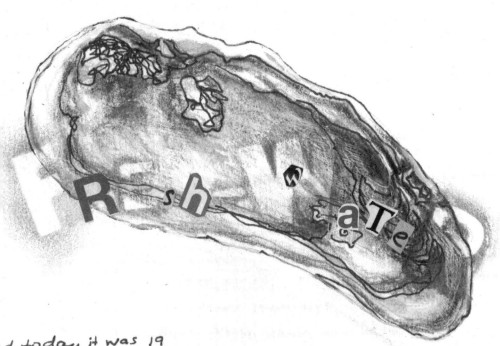

FReshwaTer

d today it was 19
was refreshing and warm.
above us, and a meadowlark called
river

Receding mounds of rock caught the light, each
cascading down the bank, separate from the natural
time-worn habitat.

This is a place where distance
is judged by maple trees, where
temperature is gauged by wind on
the skin, and seasons are read by
how close one can get to a red plastic
marker.

Wednesday     May 21/03
Schubert Drive/Halston
                    Bridge
North Thompson River

It was warm this evening. The North Thomps[on]
was flowing very swiftly. The river was
transformed at this season, with no sand to
speak of - just one spit left and rushing brow[n]
river beyond. Nowhere to walk, no way to be
close. I'll have to be content with the bike pat[h]

The feeling of the wa[ter]
self absorbed presen[t]
engrossed in the trans[...]
must travel downriver
a log be carried along
the river.

HALSTON BR.
BIKE PATH
CITY STR[EET]

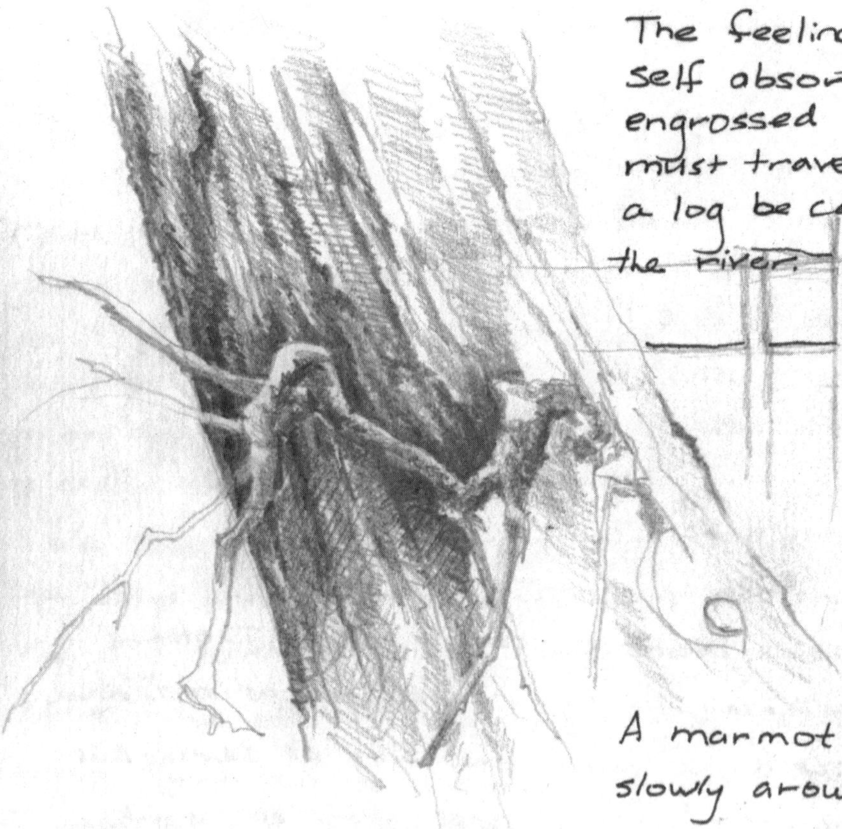

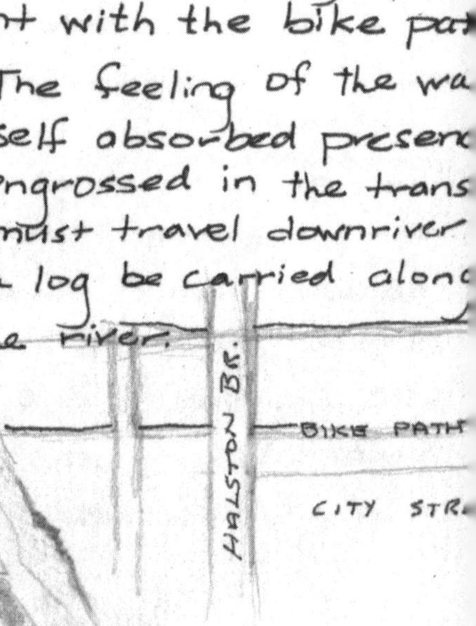

A marmot looked up
slowly around the rock

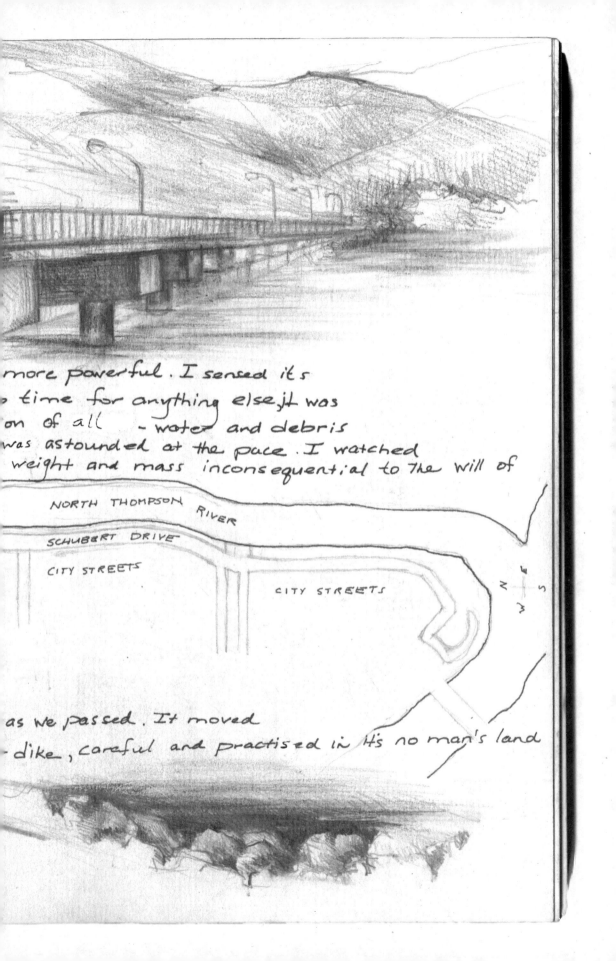

more powerful. I sensed it's

time for anything else, jt was

on of all    - water and debris

was astounded at the pace. I watched

weight and mass inconsequential to the will of

NORTH THOMPSON RIVER

SCHUBERT DRIVE

CITY STREETS

CITY STREETS

N E W S

as we passed. It moved

dike, careful and practised in it's no man's land

Right away, I realized that I should have
brought some water, but I had some
collecting to do, so pushed the idea of liquid t
a corner of my mind.

I needed to collect some earth from the sit
of the old car dike — It was something that I
kept putting off — very hot today!

We saw some sky divers, landing on the san
trying to center themselves between two flags;
gracefully wafting, their speed concealed by
elegance of movement.

We walked on with purpose through yellow sagebrush
and rosehips. A raven yelled insults from a
gnarled tree. We came across the cars, as one
might find a temple in the jungle, with a sense of
imploding stillness and shifting certainty. This

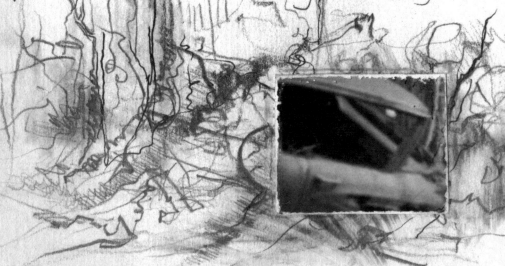

We had crossed a threshold from a land of unin
a reaction.

odd place. We had walked through the
lourful parade of parachutists and lighthearted
tertainment of passing spectatorship,

ment to one that demanded

Figure 1. Kamloops, circa 1910, Junction of the Thompson Rivers. BC Archives B-05632.

# Away from Home, or Finding Yourself Back In Kamloops: Literary Representations of the Small City

## Ginny Ratsoy

Great nutritiousness of pasturage about Kamloops. Bunch grass. Cattle brought from all around to winter. Get fat in very short time. Would not have believed this of a country which looks the colour of a lithograph.
— Dr. Cheadle, 1862

In "Making a Grass of Yourself: Small Cities Up Close," the 2003 Canadian Studies Day lecture held at The University College of the Cariboo, Robert Kroetsch and Laurie Ricou remarked that the rural template that once imprinted itself on Canadian literature has been replaced over the past several decades by the template of the big city. If, by implication, the small city does not fit in either past or present of Canadian literary history (and small cities *are* conspicuously rare in Can Lit), where does it fit? Ricou indicates marginalism as a condition of the small city: "The small city has very little place in the received Canadian imaginary." Kroetsch points to literary sensory absence: "We haven't heard the small city. How does it sound? How does it smell? How does it taste?"

We might expect the small city to have a peripheral role — to play second fiddle to the rural literature of the past and the urban literature of more recent times. How many of us — even the Canadian literature specialists and enthusiasts among us — can name even a handful of canonical Canadian novels, for example, set in small cities? We might also expect that a small city such as Kamloops, which is far from the population centres of the country (as opposed to many small cities that are suburbs or near-suburbs of large cities), would be particularly marginalized on the Canadian literary map.

Certainly, Kamloops receives passing mention in relatively few novels, even in those instances where the city seems to have been chosen arbitrarily. For example, in Margaret Atwood's *The Edible Woman*, it is one of a legion of towns home to female, part-time test marketers for the Toronto-based study that market-researcher protagonist Marian helps organize. Unfortunately, the Kamloopsian, Mrs. Dodge, "will have to be removed. She's pregnant"(24). Mrs. Dodge's condition renders her useless in the patriarchal, consumer-driven society of Atwood's first novel. Kamloops is the place to which Coyote in Thomas King's *Green Grass Running Water* refuses to return after what is depicted as a mysterious event, either a flood or a birth, or perhaps both. Kamloops is the city to which the protagonist of Marion Douglas' *Bending at the Bow* only pretends to have travelled from her Calgary home. In each of the above cases, Kamloops is at once present in but absent from the narrative.

The city's presence in Aritha van Herk's feminist road novel *No Fixed Address* is somewhat more sustained and promising. Her travelling (underwear) saleswoman/heroine Arachne, in her criss-crossing across the Canadian west, picks up a hitchhiker, a snuff saleswoman who travels with her bear, on Highway 97 at Falkland. The two women of commerce sleep together in a Kamloops motel, where "It is hot. It is always hot in Kamloops, thick" (276); and the next morning the hitchhiker, who claims to be Arachne's doppelganger, and the bear head into the Thompson River. The episode ends with Arachne fleeing farther west on the journey to return to her "gasping, squalid childhood" (278) on the coast, the promise of her Kamloops foray apparently unfulfilled. In these texts, Kamloops is either one of a succession of Canadian cities forming part of a catalogue or is given incidental mention as a convenient other place. These works are clearly about elsewhere — about large cities or the prairies.

However, even in the prose and poetry set more substantially in the Interior of British Columbia, the small city seldom occupies centre stage. From the popular histories and adventure stories found on bus station racks, to various seminal British Columbia novels, such as Sheila Watson's *The Double Hook* and Howard O'Hagan's *Tay John*, and poetry by Patrick Lane and Harold Rhenisch, Kamloops as a literary setting is peripheral to the events — present only as a mention in passing or floating just outside the narrative. Robert Kroetsch's own homage to the city, *This Part of the Country*, explores Kamloops itself only in the two poems that bookend the suite of four poems. Most saliently, Part Two, both a partial cataloguing of, and a tribute to, those who have gone before him in writing

the Interior landscape, has no distinguishing markers of the urban, nothing to differentiate Kamloops from the surrounding countryside. David Thompson, George Bowering, Roy Miki, and Sheila Watson are in the landscape and on the outskirts in the imagery of exploring and seeking. In this respect, Kroetsch follows the path of most of his literary predecessors. The historical events that loom largest in local lore (some of which are alluded to in this section of Kroetsch's poem) — the shooting by the McLean gang of Constable John Ussher and the 1906 train robbery by Bill Miner, for instance — are often depicted with little more than a perfunctory nod to the town of Kamloops itself, as in the poetry of Andrew Wreggitt, for example.

While the conspicuous absence of a Kamloops presence may, to some extent, be ascribed to the fact that the most frequently represented events associated with the area took place not in, but around Kamloops, it is nonetheless puzzling. The city is one of the most populated areas of the Interior. It is also, historically and geographically, a centre; its name, deriving from the Shuswap, means "Meeting of the Waters." Kamloops has been a transportation hub because not only the Thompson and North Thompson, but *also* the major railway lines and highways meet here.

Garrett-Petts and Lawrence locate small cities such as Kamloops in "an uncertain position, situated somewhere between the local and the cosmopolitan ... on the margin, on the edge," defined by "the borders or edges of the urban and the rural" (168). This fluid perspective provides a convenient point of departure for a discussion of literature in which this particular small city — a city that grew up not as a suburb of a larger city and not primarily because of a single resource industry within its boundaries — plays a more sustained role.

Nothing else on the literary map encapsulates Kamloops' role more succinctly than George Bowering's description (in his 1987 novel *Caprice*) of his eponymous heroine's relationship to the place: "She did not live here — she was just an uneasy presence in the town whose main purpose was to supply the surrounding ranches and the stage lines" (169). Note that the character is out of her element, and the setting in which she finds herself is one that came into existence to service the surrounding areas; it owes its comparatively urban existence to geography — to its proximity to (rural) ranchland and its fortuitous position as a transportation hub. This pattern recurs in literature about Kamloops. The town, although an important component in various novels and short stories, is rarely the main setting; that honour is left to the countryside that surrounds it. It is, in essence, the centre for the edge: the place from which to stock up on cultural and material provisions.

Because of its considerable distance from large cities, this small city is not on the edge with the large city as centre, but on the edge with the rural as centre. Kamloops, more than most places of similar size, is at once edge and centre. Perhaps, then, it is not surprising that the city's primary literary identity is as a spatial Other. In this recurrent role, it is secondary to the rural setting but central in its function as *the centre*: of activity, of culture, of protagonist growth. The rural main setting is peripheral to mainstream cultural activity; the secondary setting — Kamloops — represents that activity. As the somewhere set away from the primary setting of the literature, it is fluidly constructed, although it is more often depicted as urban centre than hinterland. The perspective of urban centre is invariably the vantage point of those writers who have inhabited, if not Kamloops itself, then areas in close geographic proximity. In

this context, one is reminded of BC historian Adele Perry's observation that "It is hard to see margins from anywhere *but* margins" as she declares that "It is no accident that scholars of British Columbia usually have lived within its borders, at least for a time: how else would we have found the place?" (59). Interestingly, those writers who have lived in the Interior landscape at once marginalize and magnify Kamloops within that Interior setting.

In these urban guises, Kamloops is about presences *and* absences: in the cityscape, the landscape as *land* is obviated when land is focal in the larger narrative. Almost invariably, it is in a juxtapositional role. Initially, the reader may perceive a simple binary opposition: the city as spatial Other contains all the rural/main setting does not, and vice versa; the rural/main setting achieves fuller definition through contrast with what it is not. However, what unfolds most frequently in prose works is the definition of identity through encounter with Kamloops as spatial Other; that is, the protagonist, usually in transit rather than a permanent resident, finds him/herself in that peripheral setting.

With a few exceptions, it is not present but past Kamloops where protagonists find themselves. Rudy Wiebe has said, "The principal task of the Canadian writer is not simply to explain his contemporary world, but to create a past, a lived history, a vital mythology" (qtd. in Jeffrey 88). Writers about Kamloops have a preoccupation with creating a past; they are still in the process of creating the "lived history." Indeed, tellingly, in works such as George Bowering's *Shoot!* and Theresa Kishkan's *Sisters of Grass*, set largely in the 19th and early 20th centuries respectively, the occasional references to the present are matter of fact and impart a microscopic view of the present, in contrast to the rather magnified view of the past. These distinct

Figure 2. The Last of the Camels. BC Archives A-00347.

ways of seeing can be fruitfully linked to Claude Gandelman's work on seeing and reading. Gandelman extends art historian Alois Riegl's "great dichotomy, the *optic* and the *haptic*," to the reading of texts. Essentially, the optic vision scans the outlines of objects, whereas the haptic focuses on surfaces and tactility (5). The optic eye, being superficial, maintains an objective distance; the haptic viewer is at once penetrative and emotionally involved in the object/text. Kishkan and Bowering view the past from a combined optic and haptic perspective, and the present from an optic scan. Ironically, it is from the present that they maintain an objective distance; the past invites tactility and involvement.

The historical perspectives of Interior literature are also, almost without exception, revisionist. Arnold Davidson has assessed western Canadian fiction as performing "an ongoing questioning of gender and race," as "insisting on the need for other narratives than the male monologues of the traditional Western that are as straight and white as a Texas highway" (7-8). Although Davidson's study focuses on prairie fiction, his observation holds true for writing about Kamloops, whose geography and history arguably have as much in common with areas of the prairies as with the Pacific coast. Aboriginal and female characters in particular, often in multi-voiced narratives, people this work, and writers such as George Bowering, Shirley Sterling, and Theresa Kishkan are in many senses unwriting the linear, Eurocentric narrative from which the traditional Western is derived. These and other writers write women and minorities into the landscape and cityscape.

With its transient, marginalized characters, in its role as a subsidiary setting, and

208

from a historical (often nostalgic) perspective, the Kamloops of fiction is a postcolonial elsewhere. Despite its peripheral position, however, it is far from one-dimensional and certainly not inconsequential. In fact, the peripheral vision is typically a combination of haptic and optic. Precisely because of Kamloops' edge position, it becomes a place of possibility — of escape, refuge, and self-discovery.

Ethel Wilson's 1954 novel *Swamp Angel* sets a template that later novels would borrow. A female protagonist, in this case Maggie, defies the conventions of her time by escaping from a stifling marriage and the city of Vancouver. Although it proves uncharacteristic in not taking the distant past as its era, the novel does depict the Interior in a nostalgic way and evokes history through, for example, the information Maggie learns on the bus trip out about the importation of camels into the Interior during the gold rush. The hilltop perspective of the townsite, echoed in subsequent work, similarly evokes history:

> As you drive up the winding ascent into the hills behind Kamloops … the passenger looks down, and still further down, and toward the beautiful confluence of the North Thompson and South Thompson Rivers which are fluid monuments to the great explorer's name. At Kamloops, the rivers join and become the Thompson River which flows westward between the sagebrush hills, spreads into a wide lake, narrows, and races on. The first Fort Kamloops was built at the vantage ground of the junction of the rivers. Kamloops is the Meeting of the Waters. (85)

Here, in a vision that synthesizes the haptic and the optic, settler history is explicitly mentioned; the Shuswap derivation of the town's name is implicit. The coyote Maggie

spots would prove to dot the literary landscape in future writing about the area: "Look! There is a coyote and his coat is the same dun color as the hill on which he runs purposefully about his business. He vanishes" (205). Kamloops is represented as a place of possibility in which history and geography meld.

After the initial detailed description, however, Kamloops is rather sketchily drawn — a distant optic outline. The small city is not Maggie's refuge from the larger city; that distinction is held by the rural — the fictional Three Loon Lake, 25 miles from the town. Kamloops is the source of provisions for the resort where she works and lives and provisional in the sense that it is where she winters — a temporary home. In his afterword to the novel, George Bowering notes, "Most of Wilson's stories are about the problem of home" (215). Significantly, Maggie begins her journey without a clear destination; if she finds a home by the novel's end, that home is where she finds herself (happens to end up and comes into her own) — near Kamloops. *Swamp Angel* depicts Kamloops as an intermediate locale, a place of refuge from the big city but without the powers of refuge of the rural — important as a stepping stone rather than possessing an identity in its own right.

Both Gail Anderson-Dargatz's *A Recipe for Bees* (1998) and Theresa Kishkan's *Sisters of Grass* (2000) present a more clearly delineated place, and the two works have much in common: historical novels set in the southern Interior, they, like *Swamp Angel*, focalize female protagonists who transcend or at least resist the prescribed social roles of their respective times. In addition, the past vision of Kamloops in each case is grand and exoticized: in an optic/haptic fusion, the journey from rural to urban is delineated, the city provides escape and growth, and the representation is infused with nostalgia (even dream and vision). Each novelist also eschews

Figure 3. Silver Grill Café, Victoria Street. Kamloops Museum and Archives 6587.

what writer Zsuzsi Gartner has called the "hermetically sealed" (qtd. in Ratsoy "Mediations" 33) approach to fiction by imbuing her respective work with varying degrees of historical references and site specificity. Furthermore, memory (sometimes multi-layered) is the prism through which the city is evoked.

At the core of the appeal of both *A Recipe for Bees* and Anderson-Dargatz's first novel, *The Cure for Death by Lightning*, is the author's magic realism. Her rural settings, sites of detailed drudgery and hardship, call to mind such literary antecedents as Susannah Moodie and Sinclair Ross. However, Anderson-Dargatz superimposes onto that template a romantic style that incorporates the supernatural, the gothic, and the magical. Ultimately, like Bowering, Kishkan, and most others who have written about the area, Anderson-Dargatz eschews

realism. I am reminded of an interview I conducted with BC playwright Joan MacLeod in which she deemed the province's "exotic … almost surreal" landscape "a great excuse for heightened language" (423).

A romantic, if not surreal, layer pervades the representations of Kamloops in *A Recipe for Bees*. A third-person narrator recounts the life of Augusta Olsen, who in the novel's present time is in retirement on Vancouver Island. In the years following World War II, living with her timid farmer husband and his tyrannical, miserly father, Augusta had a decidedly restrictive life that became progressively more limited until she took matters into her own hands and journeyed from the Shuswap farm to Kamloops for employment. Even the act of driving to Kamloops in a borrowed car "freed her so," she recalls (126).

Augusta's employment, although it provided her with a measure of psychological

Figure 4. Kamloops, Grand Pacific Hotel. BC Archives F-03633.

and financial independence, is peripheral in her recollection; the romance she encountered in the city is focal. The affair is primarily staged in three cityscapes: a café, the streets, and a hotel. The café (long represented as a hallmark of the small-town Canadian community by such writers as Alice Munro and Margaret Laurence) assumes romantic, even mythical proportions through the prism of rural reminiscence. Although Anderson-Dargatz notes parenthetically that Augusta later learned the locals dubbed the Silver Grill "The Swill," the farm woman recollects a place of wonderment, the domain of office women "dressed beautifully ... sophisticated" (135).

By establishing a hierarchy within the café, Anderson-Dargatz both amplifies Augusta's alienation and sets the scene for her rescue from that alienation. Sitting alone at a table during a busy lunchtime, Augusta is forced by a waitress to break the pattern of gender segregation by joining the men at the counter. Her visible upset at the coarse language of the men spurs an older man with "a jangle of medals that hung over his heart" to act as her knight in shining armor (136). Anderson-Dargatz employs the metaphor of dance to describe their initial conversation, and a seduction in which Augusta takes the lead is played out in the unlikely setting.

The courtship ritual unfolds against the backdrop of the romanticized city. On the city streets, with their "steady clamour" (238), the two take in a matinee on a sultry summer day, Joe behaving "as a Victorian gentleman might have" (143). The staginess of memory is underscored when Augusta recalls, "She was a movie star; he was her leading man" (145). The Kamloops Plaza Hotel, unremarkable in her memory as the location of her honeymoon, becomes, as the site of their tryst, exotic, even erotic, and romance and intrigue are amplified when she learns that Joe, too, is married. The Silver Grill is a setting to which Augusta returns long after the inevitable termination of the affair. Here Joy, the product of the relationship, asks for the truth about her paternity, but is denied it. Joe is told about Joy the following day, and Augusta later reads Joe's obituary, from which she learns that Joe had not been a soldier, but was merely acting as one. Thus, the dramatic interlude ends with the air of unreality that distinguishes the Kamloops narrative from the larger one intact. The relationship is depicted as one very much suspended in time — a world apart from the drudgeries of Augusta's "reality" — but very much in place, a place that allows Augusta freedom and makes her more able to cope with those drudgeries. The surface details of time are present, but the fairy tale-like style of the city passages — and Kamloops is very much a city here — takes the section out of time and imbues it with the qualities of dream/fantasy. The vision of the small city, peripheral to the larger narrative, fuses the haptic and the optic. George Bowering notes, "The spatial equivalent of history is geography" ("Vancouver" 127). Here the geography of cityscape is in the foreground for the more adventurous part of the double life of Augusta; the temporal aspects are a faded template on which to detail that city.

The beginning and ending years of the last century prove equally productive eras for construction of a city that is very much in place/space *and* time in *Sisters of Grass*. From letters, photographs, a concert program, a buckskin jacket, a newspaper clipping, and a length of thin, hollow bone, Nicola Valley museum curator Anna reconstructs the life of a mixed-blood ranch girl, Margaret. Kishkan's bifurcated narrative serves to examine both the allure and futility of the process

of writing memory and history, as well as to provide a stark contrast between past and present. Her style has much in common with that of such writers as Rudy Wiebe and George Bowering, a nuanced example, perhaps, of what Linda Hutcheon calls "historiographic metafiction — fiction that is intensely, self-reflexively art, but is also grounded in historical, social, and political realities" (13).

Although Kishkan's is a more reflective approach than Anderson-Dargatz's, here again the Kamloops of history is an exotic city. Riding her horse on the grasslands of the Nicola Valley, Margaret anticipates a trip to Kamloops for its cultural allure: a concert by Madame Albani at the Opera House and a stay in the Grand Pacific Hotel, site of the first running water in the area. The backdrop of the capture of Bill Miner (subsequent to the train robbery at Ducks), whom Margaret and her family encounter en route to Kamloops, serves to further the aura of authenticity and to begin a minor subplot that echoes an overriding theme: the discrepancy between newspaper accounts of the capture and her own perceptions of it. From a haptic/optic perspective, the topography of the 12-hour journey is detailed — as is that topography's own history — in the form of the 1879 murder of John Ussher by the McLean gang (and thus the two crimes that have been so frequently represented in historical and fictional writing are connected). Kishkan's comparison of the landscape to "a coiled burden basket of split root" (69) further embeds the larger history in the land, a history of the Thompson-Okanagan heritage of Margaret, whose grandmother is an expert basket maker. The first glimpse of Kamloops is as "a city vibrant with life," and the view from the balcony in the family's quarters in the Grand Pacific Hotel is of "a lively scene below" (73).

The Kamloops of *Sisters of Grass* is represented as something more complex than a site of escape; coming of age and synthesis occur here. The description of Margaret's dress and demeanour at the concert is reminiscent of a debutante's coming out, and it is here that the protagonist is permitted her first taste of champagne and her first pair of trousers. The cultural experience results in another rite of passage: the city is the nexus for the integration of her British and Aboriginal ethnicities. Margaret experiences European culture through the concert and is enthralled by a shop window displaying the photographs of Mary Spencer's studio, an experience that leads her to her eventual vocation as photographer of First Nations people.

Although Kishkan's historical Kamloops acts in some respects as a binary opposite to the surrounding ranchland that is Margaret's home, the writer's approach is more integrative than purely oppositional. Intrusions of the natural environment are presented (the "sounds of the morning" include "a rooster, even in the city") (75), and amidst the exotic wedding photographs in the window is a single representation of a Chinese camp that "captured lives lived in squalor and despair" (79). This photograph is the catalyst for an artistic and social awakening in the seventeen-year-old: "She hadn't known that photographs could do more than provide a picture, but this one seemed to speak a language whose vocabulary she could almost understand" (79).

Memories of the Kamloops visit are recounted: to her grandmother, to her lover, and in her memory before sleep. The visit is a milestone: "She had the map and now needed to learn to read its legend" (168). Although a return the following autumn cannot live up to the memory (only a few leaves remain on the tree outside her window, "so shady and green in May" (195), and Spencer's studio is closed), the historical narrative of the city maintains a romantic, inflated cast.

Kishkan's vision of historic Kamloops remains tactile and penetrative — haptic — in combination with optic.

In contradistinction to the nostalgic tone of the historic narrative are Anna's present musings. Kishkan's narrator defines the present of the 1990s by absences: there are no horses, no sounds of human voices or printing presses spewing out reports of concerts or bank robbers. Even the natural landscape is viewed through an optic eye: "the river, the golden hills rising from the town's western reach — are flattened somehow"(89). Aridity and mortality link past to present: "dust, yes, descendent certainly from the dust that settled as Margaret rode" (89). The interaction of human with natural landscape and the connection of successive generations who occupy the same landscape — the focus of the primary setting of the novel — are thus reasserted with this image of a modern, deflated city.

Both Anderson-Dargatz and Kishkan represent more detailed, even embellished, visions of Kamloops than does Wilson. Like Wilson, they employ the small city for purposes of contrast — as an elsewhere — but their images are more developed; Kamloops has a distinct entity, rather than functioning as a sketchy intermediary. In addition, both *A Recipe for Bees* and *Sisters of Grass* ground that identity in the distant past viewed both optically and haptically.

The recent past (the 1980s) is introduced from a reduced, optic perspective in Elizabeth Haynes' 1999 short story "Meeting of the Waters." (The title does double duty: both Kananaskis and Kamloops — the respective beginning and end of her journey — derive from Aboriginal words meaning meeting of the waters.) Protagonist Barb has escaped Kamloops for Calgary, but finds she cannot leave the past behind so handily. Here, memory reconstructs teenagehood: an unconsummated first love acts as a metaphor for Barb's unresolved issues in the town she cannot leave behind. The movement in Haynes' story is opposite to that in the works of Anderson-Dargatz and Kishkan: rather than the place from which the protagonist returns home, Kamloops is the hometown to which the protagonist must temporarily return. However, Kamloops' "place" in the story is once again as a spatial Other — this time, optic, static, and diminished. Barb is disdainful ("'Well, I was sure glad to leave Kamloops,' she says, 'hardly ever go back'" [83]) as she recalls logging accidents, a smoky pulp mill, drive-in movies, truck stops, and dusty shops on Lorne Street, and associates the town's present with early marriages and dead-end jobs. In the present, and in contrast to the large city, natural images dominate; barbed wire, long grasses, and "heavy bodies of cows" (96) signify the return to the former home. When the journey back from Calgary ends, the perspective shifts to haptic: Barb arrives at a meadow "where a path falls down to the river" as she "breathes in the familiar, ponderosa pine and sage. So strong it hurts" (97). Here, arrival at home is painful, and home is rural, if decidedly unromantic; but the completion of the journey to Kamloops is a hardship necessary to self-discovery/consummation.

Shirley Sterling's 1992 novel, *My Name is Seepeetza*, written for a young adult audience and based on the Salish writer's own experiences as a student of the Kamloops Indian Residential School in the late 1950s and early 1960s, similarly minimizes the city, as yet another female protagonist is on a threshold (this time of adolescence). The narrative, which takes the form of a one-year diary written by a twelve-year-old mixed-blood girl, is prefaced by maps which focalize the relational perspective that dominates the text: the first is of the Joyaska Ranch, Seepeetza's home, and the second is of the school

grounds. The city of Kamloops, renamed Kalamak City (a transparent disguise, given that the book's cover features a photograph of the Kamloops Indian Residential School), is a thin line of eight boxes to the south of the river. What loom large, in the maps and the narrative, are the outdoors of the ranch and the interior setting of the residential school.

Here, as in Tonia Funk's work, *Amnesiac*, one of the first pieces selected for *The Homeless Mind* exhibit (Garrett-Petts and Lawrence 179-194), it is necessary for the viewer to adopt a "dual perspective, a kind of double vision" to look simultaneously "across the hills and down at the lakes" (17). This same dual perspective is embodied in much of the writing about Kamloops. The written entries set in the school are infused with memories of the ranch, and the ranch settings themselves are replete with scenes of joyous interactions with family and nature. In distinct contrast, the school scenes are claustrophobic and imprisoning, so much so that the very act of writing is a defiance of authority and thus it is done in secrecy. The novel ends with Seepeetza's acceptance, at the end of a summer at home, of the inevitability, even advisability, of a return to the Kamloops Indian Residential School and the preservation of her record of the previous year in the symbols of her Native culture — a buckskin cover with bead fireweed flowers.

Sterling's Kamloops, like Haynes', is a spatial Other in a negative sense, yet it is a setting which it is necessary for the protagonist to encounter in her quest for selfhood. Although it is on the margins of Sterling's map, the city is central to Seepeetza's acknowledgement of both parts of her heritage and recognition of the reality that some sort of compromise between the two cultures is possible.

George Bowering's *Caprice* (1987) is the only novel in which Kamloops is the primary setting. Once again, however, the protagonist is from elsewhere, and the setting defines itself through its relationship with the rural area surrounding it. From the city's first mention, it is defined by negation: "Kamloops was not Tombstone (14); Kamloops was not Dodge" (15) and Bowering reiterates his anti-Western approach through further contrast ("This is not Kansas."[174]) and repeated references to the Canada-U.S. border. In Kamloops, arguments do not culminate in shootings, and there is little call for cattle theft.

Conversely, Bowering's Kamloops of 1889 typifies the western Canadian small city and stands in contrast to the eastern Canadian small city. It is an ethnically and socially diverse place; Britain, China, Italy, the U.S. and other countries are represented in its small population, and although it is part of "a wide land that didn't seem to be in that much of a hurry," a sleepy town, "the main drag was generally characterized by movement, riders riding out of town, drinkers crashing in and out of doors, harassed children trying not to keep up with their shopping ranch folks" (11). Once again, a café (this time the Canadian) is a site of community activity, as are the Nicola Hotel and Gert's Whore House. Bowering provides close-ups of the townsite's geography, such as the CPR tracks running through the middle of the main street, and culture, especially newspaper articles. As a service centre for the region, the city is a place of vitality, a vitality accentuated by Bowering's haptic/optic perspective. Nonetheless, "even in the middle of its social life the frontier could be lonely" (207). The reader is reminded of the panorama — Kamloops' place in the larger geography — and how that geography has shaped its narratives: "The entire sweep of the great Interior Plateau is fearsome in its beauty ... no single person's story could amount to much in comparison. No human being could walk or ride under that immense blue sky and remain a humanist. A human being in this place will have direct evidence of his relative insignificance" (198). Clearly, geography has primacy over civilization in this metafictional comment.

Still, the historical touchstones that infuse much of the literature about the area are very much in evidence here. Bowering makes mention of the McLean gang (the subject of his next novel) early in this work and alludes to it later. Mock stagecoach holdups serve both to further his anti-Western plot and make sly reference to Bill Miner's train robbery. The novel acknowledges E. Pauline Johnson's several public performances in Kamloops, through a parody of the poet as Emily Peachtree Guano. Furthermore, the folly of colonial transplantation is conveyed through the tale of the camels that were transported here unsuccessfully, and through a satiric depiction of the coyote hunt, an adaptation of the English foxhunt.

In addition to being an anti-Western, *Caprice* is also an anti-realist novel, and an anti-European-settler work. Not surprisingly, then, First Nations culture infuses the work, both in the presence of two Indians who act as a Greek Chorus in their running commentary on the action, and in the form of Coyote, who infuses the structure of the anti-totalizing narrative: "We have many Coyote stories, but we do not have the story on Coyote" (92). From the dedication to Manuel Louie and Windy Bone through to the feast at the novel's end, Bowering displays an acute consciousness of First Nations origins and a recognition of the fact that, as Douglas Cole writes, "Culturally and imaginatively, the native people of British Columbia have been the most significant local contributors to the world's culture" (76).

215

Bowering deploys the conventional Western revenge plot in order to subvert it: Caprice is the "bullgirl" coming from the east (Quebec) to avenge the death of her brother at the hands of an American outlaw. Against the pleading of her schoolteacher boyfriend, she travels both sides of the medicine line in her quest for justice. The climax turns into an anti-climax, as Peace, Order, and Good Government win the day over blood retribution, and the happy ending is mitigated by the absence of the romantic completion of marriage and Caprice's departure, as, in a conflation of the optic/emotionally distant and haptic/personal: "She rode eastward through the west that was becoming nearly as narrow as her trail" (266). Caprice must vanish from the vanishing West, but, like all mythological characters, she has left her mark on the town, as it has left its mark on her. As the culminating feast organized by the Kamloops community indicates, Caprice does find herself, and a sense of community, in the dusty town.

"Basically headquarters for men and ammunition and other supplies" is Bowering's unadorned summation of Kamloops in his 1994 novel, *Shoot!*. Also the site of area bureaucracy, it is to the McLean gang "the town they hated" (146). Bowering again writes the anti-Western: Ussher is "a special constable without a gun" (13) in charge of a jail that, as Charlie McLean puts it, is "a sorry cow's arsehole of a jail" that "don't keep us in much at all" (32). Like Wilson, Bowering provides a top-down, double-vision perspective of the town (through the eyes of John Palmer, the stealing of whose horse precipitates two eventual murders): "There was ice on both rivers, and wagon tracks crossed the thin snow on top of the ice. On the slope leading down into Kamloops there were hoof prints and pawprints. It was the coldest winter anyone could remember. … Kamloops wasn't much of a place in those days but it was the biggest place around" (82). *Shoot!*, like *Caprice*, depicts Kamloops as an accident of geography.

Bowering also interjects the present into his historical novel, largely through straightforward delineation of location or simple description: "In the Kamloops museum there's a display including pistols about Bill Miner the train robber. He was an American who snuck into Canadian history with a gun in his hand. People dont want to know about the McLeans. They werent Americans. They werent white people and they werent Indians. They might as well have been dead all along" (59). And this description of Ussher's grave is striking in its simplicity and detail: "At Kamloops the bones lie under rectangles of grass, differing patchwork colours joined, some lower than others, one stone in the grass. The other stones are gathered in a corner of the park, the 'Pioneer Cemetery, 1876-1900'…. The park is bordered with elms and pines. It faces the river. Behind it is the biggest bottle recycling warehouse in the city" (117). The present of the city, from the hindsight of a history it has neglected, is flattened. Like Kishkan, Bowering reserves the optic scan and close-up perspective for his depictions of the present.

Bowering also explicitly connects the McLeans to the camels. Again, the folly of the camel venture is emphasized ("Some bright bozo in the British empire got the idea of importing camels…"), but the focus is on the connection: "the Wild McLeans knew what it was like to be a camel in cattle country" (144-145). Bowering fashions the boys as "the best camel riders in the western hemisphere" (145), who ride their camels to town on a Sunday morning rampage that causes a minor stir and culminates in the boys racing out of town and letting "their improbable animals go free" (147). The difference, of course, is that the camels were imported; in many senses, the boys were exported. Their environment was made unnatural by colonization and, as mixed-bloods, they became misfits.

Kamloops itself, with its Shuswap-derived name, is a misfit. Bowering has the member of the provincial parliament questioning its name and thereby its identity and advocating a name change: "What kind of name was Kamloops? People back east were going to know the most important stop on the Main Line. They would laugh at a name like Kamloops. What the hell did Kamloops mean, anyway?" (285). Here, the town, as a hybrid of Aboriginal and British, emblematizes the McLean gang; from the point of view of officialdom, both are outsiders.

*Shoot!*, like *Sisters of Grass,* provides an historic panorama as it fuses optic and haptic perspectives. Bowering's Kamloops is at a crossroads: the gold rush is ending, and the residential schools and the railroad are coming in. Even more than the other works, this is a novel about the effects of imperialism. Not only is it an anti-Western novel, but it deconstructs Canadian myths of nation building. The railway is being built while the boys are in jail and "dynamiters blasted their way through the Province ... small Chinese men were falling down the faces of granite cliffs" (285). As James Hoffman notes, "British Columbia's small cities provide salient sites for narrative critiques of colonization" (217).

Significantly, the beginning and ending action of *Shoot!* occurs outside of town (at Monte Creek), for the murders themselves occurred in the ranchland surrounding Kamloops, and the trials and imprisonment and executions took place in New Westminster. Kamloops, thus, is at once central and peripheral, a bothersome necessity and a place of identification, misfit and representative. In this sense and because of its interior location and medial size, Kamloops is possibly an intensified illustration of its

province, which was, as geographer Daniel Clayton reminds us, "premised on the jarring and unnerving juxtaposition of different cultures in manufactured spaces that restructured local conceptions of the alien and the familiar in highly unequal ways ..." (81). Because of its specific nature as a small city, distant (and therefore distinct) from large centres and dependent for its existence and identity on the rural landscape that surrounds (and in a literary sense sometimes engulfs) it, Kamloops has had an exceptionally fluid identity in writing. The city is at once edge and centre, hinterland and cosmopolitan in setting. Above all, however, it is a literary elsewhere. Typically, characters are in transit — just visiting or passing through. Significantly, though, the marginalized characters that populate the literature about Kamloops, accidentally or otherwise, find some measure of self-identification in the place. Thereby, Kamloops achieves its literary identity.

As Laurie Ricou and Robert Kroetsch note, the space Canadian literature devotes to the small city is disproportionately small; however, such places, whatever their proximity to the rural or the urban (and I suggest that the relational location of the small city is inevitably critical to its literary identity), proffer the writer of fiction sites which represent at once the intersection of the rural and the urban and something quite distinct from either one. As Rob Shields asserts, marginalized places "expose the relativity of the entrenched, universalizing values of the centre, and expose the relativism of cultural identities" (277). The small city's very mediality and peripherality predispose it to flexible representation — and to unique ways of seeing. The "double vision" requisite to the viewer of the visual works Garrett-Petts and Lawrence examine is also called for from readers of literary representations of Kamloops. Perhaps by its very nature as a qualified urban place on the edges of the rural, Kamloops (both past and present), although mined only infrequently, offers great possibility as a subject of prose fiction.

## Works Cited

Anderson-Dargatz, Gail. *A Recipe for Bees*. Toronto: Knopf, 1998.

Atwood, Margaret. *The Edible Woman*. Toronto: McClelland & Stewart, 1989.

Bowering, George. *Caprice*. Toronto: Penguin Books, 1988.

——. *Shoot!* Toronto: Key Porter Books, 1994.

——. "Vancouver as Postmodern Poetry." *Vancouver: Representing the Postmodern City*. Ed. Paul Delany. Vancouver: Arsenal Pulp Press, 1994.

Cheadle, Walter B. *Cheadle's Journal: Being the Account of the First Journey Across Canada Undertaken for Pleasure Only by Dr. Cheadle and Lord Milton, 1862-1863*. Toronto: Baxter Publishing. 1931.

Clayton, Daniel. "Absence, Memory, and Geography." *BC Studies* 132 (Winter 2001/2): 65-79.

Cole, Douglas. "The Intellectual and Imaginative Development of British Columbia." *Journal of Canadian Studies* 24:3 (Fall 1989): 70-79.

Davidson, Arnold E. *Coyote Country: Fictions of the Canadian West*. Durham, NC: Duke UP, 1994.

Gandelman, Claude. *Reading Pictures, Viewing Texts*. Bloomington, IN: Indiana UP, 1991.

Garrett-Petts, W.F., and Donald Lawrence. "Vernacular Landscapes II: Relocating the Homeless Mind." *The Small Cities Book: On the Cultural Future of Small Cities*. Ed. W.F. Garrett-Petts. Vancouver: New Star Books, 2004. 167-178.

Haynes, Elizabeth. *Speak Mandarin Not Dialect*. Saskatoon: Thistledown Press, 1999.

Hoffman, James. "Political Theatre in a Small City: The Staging of the Laurier Memorial in Kamloops." *The Small Cities Book: On the Cultural Future of Small Cities*. Ed. W.F. Garrett-Petts. Vancouver: New Star Books, 2004. 285-301.

Hutcheon, Linda. *Narcissistic Narrative: The Metafictional Paradox*. New York: Methuen, 1984.

Jeffrey, David L. "Biblical Hermeneutic and Family History in Contemporary Canadian Fiction: Wiebe and Laurence." *Mosaic* 11.3 (Spring 1978): 86-98.

Kishkan, Theresa. *Sisters of Grass*. Fredericton: Goose Lane Editions, 2000.

Kroetsch, Robert, and Laurie Ricou. "Making a Grass of Yourself: Small Cities Up Close." Canadian Studies Day Lecture. The University College of the Cariboo. 31 January 2002.

Perry, Adele. "Presence, Absence, and the Writing of BC History." *BC Studies* 132 (Winter 2001/2): 57-63.

Ratsoy, Ginny. "Mediations: Vocations and Fiction: A Review Essay of Zsuzsi Gartner's *All the Anxious Girls on Earth*." *Essays on Canadian Writing* 72 (Winter 2000): 85-92.

——. and James Hoffman, eds. "Domesticating Social Issues: Joan MacLeod and *The Hope Slide*." *Playing the Pacific Province: An Anthology of British Columbia Plays, 1967-2000*. Toronto: Playwrights Canada Press, 2001.

Riegl, Alois. *Historical Grammar of the Visual Arts*. Boston: MIT Press, 2004.

Shields, Rob. *Places on the Margin: Alternative Geographies of Modernity*. London: Routledge, 1991.

Sterling, Shirley. *My Name is Seepeetza*. Toronto: Douglas & McIntyre, 1992.

van Herk, Aritha. *No Fixed Address: An Amorous Journey*. Red Deer: Red Deer College Press, 1998.

Wilson, Ethel. *Swamp Angel*. Toronto: McClelland & Stewart, 1990.

## Selected Annotated Bibliography

(Prepared by Ginny Ratsoy and Sherry Bennett)

### Fiction

Anderson-Dargatz, Gail. *The Cure for Death by Lightning*. Toronto: Vintage, 1997.
Anderson-Dargatz's first novel, very much entrenched in the landscape of the Turtle Valley, east of Kamloops, pays scant attention to the city itself, apart from a mention as a service centre.

MacPherson, Andrea. *When She was Electric*. Vancouver: Polestar, 2003.
Although Kamloops is outside of this narrative, set on the edges of Merritt, the novel invites comparison with the novels of both Theresa Kishkan and Gail Anderson-Dargatz. The female protagonists emerge in similar ways from striking, haunting (and somewhat haunted) landscapes — Western Gothic, perhaps?

## Non-Fiction

Lane, Red. *Letters from Geeksville: Red Lane to George Bowering 1960-64.* Prince George: Caledonia Writing Series, 1976.

From Vancouver, Vernon, and Kamloops, poet Red Lane wrote to Bowering intermittently in the four years before his premature death from a brain tumour. The first entry ends with this descriptive declaration: "For the record: If anyone in the future wishes to collect my letters this one was written on Aug. 24 1960 at 452 Battle St. Kamloops, a water hole in the great interior desert of British Columbia, Canada." Anecdotes feature, with some frequency, the Plaza Hotel beer parlour and colourful drunks at 452 Battle Street.

Rhenisch, Harold. *Tom Thomson's Shack.* Vancouver: New Star Books, 2000.

Although Rhenisch's examination of the contrasts between urban and rural Canadian life focuses on Toronto and the Interior of British Columbia's farms and hamlets, Kamloops does receive mention (usually unflattering) on occasion.

## Anthologies

Murphy, P.J., George Nicholas, and Marianne Ignace, eds. *Coyote U: Stories and Teachings from the Secwepemc Education Institute.* Penticton: Theytus Books, 1999.

These poems, stories, and personal and journalistic essays penned by students, academics, and professional writers emanate from several university courses and were compiled to mark the tenth anniversary of the Institute's partnership with Simon Fraser University. Black-and-white photos and such historical documents as "The Laurier Memorial," (see James Hoffman, "Political Theatre in a Small City: The Staging of the Laurier Memorial in Kamloops") add an important dimension to the collection.

## Legends

Tomlin, Barbara, ed. *Coyote as the Sun and Other Stories.* Kamloops: Secwepemc Cultural Education Society, 1993.

This is a collection of stories passed down orally "about the world just after it grew," at the time of the Shuswaps' "first ancestors: beings who had the characteristics of both people and animals" when the world "was not quite ready for the Shuswap people." Illustrations are by David Seymour. Some stories are adaptations of James Alexander Teit's work.

## Poetry

Bose, Chris. *Dangerous Ideologies: A Book of Psalms for the Faithless and Lost.* Kamloops: Pagan Publishing, 1999.

Bose's collection includes such works as "Sarcos," which hauntingly depicts the confluence of the North and South Thompson rivers as viewed at twilight.

———. *Works in Progress.* Kamloops: Pagan Publishing, 1998.

Bose explores such well-known Kamloops locales as Peterson Creek in "A tight knot."

Gottfriedson, Garry. *Glass Tepee.* Saskatoon: Thistledown Press, 2002.

The rural and urban frequently meet in this collection. Gottfriedson depicts the reserve and local landscape and cityscape in such works as "Naked Paths," "Kamloopa Powwow," "Dry," "Reservation Dogs," and "I'm Just Another Indian to You."

Lane, Patrick. *Poems, New and Selected.* Toronto: Oxford UP, 1978.

Amidst poems set in other Interior of BC locations (as well as South America and Mexico) are "Newspaper Walls," "From the Hot Hills," and "The Trace of Being" (dedicated to Brian Fawcett). Once again, the imported camels and the McLean boys receive mention; the action takes place in the surrounding countryside; and Kamloops is (barely) present as a service centre.

Miles, Ron. *These People.* Madeira Park, BC: Harbour Publishing, 1984.

The title poem is an acknowledgement of those who lie dead in the neglected Kamloops cemetery, where "the Chinese carried their dead to a secret acre beyond the town." In the concluding poem, "Kamloops, Late July," the aridity of the landscape acts as a metaphor for human isolation.

Puhallo, Mike. *Meadow Muffins: Cowboy Rhymes & Other B.S.* Surrey: Hancock House, 1999.

Puhallo makes use of the Kamloops landscape in such poems as "Ode to McQueen Creek."

———. *Can't Stop Rhyming on the Range.* Surrey: Hancock House, 1997.

In this collection of cowboy poetry, Puhallo includes a selection entitled "The Wild McLeans," which retraces the steps of the Kamloops outlaws prior to their rampage of 1879.

———. *Still Rhyming on the Range.* Surrey: Hancock House, 1996.

Included here is "One Shot McLean," a poem featuring the McLean boys and their lesser-known nephew, Cliff McLean.

Turner, Jacqueline. *Into the Fold*. Toronto: ECW Press, 2000.
The first of two sections in Turner's collection is a 70-page journey through the Thompson region (with brief detours to Salt Spring Island, Field, Vernon, and Vancouver). The poems are at once deeply personal and erotic and firmly embedded in geography. Here again, Kamloops, in contrast to such places as Chase, Sorrento, and Savona, is constructed as primarily urban, the site of industry and services.

Wreggitt, Andrew. *Riding to Nicola Country*. Madeira Park, BC: Harbour Publishing, 1981.
The McLean brothers are the subject of a suite of poems that occupies almost one-third of Wreggitt's 39-page book. This section provides a compact reminder of the peripheral role of Kamloops in the events surrounding the McLeans: both times the town is named, it is merely to give context to the rural location.

## Periodicals

Hofmann, Karen, ed. "Postcards from Kamloops," *Green Stone Mountain Review* 1:1 (2003).
The inaugural edition of this review features poems written by The Green Stone Mountain Writers' Collective, a disaffected group of nine poets, including Pete Smith, Patsy Alford, and Hofmann herself. As the title suggests, the poems are often linked by setting to Kamloops and the surrounding region, and present a broad vision: contemporary and historical, natural and social, rural and urban.

## Play Scripts

Downey, Brian, and David Edgington, Margo Kane, David McLeod, Cyndi Mellon, Janet Michael, Lloyd Nicholson, David Ross, Teri Snelgrove, Lenard Stanga, and Meredith Bain Woodward. *Boris Karloff Slept Here*. Unpublished script. 1984.
*Boris Karloff Slept Here* is very much in keeping with the collective creation as examined in Alan Filewod's *Collective Encounters: Documentary Theatre in English Canada*: it is community based, populist, and a response to a perceived need to define local culture. The play, which opens with a Native story about pre-contact not unlike that which begins George Bowering's *Shoot!*, also provides a panorama of post-contact Kamloops history, with excerpts from Hudson's Bay factors' journals, glimpses of Chiefs Nicola and Tranquille, references to the McLean gang, and extensive satirizing of the British settlers.

Weir, Ian. *Flyin' Phil*. Unpublished script. 1992.
This play provides an interesting, witty glimpse into the social and political climate of Kamloops through the prism of the life of Phil Gaglardi, former Socred cabinet minister and Kamloops mayor.

Weir, Ian, with Judi Weir. *The McLean Boys*. Unpublished script. 1995.
Like Bowering's, Weir's Kamloops is the antithesis of the American frontier, a place where, as his character Johnny Ussher puts it, "You didn't get much crime. … So being the constable pretty much boiled down to travelling around the district, making sure everything was nice and dull, just the way we liked it." Also like Bowering, Weir connects the McLean gang to the imported camels.

# Children, Museum, Children's Museum

## Elisabeth Duckworth

In 1998, the Kamloops Museum and Archives staff and board were restless for new direction, new vision, and a renewed purpose. The Kamloops Art Gallery had recently relocated from the building, leaving the museum with 7,000 sq. ft. of additional space. The prospect of incorporating the new space into existing museum functions provided the incentive for a complete reconfiguration of the physical and philosophical organization.

Other cultural organizations within Kamloops had recently received significant public funds to upgrade their facilities, which in turn provided the necessary initiative to nudge those organizations onto the next level in their operations. The local newspaper editor, later mayor, acknowledged, "It's now the Museum's turn." Indeed it was. Undeniably, the Museum's permanent exhibits were old and tired. The staff was caught in old roles and older job descriptions that were not reflective of its personal growth or the public's growth in expectations.

In 1999, the board and staff, through provincial and municipal funding, hired museum consultants AldrichPears Associates to help direct the process of evaluation and change. Community advisers, museum users, and interested participants were invited to join staff and board in the consulting process. Questions surfaced that were basic to the internal functioning of the Kamloops Museum as well as to its relation to the regional community. What was unique about the Kamloops Museum and its collection? Who did it really serve and how? What other related groups in the community should it serve and how? How could the representation, quality, and use of the collection be improved (AldrichPears 8)?

The consulting and visioning process took up much of 1999. During that period, a number of vision statements emerged. These ranged from the very broad ("Be an attractive, friendly, accessible location and environment"; "Reach out to the public") to the specific ("Feature live presentations"; "Offer large-format film experience") (AldrichPears 11-13).

One of the most exciting ideas, and one which was unanimously agreed upon, was the concept of a children's museum for Kamloops. This unanimity was surprising considering very few of the people present had any idea whatsoever what a children's museum was or what it might look like. Even the consultants' report was vague, for it described the children's museum as "a special place for children ... [an] informal, playful learning environment ... that appeals to children at a special time in their development" (AldrichPears 12).

It was shortly after this period, in 2000,

that the Kamloops Art Gallery (KAG), The University College of the Cariboo (UCC), and eight community partners were the successful applicants for a federal Community-University Research Alliances (CURA) grant. As one of the community partners, the Kamloops Museum was excited by the prospect of pursuing and developing the children's museum concept in partnership with the CURA and UCC. The museum allied itself with UCC's Department of Early Childhood Education. Discussions immediately began between museum staff and UCC.

The first step in the discussions was to ensure that all members of the working group had an equal or similar understanding of the children's museum concept. What was true of the community advisory group also held true for the working group. Only one member had ever stepped inside a children's museum. The remainder had vague notions, at best. To rectify this situation, two field trips were organized, one to several American children's museums and the second to Nova Scotia, where there are a number of museums with strong children's museum components and extensive children's programming.

In October 2001, two members of the working group visited several museums in Chicago, St. Louis, and Indianapolis. The third member of the working group had visited the same museums and several more the

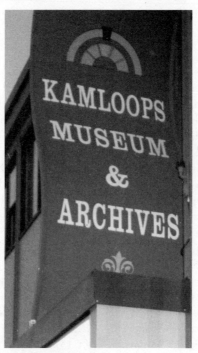

Figure 1. The Kamloops Museum and Archives Building. Photo by Bonnie Yourk.

previous year. The museums were a combination of children's, natural history, and traditional museums. They proved to be a surprise and, for the most part, a disappointment. There was no shortage of money or size or glitz. The popular Chicago Children's Museum was packed with children, noise, colour, and light. Was it a family fun centre? Absolutely. Was it a museum? No, at least not as we defined the word "museum." We wandered from floor to floor and exhibit to exhibit. We looked for examples of engaged learning, of interaction between adults and children, of worthwhile opportunities to learn about self and place. What we saw were loud, rambunctious children racing carelessly from exhibit to exhibit, followed by exhausted and bored parents.

The Peggy Notebaert Nature Museum was a welcome exception. There we found creative and exciting exhibits that required exploration, discussion, and sharing. Adults were not only necessary, but also integral and welcome partners in the learning experience. Yet, we still had no sense of place. This museum, as well as the Chicago Children's Museum, could be relocated to any city in North America with no change or loss in value.

The Magic House, St. Louis Children's Museum, presented another problem. It, too, was rich in creative, hands-on exhibits. The exhibits demanded co-operation between adult and child, and there were many examples of dialogue between children and adults and between child and child. Although the exhibit subject matters were engaging and even fascinating, there was no requirement for deeper learning. An experiment in gravity demonstrated the reality of gravity, but did not carry the principle further into practical applications. Children were not asked to consider the ramifications of gravity, how we could and do use gravity, its effect on shape, density, and size, etc. It was not long until we tired of moving from experiment to experiment. We got the picture, but there were no avenues for personal learning.

The Chicago Field Museum was an extraordinary place with an extraordinary reputation — a traditional museum at its best. Our purpose in visiting this institution was to see how successfully a traditional museum is able to integrate children's learning components into existing exhibits and galleries. The printed guide to the museum marked any child-friendly exhibits with an "open hand" symbol, an indication of hands-on activities. We concentrated our tour on these exhibits.

It was clear that a concerted effort had been made to incorporate hands-on elements and child-friendly learning stations in as many exhibits as possible. This often meant

Figure 2. This engaging exhibit at the City Museum in St. Louis, Missouri, involves several types of looms, baskets of ribbon and yarn, and an invitation to "Weave with a Friend." Photo by Helen MacDonald-Carlson.

something as simple as adding text at a lower level or setting up a corner table with books and paper. The additions were unobtrusive and harmless. Visitors with no children would hardly notice them. Parents and grandparents, however, would be delighted and relieved to find something to entertain the children while the parents enjoyed the rest of the exhibits. The quality and subject matter of the exhibits were such as to enthrall children in their own right.

One large gallery was geared specifically for children. Animal and sea-life specimens were arranged in room after room, each divided by a specific theme: "Reproduction"; "Meat Eaters"; "Saltwater Fish,"etc. There was an overwhelming array of visuals, videos, audio, text, specimens, and hands-on tables. The intentions were good, the volume of work Herculean, and the quantity of specimens and activities enormous. Strangely, the exhibit was burdened with having and being too much of a good thing. It was difficult for any substantial or sustained learning to take place. Fortunately, most of us will not find our institutions encumbered with a similar excess of money, staff, time, and artefacts.

The City Museum in St. Louis was a feast of delightful surprises. It was the child of some very creative artists who combined an interest in the fantastic with a love of the heritage and architecture of St. Louis. We were entranced, we were entertained, and we were inspired. The number and level of interactive programs and hands-on opportunities was truly impressive. Most of the ideas were very simple and inexpensive; they could be incorporated into any museum. There was a table and workbench where children and adults sat side-by-side creating clay bowls or dolls. Simple looms accommodated weaving. A blank wall was available for uninhibited painting. A puppet theatre with costumes sat ready in a corner. A glass blower, a potter, and a wood carver demonstrated their crafts and had their works available for sale on the spot. It was a lively and vibrant place where one could spend a joyful afternoon. It was not a traditional museum by any means, so the traditional expectations of a museum were not met. But the experience was still a good one.

A travelling exhibit from Reggio Emilia, Italy, was in St. Louis during our stay. Reggio Emilia is world-renowned for its preschool programs and its thoughtful approach to educating children. This particular exhibit was not for children but about children. It was a singularly moving experience to progress through the exhibit physically as well as intellectually and emotionally. It brought back the wonderment, joy and thoughtfulness of the observer's own childhood. We discerned and interpreted the success of any children's exhibits that we saw thereafter in light of the lessons and inspiration received from this simple yet profound exhibit.

The final museum of note on this tour was the Children's Museum of Indianapolis. Here we found the most successful example of a children's museum. In many ways, the Indianapolis Museum was a "traditional" museum. However, unlike the Field Museum in Chicago, the Indianapolis Museum did

not append child-friendly add-ons to preexisting exhibits. This museum did more to respect the intelligence and ability of children to learn in a dignified and deeper manner than the plastic clatter and artificial excitement of some other children's museums.

The Children's Museum of Indianapolis epitomized our vision for the Kamloops Museum: to incorporate seamlessly child and adult learning throughout the museum. Rather than limit children to a distinct area in the museum, child and adult alike could share the entire museum. This sharing could happen through exhibit design and through programs, text, and personnel. Small touches like a child's chair, a stool to stand on, and worksheets to share with an adult, a child's perspective in exhibitry, and opportunities for immediate hands-on learning signal to children and families alike the museum's desire to include everyone equally.

The children's museums we saw on this trip helped crystallize for us what a children's museum could and should be. The main area of disappointment was the lack of truly educational value in so many of the exhibits and activities. Interaction between child and exhibit was reduced to pushing buttons and lifting tabs, none of which challenged or interested the children. So many of the children's museums were simply fun centres. The word "museum" implied a quality of learning and experience that did not exist. Where a traditional museum sought to incorporate a children's space within the existing museum, it was painfully obvious that the addition was a superficial afterthought despite the significant money that may have been poured into it. There was a notable failure to acknowledge or incorporate the unique, local identity into most all the exhibits.

The following spring, in 2002, we undertook the second field trip, to Nova Scotia. There were no exclusively children's museums on this trip. Instead, we chose museums that featured strong children's programming. In the city of Halifax, the most exciting museum we saw was the Natural History Museum. Here was a happy blend of traditional and new, adult and child, scholarly learning and playful amusement. We saw complete families enjoying their visit with equal enthusiasm. Children were provoked with genuine curiosity to ask complex questions. Parents learned and discovered with their children, and together they found answers from which further questing could lead.

The Natural History Museum met many of our criteria for a successful children's museum. This was true, not only of the Halifax instiution, but also of most natural history museums we saw. The very nature of the subject seems to encourage spontaneous interplay between children and adults. Historic sites enjoy the same success. Somehow, the traditional museum must learn to translate the opportunities for impulsive and lively learning that participants find in natural history museums into its own structure.

The DesBrisay Museum in Bridgewater featured a room for temporary exhibits. On the day we visited, the room was filled with spirited drawings and paintings by local school children. There was little text, few explanations, and no photographs of the children at work. We were the only two people in the room. Yet the room was filled with the presence of children. There was energy and a real sense that this was a living, vital place. The exhibit itself cost the museum nothing more than a few hours of time. But for the visitor, it did more than anything to infuse the museum with relevancy and life.

Nova Scotia is blessed with a strong provincial education program for museums. Museums must maintain a rigorous standard of operation. In exchange, museums have access to a fully supported network of educational materials and expertise. Any museum that wishes to establish even the most basic relationship between itself and all levels of the community can do so ably and professionally by means of the provincial education program. It is an enviable asset that ensures both a minimum standard of museum excellence and a high level of local and regional learning opportunities.

The positive emphasis on museums and heritage within the province was reflected in the quality of the museums we visited.

Figure 3. This exhibit at the Museum of Natural History in Halifax, Nova Scotia, captures the interest of both children and adults. In addition to the wall-mounted displays about marine life, there is a table with the skeleton of a large marine animal. While the spine is fixed to the table sculpture, the ribs are loose, each fitting into its own individually sculpted niche. When the ribs are removed, the exhibit becomes a large puzzle as adults and children rebuild the skeleton by placing each rib in the appropriate location. Photo by Helen MacDonald-Carlson.

Figure 4. During April and May 2002, the temporary exhibit room at the DesBrisay Museum in Bridgewater, Nova Scotia, featured Celebrations 2002 – drawings, paintings, and three-dimensional artwork by local elementary school children. Photo by Helen MacDonald-Carlson.

The majority of the museums in Nova Scotia were small institutions in small towns. In the little time we could allot to each museum, we sensed pride in the unique history of their towns. However, few of these museums consciously included children in their exhibit planning. There was considerable reliance on the provincial education kits to fill programming needs. Programming outside museum walls and onto the streets of the town was limited to paper-brochure walking tours. Our questions about child-specific programming and exhibits provoked thought and considerable embarrassment. For the most part, it was a new, untried concept and one that the

museums were not yet ready to attempt.

A pivotal moment for the working group came just before our trip to Nova Scotia. We attended the Canadian Museums Association conference in Calgary, Alberta. A pre-conference workshop provided the opportunity for 30 museum educators to attend an all-day session at the Museum School at the Glenbow Museum. Only two of the members of the working group were able to attend, but a CURA research student who was heavily involved in developing potential education programs for the Kamloops Museum joined us.

The Museum School is normally the pre-

Figure 5. The classroom for the Museum School at the Glenbow Museum in Calgary, Alberta, offers a large, efficient space for groups of children from local schools. It is adjacent to the museum lobby, so the learning experiences of the children are highly visible. Photo by Helen MacDonald-Carlson.

serve of school district teachers. Teachers apply to the school, and a limited number are selected to go through a rigorous training session with Glenbow instructors. During this training session, teachers learn how to rethink, "re-view," and, ultimately, change their understanding of teaching and learning in a quite revolutionary way. Some teachers are forced to look back on a long career of teaching, only to realize that they have missed years of opportunity to teach and guide the young lives in their charge. During this training session, teachers are being prepared to bring their class to the museum and continue lessons for which the foundation was laid in the preceding months at school. Teachers learn how to release their students to learn in uninhibited and liberating ways with no set expectations or strict curriculum rules.

The inspiration of the Glenbow Museum School, coupled with the real experiences of the field trips, now had to be applied in practical, aggressive ways to the Kamloops Museum. Two things emerged from the field trips. First, because only two members of the working group had experienced the field trips together, we found that our understanding of what is a children's museum was moving in two directions. There was the original concept that the children's museum would be a distinct, physical space within the Kamloops Museum building. Now a second concept was emerging, which said that the existing museum with as-is exhibits could be used simultaneously as a children's museum. Programming, leadership, and learning through guidance would enable any exhibit or artefact to become accessible to children in wonderfully creative new ways.

A multitude of ideas for possible educational programs were put forward, each with endless possibilities for expansion and application. They needed no special place or made-to-order exhibits to work. The proposed programs were unique to Kamloops, yet could be adapted by communities anywhere in B.C. and Canada. Such versatile programming meant we could start implementing and testing ideas immediately at minimal cost. An actual children's museum "place" could be built concurrently, with each element learning from the other.

The decision was made to involve the Kamloops Museum in the "Community Mapping Project" and then to develop and test a unique museum program entitled "Jewellery for Buildings." Both projects encouraged an enlivened vision of what is a "museum." They demonstrated the unbroken interconnectedness of past, present, and future. The dusty corridors of the museum became the conduits for fresh and stimulating learning. Both projects were also the means for museum personnel to grow and stretch beyond a comfortable, simple definition of children's museum to include a philosophical approach to learning and conveying local, relevant information to museum users.

The children's museum program component has proceeded apace and will continue to do so. The entire museum staff has come to appreciate the power and potential of indepth learning possible within the museum context. Rather than taking away from the fundamental focus on the exhibit, as was feared, educational programming serves to heighten and reinforce the undeniable centrality of the exhibit, the artefacts, and the local history the exhibit seeks to portray.

The Kamloops Museum will still have a physical children's museum space, the "informal, playful learning environment" described by AldrichPears. It will form an unbroken link in a mighty chain of authentic, diverse, and multi-levelled learning in and about Kamloops.

## Works Cited

AldrichPears Associates. *Concept for the Future.* Report created for Kamloops Museum and Archives, Kamloops, 2000.

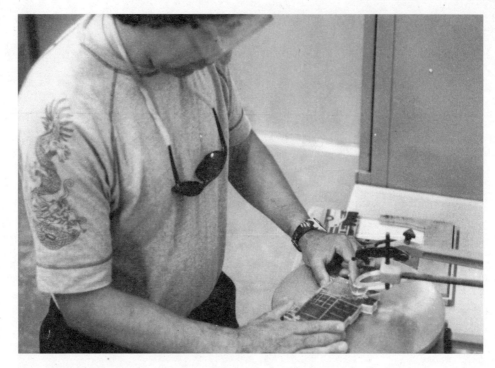

Children's Puzzle Project.

"The buildings selected for the project all make significant contributions to the story of Kamloops. Each building reveals a different aspect of Kamloops' unique character. We thought it was important to include the pit house because it is representative of the first form of architecture in Kamloops, one that dates back thousands of years. We also featured the Kamloops Indian Residential School because the establishment of these schools here in Kamloops, as well as across Canada, is telling of a dark chapter in the story of Kamloops. The old train station epitomizes the turn of the century and the flourishing western settlement. We hope the puzzles will be a good educational tool to help children learn about and remember the history of Kamloops.

"The dimensions of each of the puzzles reflect the characteristics of the buildings themselves: the narrow horizontal plane, for example, is appropriate for the residential school, while the vertical plane is suitable for the youth hostel. As a group we collaboratively chose maple-veneered plywood as the support material for the photographs for a few reasons. First, the wood is thick enough to provide some durability. The amount of handling these puzzles will experience calls for a material that is capable of withstanding heavy use. Second, the varnished wood provides a variety of tactile qualities, such as the smooth varnished bottom and the grainy edges. Finally, the maple has a unique visual appeal. The wood is light enough to provide a toned ground for the photographs and also allows the grain to remain vaguely visible."

Artists' Statement by Shima Iuchi, Sheri May, and David Tremblay.

# Children and the Small City

## Helen MacDonald-Carlson

A group of children from a local elementary school is gathered around a table, working quietly. The children are using paper, coloured pencils, and markers of varying sizes to draw a map or a picture of what they see as a significant place in the city. As they finish, they are asked to share the story of their maps with one of the adult observers. Many of the children draw maps of their yards or their neighbourhoods. Although Kamloops is a small city, it spreads out over many miles in all directions. For the most part, this group of children live in one of the outlying neighbourhoods. After one child shares her story map, which is about her neighbourhood, the adult asks: "Do you feel that your neighbourhood is part of the city, or its own separate community? Where do you spend most of your time? Is it in your neighbourhood or do you spend a lot of time in town?" The child responds: "I feel like [my neighbourhood] is part of Kamloops, but it's a lot different from other parts. [I spend time] in Kamloops, 'cause I play lots of soccer, so I have to go everywhere. We have to come in all the time."

This description of an affiliation with the city, one that ranges beyond the immediate neighbourhood, is reflected in all of the children's maps and stories. How do connections to particular spaces, such as a city, develop? Does life in a small city contribute to a stronger connection? Are there certain activi-ties that support these connections to partic-ular spaces in the community?

These questions were of great interest to our research team as we began the Children's Museum Project. The philosophy of the Kamloops Museum and Archives has always supported the importance of community through the preservation of local history and artefacts with significant local connection. We decided that this philosophy was impor-tant to maintain as we developed a vision for including more interactive programs and exhibits, but we were initially unsure what role the museum could take in supporting children's growing connections to their own community. With this initial commitment to foreground the museum's role as an educa-tional venue, we began to investigate how other museums included children in their programs and exhibits. One part of that investigation involved visits to both tradi-tional and children's museums, seeking mod-els to influence and guide our direction. As it happens, we were fortunate also to visit a travelling exhibit about the educational pro-grams in Reggio Emilia, Italy. Kamloops Museum Curator Elisabeth Duckworth described this exhibit as "a singularly moving experience" which served as a reminder of the wonderment, joy, and thoughtfulness of childhood (226). She stated that the exhibit inspired an image of the child that would help her interpret the success of any exhibits or programs for children.

Early childhood educators have been studying the innovative and thoughtful educational programs in Reggio Emilia for the last few decades. This small city in northern Italy operates more than 30 infant, toddler, and preschool programs. Their complex educational system involves a dynamic and collaborative process based on the philosophy that children are competent and capable of communicating through a wide variety of visual and verbal representations. The use of art materials is a fundamental aspect of these programs: an *atelierista*, or resident artist, works closely with the teachers and the children to prepare the environment and support the children's expression of ideas in a variety of art media. The children's work with the materials is observed and well documented by the teachers and the *atelierista*. Because of this, the children's ideas and thoughts are shared with others in a way that honours and respects their viewpoints. A visit to these beautiful schools demonstrates how this documentation process chronicles the learning that is taking place.

The schools are like galleries: the children's work is on exhibit, and their words form the didactics or story of their own learning. Most visitors to the programs have never seen preschool children's work of such high quality (Katz 11). But the teachers in Reggio Emilia are clear that these products are more than just artwork; these products represent the children's thinking and are a means of communicating ideas and thoughts that form their own unique perspective. The two travelling exhibits, one in Europe and one in North America, share thought-provoking examples of the children's work and demonstrate an educational philosophy that is more about learning than teaching. Although there are distinctive cultural and geographic differences, we found the Reggio example inspira-

tional, for the experience of the Italian children and educators provides us with two important philosophical premises to influence the development of children's programs and exhibits in a small city museum: that opportunities to visually represent ideas allow children to construct knowledge and communicate their thinking more completely; that educational programs for children are not just about teaching; that children already possess profound knowledge based on their own experiences.

Increasingly, museums are developing programs and exhibits with children in mind. Elisabeth Duckworth describes some examples of stand-alone children's museums, which are usually found in large cities. These museums have exhibits that allow for high interactivity by children of all ages and adhere to the philosophy that children must have active involvement with their environment in order to construct knowledge. They exemplify the principle that learning can be fun and entertaining. But, as Elisabeth observes, while these children's museums provide us with ideas about interactive exhibits, they have limitations (225).

Children's museum educators are aware that their exhibits are generally used by the public for entertainment rather than educational purposes (Gardner et al. 74). As part of Project Spectrum, Howard Gardner and Project Zero worked with the staff at the Children's Museum in Boston to develop an extensive educational experience for children based on the exhibits at the museum. Researchers, teachers from several preschools, and museum staff worked collaboratively to develop programs and learning experiences that would allow the children's museum to become an integral part of the school curriculum. Activities took place in the museum, and activity kits for teachers and parents were developed to provide additional experiences in the classroom and at home. All activities were developed using the principles of Gardner's multiple intelligences theory, which states that "all individuals possess, to varying degrees, [eight] areas of intellect that function relatively independently" (Gardner et al. 13). In addition, program developers wanted to ensure that the learning experiences would be resonant: the effect of encountering the same or similar experiences repeatedly over a period of time so that each encounter would "evoke and extend the previous ones" (Gardner et al. 75). Museum staff learned how to develop a more complete learning experience by combining their interactive exhibits with an educational program involving classroom teachers and parents. The Boston museum's director of education now uses the multiple intelligences theory to develop new programs and ensure that the existing exhibits and related activities are well balanced and varied (Gardner et al. 82).

Elisabeth Duckworth also outlines some examples of how traditional museums and galleries are developing children's educational programs to complement their exhibits. These museums have workshops and discovery kits for use by the children in the local community. The Glenbow Museum in Calgary has developed a program very similar to that described by Howard Gardner. Museum staff work with teachers to develop a week-long program for children at the museum. While there are no specially designed exhibits for children, the teachers and museum educators find innovative ways for the children to explore traditional, non-interactive exhibits. From an educational point of view, longer educational experiences such as this one allow children to explore a particular topic more deeply. Both Elisabeth and I felt this educational approach would be a wonderful addition to the Children's Museum Project, as either a separate compo-

nent or to complement future exhibits designed specifically for children.

In some of the small museums we visited, we found no evidence of exhibits or programs specifically for children. However, as Elisabeth observes in her description of a small museum in Bridgewater, Nova Scotia, the presence of an exhibit of children's artwork relayed a community's commitment to and enthusiasm for children (227). An exhibit such as this one, developed by the children themselves, is congruent with the philosophy of the schools in Reggio Emilia, where children's thoughts and experiences are routinely *made visible*.

Elisabeth describes the dilemma she and her staff faced as they unanimously embraced the concept of a children's museum for Kamloops: although it was an appealing idea, it was not easy to enact based on the vague commitment to develop "a special place for children" (223). Our visits to other museums, our research into educational programs for children, and our own observations of children at the Kamloops Museum and Archives provided us with information to begin to construct a more comprehensive, distinctive vision for the children's museum in Kamloops. The ongoing renovations throughout the entire museum over the last few years precluded the development of new physical exhibits in the immediate future. However, our exposure to the variety of programs for children in traditional museums inspired us to develop a series of educational programs. Like the preschools in Reggio Emilia, we decided to use artists to support the development of educational materials, and we developed a workshop format that could be used for a variety of topics about the city. At the same time, we listened — and are still listening —to children's own experiences with the city, collecting and preserving their maps and stories. Here, then, is an example of how children can study their own city, and of how we have honoured the children's own words, their impressions about growing up in a small city.

**Studying the City**

As we began to develop our ideas for educational programs and exhibits for children at the museum, we felt that it was important to provide opportunities for children to learn more about Kamloops and the local region. Since most of the exhibits and programs we observed while visiting other museums did not focus on the city, we looked for guidance from other sources. The Canadian Institute of Planners has developed a wide range of ideas to assist with teaching and learning about urban planning and community development (CIP 1). Their activity suggestions are short and discrete, although several activities can be combined or expanded into a longer educational experience. These suggestions provided us with some initial ideas, but we eventually chose a topic for our first workshop series based on our own observations of children at the museum.

During the first year of our research project, the Kamloops Museum and Archives had staged an exhibit entitled "Jewellery for Buildings." The exhibit was situated in an area undergoing renovations at the time. Developed by museum technician Cuyler Page, this short-term exhibit was a fine example of visible storage, allowing visitor access to a growing collection of artefacts, even though interpretive information had not yet been developed. With very little didactic information, this exhibit involved items — doors, windows, railings, doorknobs — from buildings in the local area. Observations of a short introductory workshop to this exhibit demonstrated strong interest in architecture by both children and the new museum educator, Tena Andersen. We felt this topic

would increase awareness of local heritage buildings, something many cities, including Kamloops, are fighting to preserve as new development initiatives threaten existing, older structures. We also speculated that the artistic perspective, which influences the educational programs in the schools in Reggio Emilia, would provide guidance in the development of activities and educational materials.

As already noted, the schools in Reggio Emilia use artists as an integral part of the teaching team. In one respect, the *atelierista* work as art educators, teaching the children about a wide variety of art media. The artists also provide a unique perspective, inspiring the children to use visual forms of representation to communicate their ideas. Under the artists' influence, the learning environment reflects not only an aesthetic sensibility, but also an educational element of such significance that the environment is considered to be another teacher in the room (Edwards et al. 177). The activities we were designing for our program on architecture would provide many opportunities for the children to create visual and verbal representations as part of active learning experiences. We also decided to use artists to support the development of educational materials with strong visual elements.

We invited a student artist, Donovan Pettigrew, to support our observation of the initial introduction to the "Jewellery for Buildings" exhibit. Donovan made architectural drawings of artefacts on display. He also developed two drawing activities allowing children to create some of their own "jewellery for buildings." As we developed educational materials for the longer program, Donovan's work formed the basis for an informational activity booklet. The development of this booklet also involved the expertise of another type of artist — graphic designer Howard Glossop. Howard used the raw materials — Donovan's drawings, text, and photographs of local buildings taken by student research assistant Jennifer Cotter — to create an attractive booklet, which encourages both visual and verbal literacy. The contribution of these artists has resulted in a locally developed product that celebrates Kamloops architecture while demonstrating both an aesthetic and educational sensibility.

Observations at the museum have long indicated that puzzles are a popular activity for children. Student artist Shima Iuchi accepted the challenge to produce a series of puzzles featuring local heritage buildings. Shima involved two other visual arts students — David Tremblay and Sheri May — to support the development of the puzzles. The three artists expanded the initial concept to include architecture representing various cultural groups associated with the historical development of Kamloops. While the puzzles could have been simple photos mounted onto cardboard, the look and feel of wood provided a more attractive alternative.

Through much trial and error, the artists eventually used liquid light to transfer the photos directly onto the wood. The result has created a wonderful look, one resembling old, sepia photographs. During the development phase of the puzzles, the artistic point of view often supported the educational goals. When cutting the puzzle pieces, Shima intuitively cut along the architectural features of the buildings. She felt this had a more artistic quality, but was worried that, for children, the puzzle pieces should be cut differently. However, cutting the puzzle to match the architectural features is a good educational strategy — additional visual and tactile reminders are, in effect, embedded in the shape of the individual pieces. In this respect, the artistic process of visual representation is sympathetic to children's desire to actively construct their own knowledge. This satisfying, collaborative experience with artists has resulted in educational materials that are interesting, innovative, and aesthetically pleasing.

This case study demonstrates a number of

## A Case Study: Jewellery for Buildings

On the first day of the "Jewellery for Buildings" pilot project, children from the school-age child care program at the Child Development Centre arrive at the museum. These five- through twelve-year-old children, and their educators, Tami Coolidge and Jennifer Cotter (who is also the student research assistant for the Children's Museum Project), will be participating in four two-hour workshop sessions. Throughout the four days, the children will explore architectural features on local buildings, and creatively express their own ideas through a variety of visual and verbal representations.[1]

Several times during the four-day workshop series, Museum Educator Tena Andersen shows children photos of local buildings. Together they identify some of the architectural features or "jewellery" on the buildings — windows, doors, mouldings, shingles, and brickwork.

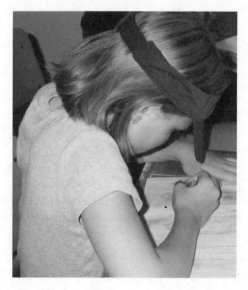

The children learn how to do rubbings as a means to replicate the texture of such ornamental features as doorknobs and key plates. On the field trip to local heritage buildings, the children will also use rubbings as a means to gather information about other textures, such as wood and brick. These rubbings will be used to add texture or "jewellery" to the three-dimensional buildings developed by the children later in the week.

These wooden puzzles of local buildings are used by the children throughout the week. This popular activity is enjoyed by all ages. The children decide for themselves if they want to make the puzzle easier by using the paper template, which allows them to match the shape of the puzzle pieces. We plan to add more information about the local buildings – name, location, date of construction, historical notes – to further enhance the educational value of the puzzles.

Prior to the field trip, children are introduced to a booklet with information about a variety of architectural elements on the buildings they will visit. The booklet also includes several activities that the children can complete over the next few days. One activity is a game to identify which building has the architectural element featured in the photograph.

The booklet also has two drawings that the children can complete by adding their own architectural elements.

During the field trip, the children visit several nearby heritage buildings. They use paper, pencils, and clipboards to draw architectural features of interest.

Drawing encourages close observation of the architectural elements. The complexity of the drawing varies depending upon each child's age level and interests. The children enjoy this activity; the field trip could be longer, or even repeated on another day, allowing visits to other heritage buildings. Photo by Cindy Piwowar.

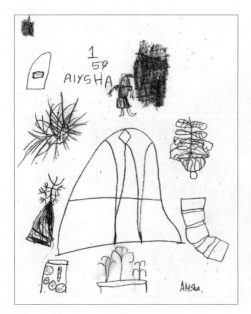

This drawing is by a six-year-old. She features many architectural elements of St. Andrews on the Square Church – a window, a light in the foyer, the steeple. She also draws the fountain and some of the plants in the adjacent park. Photo of original drawing by Al Fedorak.

This drawing of Stuart Wood School is by a nine-year-old boy. He has included the many multi-paned windows and the peaked roof entrance. Photo of original drawing by Al Fedorak.

During the field trip, the children use a Polaroid camera to record interesting architectural elements.

The children read the heritage plaques for historical information about the buildings. Photo by Cindy Piwowar.

239

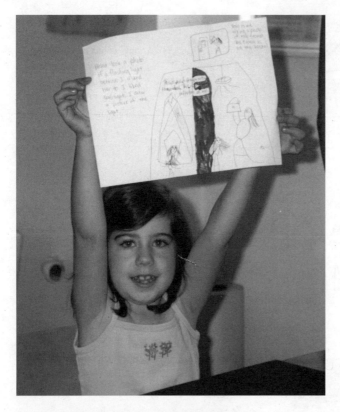

The day after the field trip, the children use visual and verbal representations to reflect upon the memorable aspects of the heritage buildings. This six-year-old girl uses drawings to represent the previous day's events, and an adult has just written down her description. She is now sharing her memories with the other children by reading aloud the story she dictated.

The children use the Polaroid photos to complete their drawings, and as physical memories of the architectural features they saw on the field trip.

240

For several days, the children develop architectural elements for their own three-dimensional models. They focus on roofing materials, textures, doors, and windows. The children are greatly influenced by what they have observed. Many children add a red door with a rounded top to their design, similar to the architectural artefact that is present in the room.

When their box sculptures are complete, the children write a story about their houses. Some children dictate their stories to an adult or an older child. The children are able to share their stories with the other children. They compile all their work – rubbings, drawings, stories, and photographs – into a journal.

key educational strategies for the development of future workshops about the city. The children had opportunities to use many visual elements to support the development of observation and representation skills. Photos of buildings and architectural features were an integral part of the educational materials — activity booklets, puzzles, interpretive signs, and overhead slides. Photos were also an aspect of the educational process — the Polaroid photos of architectural elements became visual references for the children's drawings. There were artefacts available in the room, which influenced the children when they were developing "jewellery" for their own buildings. Drawings helped identify certain architectural elements, and the children had many opportunities to draw visual representations of their own ideas. The children also had opportunities for verbal representations — writing and telling stories, conversations with peers and adults.

These educational strategies not only support children's varied interests and abilities (their "intelligences"), but they also provide children with learning choices. According to a study done by Deborah Perry, free-choice learning was among the most important variables determining successful learning from children's museum exhibits. The need to feel in control and confident about their environment, and an interpersonal need to communicate with others, emerged as other important factors in learning (qtd. in Falk and Dierking 85). The role of the adult educator is also significant, both as listener to the children's ideas and as documenter of the learning process in order to reflect the importance of the children's activities. Adults and older peers support children's learning through scaffolding — encouraging involvement with materials in slightly more complex and novel ways. The puzzles, designed to reflect the children's varying abilities, provided many

opportunities for the older children to assist the younger children.

An educational program such as "Jewellery for Buildings" is infinitely adaptable. We discovered that all ages enjoyed the activities with only minor adjustments. After observing the children sketching the historical buildings, an adult passerby remarked that she would like to take a program like this. The activities worked well together, but they can also be adjusted for shorter or longer programs. The educational materials, such as the booklet and the puzzles, were developed for the program, but they can both be used on their own. Although the presence of architectural artefacts supports the educational program, an exhibit at the museum is not a requirement. As a celebration of local heritage, "Jewellery for Buildings" embraces the city of Kamloops itself as its research venue.

**The Small City Experience**

A museum in a small city has an opportunity to do more than provide educational programs for children about the city. As Elisabeth Duckworth has observed, small city museums are finding interesting ways to collect, preserve, and exhibit children's visual and verbal representations as a celebration of the local community. This celebration of the local is certainly evident in the small city of Reggio Emilia. The children there know that people from all over the world come to view the learning environments and do short-term observations in the schools. This phenomenon prompted the schools to take on the monumental task of discovering and sharing the children's perceptions of their own city. The results of the children's thoughts and images have been compiled into the book *Reggio Tutta*. In Italian, Reggio tutta means, literally, "all Reggio," the name given by a three-year-old to her drawing, which appears on the cover. Mara Davoli, an *atelierista*, and

Gino Ferri, a teacher, explain that it was an enticing idea to ask the children to be the interpreters and narrators of their city, but it was not a simple undertaking: "The children's experience of the city is rooted in a complex web of references that are closely interconnected, where personal relationships and experiences give shape to understanding, stories, and evocations which are all permeated by a strong autobiographical connotation" (14).

*Reggio Tutta* contains many visual images of the children's perceptions of the city. Accompanying these images are the children's words and thoughts, showing what the children see as important to share about their city with visitors. There are obvious elements included in the children's impressions — the shape of the city, significant landmarks. In their own way, though, the children frame their references to these topics differently than adults might. For example, when describing the porticoes, an important architectural feature to protect residents from the intense mid-day heat, children said, "They made them to make the city beautiful;" and also, "because they hold up the houses, the windows, and the balconies, because the porticoes are underneath and the houses are on top" (Davoli and Ferri 48). To describe the circular structure of their walled city, one child commented, "In the city there are two beginnings, and in the middle, right in the middle, there's the end" (Davoli and Ferri 37). The children also try to describe the shape of Italy, explaining that a country such as Italy is bigger than the cities, such as Reggio, but that Italy is only one country on Earth. This leads one child to observe that, "the boundary is like smoke" (Davoli and Ferri 26-27). It was unique, insightful perspectives such as these that prompted Sergio Spaggiari, director of the Department of Education in Reggio Emilia, to say that this book "has the power of confounding many of the expectations we have as adults. We adults notice daily, in the Balkans, in Africa and in many other parts of the world, that drawing borders has become synonymous with massacres and violence. Ultimately, it is as if the world were saying to us: a border means bloodshed. Fortunately, the children, the utopian inhabitants of the future, surprise us and remind us that 'the boundary is like smoke'" (Davoli and Ferri 127). The children's observations are provocative; they provide a strong rationale for listening and communicating children's thoughts and ideas about places important to them.

At the same time that the Children's Museum Project is exploring ideas to support children's involvement with the city, another Community-University Research Alliances (CURA) research project, "Representing Kamloops," is asking adults to construct a communal story map detailing local attachment to personal landmarks: "These visual representations [in turn] form the 'pretext' for oral narratives, opportunities to tell the story or stories of belonging and alienation" (Dubinsky and Garrett-Petts 344). "Memory mapping [or story mapping] is one way to augment our linguistic understanding of personal experience," says researcher W.F. Garrett-Petts. "Moving from image to verbal allows us to know our subject differently, to explore and validate that which cannot be fully expressed in words" (Yourk and Garrett-Petts 16). The "Representing Kamloops Project" plans to use the visual representations, or maps, drawn by the adults and the verbal narratives, or stories, associated with the maps to develop a museum exhibit of local interest and significance.

Children are also interested in maps, and even very young children are capable of a wide range of environmental skills, including rudimentary mapping (Matthews 209).

"Here's my street and basically where I live. Barnhartvale. I put in horse corrals here because there's a field behind us – our house – and 'cause I really like horses, so that's why mainly I chose that area. This is Leanard Place. And these houses aren't exactly in the place that they're supposed to be, so my house should be around this one. I'm just guessing." Photo of original map by Al Fedorak.

Children as young as three years of age can be observed making maps — the room, the play yard, the city — and placing people they are close to on the map (MacDonald-Carlson 10). According to James M. Blaut, we know that "mapping behaviour is carried out by all individuals, of all ages in every culture: it is a natural ability, akin to language behaviour" (qtd. in Matthews 75). Children communicate their ideas and make sense of their everyday experiences through their play activities. Their natural attempts to make maps can provide insight about their relationships with particular spaces within the city. A sense of

place describes the relationship one has with a particular space, usually based upon an accumulation of experiences (Gieryn 481). Mapping activities explore children's perceptions of the city as well as their development of a sense of place.

Working with the Representing Kamloops Project, the Children's Museum Project has recently begun to collect and preserve the maps and stories of children in Kamloops. Eventually, the children's visual and verbal representations will form part of the large museum exhibit of community maps and stories. Based on our mapping experiences

"[I'm a] Snowboarder! There's the trees at Sun Peaks, so they got – like to mark off the trails – and then there's the brown mountains around Kamloops. I know that I'm going to have a fun day no matter what the conditions are. You know that you have to take Kamloops to go there, and then go to Heffley Creek, so that's why I put Heffley Creek right there. Kamloops is a fairly big city, I guess, I'd say. [The drive up is] pretty good, it's pretty scenic, too. When you start climbing up towards Sun Peaks, that's when it gets really nice. Lots of snow up by the mountains. I go up in the summer sometimes for biking. And then I go lots in the winter mostly." Photo of original map by Al Fedorak.

with school-age children so far, we have found that visual representations are an important vehicle for children to communicate their concepts and ideas about the city. They tend to focus on elements that have strong emotional connections — many of the maps are about homes or neighbourhoods. The children reflect upon special natural landmarks: "This is my maple tree and I drew my swing because, well, that's my special swing. And then, it has these branching off trees so it kind of looks like this wishbone thing and that's where I always climb up. That's where I always go after school and just read." The frequency of visual and verbal narratives about home and neighbourhood demonstrates a strong emotional connection for the children. Mapping activities with preschool children also demonstrate this strong connection to home. Young preschoolers

245

enjoy having a photo of their home available in the room, often using it as a reference in order to draw their own house onto their maps (MacDonald-Carlson 13).

The school-age children also drew maps and shared stories about favourite places to visit. These places were often associated with recreational or after-school activities: "I chose to do MacArthur Island because I go there all the time because I'm a rep soccer player and I always come here to play on the soccer fields, and I used to come to the ice rink all the time and I go to the golf course and stuff." As children move outside the neighbourhood, they are still dependent upon the adults who help them access other places within the community. Although often driven by adults, the children have a great awareness of how to get to these familiar places.

In *Lure of the Local,* Lucy Lippard describes community-based art projects that involve mapping with adults and teens. She writes that "Place history is most often recorded in maps. People from oral traditions carry detailed maps in their heads over years; the rest of us depend on outside sources" (75). Like people from oral traditions, the children seem to have internalized maps: "This is the road that I take my bus up every day to get to the college, and then these are the college residences. And this

This young boy has drawn four small maps or pictures to describe four significant locations related to BMX biking experiences, mostly shared with his dad. Once he is familiar with the sculptural map, he uses the marker to place a dot on the location of each of the four experiences.

is the Science Building where my mom and dad work. And if you keep going on the road, there's the Canada Games Pool, and I swim there every day. I like that I can get there without having to get my parents to come pick me up, and I like being able to take the bus there." This verbal narrative reflects not only the familiarity with a particular place, but the feelings associated with growing independence and an increase in responsibility.

A mapping activity such as this reveals several distinctive aspects of children's relationships to their city. The local geography has some natural features that provide a common frame of reference for residents. The children are asked to locate their hand-drawn maps on a sculptural map, which includes the main geographic landmarks — mountains, such as Mt. Peter and Mt. Paul, and both the North and South Thompson rivers. When viewing the sculptural map — which includes neither roads nor buildings — the children are initially disoriented. As soon as one of these landmarks is identified, though, the children find themselves quickly able to locate places of significant interest.

The growth and development of Kamloops has been heavily influenced by the geography of the area. Although the city has approximately 80,000 people, most of the population is concentrated in the long, narrow corridors of flat land adjacent to the North and South Thompson rivers, spreading out in several directions for many miles and limited in growth by the surrounding mountains. Neighbourhoods have also developed on the hillsides. Some of these neighbourhoods — Juniper Ridge, Rose Hill, Batchelor Heights — have limited access; size and growth are influenced by the steepness of the adjacent terrain. For most Kamloops residents, access to the nearby undeveloped, natural areas is a short walk or bike ride from their residences. Christopher Alexander and his colleagues at the Center for Environmental Structure believe this kind of balance between urban land and open countryside is an important consideration for the quality of life in urban environments. "People feel comfortable when they have access to the countryside, experience of open fields, and agriculture; access to wild plants and birds and animals. For this access, cities must have boundaries with the countryside near every point" (22). Our work with children confirms this thesis.

The geography of Kamloops has forced the urban landscape to stretch out into "long sinuous fingers" (Alexander 24), which extend into the natural landscape. This connection to the city's boundaries, or edges — grasslands, ranches, or wilderness parks — is evident in the visual and verbal narratives of the children. In some cases, the children's experiences of home include a relationship to natural areas almost in their backyards: "And this is my forest, well, the forest that's behind [my house] and we always go and walk my dog out there, and I'd always play in there. Every summer, a bear would walk through our yard and stuff." In other instances, their favourite place is a natural area within walking distance from their neighbourhood: "We walk there ["Kmart Beach" — a name given by local area residents to a secluded section of beach along the South Thompson River] because we both live in Valleyview and we just walk down and across the highway. There's this little pedestrian — it's like a pedestrian-controlled light. There's this rope swing that we always go on and sometimes we just lay there. It's really fun."

Like the artists who contributed to *The Homeless Mind* exhibition, the children "map their stories of the city at the margins of the urban landscape — often in surrounding neighbourhoods or satellite communities, in hidden places discovered through walking or hiking" (Garrett-Petts and Lawrence 169). Told from their own perspectives, the children's stories verify that this easy access to the natural environment provides the types of experiences that make their life in a small city *memorable*. Residents of neighbourhoods adjacent to natural landmarks associated with the edges of the city are likely to have a stronger emotional attachment to where they live (Gieryn 481). In their own way, the children have blurred the city boundaries, appropriating the adjacent natural landscape into their vision of the city. The children in Kamloops would seem to agree with the children in Reggio Emilia that "the boundary is like smoke" — an elusive, arbitrarily set division between, in this case, the city and the adjacent countryside.

These observations demonstrate how mapping experiences allow children to express their opinions about the city in an active way. The children in Reggio Emilia, Italy, would likely concur with the belief that visual representations are an important means of communication: "If you make a picture, they'll understand it for sure!" (Davoli and Ferri 16). Researchers involved in the community memory mapping project with adults have observed an "intertwining of place and self: sense of place anchors the sense of self, offers a way of disclosing the self, giving shape to 'where I'm from' and 'what I care about *here*'" (Garrett-Petts et al. 7). For the children, too, the mapping activities prompt the verbal narrative, emphasizing the connection between place and self.

Moreover, the children's visual and verbal narratives reflect a positive attitude. They show an enthusiasm and optimism about their experiences in the city, not unlike the children in Reggio Emilia. For children, even ordinary spaces can be places of wonder. Since many of their experiences are dependant upon the adults who care for them, children's optimistic views of their city are a factor of relationships: adults provide meaning to the experience and mediate the environment when necessary. Children's opinions and ideas need to be listened to, for listening ascribes importance to their feelings and the subject. It is the process of communicating these opinions and ideas that supports children's growing awareness of self in relation to home and community.

So what have we learned so far? As Elisabeth Duckworth points out, we have learned that there is no one right way to include children in a museum. Many large cities have developed separate children's museums devoted exclusively to highly engaging, interactive displays with little connection to local community. Given the population base, these cities can also support other museums that devote their activities to local issues of geography and history. Since small cities often have only one museum, one usually dedicated to local issues, adults and children must share the same resource. Small city museums find themselves in a position to experiment with a variety of ways to include children: children can have a separate space with exhibits designed specifically for them; children's exhibits can be integrated throughout the museum alongside adult exhibits; or educational programs can be developed espe-

cially for children. The decision regarding the best method to include children in a small city museum will be heavily influenced by resources and community support. Nevertheless, what seems clear is that small city museums should remain true to their roots: they should strive to draw upon vernacular experiences, to invest exhibits and programs with local significance. Crucial aspects of that vernacular experience are the voices and images of the community's children.

We have learned that the development of an emotional attachment to a particular space is a complex phenomenon. Educational programs such as "Jewellery for Buildings" provide wonderful educational experiences for children that will be memorable, and perhaps contribute to a growing connection to the city. However, connections to particular places cannot be taught or forced. It is possible that the very nature of a small city — with its close proximity to the natural environment and its sensitivity to boundaries — may support the development of a sense of place. In any event, the small city museum has an important role as a venue for the exploration and communication of children's perceptions about the community. Based on our experiences, it is obvious that children have a vital role in telling the story of the city.

## Acknowledgments

The Children's Museum Project would like to thank the 250 children, and the 55 teachers and parents who have participated in this research: St. Ann's Academy — Grades 3 and 4; Southshore Day Care Centre, Dallas Elementary — Grade 3; Boy's and Girl's Club South Sahali School Age Child Care; Marian Schilling Elementary — Grades 5 and 6/7; Kamloops Child Development Centre School Age Child Care, South Sahali Elementary — Grade 5/6.

## Note
1. Unless otherwise noted, all photos were taken by Helen MacDonald-Carlson.

## Works Cited

Alexander, Christopher, Sara Ishikawa, Murray Silverstein, et al. *A Pattern Language: Towns, Buildings, Construction.* New York: Oxford UP, 1977.

Canadian Institute of Planners (CIP). *A Kid's Guide to Building Great Communities: A Manual for Planners and Educators.* Ottawa: Canadian Institute of Planners. nd.

Davoli, Mara, and Gino Ferri, eds. *Reggio Tutta: A Guide to the City by the Children.* Reggio Emilia: Italy. Reggio Children srl, 2000.

Dubinsky, Lon, and W.F. Garrett-Petts. "'Working Well, Together': Arts-Based Research and the Cultural Future of Small Cities." *AI & Society* 16 (2002): 332-349.

Duckworth, Elisabeth. "Children, Museum, Children's Musuem." *The Small Cities Book: On the Cultural Future of Small Cities.* Ed. W.F. Garrett-Petts. Vancouver: New Star Books, 2004. 221-229.

Edwards, Carolyn, Lella Gandini, and George Forman. *The Hundred Languages of Children 2nd Edition.* Westport, CT: Ablex Publishing, 1998.

Falk, John H., and Lynn D. Dierking. *Learning from Museums: Visitor Experiences and the Making of Meaning.* Walnut Creek, CA: Alta Mira Press, 2000.

Gardner, Howard, David Henry Feldman, and Mara Krechevsky, eds. *Building on Children's Strengths: The Experience of Project Spectrum.* New York: Teacher's College Press, 1998.

Garrett-Petts, and Donald Lawrence. "Vernacular Landscapes II: Relocating the Homeless Mind." *The Small Cities Book: On the Cultural Future of Small Cities.* Ed. W.F. Garrett-Petts. Vancouver: New Star Books, 2004. 167-178.

Garrett-Petts, W.F., Donald Lawrence, and David MacLennen, eds. *The Homeless Mind: an Exploration Through Memory Mapping.* Kamloops: B.C. Cariboo Bookworks Press, 2003. 179-194.

Gieryn, Thomas F. "A Space for Place in Sociology." *Annual Review of Sociology* 26 (2000): 463-96.

Katz, Lillian. "Impressions of Reggio Emilia Preschools." *Young Children* 45.6 (1990): 11-12.

Lippard, Lucy. *The Lure of the Local: Senses of Place in a Multicentered Society.* New York: New Press, 1997.

MacDonald-Carlson, Helen. "Developing a Sense of Place: Exploring Ideas of Home and Community." *Canadian Children* 28.2 (2003): 10-16.

Matthews, Michael Hugh. *Making Sense of Place: Children's Understanding of Large-Scale Environments.* Hertfordshire, England: Harvester Wheatsheaf, 1992.

Yourk, Bonnie, W.F. Garrett-Petts, et al. "Representing Kamloops." Unpublished report prepared for the Social Sciences and Humanities Research Council of Canada. September, 2002.

# Part III

# Cultural Symbols
and Identities

# Naked Paths

## Garry Gottfriedson

you, silent sapphire love
perched
on wood at Riverside

calling Raven
to Crow Hop to the edge
of phantom lane below Paul Mountain

there, a willow full of tears
gave a refuge to Raven

later, delicate words softened
Raven's heart
& you kissed radiant black love

then, you invited the Sun
to weave shadows
along the naked path
home

Figure 1. The Two River Junction Dinner and Musical Revue cast performs *Tales From the Rails*. Photograph courtesy of Rocky Mountaineer Railtours.

# Upstaging History: Outlaws as Icons

## Sherry Bennett

Entering the Two River Junction Dinner and Musical Revue for the first time, visitors are greeted in the lobby by matrons dressed in early-20th-century costumes and by Bill Miner's glaring eyes staring out from a wanted poster that sits perched above the venue's guest book. While filing into the facility to be seated, guests can view a dozen photos of Kamloops cityscapes and scenes related to the notorious outlaw's capture and trial, all recorded a hundred years ago by Kamloops photographer Mary Spencer.

After enjoying a western-style buffet dinner, guests position their chairs to view a cast of five re-create Bill Miner's Kamloops escapades in a hilarious musical revue entitled *Tales From the Rails*. The cast consists of a svelte and crafty Bill Miner; his two bumbling accomplices (Tom and Harry); an over-confident, proud North West Mounted Police officer (Constable Bernie); and Mary Spencer, a dedicated *Kamloops Sentinel* reporter. The performance begins with dimmed lights, the sound of a train whistle echoing off in the distance, and a brief narration detailing Bill Miner's historical connection to Kamloops. The spotlight then shines in on Miner and his cohorts performing a comedic rendition of "The Miner Bunch," sung in harmony to *The Brady Bunch* theme song.

Spencer, in turn, calls upon audience members to provide her with information about the masked man who robbed the train, an exercise that mimics the game of Chinese whispers. We learn that, after deciding to hide out in Kamloops, Miner assumes the alias George Edwards and immediately finds himself a target of Mary Spencer's romantic affections. Throughout the production, Miner's bumbling sidekicks appear on stage in a number of disguises, ranging from a train conductor, Little Bo-peep, and a bar wench in pink satin. Cast members belt out old-time favourites, including "O' Susanna," and play a range of instruments, from the mandolin to the kazoo. At various moments the waiters join in the singing and dancing, taking their places on stage.

Bill Miner has been part of the Rocky Mountaineer Railtour's Kamloops entertainment promotion — *Two River Junction* — for five years, with a remarkable 190,000 visitors passing through its doors since the show's inception eight years ago (Venture Kamloops 35). What makes this production even more remarkable is that it has remained virtually invisible to locals. Most of the venue's patrons are international travellers, the majority travelling from the U.S., Australia, and Britain, with a handful of local residents showing up for each of the three performances the venue stages each week. As a vehicle for cultural tourism, the *Tales From the Rails* musical revue has, like events staged in other small BC communities, successfully embellished and promoted the story of the outlaw Bill Miner.

"Bill Miner" presents a prime example of manufactured heritage. The American-born Miner, whose only true affiliation to Kamloops is a botched train robbery and trial, has been moved across space and time to become established as a popular folk hero. In contrast, indigenous outlaws such as the McLean boys, three brothers born and raised in the Kamloops area, who killed two locals in the late 1870s, have gone largely ignored by the cultural tourism industry. Allen, Charlie, and Archie McLean, and their friend Alex Hare, seem rooted in local history but remain unattractive candidates for the kind of musical revue that the *faux* Miner enjoys. Why would an elderly train robber, who spent only a few weeks in Kamloops, so dominate the local heritage stage? How is it that historical figures such as the McLeans can virtually disappear for long periods from public view? What makes historical figures either eminently marketable or mere archival curiosities?

It is not unusual for Canadian cities to capitalize on, even exploit, or make up, local history. The western/outlaw theme — with

Figure 2. Bill Miner after his arrest for train robbery near Kamloops, 1906. Photograph courtesy of the Kamloops Museum and Archives (137).

Bill Miner as a central character — has also become an important means of promoting the consumption of place in Princeton during the late 1990s. The small BC town of 4,200 residents represents the place where Miner chose to settle down (to elude American law authorities), and thus is said to represent Miner's "most favourite" BC town. Similarly, Moose Jaw, Saskatchewan, has adopted American outlaw Al Capone into its local history as a means to propel a highly successful cultural tourism industry. Despite the fact that no historical records exist verifying Capone's visits to Moose Jaw, the city has been able to develop a thriving, multi-million-dollar tourism industry.

Examples of such promotion strategies abound. Tom Paradis notes that "scripted themes," the constructed images cities use for tourism promotion, provide insight into a community's sense of place. Well-chosen themes can draw communities together; ill-chosen themes can create inter-community conflict ("Top-Ten Reasons"). What I find interesting is the dynamic, highly social nature of "theming": how, as the community changes over time, new community associations and attachments are formed. What sets the Bill Miners and Al Capones apart is their seemingly incidental or tangential relationship to the communities they have come to represent.

I should note that, in and around

# Bill Miner

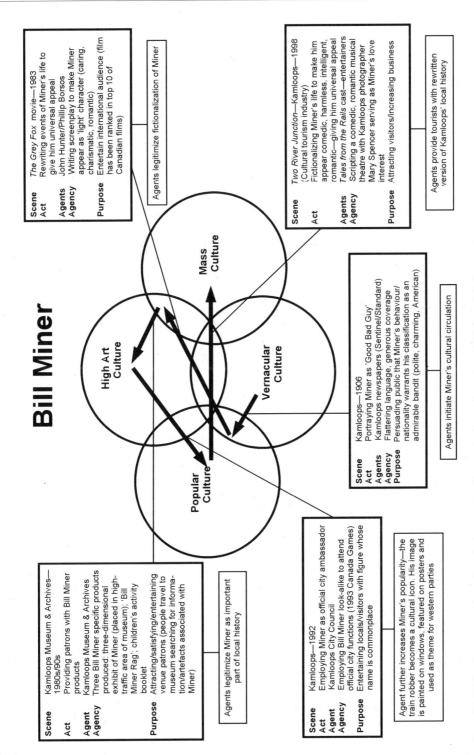

**Scene** *The Grey Fox* movie—1983
**Act** Rewriting events of Miner's life to give him universal appeal
**Agents** John Hunter/Phillip Borsos
**Agency** Writing screenplay to make Miner appear as 'light' character (caring, charismatic, romantic)
**Purpose** Entertain international audience (film has been ranked in top 10 of Canadian films)

Agents legitimize fictionalization of Miner

**Scene** *Two River Junction*—Kamloops—1998 (Cultural tourism industry)
**Act** Fictionalizing Miner's life to make him appear comedic, harmless, intelligent, romantic—giving him universal appeal
*Tales from the Rails* cast—entertainers
Scripting a comedic, romantic musical theatre with Kamloops photographer Mary Spencer serving as Miner's love interest
**Agents**
**Agency**
**Purpose** Attracting visitors/increasing business

Agents provide tourists with rewritten version of Kamloops local history

**Scene** Kamloops—1906
**Act** Portraying Miner as 'Good Bad Guy'
**Agents** Kamloops newspapers (Sentinel/Standard)
**Agency** Flattering language, generous coverage
**Purpose** Persuading public that Miner's behaviour/nationality warrants his classification as an admirable bandit (polite, charming, American)

Agents initiate Miner's cultural circulation

**Scene** Kamloops Museum & Archives—1980s/90s
**Act** Providing patrons with Bill Miner products
**Agent** Kamloops Museum & Archives
**Agency** Three Bill Miner specific products produced: three-dimensional exhibit of Miner (placed in high-traffic area of museum); 'Bill Miner Rag'; children's activity booklet
**Purpose** Attracting/satisfying/entertaining venue patrons (people travel to museum searching for information/artefacts associated with Miner)

Agents legitimize Miner as important part of local history

**Scene** Kamloops—1992
**Act** Employing Miner as official city ambassador
**Agent** Kamloops City Council
**Agency** Employing Bill Miner look-alike to attend official city functions (1993 Canada Games)
**Purpose** Entertaining locals/visitors with figure whose name is commonplace

Agent further increases Miner's popularity—the train robber becomes a cultural icon. His image is painted on windows, featured on posters and used as theme for western parties

Figure 3. Bill Miner's movement throughout the last century. Diagram by Sherry Bennett and W.F. Garrett-Petts.

Kamloops, the McLeans have not been entirely erased from popular culture; they have been referenced occasionally in song, theatre, and books. But their fame pales in comparison to Miner: Kamloopsians are evidently happy to rehearse an imported, theatrical version of local history. Kenneth Burke's theory of "dramatism" — which maintains that life is not *like* a drama; life is a drama (vx) — seems especially well suited to help explain this staging of local history. Burke encourages us to seek evidence of motives in the cultural dramas that both inform and represent our communities. He argues for a "pentad" of social focal points, five crucial elements central to all human drama:

Act: what takes place, in thought or deed;

Scene: the background of the act, the situation in which it occurs;

Agent: what person or kind of person performs the act;

Agency: what means or instruments he or she uses; and,

Purpose: why something is done. (xi)

Burke believes that narrative acts — including exhibitions, historical displays, formal histories, conversations, and musical revues — find their social motive in one or more of these five elements. In this chapter, I employ Burke's method to analyze textual and verbal representations of the outlaws in a specific rhetorical situation: the small city. What interests me here is less the actual events "performed" by the outlaws than the representations of those events. My intent is to explore the motives behind such historical representation and misrepresentation: to explore what is gained, and what is lost — and what it all says about the roles of cultural tourism and heritage in the small city.

Using Burke's methods, I will determine the nature of the scene, the construction of the agent as communicator, the act being performed, and the underlying community motives — especially in terms of the community's rationale for linking local heritage to place promotion. I begin with the premise that historical representations do not stand still. Reputations rise and fall as new information either comes to light or is reevaluated in the light of new values, new motives. The outlaw *actors* focused on here have experienced varying but significant movement over the past 125 years. To chart their historical movement we need to refine one of Burke's key categories: *scene*.

According to W.F. Garrett-Petts and Donald Lawrence, there are four principal cultural scenes: *vernacular culture*, involving representational strategies indigenous to the local; *popular culture*, involving highly conventional representational strategies, ones that link the local to the larger scene; *high culture*, involving the discourse of museums, academe, and heritage; and *mass culture*, involving promotional strategies that fictionalize and commodify local experience. Garrett-Petts and Lawrence, echoing Burke, speak of the flow of cultural exchange, reminding us that, "as Andy Warhol made clear, yesterday's soup can may become tomorrow's cultural icon" (19). Similarly, the iconic figures of history (including outlaws) "migrate and adjust to the shifting rhetorical situation of each cultural domain" (20). It is my contention that to gain cultural currency, to become a likely subject for cultural tourism or "theming," the objects of vernacular history need the validation of high or popular culture. The vernacular — which is rooted in the local — exists as a trace memory, as that which cannot be fully recovered or objectified without either an elaborate academic apparatus (scholarly writing, the

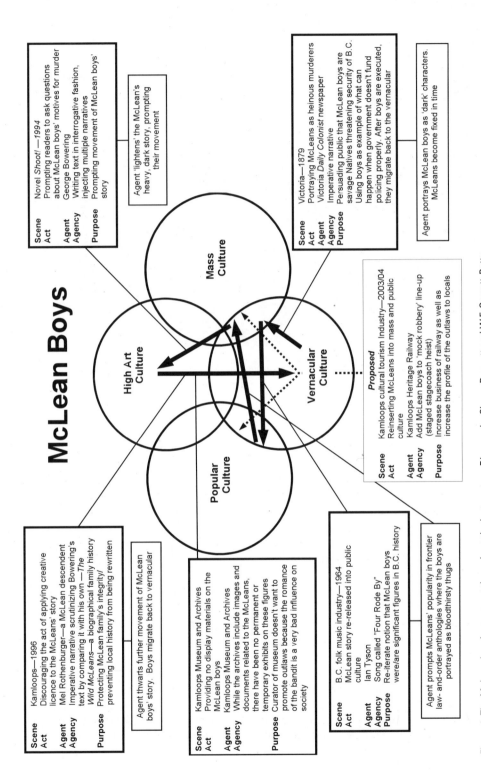

Figure 4. The McLean boys' movement throughout the last century. Diagram by Sherry Bennett and W.F. Garrett-Petts.

Figure 5. Miner, Dunn, and Colquhoun arriving at Kamloops, B.C. after being captured by North West Mounted Police on May 14, 1906. Miner sits in front with blanket wrapped over his body. Photograph courtesy of the Kamloops Museum and Archives, No. 881.

imprimatur of museum display, and so on) or a substitute narrative drawn from popular culture (from tall tales, legends, newspaper accounts, and the stereotypes promoted by mass market publications).[1]

## Bill Miner:
### An Historical Figure "Within Reach"

Miner jumped into Kamloops history books on a Canadian Pacific Railway (CPR) train headed west in 1906. Born Ezra Allan Miner in Vevay Township, Michigan, on December 27, 1846, Miner had been convicted of 17 assorted robberies, assumed 7 aliases, and spent 33 years behind the bars of San Quentin before setting foot on Canadian soil in October of 1903 (Bossenecker and Dugan 213-218). After robbing a CPR train at Mission Junction, BC, on September 10, 1904, Miner fled to the hills in the Princeton area, posing as "George Edwards" and using his gentlemanly prowess to woo locals into believing he was an American prospector who had come to Canada to strike it rich with gold. After spending two years in the Princeton/Aspen Grove area, he made his way to Kamloops with accomplices Shorty Dunn and Louis Colquhoun and proceeded to rob another CPR train on May 9, 1906, at Ducks (now called Monte Creek), a small community on the eastern outskirts of Kamloops ("Train Held Up"). Though Miner managed to escape with $7,000 in cash and gold dust and $300,000 in bonds from his Mission Junction heist (Bossenecker and Dugan 110), he was not so lucky in Kamloops: his second BC train robbery was a botched one, yielding him a paltry $15.50

and a bottle of liver pills ("Landed in Penitentiary"). Miner was apprehended by Provincial Constable Fernie and his posse at Douglas Lake, five days after his robbery, and was transported back to Kamloops, where he was tried and sentenced to life imprisonment in the BC Penitentiary. Miner escaped from BC's provincial gaol 14 months into his sentence, an escape alleged to have been orchestrated with the CPR (Bossenecker and Dugan 142-148). He worked his way down to Georgia, robbing trains along the way, eventually performing the state's first train robbery in February of 1911, being apprehended by Georgia officials shortly thereafter. After a few failed escapes from Milledgeville prison over the next two years, the elderly train robber died in the Georgia jail in 1913 at age 66. Over the years, the train robber's folklore status has increased exponentially, being celebrated in Georgia, Mission, Princeton, and Kamloops. Miner is currently referred to in Kamloops variously as the "gentleman bandit," "The Grey Fox," and the "Robin Hood of the North."

Figure 6. Allen McLean. BC Archives A-04956.

## The McLeans:
## Historical Figures "Too Close"
The McLeans drama was played out in 1879, when three McLean brothers (24-year-old Allen, 17-year-old Charlie, 15-year-old Archie) and their 17-year-old friend Alex

Hare began a crime spree in and around the Nicola Valley of BC's interior. Born to an Aboriginal mother, Sophia, and a Scottish Hudson's Bay Company trader, Donald McLean, the boys lost their father when he was shot dead in the Chilcotin War of 1864 ("News from the Chilcotin Expedition"). Classified as quarter-breeds, the McLean boys found themselves straddling two races and unwelcome members of both the Aboriginal and white communities. Allen, Charlie, and Archie McLean, and Alex Hare, started out on a horse stealing and robbing spree in the fall of 1879. They stole horses, saddles, liquor, and other property from local ranchers in the vicinity of Cache Creek, and were subsequently jailed for their thefts. Easily escaping from the flimsy, unsupervised Kamloops gaol (operating under the supervision of Constable John Tannatt Ussher), the boys fled to the hills of the Nicola Valley. Despite a $500 reward offered for the capture of the boys, few were able to track them down. On December 6, 1879, Nicola Valley rancher William Palmer ran into the McLeans on the trail and spotted them with his prize gelding. He pretended not to notice the horse and fled back to Kamloops, demanding that authorities do something to get his horse back. A few ranchers were sworn in as constables, and a posse was quickly assembled, consisting of Ussher,

Palmer, Amni Shumway, John McLeod, and Bill Roxborough. The posse met up with the McLean boys at their camp near Brigade Hill on the morning of December 8, 1879. It is alleged that the boys began shooting at posse members, and Constable Ussher, who allegedly left his gun in the holster on his horse, approached the boys and asked them to surrender. Upon reaching out to Alex Hare, Ussher was taken down to the ground, and it is alleged that Archie McLean approached Ussher and shot him point blank in the face. Ussher was reportedly finished off by Alex Hare's Bowie knife ("The Kamloops Outrage").

Both Palmer and McLeod were shot in the ensuing gun battle, one bullet penetrating Palmer's beard before entering and exiting the cheek of John McLeod. Palmer and McLeod returned to Kamloops, where a party was sent to retrieve Ussher's body, and a large posse prepared to apprehend the boys. The boys fled to find refuge, stopping at several ranchers' homes along the way to collect provisions and weapons. Shortly after killing Ussher, the boys ran into sheepherder James Kelly and killed him, it has been said, for "no apparent reason." The boys sought refuge in a log shack on the Douglas Lake Reserve, where they spent two days surrounded by ranchers and officials. The boys surrendered on December 13 and were subsequently shipped down to New Westminster to the jail, where they would be housed until their hearing.

The McLeans and Alex Hare were tried twice; the first trial, carried out in March of 1880, was declared a mistrial because official permission had not been granted to try the boys outside of Kamloops. The boys were found guilty at their second trial in November of 1880 and were hanged at a mass execution on January 31, 1881, in New Westminster.

## Newspaper Stories as Agency

Both Bill Miner and the McLean boys acted out some part of their dramas in Kamloops. The McLean boys achieved notoriety during the time of their misdeeds, with the Victoria *Daily Colonist* providing daily coverage of the boys' capture, trials, and execution. Hundreds of inches of newspaper copy were devoted to the McLeans's story. From the moment the news of Ussher's and Kelly's deaths became public, the boys were cast, first, as local murderers (vernacular figures), and later as savage animals (generic or popular clichés) posing a threat to the safety of the entire province of British Columbia, as illustrated in Hudson's Bay Company factor John Tait's monthly communication to his supervisor in Victoria: "I presume you have heard of the exciting time we had here last week and a part of this, which was all caused by the most worthless set of vagabonds that ever lived in any country, i.e., Allen McLean,

Figure 7. Charlie McLean. BC Archives A-01458.

Charles McLean, Archie McLean and Alexander Hare. … It is most fortunate … the murderers were arrested as soon as they were. A few days more and many more would have been butchered and property destroyed" (102).

The scene (Tait's correspondence), the agent (Tait), and the act (portraying the McLeans as murderers, butchers, and the most worthless set of vagabonds that ever lived) set the tone for how British Columbians would receive the boys. Tait's account of the boys would be mirrored in several BC newspapers, the *Daily Colonist* publishing such headlines as "Robbery and Murder — Fearful State of Things at Kamloops" ("Double Murder and Arson"). The *Daily Colonist* showcased the McLean boys and Alex Hare as poignant examples of what can go wrong when a government loses sight of its responsibility to provide resources for a colony's security: "The removal of the police force from the Interior, in pursuance of a pennywise and pound-foolish policy, has created a feeling of contempt for the law in the minds of the aborigines and half-breeds" ("The Grave Emergency").

The McLean boys became the socially constructed by-product of what the newspaper identified as years of government neglect. Reportage of the McLeans was exaggerated to mythical levels, with news accounts originating in Victoria telegraphed to newspapers

Figure 8. Archie McLean. BC Archives A-01459.

throughout the nation. The scene (Victoria), the agent (*Daily Colonist*), and its reportage of the McLean boys (the act) worked in unison to present the McLeans as heinous, evil murderers spurred on by government negligence (the agency). Because the McLean boys were part Aboriginal, and because they had once threatened to incite a Native uprising, the newspaper alluded to the Chilcotin War of 1864 (a conflict that left 19 whites and 9 Aboriginals dead) as an example of what could happen if the McLeans were left at large. According to the *Daily Colonist*:

"A band of desperadoes armed to the teeth, who have started out to rob, plunder and destroy. Two victims have already fallen. Others may be marked for destruction. A whole community of industrious settlers, with their wives and little ones, their flocks and buildings, are threatened. Everything depends, as we have said, on prompt action, for should the Indians rise the country will be devastated. The hands of the government, weak and incompetent as they are, must be strengthened by the sympathy and active cooperation, if need be, of every good citizen. When the commonwealth is threatened, all must assist in saving it…. Perhaps from Kamloops to Osoyoos 1,500 warriors might be collected who speak one language and acknowledge a common origin" ("Mounted Police for the Interior").

Though not a perfect fit, the Chilcotin

narrative reframed the McLeans's story, making it accessible as an exaggerated topic of popular culture. The local story dilates, drawing in a "whole community of industrious settlers," "the country," and, finally, "the commonwealth." There is no interest here in what may have actually motivated the violence — in what combination of racism, social neglect, and accident may have conspired against the boys. There is no mention here, for example, of Annie McLean's pregnancy — of local politician and landowner John Mara, who the boys believed raped their sister. Instead, the McLean Gang was cast as a possible national threat, as the potential catalyst for an uprising.

The presiding judge further elaborated this theme, sending a firm message to other would-be outlaws: "The jury had now the opportunity of redeeming the good name of that portion of the province, and enforcing the lesson that even in the most isolated places the law must be implicitly obeyed. A failure to do that would encourage the settlement of disputes by the Bowie knife and revolver" ("The Kamloops Murders, Address of Counsel, Judge's Charge"). The moment Judge Crease uttered the words "You have caused great terror throughout the whole country, and by a system of robbery and outlawry have disgraced British Columbia" ("The Closing Scenes"), the McLeans' cultural position shifted once again, splitting into a general object of fear and a local subject of

Figure 9. Alexander Hare. BC Archives A-01455.

shame. After the trial, the boys migrated back to the vernacular (as figures of local disgrace), where they would attract little attention until the 1960s.

Quesnel author F.W. Lindsay reintroduced the boys as British Columbian folk heroes in 1963 in his book *The Outlaws*: "These were true sons of the frontier who rode before they could walk and learned to shoot before they could use a knife and fork. They had a heritage of wildness equalled by few men before or since" (27). Just one year, later Canadian folksinger Ian Tyson carried on where Lindsay left off, resituating the McLeans in popular culture via the folk music scene with his song "Four Rode By," a cut from a highly successful album titled *Northern Journey*.

During Canada's 1967 centennial celebrations, a permanent reminder of the McLeans's villainous acts was erected in a highly publicized ceremony. A cairn honouring Constable Johnny Ussher was unveiled in the hills south of Kamloops in August 1967, spurring a myriad of BC- based "factual" McLean boys stories in newspaper features and law-and-order anthologies.

There would be several additional murders within the Kamloops region before the end of the century. There would be no crime, however, that would captivate the attention of the public and newspapers more than Bill Miner's 1906 train robbery. Whereas the *Inland Sentinel* (established in May 1880) showed very little interest in the McLean boys' second trial and execution, the paper found itself wholly captivated by the American train robber. It would be through newspapers, and Miner's apparent skill at charming reporters, that the bandit would gain his notoriety and gentlemanly reputation. Just as the McLeans's acts were exaggerated in newsprint, so too were Miner's deeds. Newspaper accounts of Miner portrayed him as a criminal with a twist. Miner performed the Monte Creek heist with two accomplices, Shorty Dunn and Louis Colquhoun, but his cohorts quickly became minor players: Miner was singled out by reporters as the only outlaw worthy of attention and admiration. Miner caught the attention of many a reporter during his day, including one working for the *Kamloops Standard* in 1906: "He is a rather striking looking fellow with grizzled hair and moustache, erect and active and does not appear to bear within ten years of the weight of age which the prison records now credit him with. He claims to be 62, looks like a man of 50, and moves like one of 30. He answered all the questions put to him coolly, but sometimes hesitatingly, evidently considering his answers well" ("The Chase, Capture and the Committal").

Contrast this with a Victoria reporter's description of Allen McLean at his 1880 trial:

> Allen and Archie were unmoved, the former during the pathetic narrative, yawning audibly and keeping his eyes fixed on the face of the Judge with apparent unconcern and chewing tobacco vigorously. In his stalwart frame, swarthy complexion and air of savage unconcern he is a fitting prototype of Hugh, the half-gypsy, whose character Dickens so vividly describes in *Barnaby Rudge* ("The Trial of the Kamloops Outlaws").

The words reveal a powerful bias, a tendency to import and impose a colonial cultural frame. The agents (newspaper reporters) with their acts (portraying one outlaw as admirable and one as derelict) use language as the agency to prompt readers on how to "read" the outlaws. Much more than the facts of the trial were reported, and the reporters' "sentences" were inked onto newsprint and filed away in archives. The same historical documents would play a major role in determining how the outlaws were to be read throughout the 20th century.

Graham Seal, in his book *The Outlaw Legend*, argues that there exists an outlaw code that determines whether or not an outlaw will be elevated to a hero or legend. Seal argues that "all outlaw heroes operate outside and against the official legal system of the state, but remain within the unofficial legal and moral code of those who see them as one of their own … In order to maintain respect, sympathy, and the active support of his own social group, the outlaw must adhere to, or at least be seen to adhere to, a relatively rigid set of guidelines. Some actions are appropriate, even laudable, while others are reprehensible, and may not be countenanced if the outlaw is to become a hero." "Outlaws," he says, "who disregard these rules are unlikely to have the sympathy and therefore the sustaining support of their own social group" (7). The outlaw hero tradition consists of ten motifs or discrete but interacting narrative elements: friend of the poor, oppressed, forced into outlawry, brave, generous, courteous, does not indulge in unjustified violence, trickster, betrayed, and dies a valiant death (5-11).

It was through linguistic skill and personal charm that Miner was able to disseminate his fictional stories. Because Miner's stories were communicated to newspapers — the so-called first drafts of history — his stories would be legitimized as popular "facts." Still, many myths surround Miner, and many of the myths were created by Miner himself, including the one that he was born in

Bowling Green, Kentucky (Bossenecker "Interview"). The bandit committed dozens of robberies before crossing the US border into Canada, and it was through those robberies that he learned the importance of public perception. John Bossenecker, co-author of Bill Miner's biography — *The Grey Fox* — claims Miner was cognizant of the need to maintain a courtly Robin Hood image because he knew it would elicit sympathy from the public, and the public would be the same people who would eventually serve on the juries for his trials (Bossenecker).[2]

The agent (Miner) used his act (presenting himself as a gentlemanly social bandit) as the agency to attract public admiration, with self-preservation being his ultimate purpose. One could also argue that Thomas Edison's 1903 production *The Great Train Robbery* also played a role in his public popularity, as the 12-minute production introduced the notion of the romantic American train robber to the public three years before his Monte Creek heist ("The Great Train Robbery"). Unlike the McLeans, Miner would remain in the popular culture sphere for decades after Monte Creek because his act of portraying himself as a "good kind of bad guy" allowed him the ability to disguise his real, not-so-nice attributes.

The McLean boys and Alex Hare shared virtually none of the media savvy that Miner did. As figures caught between two cultures, the boys might seem ready candidates for celebrity status as symbols of racial oppression — or, at least, racial ambiguity. Some people viewed the McLeans as brave and courageous, but the public has been unable to see beyond the boys' brazen public behaviour. There are, as we might expect, competing theories as to why the McLeans and Alex Hare murdered Ussher and Kelly. The two most popular theories cite anger caused by John Mara's act of impregnating the boys' sis-

ter Annie (Balf *John Andrew Mara* 8), and lack of direction caused by the death of their father (Balf "Law and Order" 75). Despite the theories, no concrete motivation has been discovered that justifies the murders. Through the Kamloopsian lens, the McLeans were seen to murder in cold blood; apply unjustified violence; boast of their murderous acts; lynch, beat and rob an innocent Chinese man walking down a street ("The Kamloops Tragedy"), thus violating a number of outlaw moral codes, and in turn giving up their right to become legends. Unlike Miner, who wasted away in prison, the McLean boys departed the world in a spectacular fashion — suspended from nooses — but any bravery they may have exhibited at this event has been overshadowed by their behaviour during their capture at Douglas Lake: "seeing the uselessness of the struggle or becoming faint-hearted, they threw out a signal of surrender and agreed to lay down their arms" ("The Kamloops Tragedy").

There are few written accounts of the McLeans' version of events (their motives and other particulars). There is some evidence that their story went untold because the boys decided to speak in a Chinook dialect ("Kamloops Outlaws Reach the Royal City"), though it is still unclear whether the McLeans were not speaking up, or the newspaper reporters were not listening. There is, however, much documentation to argue that Miner possessed both the charm and the literacy skills to attract positive public and media attention.

According to Burke, a particular pentadic pattern (ratio) in a text is both a "selection" and a "deflection": a text deploys selected pentadic resources, and the elements can combine in different ways, each leading to a different construction of motive (Stillar 64). The scene, the acts, and the agents are important here, but agency (in particular, the rhetorical stance taken by the newspaper coverage) assumes an agent-like role, both reporting the news and rather deliberately shaping public opinion. The papers and the judge treated the McLeans as a form of metonymy: they were characterized in terms of association, as a part (or symptom) representing the whole (a perceived Aboriginal problem). The coverage of Miner, on the other hand, was characterized by metaphor: Miner *was* and *is* the Robin Hood of the North.

## Museums, Popular Culture, and Marketing

Both the McLeans and Bill Miner migrated to the high cultural domain through the museum and archives, thus becoming legitimate cultural icons within the Kamloops community. While museums can propel a cultural icon or cultural object into other cultural domains, such was not the case with Bill Miner, for the reverse seems to have occurred. I argue that his circulation as an object of mass culture increased Miner's profile in the museum. One could in fact argue that both sets of outlaws gained their entrance to high culture via the entertainment industries that romanticized them.

Both Miner and the McLeans have been celebrated in song and have been featured in several frontier law-and-order anthologies throughout the years, mainly because of the Anglophone culture's fascination with the activities, trials, and executions of great criminals (Seal 191). Miner began a major trajectory into mass culture in 1983, mobilized primarily by Phillip Borsos's feature film — *The Grey Fox*. He gained significant notoriety throughout North America after the Canadian film (showcasing Miner's adventures in British Columbia) was released into theatres. The response to the movie was monumental: the public came to view the names

Bill Miner and the Grey Fox as synonymous.

John Hunter, the film's screenplay writer, admitted that after reading the "factual" accounts of Miner, he found "characterizations minimal," and hence made the decision to depart from the truth and mythologize the robber (Bowie and Shoebridge 47). He planted several fictitious items into the screenplay; the most major deviation from Miner's life was the addition of a fictitious love interest — a photographer named Kate Flynn. Hunter goes on to state that since the movie debuted, he has come across published items about Miner, which "quote little facts about him that were invented for the screenplay." Hunter claims such is the power of film (Bowie and Shoebridge 147-48.) The scene (*The Grey Fox* movie), created by the agent (Hunter), portraying Miner as a pseudo Robin Hood figure and a romantic gentleman (the act), has served both to transfer Miner to the mass culture and, more importantly, legitimize the act of fictionalizing Bill Miner narratives.

Miner's popularity after *The Grey Fox* movie increased exponentially, to the extent that his character was adopted by the City of Kamloops for public campaigns. Aiding Miner in becoming common currency was his use as the city's ambassador during the city's 100th birthday celebrations and 1993 Canada Summer Games. In 1992, Kamloops resident Neil McLean (a Bill Miner lookalike) was sanctioned by the city's tourism manager as the city's official welcoming delegate for visitors to the 1993 Summer Games ("Train Robber"): "Throughout this year, Miner will be a visible figure around the city tracked by a North West Mounted Police officer … Miner is being introduced as an official ambassador for the City of Kamloops for this year and the future" (Jones A3).

Once Bill Miner entered into mass culture (film), he became an ideal subject for creative non-fiction. One cast member of the musical revue stated that the *Tales From the Rails* performance was modelled after the movie *The Grey Fox* in order to make it more entertaining for the audience. Cast members inserted a love interest into the performance, but rather than fictionalizing her as John Hunter did, they selected a real historical character — Kamloops photographer Mary Spencer. The cast of *Tales From the Rails* said they believed visitors came to the venue to be entertained, not to receive a history lesson, thus they did not believe accuracy was something that should be adhered to in their performances. Cast members' sentiments are shared by others, including researchers McKercher and du Cros. They too argue that the cultural tourism experience is one that must be carefully manufactured: "Indeed, as reprehensive as it may sound, the manufacturing of experience typically involves distortion, myth, and fabrication in the social construction of tourist assets to ensure that the message is received" (128). The revue was more factual in the early days of the show, but the performance became more successful once a love interest was added. Again, according to Burke's theory of dramatism, narrative acts that inform and represent our communities find their social motive in one or more of the five crucial elements central to all human drama: act (what), scene (where), agent (who), agency (how), and purpose (why) (xi).

The Two River Junction — a revenue-generating cultural tourism venue that wanted to increase its popularity (the scene)—realized its need for a love interest (act), and injected Mary Spencer into the story as Miner's lover (the agency) in order to increase entertainment value for the show's consumers, thus increasing the venue's popularity (the purpose). It was convenient for Rocky Mountaineer Railtours to employ the services of Miner, for he was, after all, a train robber. It was also convenient to employ the historical figure of Mary Spencer because she both mirrored the female photographer portrayed in the fictional biography *The Grey Fox* and was also a real local photographer who was affiliated (through photography) with Miner while he was in the city. The *Tales From the Rails* cast cannot be credited with being the first to modify Miner's story for entertainment purposes; they merely grabbed the baton from Philip Borsos. They rewrote Mary Spencer into the musical revue to make Miner's story more universally appealing to the masses.

The vast majority of those who attend the venue are tourists from outside of Kamloops. They will, after viewing the performance and the collage of Mary Spencer photographs on the wall, leave the city with the impression that Mary Spencer and Bill Miner were romantically involved. While it was not the Two River Junction's motive to rewrite history, that has been the end result, therein lying the power of cultural tourism venues to accentuate the mass culture sphere. Cultural tourism industries, like the film industry, possess the power to propel and perpetuate myths and urban legends.

Most successful tourist attractions share the following common features: they tell a story; make the asset come alive; make the experience participatory; make the experience relevant to the tourist; and focus on quality and authenticity (McKercher and du Cros 122). But McKercher and du Cros also argue that "tourists want a taste of 'authenticity,' but not necessarily reality" (40). Their ties to the community are loose, not close: "Authenticity is a social construct that is determined in part by the individual's own knowledge and frame of reference.... [M]any tourists have a passing interest in cultural heritage, but most have minimal knowledge about the specific past of any given place they visit. As such, they may be travelling to have their stereotypical or romantic images of a

Upstaging History: Outlaws as Icons

destination reinforced or possibly challenged, depending on their political learning" (40). "Much of cultural and heritage tourism," say McKercher and du Cros, "serves a covert role in creating or reinforcing national myths, cultural symbols and ethnic identities" (127). In other words, cultural tourism depends upon generalities tied more to popular culture than to the vernacular culture of lived experience.

It is the generalities of romantic western experience that attracts travellers to such venues as the Two River Junction and the Kamloops Heritage Railway because they offer the consumer the opportunity to "experience" the Wild West. According to Howard Grieve, the developer behind the Heritage Railway, passengers are afforded an experience that stimulates all the senses: feeling the wind blow through one's hair on the open-air coach; feeling the vibration of the train clanking over the tracks; hearing the loud guns go off; seeing the horses rear up; tasting the dust created by the horses; feeling the confusion, panic, and fear (Grieve). Rather than sitting in a lecture hall, or reading a textbook about Bill Miner, people are given the opportunity to not only hear his story in its location of origin, but to interact with him as well. Such face-to-face encounters produce a safe sublime — a literal enactment of what is metaphorically a broader merging between past and present, here and there, "them," and "us" (Desmond xvi ).

Herein lies the logic of cultural tourism: the tourism industry represents a vision of a world in harmony, a vision that is at once nostalgic and highly marketable. Interestingly, the director of the Kamloops Archives and Museum believes it is this romantic appeal that lures visitors into the museum to seek out "the bad guys" (Duckworth). Once inside the museum, however, visitors are exposed to a variety of competing narratives. Here the motive for

representation is quite different; as local historian Mary Balf explains: "A museum can limit itself to purely local concerns, covering only a relatively small territory, but covering it in detail and with accuracy, and providing a first-class picture of the past and present of its own district" (*History in the Museum* 2).

Both Bill Miner and the McLeans have claimed their space in the museum, but their presence there has not been an equal or static one. A trip to the Kamloops Museum and Archives in 2004 provides visitors with a comprehensive representation of American Bill Miner as soon as they enter the museum's third-floor entrance. Upon leaving the museum, a visitor can purchase a copy of the museum's *Billy Miner Rag*, a 28-page collection of newspaper articles dealing specifically with Bill Miner during the years 1906 to 1911. In contrast, a visitor to the museum will find no mention of the McLean Boys, unless he or she finds the archives and is willing to sift through 19th-century newspaper articles stored on microfilm. Although the museum is supposed to represent a place to learn a town's "natural" history, the representation each Kamloops outlaw receives is noticeably disproportionate.

Both the Kamloops Museum and Archives' curator and director reveal that they are not fond of the notion of promoting outlaw figures because their promotion sends the message that crime does pay (Page; Duckworth). However, the director states visitors do in fact come to the museum looking specifically for Miner-related items (the museum houses two of Miner's guns). The museum boasts a major exhibit of Miner containing a series of three large black-and-white posters positioned above a large diorama of the community of Monte Creek enclosed in a Plexiglas box. Noticeably absent from the display are adjectives that commonly accompany his name (adjectives I've seen in almost every text dealing with him): "gentleman" bandit, "notorious and loveable" scoundrel, "courageous," "sly," and "Robin Hood-like." We are told instead that "Wild West Kamloops has its fair share of gun-toting outlaws and famous bad guys. But none is as popular as train robber Bill Miner" (Kamloops Museum and Archives display 2003).

Miner's display is grand and given preferential status in the museum, but Miner is not presented as a hero. He is "popular" rather than admired. As part of a museum exhibition, he shares the company of many other "gun-toting outlaws," thus he is not unique. Miner is not presented in an exclusively positive light. On the contrary, there are two photographic silhouettes positioned in the display that have been reproduced to mimic undeveloped prints — both in a negative light — perhaps hinting that the exhibit is designed to counter the general celebratory tone found elsewhere in the city. The museum's staff use Miner's train robbery primarily as a means to educate visitors about the nearby community of Ducks (where Miner robbed the train).

The scene (Kamloops Museum and Archives — the high culture medium which acts as an official legitimizer of the icons) is directly influencing the way the agents (outlaws) are being represented. The museum's director states that Miner is being over-represented, yet his display still features prominently in the cultural facility. This reality is due in part to the fact that visitors, who have become familiar with Bill Miner via popular and mass cultures, come to the facility expecting to find "authentic" items associated with Miner: they have seen and heard narratives of Miner's exploits, narratives that imply he played a major role in the city's historical past.

What, then, of the McLeans?

Burke reminds us that when we are inca-pable of either acknowledging or justifying an act, we tend to experience guilt and shame. We seek release from this guilt to the extent that we will name scapegoats and claim "victimage" to establish our shared innocence (19-20). Officially, the McLeans are not displayed visually in the museum because people do not come to the venue looking for information on them to the extent that they do with Miner (Duckworth). "Most people outside of our area really don't know their story," says the museum's archivist (Cross). With the exception of a few school children working on heritage projects, few visitors ask questions about the boys. Though the museum's mission statement says that its primary purpose is to provide residents and tourists with a detailed account of local history, the museum is, at the end of the day, a cultural venue that must generate revenue in order to exist. A museum must respond to public expectations, and the Kamloops Museum, given its professed dislike for promoting outlaws, appears to be featuring Bill Miner so prominently only to satisfy the curiosity of visitors.

Miner's celebrity has, in this instance, created an implicit rewriting of history. Miner's actual role in Kamloops was a very limited one, yet his display is a major one commanding centre stage in the facility. Tourists visiting the venue could easily conclude that Miner played a major role in the city's history; and these same visitors could be forgiven for leaving the museum (and Kamloops) without ever learning anything but a hearsay account of the McLeans.

## Poetic Licence and Accuracy in Representation
The McLeans's limited migration into the high cultural domain has been more successful outside the museum. During the 1990s, the McLeans enjoyed a major resurgence of

attention; there were promising signs that their story would be welcomed into mass culture. At least four works were created around the McLean boys' story between 1993 and 1996: Mel Rothenburger's *The Wild McLeans* (1993), George Bowering's novel *Shoot!* (1994), Ian Weir's play *The McLean Boys* (1996), and Bill Gallaher's folksong *The Wild McLeans* (1994). Three of the works clearly aspired to the high cultural sphere — the folksong, novel, and play; the McLeans seemed poised to escape their vernacular limitations.

Rothenburger's local history book, centring on the boys' 1879 exploits — "a story about the family for the family" (qtd. in *Exposing Culture* 121) — represented an updated version of his first biography on the McLeans, published in 1973, titled *We've Killed Johnny Ussher!* The 1990s fictional works depicted the boys with well-rounded characters, and with motives for their actions (a tactic similar to that employed by John Hunter). Prior to the publication of Bowering's novel, few authors had provided speculative details on the McLeans' personal lives, personalities, and motivations — what their characters might have been like, or whether they had gentle sides (Duckworth).

Only one author before Bowering — playwright Ken Smedley — used poetic licence to provide the McLean boys' story with a personal slant in his 1971 theatre production *Renegades*. Smedley claimed his motivation for writing the play — "a powerful indictment of the attitudes of a white society towards the Indian and half-breed" (Kellett 13) — was to "to try to get some of the truths about what really happened and why" (qtd. in *Exposing Culture* 130). "One of the things that … I was looking to understand," he said, "is what makes these people do what they did? Look at them and the environment that they were living in, and what

they had grown up with and the kind of treatment and abuse that they received and historically what had proceeded" (130).

Smedley sought to rehabilitate the 19th-century vernacular by giving it contemporary relevance. In order to do so, Smedley sacrificed some elements of historical accuracy, prompting Mel Rothenburger, then writing for the *Kamloops News Advertiser*, to note: "It's probably only a little bit more historically faithful than the tales of Sherlock Holmes, but it's local" ("Play Sacrifices"). Rothenburger went on to criticize the play's producers for "having taken dates, ages, characters, and actions, tossed them together, mixed them around and burped them out as a centennial play with a message…. When people go to see this play next week they should be aware of what they are seeing. Unfortunately it seems unlikely that if plans to present the play in other parts of the country materialize, other audiences will take it for anything but the gospel ("Play Sacrifices").

Bowering, too, penned his novel *Shoot!* with an eye more intent on the probable than the actual. Like Smedley, he provided the McLean boys and Alex Hare with something previous authors had not — a sympathetic if speculative narrative to contextualize and explain the outlaws' actions. Bowering portrays the boys as young outcasts unable to find employment and acceptance from either white or Aboriginal society. Rather than simply reiterating what the outlaws did, Bowering goes further and provides plausible motives.

It was Ian Weir's play *The McLean Boys*, staged two years after Bowering's novel *Shoot!*, which incited Mel Rothenburger, who, as it turns out, is a descendent of the McLeans, to again publicly express dissent with the way the boys were being misrepresented. Rothenburger's argument involved some element of personal response: he took

271

Figure 10. Kamloops actor Larry Foss performs a train robbery re-enactment for guests riding the Kamloops Heritage Railway's 2141 train. Foss boards the train during the performance and provides tourists with a narrative explaining Miner's connection to Kamloops. Photograph courtesy of Terry Butcher.

offence at the works of artists such as Weir and Bowering because they played fast and loose with the facts: "He [Bowering] was laying down the stuff in there that sounded like it was fact. ... I took it somewhat personal at the time because I must admit, our family has always been highly sensitive about the portrayal of the McLean brothers" (Rothenburger). The subjects of vernacular culture, invested as they are with personal histories, are not easily transplanted to other cultural spheres.

In a video produced by the English Department at the University College of the Cariboo in 1996, Rothenburger stated that he was upset with the way Weir manipulated facts regarding the McLeans in order to make their story more entertaining (an element common to both creative writing and tourism promotion). In particular, Rothenburger took offence with the play because it both misrepresented history and upset descendents of the McLeans. Rothenburger summed up his thoughts on the fictionalizing of the McLean boys in a 2001 interview. "I've worked for thirty years or more now at undoing those myths, but people keep coming along and rediscovering the story" (qtd. in *Exposing Culture* 122).

Rothenburger's public statements spurred

a public debate around the issue of whether historical accuracy was an important component of creative productions, with a back and forth dialogue being carried out on the editorial page of the *Kamloops Daily News* throughout the month of February in 1996. An editorial written by reporter Susan Duncan echoes the review of Smedley's play written 25 years earlier:

> It's troubling when playwrights don't realize the power they hold. People will leave Sagebrush Theatre after seeing *The McLean Boys*, believing they know the story about a piece of local history. In later conversations, they will talk about that play as if it were the truth. That's how history gets rewritten. It's no use saying people will realize that artistic license was used. They won't. ("When Creative License Goes a Little Too Far")

The rhetorical consistency of such views suggests a community consensus regarding how the McLeans should be represented: in an accurate, that is, "factual," manner. Others within the cultural community and the tourism industry also feel that accuracy should be strictly adhered to as a criterion for representation (though, ironically, many are not aware of the accurate versions of history because they have not investigated them in as thorough a manner as historians such as Rothenburger). Rothenburger sees the rewriting of local history as a dangerous pursuit, for it allows characters to be inaccurately promoted to folklore status (precisely what has occurred with Bill Miner). In making such a public statement (the act), Rothenburger (the agent) is sending the message (the agency) that other artists must act more "responsibly" than either Bowering or Weir. Rothenburger's purpose is to maintain an accurate public record and protect the

McLeans's story from willful or careless misappropriation.

The stakes for cultural representation are high given these very public interventions. Kamloops has become a scene where it is very difficult to mobilize the McLeans (in a way similar to Bill Miner) into either high art or mass cultures. The "facts" of the McLeans's story are incomplete and still subject to often contentious local debate. Faithful adherence to local facts ensures authenticity, but until these facts are generally agreed to, such adherence limits the logic of analogy and association that tourists depend on to frame the initially unfamiliar and to develop a passing appreciation for local cultures. Those tourists riding the train or viewing *Tales From the Rails* may have no prior knowledge of Bill Miner, for example, but they are familiar with Robin Hood, because the name is instantly identifiable and instantly elicits a notion of a "warrior of oppression." By labelling Miner as a Robin Hood figure, the bandit is transformed from a criminal to a hero in an instant, his admirable qualities allowing him currency within a variety of cultural domains. The McLeans, to date, appeal to no similar popular stereotype.

Social issues connected to the McLean boys's story still elicit shame and guilt from Kamloopsians. This shame and guilt thwart the McLeans's ability to migrate effectively into the popular and mass culture. To the residents of Kamloops, the McLeans are murderers first and foremost. Their story is a dark one, with racial turmoil attached to it. Despite these reservations, the Kamloops Heritage Railway is the one cultural tourism industry in Kamloops that would like to see the McLeans given a higher public profile. The railway claims to have plans in the works to add the boys to their "robbery line-up" (Grieve). We have to wonder, though, whether the community of Kamloops will allow some necessary fictionalization of the boys. The Kamloops Heritage Railway (the agents), by writing the McLean boys into their staged show (the act) as stagecoach robbers so that they will be "convenient" for their purposes (the agency), will further promote local history and elevate tourist interest (the purposes), but in turn will misrepresent local history (the scene), because historically the McLeans did not rob stagecoaches. Employing the McLeans as stagecoach robbers is seen as the only way the railway can draw the boys into their cultural tourism venue.

Those promoting the railway venture are well aware that there are many in the Kamloops community who would prefer to see the "evil, murdering" McLean boys left in solitary confinement. When Rothenburger was informed of the Heritage Railway's plans to employ the McLean boys in a mock stagecoach hold-up, he replied that he would love to see them added to the show, but he was quick to point out, "they weren't stagecoach robbers" (Rothenburger "Interview"). The McLeans' movement from the vernacular to mass culture may still be premature.

## Some Tentative Conclusions

Outlaw figures have played a definitive role in Kamloops' Wild West history. Both the McLean Gang and Bill Miner can be credited with luring international eyes and ears to the city over the years. However, while both the McLeans and Miner are bona fide outlaws, Miner has been deemed a "good" outlaw and the McLeans have been deemed "bad" outlaws. Miner's decision to hold up a train at Monte Creek was a blessing in disguise for the city, for it allowed the community the opportunity to create and nurture a scene where an outlaw heritage could be promoted publicly without having to commis-

sion the assistance of the "disgraced" McLean boys.

Burke says that when we experience guilt, we seek redemption by establishing a scapegoat (19-20). Kamloops has two sets of outlaws — four young men who disgraced the city through acts of seemingly unmotivated violence, and an American train robber who got caught stealing from a corporation perceived as gouging the public. Bill Miner is a generic outlaw figure whose presence helps promote the city's Western heritage and, at the same time, deflects attention from the city's true outlaw heritage. The McLeans, on the other hand, were sentenced twice for their deeds — once in a courtroom in New Westminster, and now in the city's cultural tourism arena. In contrast, 98 years after Bill Miner wandered into Kamloops' city limits, he is still very much a "wanted" man.

There seems a general understanding in Kamloops that the McLeans story is a dark one, something that symbolizes the tumultuous race relations the city experienced in its early days. When Judge Crease sentenced the McLean boys, he sentenced the city of Kamloops as well: "a system of robbery and outlawry [has] disgraced British Columbia," he said ("The Closing Scenes"). The word "disgrace," uttered 125 years ago, still echoes loudly in the ears of some local residents. The McLean boys are outlaws, but they also symbolize an era of racial dissent. They are figures too close to be objectified. Descendants of the McLeans still reside in Kamloops, and thus the vernacular aspect of their story remains always close to the surface. In contrast, because Miner was born 3,000 kilometres to the east, in the state of Michigan, there are no local descendents to question or defend his motives. In many ways, it is Miner's lack of connection to Kamloops that makes him a ready candidate for tourism promotion.

That which is too close to us (that which remains situated in the vernacular) cannot be easily separated from private and personal association; that which is merely familiar or generally known can be more easily shared, rewritten, and promoted. As Nelson Graburn argues in "Learning to Consume," the "tripartite structure — too close, within reach, and too far — is a useful paradigm to look at heritage" (72). Graburn draws a telling comparison between eating animals and consuming culture: animals close to us (pets) may not be eaten, while those that are familiar but more distant (farm or field animals) may be eaten within certain guidelines; more strange or distant animals (those found in the wild or in zoos) are not usually eaten. Similarly, consumption of cultural icons and narratives depends upon points of "proximity and familiarity" (73).

According to Graburn, and I think the Kamloops examples support this idea, the conventional logic of cultural consumption moves us to domesticate the exotic and to distance ourselves from the personal. The question remains whether we need to let conventional thinking and market forces dominate. History and heritage may provide wonderful raw materials for tourism promotion, but once visitors have been entertained, many may also seek to gain more insights into the city's vernacular past. As this chapter has detailed, the McLeans's story is one that says a great deal about local history — and about the larger narratives of 19th-century racism, politics, media coverage, law, and colonial imperialism. The challenge for small cities like Kamloops is to find an appropriate way to share vernacular heritage: when figures like the actual McLeans feature as prominently as the largely fictional Miner as vehicles for both tourism promotion and heritage education, the city will have tapped into an important, truly authentic cultural resource.

## Acknowledgments

Research for this chapter was supported by a Comprehensive University Enhancement Research Scholarship (from UCC). My many thanks, also, to my research supervisor Will Garrett-Petts.

## Notes

1. I have drawn extensively from Garrett-Petts and Lawrence's theory of the vernacular as detailed in *PhotoGraphic Encounters*. In addition, my understanding of vernacular representation has benefited from several personal interviews with Garrett-Petts.

2. Cultural tourists have a thirst for what McKercher and du Cros call "edutainment" (17). Documentaries and biographies do not elicit the same interest that romanticized versions do. Two American authors penned a scholarly biography on Bill Miner in 1993, but the response to the book, according to co-author John Bossenecker, was "ho-hum" (Bossenecker). The authors titled their book after Phillip Borsos's movie, believing that people would seek it out because of its familiarity, but the non-fiction account of Bill Miner's life was not nearly as popular as the movie (Bossenecker). A comment made by Bossenecker regarding his biography on Miner may offer another clue as to why Miner has been able to gain legendary status and why the McLeans have not. Bossenecker claims that the public did not greet co-author Mark Dugan's evidence that Miner was a homosexual with fanfare, perhaps because such an attribute failed to fit well into the Hollywood notion of the outlaw.

## Works Cited

Balf, Mary. *History in the Museum.* Kamloops Museum and Archives. Article N85. 2.

———. *John Andrew Mara.* Kamloops Museum and Archives. Article N100. 8.

———. "Law and Order." *Kamloops: A History of the District up to 1914.* 3rd ed. Kamloops: Kamloops Museum Association, 1989. 75.

*The Grey Fox.* Dir. Philip Borsos. Prod. Barry Healey, Philip Borsos, Peter O'Brian. Perf. Richard Farnsworth, Samantha Langevin. Mercury Pictures, 1982.

Bossenecker, John. Personal Interview. 12 Aug. 2003.

Bossenecker, John, and Mark Dugan. *The Grey Fox: The True Story of Bill Miner, Last of the Old-Time Bandits*. Oklahoma: U of Oklahoma P, 1992.

Bowering, George. *Shoot!* Toronto: Key Porter Books, 1994.

Bowie, Douglas, and Tom Shoebridge, eds. *Best Canadian Screenplays*. Kingston, ON: Quarry Press, 1992. 147-48.

Burke, Kenneth. *A Grammar of Motives*. California: U of California P, 1969.

Canadian Studies. *Exposing Culture — In Conversation with Interior Artists*. Kamloops: University College of the Cariboo Department of English and Modern Languages, 2001.

"Committed for Trial." *Inland Sentinel* 22 May 1906: 2.

Cross, Susan. Personal Interview. 6 Aug. 2003.

Desmond, Jane. *Staging Tourism: Bodies on Display from Waikiki to Sea World*. Chicago: U of Chicago P, 1999.

"Double Murder and Arson." *Daily Colonist* 11 Dec. 1879: 3.

Duckworth, Elisabeth. Personal Interview. 31 July 2003.

Duncan, Susan. "When Creative License Goes a Little Too Far." Editorial. *Kamloops Daily News* 1 Feb. 1996:

Gallaher, Bill. "The Wild McLeans." *Across The Divide*. Socan. 1997.

Garrett-Petts, W.F. Personal Interviews. Sept.-Dec. 2003.

Garrett-Petts, W.F., and Donald Lawrence. *PhotoGraphic Encounters: The Edges and Edginess of Reading Prose Pictures and Visual Fictions*. Edmonton: U of Alberta P, 2000.

Graburn, Nelson H. H. "Learning to Consume: What is Heritage and When is it Traditional?" Ed. Nezar AlSayyad. *Consuming Tradition, Manufacturing Heritage: Global Norms and Urban Forms in the Age of Tourism*. New York: Routledge, 2001. 68-89.

Grieve, Howard. Personal Interview. 1 Aug. 2003.

"Honor to Whom Honor is Due." *Daily Colonist* 19 Dec. 1879: 2.

Jones, Sydney. "Bandit is Back For Year-long Chase." *Kamloops Daily News* 15 Jan. 93: A3.

Kamloops Museum and Archives. *The Bill Miner Rag*. Kamloops, 1990.

"Kamloops Outlaws Reach the Royal City." *Daily Colonist* 28 Dec. 1879: 3.

Kellett, Gordon. "Renegades Ride Again." *Interface*. Dec. 1971:13.

"Landed in Penitentiary." *Kamloops Standard* 9 June 1906: 1.

Lindsay, F.W. *The Outlaws*. Quesnel, BC: F.W. Lindsay, 1963. 25-34.

McKercher, Bob, and Hilary du Cros. *Cultural Tourism — The Partnership Between Tourism and Cultural Heritage Management*. New York: Haworth Press, 2002.

"Mounted Police for the Interior." *Daily Colonist* 13 Dec. 1879: 3.

"News from the Chilcoaten Expedition." *Daily Colonist* 1 Aug. 1864: 3.

Page, Cuyler (Kamloops Museum Curator). Personal Interview. 14 Aug. 2003.

Paradis, Thomas. "The Top-Ten Reasons Kamloops is No Vancouver." A paper presented at The Small Cities Forum, Kamloops, B.C., May 9, 2004.

*Renegades*. By Kenneth Smedley. Dir. Tom Kerr. Perf. Eric Schneider, Michael Bianchin, Frank Atlin. Kamloops Secondary School, Kamloops. 7 Dec. 1971.

*Representing and Misrepresenting History*. Prod. University College of the Cariboo Modern Languages and English Department, 1996.

Rothenburger, Mel. Personal Interview. 8 Aug. 2003.

——. "Play Sacrifices Historical Accuracy." *Kamloops News Advertiser* 10 Dec. 1971; sec.: 2.

——. *The Wild McLeans*. Victoria: Orca Book Publishers, 1993.

——. *We've Killed Johnny Ussher!* Vancouver: Mitchell Press, 1973.

Seal, Graham. *The Outlaw Legend — A Cultural Tradition in Britain, America and Australia*. Cambridge: Cambridge UP, 1996.

Stillar, Glenn. *Analyzing Everyday Texts. Discourse, Rhetoric, and Social Perspectives*. California: Sage, 1998.

Tait, John. Letter to William Charles Esquire. 30 Dec.1879. Hudson Bay Company. Kamloops Museum and Archives. Kamloops.

"The Chase, Capture and the Committal." *Kamloops Standard* 19 May 1906: 1.

"The Closing Scenes." *Daily Colonist* 21 Mar. 1880: 2.

"The Grave Emergency." *Daily Colonist* 13 Dec. 1879: 2.

"The Great Train Robbery 1903." *Teddy Blue's Bunkhouse*. 10 Aug. 2003. <http://www.wildwest-web.net/great.html>

"The Kamloops Murders — Address of Counsel — Judge's Charge." *Daily Colonist* 20 Mar. 1880: 3.

"The Kamloops Outrage — Succinct Account of the Atrocities." *Daily Colonist* 1 Jan. 1880: 3.

"The Kamloops Tragedy." *Daily Colonist* 13 Dec. 1879: 3.

"The Trial of the Kamloops Outlaws." *Daily Colonist* 19 Mar. 1880: 3.

"Train Held Up." *Inland Sentinel* 11 May 1906:1.

"Train Robber From City's Past Vows to Return For Some Fun." *Kamloops Daily News* 23 Dec. 1992: A3.

Venture Kamloops. *2004 Official Kamloops & the Thompson-Nicola Adventure Guide*. Kamloops: Venture Kamloops, 2004. 35.

Weir, Ian. *The McLean Boys*. Unpublished play. 1996.

# Directing the Small City

## David Ross

I don't usually think of myself as a writer, but being an actor I am pretty sure I can talk. So maybe I'll talk this contribution to *The Small Cities Book.*

What I've been asked to talk about is: where did the play *Ernestine Shuswap Gets Her Trout* come from; how was it developed; what's the scoop on the BRAVOTV documentary video on the making of the play; how did I feel about the premiere production, particularly opening night; and, finally, what are the pros and cons of producing and directing theatre in a "smaller city"?

The origins of the play really go back 20 years, to my arrival with my wife Janet and our then-young family. We had only expected to stay a few years, but when we talked about leaving, one of the many things that held us in Kamloops was the close proximity of a true Aboriginal culture. Coming from Newfoundland, we had been used to a strong, unifying sense of culture, of English and Irish roots in particular. There are some Aboriginal people in Labrador, and a few late arrivals from Nova Scotia who have created a small Micmac community in the relatively isolated area around Conne River, but the indigenous people of Newfoundland, the Beothuk, finally disappeared in the early 19th

century through an official policy of benign neglect, and active slaughter. Here in Shuswap territory, the Aboriginal people have somehow survived these forces, and we gradually came to know some of them.

One of the first artistic connections we made with the people of the area happened because of an impulsive promise I had made during my interview for the job. I don't remember who, but one of my four interviewers asked in about the third hour, "What kind of plays would you create that would be different from the work of your predecessors?" For some reason, I hadn't expected the question and therefore was not prepared for it, but my scrambling brain went to my most recent work in Newfoundland, where a lot of our work presented the past to audiences in a way that Newfoundlanders really appreciated.

So, improvising quickly, as I love to do, I thought of the two hills I had just learned the names of — Mounts Peter and Paul — and I said I would create a show that gave the history of this area from both the Aboriginal and the European points of view. The interviewers seemed a little puzzled, but pleased, and I made a note to myself that that was one promise I would have to keep.

The first challenge was putting together the creative team. I couldn't immediately find a writer who seemed qualified for the task, and I didn't want to take the two to four years that new play development usually takes, so I settled on collective creation, which, if you're not familiar with the term, means a group of people, usually six or seven, after researching an issue, improvise dialogue and scenes, usually under the guidance of a director. In four to six weeks you assemble what's been created into something that resembles a show. It's a crude technique but it allows immediate attention to an issue, and often creates a great impact on the audience.

The team itself was made up of two excellent improvisers from Vancouver I had just met — Meredith Bain Woodward and David McLeod; a Newfoundland improviser I knew I could count on named Brian Downey (who later became a bit of a TV star through the series *Lexx* that you can still see in Spanish on the Latino channel); a fine composer and music director from Vancouver, Lloyd Nicholson; and Margo Kane, who was and still is one of the prime movers and shakers in First Nations theatre. The final member of the team was my wife, Janet Michael, who, in addition to her singing and acting talents, is a "person of colour," which means that, despite being by blood an Anglo-Lebanese Newfoundlander, she can pass for anything. She and Margo played the women of all races.

Before the actors came, I collected a lot of research, mostly from the Kamloops Museum and Archives. With the actors, I visited the archives in the old residential school, but the collection there was very much in its infancy. What we found, of course, was that the "white" history could be inferred from various documents, often records of business dealings, but in the Aboriginal world the received wisdom, other than from living eld-

ers, came in the form of legends. The play that was created reflected these two very different ways of thinking: the one factual and often mercantile, the other allegorical and folk philosophical in nature. The play was called *Boris Karloff Slept Here*, and while I remain proud of the show to this day, the different ways of thinking that it was born from did not blend easily. On closing night I took notes to be used when we moved the project along from a work-in-progress to a finished piece. The opportunity to complete the work didn't happen immediately, but the ideas did remain in the back of my mind.

When you run a professional theatre company in a small city, there is a tendency to want to be all things to all people. Persons who care about theatre know you and they often let you know what they would like to see, so other branches of our constituency got the focus for the next while. We did continue to present the work of Aboriginal artists, including plays by Drew Hayden Taylor and Margo Kane, and we did continue to watch for another opportunity to engage our neighbours, the Shuswap people, with a work created about them.

The next creation that I envisaged that related to the Shuswap people came from the then editor of our daily newspaper, now the Mayor of Kamloops, Mel Rothenburger. The story of the McLean Gang was about as theatrical as we get in Canada. The story had been treated in plays and novels before, and Mel himself had written two books about the boys, but I wanted a theatrical treatment that started with primary source materials. To me, the story of the boys being caught between the two races that made up their own blood was a theme that still has great relevance in the Canada of today. So we commissioned Ian Weir, an established playwright from Kamloops, to write the play. We didn't collectively improvise, but we did allow the several years of development for the play to be refined beyond what had been possible with *Boris Karloff Slept Here*.

Casting is always important, but in this production I wanted to achieve a very specific result. I wanted the four actors, who played Alan, Charlie, and Archie McLean and Alex Hare, to be of mixed Aboriginal and European blood, and after much scouring I did find them. All four actors were excellent in the show, as were the other four actors who completed the cast, and I was glad I had committed to the exercise, but it was very clear to me, after spending a month with these men, that an actor's soul is far more important in the casting than his or her bloodlines. After all, an actor's job is to convincingly play someone he or she is not. Experience is the great teacher! And that has remained my mantra with regard to casting. If a play has connections to a Jewish world, an Aboriginal world, or an Italian world, that play will be best served by having some of the actors "be" of that world. On the other hand, a director's responsibility in the final analysis is to cast the best actor available in the part, regardless of race, ancestry, etc.

Eight or nine years ago, my friend Ron Ignace, then Chief of the Skeetchestn Indian Band, handed me a document called the Laurier Memorial, which the chiefs of the Shuswap, Thompson, and Okanagan tribes had presented to Sir Wilfrid Laurier, prime minister of Canada, in 1910. I found the document intriguing because it was a record of the first 100 years of contact between the "whites" and the Aboriginals of this area, but, from the Aboriginal point of view, the very thing I couldn't find more than a decade before when we had created *Boris Karloff Slept Here*. Now we knew the Aboriginal concepts of kinship, land ownership, and basic hospitality. Now we knew for sure that the use of the land by Aboriginal people had not

been, as Stephen Leacock had suggested, "scarcely more than that by crows and wolves" (Leacock 19). Or as former British Columbia Premier William Smithe had told the Aboriginal people of BC: "When the whites first came among you, you were little better than the wild beasts of the field" (BC Legislature 264). But how best to treat the document was the question. Perhaps it was a short film. Perhaps Ron and his cousin Manny Jules, who was Chief of the Kamloops Indian Band at that time, could play their forebears, and I would play James Teit, the young Scot who had married into the Thompson people and who had acted as secretary and translator to the chiefs for this Memorial. It could be the 15-minute short that played before the main feature at all those Canadian film festivals.

All three of us being very busy, we sat on that idea for several years, until one morning when John Dormer, a former mayor of Kamloops, phoned with an offer to buy me coffee. But before we get to the coffee, I have to fill in another piece of the puzzle. As I mentioned earlier, Janet and I had developed friendships among the Shuswap people from several bands, but when it came to the creation of art, our philosophy was to be reactive rather than proactive. What I specifically mean is that it was obvious the Shuswap Nation had had almost two centuries of non-Aboriginal cultural influence, which had almost obliterated the indigenous culture. We didn't want to be part of any kind of continuation of that. If Keith Matthew and Linda Jules of the Shuswap Nation called up to see if we would meet and help them form a young Shuswap Theatre Company, we would give what help we could. If a Native theatre company in Penticton needed a workshop on a play that they had created, we were there. We wanted to help, not lead.

Some months prior to the John Dormer

phone call, I had hired Lori Marchand as our new administrative director. I could write another paper on all the reasons why I wanted Lori in our key administrative position, but what is especially relevant to this story is the fact that, although her mother looks like my slightly older sister, Lori is a member of the Okanagan Nation and has a great understanding of Aboriginal history. This understanding gave us the opportunity to be slightly more proactive on Aboriginal issues.

Now back to John's offer of coffee. He was phoning because he had a connection (one I've never fully understood, but that's just John) with the Sun Rivers project. He wanted me to meet Robert Simon, who was then Executive Director of the Secwepemc Cultural Education Society. I agreed, and Lori and I met with John and Robert at the Grind Coffeehouse on a sunny fall day — at least I think it was the fall. I know we sat outside, and it was invigorating. Anyway, Robert talked about a television project that he was planning concerning the Laurier Memorial. We said we would help in any way that he thought appropriate, but that we were in the business of making plays, and how about a play that was somehow based on the Memorial, and how about a co-commission from both of our organizations to create the script, and how about approaching Tomson Highway, who I had met some years before at the Banff Playwrights' Colony, and who had visited Shuswap territory several times since, and whom we all admired? My charge to Tomson, along with fistfuls of research from Simon and the now-significant Secwepemc Museum, and the document itself, was to examine the first 100 years of contact leading up to the Memorial and see where his muse took him.

Over the next four years there were eight or nine drafts and six workshops: two in Kamloops; one in Vancouver; one in Ottawa;

and two in Banff, the last one for two weeks leading to a staged reading before an invited audience. I directed all of the workshops with dramaturgical advice from many people, including the 16 women who read the parts at different times.

Shortly after we started on the commission, another partner joined, or we joined it, depending on your point of view. Kamloops received funding from the Community-University Research Alliances (CURA), a granting program initiated by the Social Sciences and Humanities Research Council of Canada, and its support for our project has been critically important. Without CURA's help, the two-week residency at Banff couldn't have happened. Neither could the documentary on the making of the play that aired this fall on BRAVOTV. In fact, the idea and most of the funding for the documentary has come through Lon Dubinsky, a CURA research associate at the Kamloops Art Gallery, and Will Garrett-Petts, an English professor at the university and co-director of the CURA-funded Small Cities project.

I should also add that the cast members for the premiere were the results of auditions in Vancouver, Calgary, and Toronto and reflect a balance of Aboriginal knowledge and identity and a strong sense of this region. They are in my opinion the four best actors for these roles. And boy, did they look great on opening night!

It certainly was a night to remember. Lori had led a group to create the gala, which was exciting and moving. When old friends like Ron Ignace gave the prayer and John Jules sang the welcoming song, and when the chiefs and/or councillors of 17 bands of the Shuswap Nation were present with a number of theatre colleagues from across the country; and when the Western Canada Theatre staff and Board and so many other dignitaries and friends showed up; and when the show, which just sang on that night … well, nothing's perfect, but on that night it all felt very, very good.

As far as the pros and cons of producing theatre in smaller cities go, the pros are all the things you might imagine: knowing people from one end of the community to the other; being able to call on those people for help and advice; being seen as a key player in the community instead of struggling to be noticed; and having a major influence in the community. Think about it this way. A Western Canada Theatre hit can play to 10% of the population; a hit in Vancouver would have to run for years to have the same influence on the community. We are a big part of the community dialogue.

The cons, on the other hand, don't really exist anymore. We are not ignored by the rest of the country. In fact, our work is highly regarded, which is why our funding is significant and stable. We don't have trouble getting the best artists to work here, because our reputation is: "You won't get rich, but you'll have fun and you'll do challenging, rewarding work." This is the same reason we don't have trouble filling all of the other positions within our company and the reason why, 20 years later, Janet and I still think this is the best place in the country to base our work in theatre.

## Works Cited

BC Legislature. *Sessional Papers*, Victoria, BC, 1887.

Leacock, Stephen. *Canada, The Foundations of its Future.* Privately Printed, 1941.

Figure 1. Opposing performances: Following colonial models, local chiefs and Prime Minister Laurier enact the protocols of colonial deference. At the same time, as noted in the behaviour of the people along the bench, a counter-performance takes place that anticipates *Ernestine Shuswap Gets Her Trout*. Drawing courtesy of David Seymour.

# Political Theatre in a Small City: The Staging of the Laurier Memorial in Kamloops

## James Hoffman

Etymologically speaking, all theatre is political, as it presents protagonists within a town or group.
Patrice Pavis, *Dictionary of the Theatre*

There's an ecology of theatre in this town.
David Ross, Artistic Producer of Western Canada Theatre, Kamloops.

Two gaslights dangle from the ceiling of an austere public hall. At one end, three men in deep concentration sit around a long table, while three others in Aboriginal dress stand close by. All are formally dressed and very still; all gravely focus on a man in black who reads aloud. The reader has a large crucifix jutting from his black cincture: he is an Oblate priest and reads from a paper, directing his message — apparently a lofty one — to one sitter in particular, a distinguished gentleman positioned exactly at the centre of the room. This man seems familiar, important. Then, to the right, along a bench, there is another group: nine people sit, stand, and slouch. They are a mix of First Nations boys, adults, and white-haired old men in various contortions of daydreaming, conversing, and thinking. Positioned as audience for those at the table, they generate a different performance of their own — thereby subverting the formal reading and engaging in an authentic

act of British Columbia theatre.

The above paragraph describes not the actual but an imagined performance of the Laurier Memorial, in this case a drawing made in 1988 by First Nations artist Dave Seymour, which is now the centre of a permanent display at the Secwepemc Museum in Kamloops, along with accompanying documents and descriptions of the Memorial. Although the artist used a degree of "free rein" (Seymour) — such as the inclusion of the people on the bench — his staging of the event is based on a documented historical moment. In his creative inclusion of the nine on the bench, Seymour graphically articulates a discursive context for an alternate perception of history, one that was also powerfully evident in Kamloops in 1910 when the first performance of the Memorial took place. These, along with a play based on the Memorial staged in 2004 in Kamloops, demonstrate that a small city in British

Columbia can be uniquely placed to generate powerful performative acts responding to the experience of colonization.

What actually did happen? On an evening in late August 1910, chiefs of the Shuswap, Okanagan, and Thompson tribes gathered in the Oddfellows Hall in Kamloops to perform a political act for an audience of one: the prime minister of Canada, who was visiting the city on a pre-election tour. As Wilfrid Laurier sat and listened, the chiefs stood nearby — effectively playing both audience and performers — while Father Jean-Marie Raphael Le Jeune read aloud what is now called the Laurier Memorial, a 3,000-word petition outlining 100 years of increasingly troubled relations between the First Nations peoples and the immigrant-settlers. Addressed to Laurier as potential ally — "Dear Sir and Father" — the document is forthright in its political position, "We condemn the whole policy of the BC government towards the Indian tribes," and resolute in its demand for change, "We expect much of you...." The reading had immediate effect: Laurier seemed impressed, promising afterwards to look "carefully" into the claims of the chiefs, while the local newspaper, the *Kamloops Sentinel,* reviewed the event positively: "The Memorial is an excellently drawn up presentation of their case in support of their demand for treaties" (26 August 1910).

This well-staged reading was only one of a series of dissonant readings articulated that evening in the spaces between the city's routine obeisance to the authority of Empire and a confident measure of local, postcolonial assertion. Many civic groups, from the mayor to the chiefs, took part in an imaginary spectacle reflective of a durbar in colonial India: not only were there the familiar accoutrements of Empire — a high-ranking official on tour, a guard of mounted soldiers, a loyalty arch, a patriotic chorus of young women

— but there was emphasis on the homogeneity of the dominant community. By means of a performance structure that included receptions, entries, parades, tableaux, and formal addresses, the citizens of Kamloops were regulated as loyal citizens of the Dominion of Canada.

Along with this localized, on-site enactment of colonial allegiance, however, there was a subversive difference: the people of Kamloops also wanted specific political results — and were quick to complain the following day when these were not obtained. So what was traditionally conceived of as a passive show of loyalty, a civic spectacle with its presumed absence of serious local contestation, was in fact a piece of political theatre also staging an oppositional stance between the city and the other — the latter in this case the federal government represented metonymically by Laurier. What is striking in these performances, including that of the chiefs, is the high degree of political effect: what at first appear as routine acts of loyalty, with *pro forma* protocols and petitions, upon closer examination take on a much more sophisticated aspect — in Kamloops. Indeed, the particular *size* of the city seems to matter: the city's comparatively long history, the configuration of its different organizations, the proximity and relationship between Aboriginal and non-Aboriginal peoples, even the landscape that divides yet transports them, all seem in conjunction for the staging of a vital theatre.

Taken together, these performance activities suggest both a typology and efficacy of political theatre in a small city. As we learn from Ginny Ratsoy, however, the literature on small cities is not large; it is virtually silent on the subject of a theatre of consequence specific to small cities. Thus, we are left to ponder: Can a small city in British Columbia generate a vital theatre? A political theatre? It is conventionally understood that they cannot, that the theatre produced by small cities is inferior to and imitative of that produced in large cities, where theatre is seen as professional and meaningful (the two terms are too often non-problematically conflated), and that if there is value in the cultural performance in a small city, it is negotiable only in relation to metropolitan formations — Kamloops looking to Vancouver for its performative issues and models. Small city theatre often focuses on amateur activities and emphasizes Broadway musicals, light comedy, and mystery-thrillers, all based on published plays that have been successfully staged — and therefore validated — in major cities. Not surprisingly, much of the written theatre history of the province is Vancouver-centric (Hoffman, "Shedding"); when small cities do enjoy a professional theatre, with its presumed adherence to high standards and potent issues, they get it from a large centre: "the interior of the province has benefited from the touring undertaken by Vancouver based companies" (Todd 63).

According to the literature, the only other locus of a vital, political theatre is antipodal: a rural theatre. Located on ten acres near Armstrong, the Caravan Farm Theatre, with its romantic image of Clydesdale horses pulling colourful, gypsy-like caravans on tour through rural British Columbia, seems to signify a Native culture of authentic, rural innocence. In its politics, however, the Caravan is seen as an anarchistic theatre (Kirkley 35). In the Kootenays, Theatre Energy similarly attempted to provide a locally based theatre, recruiting actors to visit people living in the Slocan Valley, then, through collective creation, presentational acting, and simplified *mise en scène*, performing local stories and touring to small venues, earning a reputation as "a vital theatre" (Hoffman "Theatre Energy" 14).

Small cities like Kamloops, then, are left to occupy an uncertain middle terrain, caught between aspiring to the theatrical ferment of the big city while being too urban to claim the performance essence of the rural. If the theatre of the province's big cities is contested, emergent, and noteworthy, in small cities it is contrarily seen as a fixed object drawn from external sources, symbols, and language. If a big city is charged with discovering the political realities of a play production, along with aesthetic breakthroughs, the small city is content to replicate the political and fictional realities of somewhere else. While theatre in the former, at its best, is viewed as cultural practice, theatre of the latter is typically seen as innocuous entertainment. Not surprisingly, the theatre of large cities is much studied while that of small cities is ignored in the critical literature. In their summation of the history of western Canadian theatre, Benson and Conolly (23 ff) dwell almost exclusively on Vancouver, especially its theatre buildings and foreign touring stars, devoting only passing reference to the existence of an important Little Theatre near Naramata (the Home Theatre) and a resident stock company in Kamloops (the Ray Brandon Players).

It must be remembered, however, that these constructions are made largely by big city critics writing for, by and large, big city audiences. Andrew Parkin, in his survey of the resources available for the study of British Columbia theatre, under the rhetoric of "beginnings," "emergence," and "founding," focuses almost exclusively on activities in Victoria and Vancouver (New Westminster gets a brief mention), where all significant theatre apparently occurs. Writing from a metropolitan centre and refusing to acknowledge either a local settler or indigenous culture, they remind us how closely our theatre history is inflected with the experience of colonialism. Much of our theatre history in the province is a record of attempts by the two major cities to replicate the theatrical styles and content of professional theatre in the Imperial centres of Britain and the United States.

A reading of those who have written the theatre history of the province reveals an obsession with beginnings, buildings, and, above all, the markers of professional theatrical culture. Their silence on small cities is not evidence of the lack of a vital theatre, but rather that the critics themselves have been writing within colonizing tropes of discovery, exploration, and settlement, the smaller cities and towns standing in for the colonial margins. Indeed, this silence reveals a space for alternate critical strategies, especially as we examine the performance in Kamloops in 2004 of Tomson Highway's *Ernestine Shuswap Gets Her Trout*, which powerfully replays a performance that was originally staged in 1910.

Since its first performance, the Laurier Memorial has persisted as a central script in the ongoing presentation of local First Nations' struggle for land claims and cultural assertion. It has appeared in full text in newspapers and in a book dedicated to asserting Secwepemc culture (Murphy). In 2004 the Western Canada Theatre (WCT) of Kamloops, in association with the Secwepemc Cultural Education Society, commissioned and premiered a major new play written by a leading Canadian playwright, Tomson Highway, then sent it on to play on major stages in Vancouver and Calgary. Other performances in other Canadian cities will doubtless follow. The content of *Ernestine Shuswap Gets Her Trout* entirely concerns local history and has a political agenda: it is focussed on, and concludes with a partial reading of, the Laurier Memorial. It demonstrates that many of the negative political realities of the Memorial are still in effect: according to anthropologist Marianne Ignace, "the beliefs and principles that guided the struggle in 1910 were the same ones that are at the forefront today — Aboriginal title, Aboriginal rights, and inherent sovereignty as a nation" (qtd. in Murphy 11).

The play, however, is not structured on a widely known narrative, nor is it based on familiar historical characters; furthermore, it is not constructed along melodramatic plot turns but on two imagined events: the preparation of a banquet for the prime minister and a rehearsal for the reading of a political prose document written almost 100 years ago. The Laurier Memorial is surely unique: few other scripts in British Columbia theatre have proven so long-lasting and so vital. In so many ways, the production of *Ernestine* chal-

Figure 2. Janet Michael plays Ernestine Shuswap. As in the original presentation of the Memorial in 1910, a non-Aboriginal surrogate articulates linguistic resistance to imperialism. Photo by Murray Mitchell.

lenges us to rethink the nature and operations of theatre in a small city as sources of a vital, political theatre.

More specifically, we can ask: What role does *Ernestine Shuswap Gets Her Trout* play in repositioning theatre within its conventional framings, especially in the context of its small city ethos? Are there special alterations or expansions in how theatre operates within its boundaries that are peculiar to a small city? Are there special contexts or considerations available in Kamloops that alter the borders of theatrical performance as cultural catalyst? In its interaction with a small city environment, are there certain interventions available? That other politically significant productions have occurred in small cities, such as the unique (but little known) First Nations opera *Tzinquaw*, performed in Duncan in the early 1950s (Hoffman *Tzinquaw*), is further evidence. These questions suggest that Kamloops is uniquely placed for the creation of a vital, political theatre. To make this argument, I will examine the implications for an indigenous theatre according to several key characteristics of a small city. I will then hypothesize a historical site and model for a British Columbia theatre. In doing so, I will look at the two performances of the Laurier Memorial (1910 and 2004) for evidence of continuities.

Generally speaking, what can we say about the phenomenon of artistic culture in a city like Kamloops? Certainly culture can be a powerful force in a community — indeed it has the ability to help shape a city. Sharon Zukin, in *The Cultures of Cities*, has noted culture's *increasing* influence in the modern city: "The cultural power to create an image, to frame a vision of the city has become more important as publics have become more mobile and diverse, and traditional institutions — both social classes and political parties — have become less relevant mechanisms

of expressing identity" (2-3). Today, even as we examine its theatrical culture, Kamloops is already reimagining itself as a centre for the performance of sports. Well known as a hockey town, as well as for many other sporting activities, the city in 2001 adopted the slogan "Tournament Capital of Canada." In 1993 the Canada Summer Games were held in Kamloops; the city has also hosted the Labatt Briar Curling Championship, the World Fly Fishing Championship, the B.C. Seniors' Games, and others.

As Lon Dubinsky articulates in "The Culture of Participation," Kamloops has also supported almost 30 years of uninterrupted professional theatre — an achievement that is unique in British Columbia. Cities of similar size, such as Kelowna, Prince George, and Nanaimo, while they presently have professional theatre companies, have had less success than Kamloops in sustaining them. Most Kamloopsians would agree that the city environment would be unthinkable without the presence of the Western Canada Theatre. Indeed, the company actively reaches out to a wider demographic: "we appeal to such a broad cross-section of people," says David Ross ("Interview").

Does the company attempt to "create an image, form a vision," as Zukin suggests? At one level it does: like most professional theatre companies, WCT offers a season of plays carefully selected to appeal to its audiences. The plays are packaged in a promotional brochure making claims to take the audience to specified spaces — such as this year's "See the World from the Edge of Your Seat!" In this way, Ross fulfills his mandate to offer his audiences, which he sees as having an "urban mentality," the normative qualities of big city theatre. Each season he announces a season of plays, with conventional posters and live promotions (in effect, additional performances) claiming to provide a year of quality theatri-

Figure 3. Western Canada Theatre brochure for its 2003-2004 season promises to take audiences away from Kamloops, but more and more the theatre company is imagining the potential of the small city. Graphic design by Bonnie Mclean. Reproduced courtesy of Western Canada Theatre.

cal entertainment — on a par, say, with that of Vancouver. On the other hand, Ross believes that Kamloops' audiences also prefer the scale and local identity of his company. WCT, while presenting the conventional fare of theatre companies in other cities, has also attempted to engage its community by presenting a season made up of 60% Canadian-authored and important works based on local figures, such as *Flyin' Phil* (1991) by Ian Weir and Judi Bryson, *The Trials of Eddy Haymour* (1994) by John Lazarus, and *The McLean Boys* (1996) by Ian Weir and Judi Weir. In addition, as evidence of his confidence in his community audience, Ross has often included one or two plays that can be described as "risky," plays such as *Sex Tips for Modern Girls* (1985) by Edward Astley et al. and *Respectable* (2000) by Ron Chambers, both of which received strong audience reaction, the former moving city council to consider withdrawal of funding for WCT. On the other hand, many people rose to the controversial play's defence, resulting in a healthy debate and a better-educated audience. Other recent WCT practices include printing each play's program in the general culture magazine *Grasslands* and using members of The University College of the Cariboo's academic community to write program notes for each production, the idea being to provide extra "food for thought." In addition, more provocative theatre is presented regularly at the smaller Pavilion Theatre, where a black box performing environment allows for experimental and *avant-garde* productions from both locally generated and touring shows. Western Canada Theatre is only one of a number of strong community organizations that give performative identity to Kamloops. The prominent role played by local institutions is central and, as we will see below, has been so since 1910.

## The Laurier Memorial

Arriving at seven o'clock in the evening, Prime Minister Laurier was met at the train station by a reception committee of the city council, the Kamloops Board of Trade, and the Liberal Association. He was then driven through town, escorted by a detachment of the British Columbia Horse, to meet with representatives from various commercial and service organizations as well as the wider Aboriginal community. Along the way, the city band played, flags and bunting hung from numerous stores and houses, and at the corner of Victoria and Second Streets hundreds of electric lights illuminated a grand double arch that proclaimed "Welcome" and "Kamloops" in large letters. Beneath the arch, on a platform, a choir of young women sang "The Maple Leaf."

At the Kamloops Opera House, the prime minister met more dignitaries, listened to the mayor's speech, and received a formal paper written by the Kamloops Board of Trade. The city petitioned Laurier for federal help regarding a vital connection to the Grand Trunk Pacific Railway then under construction, for improvements to navigation on the North and South Thompson rivers, for expansion and relocation of the post office building, and for the establishment of an experimental farm. Afterwards, the Prime Minister was taken to the IOOF (International Order of Oddfellows) Hall for a meeting of local Liberals. It was here that the chiefs performed their Memorial. Laurier's response, duly reported in the next day's *Standard*, was characterized as polite but "vague."

"Sir Wilfrid Laurier is Royally Welcomed by the Citizens" headlined the *Kamloops Standard* (26 August 1910) — but the city's performance was immediately seen to have failed. The same newspaper, reviewing the events of the evening, asked what had really been achieved politically and concluded: "Nothing, absolutely nothing." Despite the prime minister's immediate response, promising "to look carefully into the representations made," (*Kamloops Sentinel*, 26 August 1910), the chiefs' Memorial also failed to achieve any political gains. At this time, Laurier's career was in decline: shortly after returning to Ottawa, he faced an election, which he lost. The next government, the Conservatives under Prime Minister Borden, continued a policy of ignoring the petitions, while the British Columbian government formed the infamous McKenna-McBride Commission, which further set back the claims of First Nations. Nonetheless, both the Kamloops and the First Nations peoples had staged an act of political theatre — and it seemed especially effective in a small city. Why was this?

Gerald Hodge and Mohammad Qadeer have identified the unique and highly varying nature of local institutions as crucial in a small town's identity: "Such variations in the mix of institutions are the basis of a small community's individuality" (114). Clearly, Kamloops in 1910 was a city with widely different but highly complementary interests: although primarily a cattle ranching and railway centre, the city also had a strong Aboriginal, white collar, and military presence. Rather than a limiting dominance such as is found in a one-industry town, the city presented a multi-faceted economic, political dynamic: the Board of Trade was looking for more land on the Indian Reserve, the military was concerned with presenting a new regimental appearance, while the Shuswap were seeking land title agreements. In addition, two new forces were promoting the area to the outside world as a health and settlement centre: the new hospital at Tranquille was establishing itself as the province's premier long-term care facility, and orchardists were looking to transform stock-raising lands into fruit-growing meccas at Walhachin and Sunnyside.

This crucial play of forces continues today, with the addition of a major post-secondary institution, The University College of the Cariboo, and a growing tourism industry, especially at the nearby Sun Peaks ski resort. This growth translates into a city looking inward and outward in equal measure, a city close enough to its landscape and heritage yet not bound by conservative restraints such as the "old versus new" identified by Qadeer and Hodge. As suggested earlier, this rhetorical situation opens a space for a postcolonial voice: if the small city is conventionally figured as a colonized subject, silent in relation to the authority of the large city, then that very silence must be re-examined — and the two productions of the Laurier Memorial are illustrative.

Indeed, their most striking characteristic is the powerful *use* of silence. In 1910, it was *not* the chiefs who recited the Memorial to Laurier, as might be expected, but a non-Aboriginal, a priest, acting as their surrogate. In 2004, the Memorial is again mediated, this time by a nationally known playwright working primarily in an imagined presentation of the Memorial. This mediation might be seen initially to confirm the stereotype that the First Nations peoples are historically muted and linguistically marginalized, limited to communicate only by the dominant discourse, but muted peoples can also speak subversively. As Helen Gilbert and Joanne Tompkins suggest, "the silence of the colonized subject is less clear and less total … [it can suggest that] the silence has been *imposed* on the colonized subject rather than simply 'discovered'" (189). Thus the chiefs, as well as Tomson Highway, are involved in a complex communicative strategy: by not speaking the Memorial directly, they avoid interpellation

by Imperial discourse while, in their proximic appearance, they are inscribed as expressive with a powerful *other* voice, one more far-reaching than direct speech. At the same time they demonstrate a mastery of English: in Highway's well-known plays, *The Rez Sisters* and *Dry Lips Oughta Move to Kapuskasing*, English is inflected with Cree; in *Ernestine*, it is grounded in Shuswap language rhythms. Even the Laurier Memorial, while officially written by James Teit, is similarly infused with the locutions of First Nations people. According to Marianne Ignace: "While written in the English language, [the Memorial] nonetheless reflects the way of speaking of the Secwepemc, Nlakapmx, and Okanagan people. This is clear from the simple, but eloquent style of speech, the expressions and metaphors used, and, of course, the concerns that are addressed. Some of these expressions can be best understood in light of Shuswap customs" (12-13).

Moreover, the chiefs actually *did* speak, but they did so in their own language, on their own terms: they had met earlier that summer at Spences Bridge, where they agreed upon a common history of contact and set out their concerns. James Teit, a botanist, was present and transcribed their vision, acting as secretary. Chief Louis of the Shuswap people was not only an experienced political leader but also a gifted orator. We can assume that he spoke the Memorial — that is, *his authentic version of it* — thus positioning both Teit and Le Jeune as subsequent interpreters, even possible mis-translators, thus producing a powerful metonymic gap. Interestingly, this gap is used again in *Ernestine*, where audiences hear authentic Shuswap language, carefully recorded under the direction of Chief Ron Ignace. In this way the Shuswap chiefs *do* speak, while their non-Aboriginal surrogates effectively increase the complexity and power of the voice and alter the anticipated

Figure 4. "Read it. Read the sign." But Ernestine Shuswap (Janet Michael) and Isabel Thompson (Lisa Dahling) can make only a partial reading ("NO …") of the signposts erected by the settler-invaders. Their inability amounts to a refusal to enable the markers of colonial authority. Photo by Murray Mitchell.

roles in the presentations. The chiefs in effect put words into the mouths of others who speak as disharmonious partners in the project; *all* now speak counter-discursively, not about a settler but an indigenous peoples' history. By disrupting the expectations of who is speaking, who is listening, and what the message ultimately means — in short, by giving the Memorial a multi-voiced enunciation — the authors/performers open the Memorial to continuing replay, to present and future meanings. Each performance demonstrates a refusal to speak according to conventional performative genres, but instead in a more local and complex configuration in which the

circulations of power are realigned and made contestatory. The result, in each case, is a highly complex and very local hybrid creation, one that seems particularly available in a small city with a sufficient number of strong institutional voices — particularly those of the First Nations.

First Nations performance culture is embedded in both productions of the Memorial. At first glance, the chiefs' 1910 presentation followed similar presentations made to Laurier in many cities on his western Canadian journey. In Kamloops, for example, both the mayor and the Kamloops Board of Trade presented petitions of their own.

However, from the evidence of the Memorial document itself, the chiefs' presentation followed indigenous First Nations practice. When, for example, a visiting chief, or indeed an important white visitor, came to the Shuswap, he would be formally greeted and welcomed to the area by means of strict performance protocols such as a welcoming speech, dances, and feasting. While the Memorial presentation may have looked like a standard petition to non-Aboriginal peoples, it was clearly reconfigured by the presenters.

Unlike other presentations with their *pro forma* recognition of colonial hierarchies, enunciated in a flattering address, followed by promises of loyalty and a list of requests, the Chiefs' Memorial engages in a dramatic reassigning of the roles and expectations between the parties. The chiefs, as they would do at a gathering, first assume a strong speaking position, forcefully claiming knowledge and full possession of the issues and major players in the regional politics. Rather than positioning themselves as subjects, they assume the role of equals, of heads of state welcoming another head of state — Laurier is welcomed to "our country." The address is further complicated by their assigning Laurier a mythical, imagined role, someone from a different era: the prime minister is identified specifically as someone *not* like those accompanying him, nor presumably like local politicians, but as a "real white," the kind of whites the First Nations dealt with during the fur trading days of the early 1800s, a white who dealt fairly with First Nations and who made no claims to their land. Constructing themselves centrally in history, the chiefs narrate a story of 100 years of contact, articulating their complex subjectivity in pre-contact, contact, and the postcolonial present.

What is important is that the chiefs made no strong effort to conflate the formalities of official western presentation with First Nations reception protocols: literally, by standing aside in strategic silence they maintained a crucial distance even as they engaged, and masterfully appropriated, non-Aboriginal performance modalities. In this way the 1910 Memorial was a contestatory hybrid performance: utilizing strong elements of both non-Aboriginal presentation and First Nations performance, not so much to blend the two or erase differences into one, but to explore the two in creative, unassimilated disjunction.

The silences in *Ernestine Shuswap Gets Her Trout* are greater than in the 1910 presentation, yet they also speak more eloquently. There is now less connection to historical fact: all the characters are fictional; their central action of preparing the feast is imagined; even their individual problems, such as Delilah Rose's marriage to a white colonizer or Annabelle's distress over the shooting death of her husband, have only a generalized background in fact. In this play, the key players of 1910 are nowhere to be found: there are no chiefs, no Laurier, no civic dignitaries, no Oddfellows Hall. The only continuity is the Memorial itself, which is read over by the women — not as a finished, formal performance but as a rehearsal. Highway has taken several steps backward to move the Memorial forward.

*Ernestine Shuswap Gets Her Trout* is about welcoming Laurier, and, as in 1910, there are provocative departures from expected norms of performance. Tomson Highway also reassigns roles: rather than the chiefs, he has four women representing the three regional tribes, the Shuswap, Okanagan, and Thompson, who were signatory to the 1910 Memorial. They are not high-ranking but ordinary women; nor are they participating in ceremonial formalisms but in gathering food and

Figure 5. Delilah Rose Johnson (Cheri Maracle) obsessively knits an oversized tablecloth while the hat of her absent white husband hovers overbearingly. She and Annabelle Okanagan (Lisa C. Ravensbergen) similarly adopt the dress code of the dominant culture, but their race and gender belie its apparent neutrality. Photo by Murray Mitchell.

preparing a feast for Laurier and, presumably, the chiefs. The prime minister is again refigured as an equal: frequently calling Laurier the "great Kahuna," the women deflate the role of the Prime Minister — he is what they want him to be; he could be one of them. In what is perhaps the play's most spectacular creation, the play re-imagines history from a First Nations perspective. Although there never was a First Nations feast served up to Laurier when he was in Kamloops, there *should have been* under normal, pre-contact protocols. By basing the play on the preparation for a meal, Tomson Highway re-inscribes the truth of the presentation by focusing on the exigencies of food gathering within local First Nations culture rather than the apparently static, largely unknown for-malities of the Oddfellows presentation. Highway's choice of four women from different regional bands also alludes to the vast political program undertaken by the regional chiefs. The Shuswap and the Okanagan, for example, were longtime foes; their cooperation in presenting the Memorial in 1910, even Highway's premise today that they might cooperate to prepare a feast, represents a considerable political initiative.

Environmental and historical factors also play particularly strong roles in a small city's self-identification. Similarly, spiritual and material connection with their territory has always been fundamental for First Nations peoples and is the basis for their oral histories: "The *stspetekwll* (ancient stories) told within each Nation on the Plateau and

Figure 6. Regional variants: Annabelle (Lisa C. Ravensbergen) and Isabel (Lisa Dahling), with a muted colonial speaker behind them, speak in registers that verbally and bodily restore elements of Aboriginal culture. Photo by Murray Mitchell.

shared among Nations, create a network of connections to place, as embedded in past events and past occurrences" (Ignace and Ignace "A Ranch" 6). Located at the confluence of the North and South Thompson rivers, two of the largest rivers in the province, Kamloops has a long history as an important meeting place for economic, social, and cultural transactions, particularly during contact years when, as James Teit reported in 1909: "The Kamloops people has the most intercourse with the other divisions … for the members of most bands repaired there with their furs" (467).

Kamloops is one of the oldest settlements in the province, its fur trading fort having been established in 1812, over three decades before Victoria. Mounts Peter and Paul, lying closely to the north, are prominent but are only two of a number of mountains that crowd and divide the city into a number of pocket communities, each having its own distinct identity and connection to other communities. Local inhabitants have long contended with crossing the waters, both literally and symbolically: bisected twice by large rivers, the city of Kamloops has seen a history of traversing cultures. Even today, the rivers continue to impose divisional lines, with the Aboriginal reserve in the northeast sector and the non-Aboriginal sectors in the west and south. The shifting locale of the various fur trading posts, along with the ongoing — but not uncontested — presence of the Shuswap have been key elements in the city's formation. Even while the Memorial was being presented in 1910, the city's Board of Trade, no doubt inspired by Victoria's recent relocation of the nearby Songhees reserve, sought to move the Shuswap from the city to a reserve ten miles north.

The waters have been the source of mythological as well as more contemporary narratives. According to Rachel Nash, Kamloops' formal iconography "comes from reliance on … the city's setting, especially the rivers and the sun" (324). Recurring images from Kamloops' history cluster around the early trading forts, with their varying locations on either side of the rivers, the Overlanders rafting down the North Thompson, and the CPR trains hauling along the city's main street. The Thompson River, and its sources, has long been the site of the Shuswap peoples' most important food source, the salmon; one of the central originary myths tells how the fish first came into Shuswap Lake (Willard 42). Each of these rivers participates in a unique flow and movement of cultures in close, dynamic relationship; in a particular scale and juxtaposition of cultures, on a terrain that MacKinnon and Nelson characterize as "an important crossroads function" (9). The landscape of Kamloops powerfully provides the setting for a creative hybrid performance, for what I am calling an authentic British Columbia theatre.

The performance history of the province can be divided roughly into the pre-colonial, the colonial, and the postcolonial periods. Significantly, although the 1910 staging of the Memorial took place during the colonial period, it anticipates the postcolonial period of *Ernestine* because the Memorial was conceived and presented not as a finished, stable script or even as an ideal production of conventional theatre but as a *pre-text* for wider cultural effects. In this way, it is to be seen as one of the "performance texts that serve spe-cific cultural and theatrical communities at particular moments as sites for the negotiation, transmission, and transformation of cultural values" (Knowles 259). This historical designation links the Memorial to a British Columbia meta-performance that crosses all periods, one that performs the ongoing story of arrival and display, of immigrant and Aboriginal cultures contending for ceremonial space on constantly shifting stages — as embodied locally by the waters of the Thompson rivers (see Hoffman "Captain George"; Hoffman "Shedding" for elaboration of this meta-performance).

The original model for this ceremonial theatre is the staging of *Nootka Sound; Or, Britain Prepar'd* in London in June 1790 at the Theatre Royal, Covent Garden. This extravagant, jingoistic musical production depicted events that had taken place one year earlier at Nootka Sound, on the west coast of what we now call Vancouver Island, as well as activities that were taking place as Britain readied itself for war with Spain over trading rights in the Northwest Pacific. London audiences watched and cheered as stout English tars contended with shifty Spanish sailors, while, nearby, the First Nations people — their habitat spectacularly depicted in "new and selected … scenes and decorations" (according to a poster advertising the show) — observed and reacted, embodying the triple roles of audience, performer, and setting. In this formal stage performance, however, at one of London's major theatres, Britain's colonizing venture in the northwest Pacific was ambivalent, even in the heart of Empire, evidenced in how generically dispersed the production was.

The performers play naval marines in rehearsal to stage the scenes of capture at Nootka Sound (the Spanish had captured several British merchantmen, their crews, and cargoes), then scenes of press gangs at work in

Portsmouth where a large war fleet is being assembled. But the lieutenant in charge tells several guests who have come to watch the rehearsal that the work is only "a slight specimen of Pantomime, Tragedy, Comedy, Opera and Farce, all together, egad!" (Hoffman "Captain George" 144). What are we to make of this devaluation: the overall "slight" show, its mishmash of genres, and its construction as a mere rehearsal, especially when juxtaposed with the play's jingoistic lyrics? The whole colonizing venture, even in its metropolitan application, was fraught with hesitation, especially as perceived by one possible member of the audience, George Vancouver, who had been to Nootka Sound earlier with Cook in 1778 and was soon to return and make his own famous voyages of exploration. Even the London newspaper critics found the piece wanting: while acknowledging the need for a patriotic gesture, they saw the work as unwieldy, *The Public Advertiser* (5 June 1790) declaring the work, "not of such a nature as to do any credit to the Royal Theatre." Thus began, if we need "beginnings," the representation of British Columbia on an Imperial stage, as a participant in a highly-charged political setting that was highly compromised by generic and thematic uncertainty.

What was actually occurring, however, was *the event* of British Columbia theatre, modelled in this early realization, which was based on widely divergent peoples performing essentialist aspects of their culture on shifting, improvised stages. During this precolonial period — about 75 years in length — Aboriginal peoples and the small white population co-existed as sporadic trading partners well before the intense colonizing pressure to acquire land and establish settlements that commenced in the 1850s. As dozens of mainly British and American vessels visited these shores during the late 18th century, establishing trading forts on land, there were numerous performative acts on ship, on shore, and on land, which were employed by both Native and visitor alike in the ritual acts of trading. Cole Harris has described how the maritime fur trade had "little … fixity and stability. It was always highly mobile" (60). These trading practices were improvisatory, typically including processions, the approach of dignitaries, the ceremonial offering of presents, followed by invitations to feasting, dancing, and storytelling, all in the service of successful bartering. All parties, Aboriginal and non-Aboriginal, utilized strong performative elements from their own cultures, carefully altering certain aspects and adding others to suit the occasion for political and economic ends. It was assumed that, at the end of the day, each would return to his or her home, and that all cultures would remain politically intact, especially as they were adapting to meet the changing performative dynamics of the present.

Thus a vigorous, hybrid theatre tradition evolved in British Columbia. It was improvisatory, contestatory, forceful, as mobile and assertive as the constantly shifting ships, canoes, and forts upon which it was staged, and it was characterized as much by linguistic disjunction, mistranslation, and mistakes, as it was by creativity and experiment. We can assume that many of these features continued into the colonial period, from 1849 to 1871, which Adele Perry has characterized as "racially plural, rough, and turbulent"(3). Without a common language, it was largely an oral culture, and a whole set of unspoken, paralinguistic signs and practices were literally set in motion, with the rules of the discourse constantly altering.

For example, while the nomenclature of "Memorial" was used — a common term for a common practice in those days — the presentation was/is not to be conceived of as simple petition, but as a form of oratory commonly used at gatherings and meetings of Plateau peoples of the Interior. The Memorial, along with other written documents from the same period, is to be approached as oral history rather than written history. That is, "the meanings and style of these documents must be understood in terms of the cultural conventions and protocols, and the style of discourse of Interior Salish peoples, as well as from the vantage point of their sense and experience of history" (Ignace and Ignace).

Robin Ridington calls this oral performance "storied speech" (278), in which people in hunting and gathering cultures speak both in relation to immediate, temporal concerns and in relation to the totality of the community's mythic understandings: "Storied speech makes subtle and esoteric references to common history, common knowledge, common myth" (278). More specifically, the Laurier Memorial is a script of particular rhetoric that may not be apparent to many non-Aboriginal readers. The Memorial bears no specific names in the signatures (unlike the Oliver Memorial signed the following year); only "The Chiefs of the Shuswap, Okanagan, and Couteau or Thompson tribes" are listed. The sole name attached to the document is that of J.A. Teit, listed as "secretary." Teit had long worked with the Plateau peoples and had supported their political efforts on other occasions; in the case of the Laurier Memorial, he had acted as translator. Despite his intervention, plus the fact that the Memorial is in English, the script is written in a hybrid language that reflects Aboriginal language. Comparing Teit's own writings, as in his ethnographic monographs, Ignace sees a striking difference: "They easily translate into the Aboriginal languages, and make use of English terms, meanings and concepts familiar and common in the Aboriginal languages ... [they] reflect the way of speaking of the Interior Aboriginal peoples" (17).

Clearly, in terms of performance genre, this is storytelling. When it was first presented in 1910, we can assume that the single speaker, Father Le Jeune, intoned the words with great power and passion. His word, gesture, and appearance, as well as his proximity to the chiefs, marked him as a surrogate chief, as both player and narrator for his peoples, creatively playing his own and their voices as well as that of the white settlers. Important First Nations traditions were maintained: the primary language of delivery was a sophisticated hybrid of English and Shuswap, the latter informing the other through subtle rhythms and gestures. Thus, powerful statements were made in a mode of delivery that was richly, multiply coded.

Similarly, Tomson Highway, as storyteller, masterfully asserts a controlling power in *Ernestine Shuswap Gets Her Trout* in a number of ways. In his role as a well-known First Nations playwright, he acts as surrogate chief and master of ceremonies, carefully stage managing the play's enunciation and its utterance. Similar to the chiefs in the first Memorial presentation, he speaks for a number of First Nations peoples in welcoming audiences and setting out a creative agenda. While the 1910 chiefs welcomed the prime minister to "our country," Highway begins his play by establishing a strong welcome to "our theatre" — that is, a theatre that evokes both an Aboriginal and a non-Aboriginal culture. In the beginning, a cello is heard; later, a piano is added when Beethoven's *Sonata for Cello* is played. In his first image, Highway centrally positions a group of storytellers who evoke a broad Aboriginal culture: the three women, each from a different tribe. Only their faces are lighted, done "so that these faces look like masks in a Greek tragedy ...

their voices should sound like ... those in a play by Euripides" (stage directions). By means of the women's storytelling monologues, Highway controls the moment-to-moment dynamic: each performer can speed up or slow down for effect and according to audience feedback.

In effect, each performance group, in 1910 and 2004, participates in an "indigenizing" process wherein the circulation of many different cultural values, under as many social registers, takes place in a situation where the only common denominator is a sense of potent, shared space. As Gilbert and Tompkins have observed, "Oral cultures emphasize not only the sound and rhythm of language and its accompanying paralinguistic features, but also the site from which it is spoken" (167). In this liminal space, the production of meaning is always ambivalent and at the same time full of possibility for creative, local formations. And always, however the land is conceived, geographic determinisms are crucial.

As in its early modeling in the 18th century, with the staging of *Nootka Sound; Or, Britain Prepar'd*, the two presentations of the Laurier Memorial participate in a British Columbia ur-performance that draws its essential character from both metropolitan and regional elements but is creatively a third type of theatre with possibly its greatest potential in the small city. Linked by mutually profitable economic relationships, the various groups displayed complex hybrid forms of performance as they appropriated and adapted aspects from their own and each others' cultures but remained creatively distinct. Thus, the nature of this hybridity, like the divisive politics of the province, has been one of resistance and oppositionality, rather than assimilative mutuality. On these interior waters, on in-between space, interculturation took place with its attendant negotiation,

contestation, and appropriation; in other words, intricate, localized forms of hybridity were set in motion that seem unique to a small city like Kamloops. I am suggesting that these closely model the kind of postcolonial theatre that the province has seen slowly developing, and, in the two performances of the Laurier Memorial, we see compelling evidence.

## Works Cited

Benson, Eugene, and L.W. Conolly. *English-Canadian Theatre*. Toronto: Oxford UP, 1987.

Chiefs of the Shuswap, Okanagan, and Couteau or Thompson tribes. "Memorial to Sir Wilfrid Laurier, Premier of the Dominion of Canada, August 25th, 1910." *The Daily News*, Kamloops, B.C., 24 October, 2001: A11.

Davis, Kingsley. "The Urbanization of the Human Population." *The City Reader*. Ed. Richard T. LeGates and Frederic Stout. New York: Routledge, 1996.

Dubinsky, Lon. "The Culture of Participation." *The Small Cities Book: On the Cultural Future of Small Cities*. Ed. W. F. Garrett-Petts. Vancouver: New Star Books, 2004. 65-84.

Gilbert, Helen, and Joanne Tompkins. *Post-Colonial Drama: Theory, Practice, Politics*. London: Routledge, 1996.

Harris, Cole. "Social Power and Cultural Change in Pre-Colonial British Columbia." *BC Studies* 115/116 (1997-98): 45-82.

Highway, Tomson. *Ernestine Shuswap Gets Her Trout*. Dir. David Ross. Western Canada Theatre. Sagebrush Theatre, Kamloops, B.C. January 22-31, 2004.

Hodge, Gerald, and Mohammad A. Qadeer. *Towns and Villages in Canada: The Importance of Being Unimportant*. Toronto: Butterworths, 1983.

Hoffman, James. "Captain George Vancouver and British Columbia's First Play." *Theatre Research in Canada* 21.2 (Fall 2000): 135-148.

——. "Theatre Energy: 'Doing Our Own Theatre.'" *Canadian Theatre Review* 39 (Spring 1984): 9-14.

——. "*Tzinquaw*: A Site of Postcolonial Performance in British Columbia." Unpublished Paper, presented at BC Studies Conference, University of British Columbia, May 2003.

——. "Shedding the Colonial Past: Rethinking British Columbia Theatre." *BC Studies* 137 (Spring 2003): 5-47.

Ignace, Marianne. "A Commentary on the Laurier Memorial." *Coyote U: Stories and Teachings from the Secwepemc Education Institute*. Ed. P.J. Murphy, George P. Nicholas, and Marianne Ignace. Penticton, BC: Theytus Books, 1999. 9-17.

Ignace, Marianne, and Ron Ignace. "A Ranch of Our Own: A History of European/First Nations relations as told through the Memorial to Sir Wilfrid Laurier, 1910." Paper presented at "Worlds in Collision" Colloquium, University of Victoria, February 22-23, 2002.

Kirkley, Richard Bruce. "Caravan Farm Theatre: Orchestrated Anarchy and the Creative Process." *Canadian Theatre Review* 101 (Winter 2000): 35-39.

Knowles, Richard Paul. "Reading Material: Transfers, Remounts, and the Production of Meaning in Contemporary Toronto Drama and Theatre." *Essays on Canadian Writing* 51-52 (Winter 1993-1994): 258-295.

MacKinnon, Robert, and Ross Nelson. "Urban and Economic Change in Kamloops: Postindustrial Adjustments in a Staples Economy." *The Small Cities Book: On the Cultural Future of Small Cities*. Ed. W.F. Garrett-Petts. Vancouver: New Star Books, 2004. 23-47.

Murphy, P.J., George P. Nicholas, and Marianne Ignace, eds. *Coyote U: Stories and Teachings from the Secwepemc Education Institute*. Penticton: Theytus Books, 1999.

Nash, Rachel. "Change and Resistance: Kamloops' Civic Symbols and Identity in the 1990s." *The Small Cities Book: On the Cultural Future of Small Cities*. Ed. W.F. Garrett-Petts. Vancouver: New Star Books, 2004. 319-331.

Parkin, Andrew. "The New Frontier: Towards an Indigenous Theatre in British Columbia." *Theatrical Touring and Founding in North America*. Ed. L.W. Conolly. Westport, CT: Greenwood Press, 1982.

Pavis, Patrice. *Dictionary of the Theatre: Terms, Concepts, and Analysis*. Toronto: U of Toronto P, 1998.

Perry, Adele. *On the Edge of Empire: Gender, Race, and the Making of British Columbia, 1849-1871*. Toronto: U of Toronto P, 2001.

Ratsoy, Ginny. "Away from Home, or Finding Yourself Back In Kamloops: Literary Representations of the Small City." *The Small Cities Book: On the Cultural Future of Small Cities*. Ed. W.F. Garrett-Petts. Vancouver: New Star Books, 2004. 205-220.

Ridington, Robin. "Cultures in Conflict: The Problem of Discourse." *Canadian Literature* 124/5 (1990): 273-289.

Ross, David. Personal Interview. 21 May 2003.

Seymour, Dave. Personal Interview. 27 May 2003.

Teit, James Alexander. *The Jessup North Pacific Expedition*, Vol. 2, Part VII, The Shuswap. New York: E.J. Brill, Leiden, G.E. Stechert, 1909.

Todd, Robert B. "British Columbia, Theatre." *The Oxford Companion to Canadian Theatre*. Ed. Eugene Benson and L.W. Conolly. Toronto: Oxford UP, 1989. 60-63.

Willard, Ike. "Shuswap Dances." *Shuswap Stories*. Ed. Randy Bouchard and Dorothy I. D. Kennedy. Vancouver: CommCept, 1979. 129-131.

Zukin, Sharon. *The Culture of Cities*. Cambridge, MA: Blackwell, 1995.

Figure 1. Bone game at the Evan Deneault memorial celebration, Skeetchestn 2004. Photo by Marianne Ignace.

# Tagging, Rapping, and the Voices of the Ancestors:
# Expressing Aboriginal Identity Between the Small City and the Rez

Marianne Ignace,
with George Ignace

[Aboriginal young people] are the current generation paying the price of cultural genocide, racism and poverty, suffering the effects of hundreds of years of colonialist public policies. The problems that most Aboriginal communities endure are of such depth and scope that they have created remarkably similar situations and responses among Aboriginal youth everywhere. It is as though an earthquake has ruptured their world from one end to another, opening a deep rift that separates them from their past, their history and their culture. They have seen parents and peers fall into this chasm, into patterns of despair, listlessness and self-destruction. They fear for themselves and their future as they stand at the edge.

— *Report of the Royal Commission on Aboriginal Peoples*

## Introduction

While attending an academic conference in a large U.S. city, I became engaged in conversation and "comparing notes" with a Lakota mother about raising First Nations youth between the reserve/reservation and the city. As we were sharing our experiences, the full degree to which Afro-American rap culture and graffiti art had penetrated the lives of our youth on both sides of the border hit home to me. Our 21-year-old son, before he was killed on New Year's Eve 2002, loved rap. Among the cherished possessions we found were his own rap songs sung into a small tape recorder a few days before he died. Our 16-year-old son's pastimes and artistic pursuits are consumed by tagging and rapping, like every one of his peers on the "rez" we call our home, Skeetchestn, a reserve community some 60 kilometres east of Kamloops. Graffiti art with distinct hints of Aboriginal motifs now adorns our horse barns, various walls at the reserve community, and places in the city of Kamloops.

In this chapter, we will explore the contemporary expression of cultural identity — and the simultaneous seeking of identity — among youth who live in the rural First Nations reserve community connected with Kamloops, the small city. The medium of expression of this emerging Aboriginal identity, as we will describe it, involves the "culture" of rap music and tagging, usually associated with Black ghettos, but beyond that, with all marginalized youth in the cities generally. As a visual and oral art of protest, graffiti or "tagging" represents a defiant mode of artistic self-expression, consisting of the simultaneous concealment and flaunting of individual and collective sense of self through the act of inscribing messages into the public landscape, in defiance of the hegemony of middle-class culture. More than a rebellious means of leaving random marks in the public landscape of the city — and now the reserve — it is an elaborate and intricate art form, a complex layering of thought and experience in verbal and visual messages.

Superficially, graffiti appears to be an art form that is removed from the cultural traditions of Canadian Aboriginal peoples, including the Secwepemc. We must remind ourselves, however, that all art, all culture, rests on the continuous creative rethinking of personal and collective identity. Graffiti art between the small city and the rez presents an instance of this.

In a wider sense, this chapter explores the ways in which Aboriginal culture relates to, reacts to, and is informed by the global culture of visual art and music. It may be tempting to suggest that these ways of cultural expression are yet further ways Aboriginal peoples' lives have been acculturated, and further ways indigenous traditions and patterns of living, thinking, and being have been pushed aside by Western culture. Our point here, however, is that finding new media of expression provides unique ways of integrating Aboriginal self-reflection and expression of culture. Our youth are subjected through the media to the steamrolling effect of modern "pop culture." Yet, at home on the rez, they maintain traditions of playing the Secwepemc bone game, sweating, hunting, and fishing. Through a lived connection to

the traditions of the Aboriginal past, the practices of the elders and their voices are woven forward into the present. In synthesis, both the meaning of Aboriginal tradition and the meaning of graffiti art are elevated to a new level.

Contemporary youth also live in the world of multiple cultural and ethnic identities. Aboriginal identity is connected to multiple ethnic groups within and outside of the Aboriginal community, in the neighbouring small city, and in larger cities across North America. Youth identity is also connected to multiple layers of experience. At the same time, we must understand that rap and graffiti are artistic expressions that emerge from experienced marginalization, violence, anger, and frustration. Aboriginal youth in the city, and on the contemporary reserve connected to the city, grow up in a context that includes experiences of racial discrimination and marginalization — often in subtle forms of symbolic violence (Bourdieu). Moreover, North American statistics on Aboriginal life and death expectation, accidental death rates, violence, and suicide show that all of them far exceed those in the non-Aboriginal population. Our youth are the living statistics who, within our communities, have to come to terms all too often with grief, loss, and the fallout of violence, while surrounded by the traditions of the Aboriginal community, elders, and what remains of the comforting practices of the past.

We present this topic from a multiple perspective as members of the Aboriginal community, parent, youth, artist, and social researcher. As Renato Rosaldo has so aptly shown, in writing about culture, the author's experience and one's immediate connection to the multi-vocal subjects of our enquiry inform and influence our understanding of what we write and how we write about the experience of "other." Writing this essay also reflects a process of recent experience. As co-author (Marianne Ignace), I admit that not long ago I shared the attitudes and reactions of middle-class culture around graffiti art, which constituted itself as an anthropological "other." I did not know it, was alienated by it, associated it with the vandalism of public places, and thus did not learn to understand it, blinding myself to the connection it has with contemporary Aboriginal culture, the reservation, and the small city that is a point of connection for members of our reserve community. Personal experience taught me to look for layers of meaning in forms of expression that previously escaped me.

## Aboriginal Youth in the 21st Century

My explorations, destinations, have often led to devastation,

I've been across the nation, no appreciation,

Occupations none I'm facin'

Time is wasted, how I hate this.

— George Ignace, Rap Beat 2004

In 1996, the Royal Commission on Aboriginal Peoples (RCAP) provided the Canadian public with qualitative and quantitative research that highlighted the situation of Aboriginal youth in Canada, noting that 56.2% of Aboriginal people in Canada are under the age of 25, with Aboriginal youth (15-24 years of age) accounting for almost half of the under-25 population, 14.2% of the Canadian population, but nearly 20% of the Aboriginal population. Nearly half of Aboriginal youth live in non-reserve urban centres, a significant portion of them living near large urban areas like Montreal, Toronto, Winnipeg, etc. In other words, Canada's Aboriginal population is a young population dominated by a large portion of youth; it is also an increasingly urbanized population. While this article does not deal with Aboriginal youth primarily living in urban centres, it will contribute to our understanding of the connection between global culture, urban centres, and rural reserve communities.

As the extract from the RCAP report at the beginning of this chapter shows, contemporary Aboriginal youth also live in an era of fallout from the cultural genocide produced by more than 100 years of internal colonization and oppression through state policies that have affected Aboriginal people as individuals, their communities, and their Nations. The tremors of the "earthquake" of cultural, political, and social dispossession and marginalization are experienced by Aboriginal youth across Canada in their day-to-day lives; whether in the ghettos of contemporary reserve communities, or in the ghettos of urban centres, the rates of suicide and violent deaths among the Aboriginal population dwarf those of non-Aboriginal communities. For example:

- The death rate from injury in the Aboriginal population is three to four times higher than the national rate.
- The suicide rate among First Nations male youth is eight times higher than the national Canadian average for females and five times higher than for males.
- In 1996, the unemployment rate for Aboriginal youth was 32%, almost double the rate for non-Aboriginal youth.
- The average income for Aboriginal people in 1991 was $14,561, compared to $24,000 for all Canadians.
- Only 42% of Aboriginal children complete Grade 12, compared to 74% of Canadian children overall.

Other kinds of social, economic, and personal trauma experienced by Aboriginal youth also exceed those of the mainstream

305

Canadian population. In that sense, Aboriginal youth are "living statistics," having experienced the uprooting and devastating influences of physical violence, the occurrence of death in the family and community, and the fallout from the many facets of the "residential school syndrome" of their parents and grandparents.

The above statistics show their human faces in Aboriginal communities throughout Canada, including the south-central Interior of British Columbia. Aboriginal communities here and elsewhere have worked hard to overcome the multiple traumata produced by dispossession from land, government policy, racial discrimination, the residential school system, chronic unemployment, alcohol and drug dependency. Last, but not least, the degradation of the environment and the hazards of the personal and collective challenges to safety and well-being imposed by terrorism and war all occupy and impact on the sense of identity and well-being of Aboriginal youth.

The Royal Commission report noted that Aboriginal youth are often wary of government-devised solutions, including those devised by their own First Nations governments. As the report states: "When they speak out, their voices go unheard. Feeling marginalized, excluded and devalued, some have lost faith in their communities." The sense of marginalization and loss expressed by Aboriginal youth across the country is also connected to a "search for culture and identity" (151). Rather than locating this search for culture and identity in simple (and perhaps impossible) connections with one's ancestors, we need to ask whether seeking Aboriginal culture and identity in an elusive pristine past is the only alternative to cultural survival of Aboriginal youth. Although the realities of contemporary life and the exposure to global culture have done their work, they can be a

source of creative power for the expression of cultural identity.

## The Rez and the City
## — Skeetchestn and Kamloops

The city of Kamloops, situated at the confluence of the North and South Thompson rivers, is the site of the ancient Secwepemc village of Tk'emlúps ("confluence"), one of the main villages at the hub of indigenous trading activity in the southern Secwepemc Nation. The Secwepemc Nation, in turn, represents the northernmost Aboriginal Nation on the Canadian Plateau, its boundaries stretching from near Jasper and Tête Jaune Cache to the Quesnel Lake area, along the Fraser and Thompson River plateaus to Ashcroft, across the ridges south of Kamloops Lake to the Shuswap and Adams Lake plateaus, and eventually over to the Arrow Lakes, and along the upper reaches of the Columbia River to Jasper.

With the allocation of Indian reserves in the south-central Interior of British Columbia during the late 1870s, less than 2% of Secwepemc territory came to comprise the reserve lands of 17 Indian reserve communities or Bands within the margins of the Aboriginal territory of the Nation. Several of these reserves are situated within a 75-kilometre radius of Kamloops, including the Kamloops Indian Band itself, comprising an on-reserve population of about 600, whose lands are on the northeast shore of the confluence: the Skeetchestn Indian Band (on-reserve population about 250), situated some 60 kilometres to the west of Kamloops, as well as several other reserve communities located in a 60-mile radius of the city. Although the Kamloops Band can be characterized as an urbanized community, separated from the city of Kamloops by a bridge across the river, the lives of Secwepemc people in the above reserve communities and other reserves farther away from Kamloops are separated from the lives of residents of the city by legal categories, lifestyles, social connections and, especially, cultural values and social practices.[1]

Youth and adults from Skeetchestn maintain ongoing connections to Kamloops; they rely on services not available on the reserve, including schooling, shopping, medical care, as well as all facets of entertainment: movies, concerts, hanging out in the streets and malls, visiting friends, all of which creates ongoing and significant physical exposure to North American consumer culture in all its dimensions. The high school bus, on a daily basis, transports more than a dozen youth from the reserve to the city; most families from the reserve travel to Kamloops at least once per week to shop, access medical services and other government services, seek entertainment, or "hang out." Since the Skeetchestn Indian Band office, similar to that of other bands in the area, is by far the largest employer of the community, many band members commute to Kamloops itself, or to the many First Nations service organizations on the Kamloops Indian reserve, on an almost daily basis.

The connection to mainstream North American culture is also maintained through the media: all households on the reserve are hooked up to the wider world by satellite televisions; most households with younger people have computers with internet access; all households have VCRs; many have DVD players; and most young people have portable CD players and other electronic music devices. Thus, youth from the reserve are consumers of modern media pop culture, including music, and other forms of mass media entertainment, fashions, and fast foods. Kamloops, in this sense, is the physical manifestation of the world beyond the reserve, and is an ongoing, if not daily presence in the lives of youth from the reserve.

The physical connection with larger cities, including Vancouver, is far more remote for most of the youth, with only some of them having spent any significant amount of time there or being connected to these large cities on an ongoing basis, although television, video, Internet, and radio provide frequent and ongoing electronic exposure to the big cities beyond Kamloops. Youth from the Skeetchestn reserve express a progression of connections between "the rez" and the outer world: the Kamloops Rez as connected to the small city (Kamloops), the Big City (Vancouver), and the urban world beyond. In turn, the familiarity with people, people's ability to trust others, the dangers of drugs and crime, all change as one moves from the local reserve, to the urban reserve, to the small city, and to the big city. Young people express concern that the negative influences of the city are having more and more impact on the ability of members of the reserve community to trust one another, to stay away from the realms of crime and addiction. For youth and adults from a rural reserve community like Skeetchestn, the connection to Kamloops as a city is also interwoven with the connections through kinship to the Kamloops reserve community and other reserve communities, which encompass off-reserve members who live in Kamloops, most often on the North Shore.

## Life on the Rez — The Voices of the Ancestors, Death, and Alienation

Aside from their connections with the outside world, Skeetchestn, like any reserve, remains a close-knit community of interrelated members of about a dozen extended families. Youth from the community still participate widely in traditional resource harvesting activities of the Secwepemc people: nearly all youth participate in their families' summer and fall spearfishing of salmon from the Thompson Rivers; many partcipate in late spring camp-outs at the ancient trout fishery at HiHium Lake; and most youth also accompany their fathers and uncles to go deer and moose hunting for their families' subsistence, with some of them undergoing the Secwepemc male coming-of-age ceremony — killing their first animal and distributing the meat among their elders and relatives. A few young people have also fasted and stayed in the mountains, carrying on ancient traditions.[2]

During the past decade, the Salish bone game or lehal, *llek̓mew̓es*, has made a comeback among younger people. This traditional guessing game, played to the accompaniment of drum songs, in sets of two opposing teams, has become a frequent pastime among youth from Secwepemc communities and other Interior Plateau communities, who carry out bone game tournaments — often with cash prizes for the winning team — as often as floor hockey or basketball tournaments. Pow wows are also important events for the celebration and practice of cultural traditions. Youth from all Secwepemc communities attend and participate in the Kamloopa Pow wow and other smaller regional pow wows.

The enactment of practices and values that are connected to the indigenous past manifests the most in the rituals and ceremonies associated with funerals in Secwepemc communities. Both male and female young people participate in all aspects of funeral preparations and ceremony. Upon the news of a death, a fire is lit and maintained, guiding the spirit of the deceased person along the journey and comforting the survivors. Young people stay to tend the fire, to help out, to just be there to comfort the family members, and to do chores for them. Young girls help to mind children, to clean the house where the wake will be held, and to cook. Other young people go hunting for deer and moose to feed the people gathered at the wake and for the feast that follows the funeral. In Secwepemc belief, the animal that is hunted and killed is thought to give its life for the mourners, and the way it lets itself be killed gives signs or messages from the deceased that are in turn witnessed and interpreted by the hunters. The young men also help as gravediggers and pall-bearers, and with other practical and ceremonial tasks, including a final bone game and card game in honour of the deceased (see Figure 1).

Besides the power of grief and the spiritual meanings around death that the entire community experiences, funerary ceremonies represent an important socializing power in First Nations communities: they put young people in touch with the ceremonies, songs, and voices of their ancestors and give them a meaningful role in powerful events that affect most everyone in the small reserve community. This connection to the spiritual and cultural ways of the ancestors is tacit and matter of fact. As young people themselves observe, in times like these, "Everyone steps in; everyone knows what to do" without having to be reminded. Some young people, dropouts from school and without tasks that validate them in everyday life, find validation from elders and other community members in the roles they play during such times and take pride in being reliable through following their tacit roles during funeral rites.

While the work of grieving takes place in ritual acts which give comfort to the survivors, it also takes place in everyday reactions among the survivors, and in ever-different forms. The messages of anger and alienation in graffiti art and rap music serve as ways for youth of the community to live with grief. Aboriginal young people listen to these media in light of their individual and collective experience with grief in all its dimensions

Figure 2. Graffiti on a barn at the rez, 2004. Photo by Marianne Ignace.

and with the angered frustration of collective marginalized existence as it affects Aboriginal youth, Black Americans, and many others. The aesthetic and entertainment functions of these forms of art exist beyond the act of mourning; but in so far as they give expression to multiple levels of feeling and being experienced by youth in the Aboriginal community connected to the city, the lyrics of rap songs and the images of graffiti art have become connected to the collective memory of the community as it is shared by youth (see Figure 2).

## The Connection of Aboriginal Youth Culture to Rap and Graffiti Art — "How I Came to See Graffiti and Rap in a Different Light"

Like the writers of the 1996 *Report of the Royal Commission on Aboriginal Peoples*, most of us think of the reconnection with and thus survival of Aboriginal traditions as "going back to the old ways" — reconnecting in an unquestioning way with the traditions, practices, world views, and values of the past. For Aboriginal youth, however, the connection with tradition is also connected to living in a contemporary world, a world full of contra-

dictions with the past, and one that begs the rethinking of individual and collective identity.

For me as mother, anthropologist, and member of the Secwepemc community, the connection with tradition in my own family had languished for years: hunting, fishing and plant gathering; participating in community events; encouraging our children to *etsxem* — sweat and seek out the company of elders; trying to speak Secwepemctsin with them. Moreover, I was privileged to reflect on the continuation of Aboriginal traditions in an academic context through my involvement as instructor and coordinator of an Aboriginal university program. However, I did not conceive of a connection between Aboriginal traditions, youth, their future, and graffiti art until experience taught me otherwise. As Renato Rosaldo reminds us in his essay "Grief and the Headhunter's Rage," profound human experience, including death, whose connection with not only grief but also rage is often suppressed in Anglo-American society, allows us to re-evaluate social and cultural connections in a different light and gain perspectives on how others construct meanings of events. This is where

309

graffiti art comes into play.

Graffiti (from *graffito*, "scratched or scribbled messages") have been defined as drawings or inscriptions made on a wall or other surface, usually to be seen by the public. Graffiti writing rests on the artistic and aesthetic distortions of letters to produce messages, similar to a secret code, indecipherable to outsiders. Graffiti, especially in its popular image sustained by the dominant culture, is associated with vandalism and the defacement of public walls through the random "scribbling" of spray-painted messages. While "bombing" — the secret and hurried inscribing of spray-painted messages and images in public places — is connected to the social and artistic connotations of graffiti art; elaborate "graphing" of authorized public spaces through the detailed multiple layering of intricate scripts and images has gained popularity as an art form rather than as "crime art."[3] The essence of graffiti, of course, is the *unauthorized* and thus defiant nature of its production, which resists and opposes bourgeois culture.[4] Public perceptions of graffiti art, whether on unauthorized murals, on trains, and in other public places, have the connotations of "vandalism art," "guerilla art," produced by individuals who feel marginalized and without voice, and who thus give themselves voice by leaving their visual tracks in the landscape. The visual tracks, however, are like coded messages, decipherable to those who have learned to read them; undecipherable, and hence shrugged off, by mainstream society.

Art historians, archaeologists, and folklorists have pointed to the connection between contemporary graffiti art denoting in semi-coded messages that "so and so was here" and ancient cave art of indigenous peoples. Within the traditions of the Plateau Aboriginal peoples, rock paintings throughout the landscape of the Aboriginal territories

of the Secwepemc and surrounding nations were often associated with spirit guardian quests or other experiences of visits in far away yet familiar places. Symbolic images of people, animals, and natural phenomena, rendered in an artistic style that requires insider skill to decipher the message left by the sojourner, remind us of the travels, encounters, thoughts, and experiences of long-ago ancestors. In the modern style of graffiti art, "bombed" messages are left in the urban or reserve landscape as clues to the travels and experiences of urban youth, but also Aboriginal youth.

I remember my consternation when these marks in the landscape began to invade the spaces of our barns, our walls, and our belongings, aggravated by my inability to decipher them. Graffiti art, with its angry allusions, also looked like violent art and found its acoustic counterpart in the reverberations of rap beats emanating from the ghetto blasters in our teenagers' rooms and those of their peers, friends, and cousins. As angry "black noise," it accompanied the visual messages inscribed into the landscape of the rez and the urban landscape (Rose). It appeared that, in complementary visual and acoustic art forms, graffiti and rap were typical cases of marginalized art forms attracting youth. Had our reserve youth become so ghettoized that they sought identification with the pop culture of the ghetto?

In late December 2002, our 21-year-old son Gabriel "Skooks" died a violent death at the hands of others. Only two months later, a 16-year-old boy from Skeetchestn, cousin or friend to all youth from the reserve, took his own life. Soon after, Sam Camille, a male elder who was a pillar to our community, passed away.

In the time that followed, especially the time after the two violent deaths, the grief that consumed our family, community, and

Figure 3. *Inner City Bandits* by George Ignace, 2002. Pencil drawing on paper, 40 x 40 cm. Photo by Marianne Ignace.

all those connected with the living and the dead took many forms: rage and anger among them; numbing pain at other times. The rap lyrics of Tupac, "They killed my Brother," took on a new meaning; so did the graffiti message, "Skooks," left on our son's carved headstone, and the messages of grief, anger, and alienation that were left by community youth on buildings of the rez and, eventually, on places in the urban landscape.[5]

The angry messages of graffiti art made sense when seen in a new light and a new context, as did the angry messages of rap music: in the same way that graffiti art gives visual expression to the voices of marginalized others, rap (hip-hop) culture represents

the marginalized voices or "vernacular ethos" of the struggle for voice among the urban ghetto populations in North America.[6] The lyrics and rhythms of rap music — often represented in the music of Black artists — give voice to their experiences with, and fear of, violence, their alienation from social and political power.

## "What the art means" — Examples of Graffiti Art Produced by First Nations Youth

The images that accompany this chapter were produced by First Nations youth from Skeetchestn and Kamloops at St. Ann's Academy in Kamloops, as a project providing

Figure 4. *Inner City Bandits II — Kids with Cans* by George Ignace, 2003. Felt pens on paper 80 x 60 cm. Photo by Marianne Ignace.

outlets for young artists to express their sense of, and search for, identity through visual art. Figure 3 is a pencil drawing titled *Inner City Bandits* (George Ignace, ca. 2002). In form and organization, it invites comparison with Secwepemc artist David Seymour's oil canvases from the 1980s that reflected on the contrasts and continuity between the Aboriginal traditions of living on the land, in harmony with nature, and the changed material culture of contemporary Secwepemc in the late 20th century. In *Inner City Bandits*, the trees are intricate tags containing messages of the alienated "abnormal" inner city kids and allusions to people and events in the landscape, mixed with the pain of losing them. The pristine nature of David

Seymour's art has become the "sunk in scriptures" tag of the modern landscape between the reserve and the city that young people live in and take inspiration from. The person in the centre stands within a sprawling landscape; the "inner city bandit" to the left, a young person who lives at the margin of the urban sprawl. Strangers and "aliens" occupy the spaces on the margins.

*Inner City Bandits II — Kids with Cans* represents a reflection on biohazards, the threat of nuclear war, the impact of 9/11, and the red-orange destruction of cities (see Figure 4). The "kids with cans" on the left are the Aboriginal and non-Aboriginal youth who react to the destruction of the world by spray-painting their messages of frustration,

Figure 5. *Road Puzzle* by Lyle Paul, 2003. Pencil drawing on paper 40 x 40 cm. Photo by Marianne Ignace.

grief, and anger into this landscape informed by destruction, the encroachment of the city, and the fact that those in power play dice with the fate of the kids with cans in the large city. The "Whoa" tag asks for a halt to the destruction beyond the control of the kids with cans.

The puzzle-piece pencil drawing by Lyle Paul represents another reflection on the search for identity (see Figure 5). Roads and railways lead to the city and then contort and crumble in the spaces away from the city. The individual, on a quest towards understanding not unlike the spirit guardian quests of his ancestors, has the road/railway to the future coming from within him; he seeks to find the path to the places in all four directions. In a new guise, he has become a "kid with a

[spray] can"; the road turns into a precipice, with destruction in all directions. A "stop" sign that warns the traveller is contorted and displaced.

George Ignace's pencil drawing *In The Beginning There Was Death* was produced in 2003, following the homicide death of his brother, Skooks, the suicide of his friend Evan Deneault, and the death of a community elder, Sam Camille (see Figure 6). The themes and tags in this drawing move in a counter-clockwise direction: the beginning of all is death, and the lost souls (in the perception of the survivors) at the top; in the right-hand corner, the unknown and uncertain imagined realm of after-life: "You don't know what happens next," the names of the significant dead as victims inscribed as tags. The

313

Figure 6. *In the Beginning There Was Death* by George Ignace, 2003. Pencil drawing on paper 40 x 60 cm. Photo by Marianne Ignace.

dangers for the survivors are depicted on the bottom: crack heads, numbed by drug use, without the ability to feel, see, or listen. The inscription reads:

> My eyes are open, but I cannot see, I am carefully listening though I can't hear,
> There is no feeling in my touch, and no essence when I breathe,
> Not a taste comes to mind, what am I?

I'm unaware of my surroundings, lost and wouldn't know if someone had found me.

The counter-clockwise movement leads back to an unknown afterlife in the top left, symmetrical with the one on the top right. Intuitively to the observer, there is again a resemblance in form to the 1980s oil canvases of Secwepemc artist David Seymour. The present and future that emanates from

314

Figure 7. Mural of St. Ann's Academy First Nations arts students, 2003. Acrylic paint on concrete 4 x 2.4 m and 3 x 2.4 m. Photo by Marianne Ignace.

George Ignace's drawing, however, is grim, marked by the experience of violent death, the observation of drug use, and the double uncertainty of origins ("In the beginning, there was death") and of the fate in afterlife of sibling, friend, and elder. Although there is a desire to find out "What am I," grief has numbed the artist; the knowledge that drugs further numb perception, and a sense of the "abnormal" — inscribed into the centre of the artwork — permeates the artist's sense of self.

The sense of bewildered and uncertain identity also permeates the mural by First Nations art students at St. Ann's Academy.[7] In the foreground of a river and the earth tones of the physical landscape, a Black rap-per and a "city bandit" populate the land-scape. The smoke that rises from the high-rises of the city reads: "accept abnormal skills" (see Figure 7).

## Conclusions: Tradition and Innovation — The Complex Destiny of Aboriginal Culture

The examples of drawings, murals, and paintings show the intense emotions which growing up at the margins of the rural reserve and the city evokes in First Nations youth. Young people in the early 21st century express their grief and anger at community violence and loss, but they also reflect on being increasingly connected to the urban landscape, and beyond that to the fortunes of

315

Figure 8. *Native Issues* by George Ignace, 2003. Acrylic pens on canvas paper 80 x 60 cm. Photo by Marianne Ignace.

the global landscape. The reflection on their traditional cultures asks questions about the past and destiny.

Amidst the immersion in graffiti art to express youths' concerns about loss, grief, alienation, identity, and the future, the art presented here shows a fusion of the urban and the traditional in both form and content. In form and iconography, in the shape of the images, this graffiti seemingly bears little resemblance to what we expect of Aboriginal art: the Aboriginal youth in these drawings take the shape of "city bandits" and "kids with cans"; even the ancestors are not attached to visible images of Secwepemc culture. In the depiction of landscape or

humans, we find little evidence of symbols, icons and images that we usually associate with Aboriginal culture in general, the culture of the Secwepemc in particular, or even the iconographic images of ancient pictographs.

If one looks beyond conventional expectations of what Aboriginal iconography ought to be, however, the social and cultural messages of the art are intensely connected with the social meanings of Aboriginal and Secwepemc culture: most of the drawings discussed above, perhaps intuitively, make use of *cyclical connections* between the collective "us" of young people, and the past of the ancestors, of deceased family, and the world around. In Lyle Paul's *Road Puzzle*, the concern is with the paths between the self and the roads and railways to other people and places, although they are broken. In the drawings of George Ignace, the concern is with the collective rather than with the individual, nucleated self, and with the connections to others within one's own past and the places of others' pasts, which at the same time have become places of connection for youth. The drawings also express concerns with landscape, although that landscape has been fused to the urban landscape of buildings, Black ghetto images, and "city bandits." In the end, in the meanings that underlie the images rather than in their overt form, the drawings represent points of fusion between the world of Aboriginal reserve culture and the world of the city.

What is the role of the small city in this emergent sense of identity and expression? As we noted earlier, the small city represents the *real* point of connection between the reserve culture (with its still intact social networks in a flood of grief that derives from the very forms of its past oppression) and the urban ghetto culture whose vernacular message of marginalization and alienation provide affinity and inspiration. For most of the Aboriginal youth from reserves in the Kamloops area, the small city provides the ongoing experience of somewhere connected to, but separate from, life on the rez. It enables them to continue to live the distinct cultural life of reserve communities that we explained above, while partaking of the images and attractions of city life. The small city, with the semi-urban reserve connected to it, also represents the connection to the dangers and vices of city life: it is viewed as the source of drugs, of crime, and the perceived nucleation of social identity and separation of connections with the past. In short, the positioning of youth vis-à-vis the small

city is marked by ambivalence and flux. It is an emergent positioning, which transcends the art, and which will continue to grow in the lives of young people.

Finally, beyond the real and symbolic connections to the small city, this chapter has also explored what "artistic shape" the emergent sense of individual and collective self is taking among Aboriginal youth. For a final reflection on how the past is perceived as connected to the future, we can turn to George Ignace's drawing *Native Issues* (see Figure 8). This drawing is a reflection on the overwhelming and profound influence of residential schools as representing the crux of "native issues": at the bottom left are the tepees and blue-green landscape of the culture of the past, representing a time before the impacts of colonization. The imposing building, the Kamloops Indian Residential School, is surrounded by the people who attended and suffered its impacts, their eyes hollow or downcast, their faces defeated. In the blue waves of the destruction of their identity and culture is the face of the priest, who "only gets a brief view, he can't really see what's happening." In the end, he does not succeed in either grasping or destroying the essence of Aboriginal culture and existence. Ghosts and spirits of the past wash past him in waves. On the right side of the drawing, however, are empty blue waves: the drawing is incomplete on the one hand, but on the other hand it leaves open the question of the future: will the future be controlled by the demons of the past, or will there be new images shaping the future? The youthful reflection on the past and its consequences gives hope for the future and continues the reflection on what that future may become.

In this chapter, we have explored how unexpected and novel art forms connect to the lives and identities of Aboriginal youth in the Kamloops area. In questioning the past, and the meaning of life and death, youth have created ways to reflect on "Who are we?" and "Who will we become?" Even in settings like the rural reserve community of Skeetchestn, where traditions associated with Secwepemc "traditions" are still widely practised by youth, the experiences of Aboriginal youth pass through the city and are reflections on their experiences with the external world, incorporated into their sense of self. In order for culture to carry on, it must re-invent itself in continuously new ways and forms. Kamloops as a small city is the place that connects the reserve to the large city, but it also provides one of the real arenas for the seeking and finding of self-expression among Secwepemc youth.

## Acknowledgments

This paper is dedicated to Skooks and Evan. We thank Ron Ignace for feedback and information on Secwepemc ceremonies; youth from Skeetchestn for providing comments and feedback, and Rickie Greenwood and Margaret Gardiner from the Simon Fraser University library in Kamloops for help with statistical data. We also thank Ms. Kathie McKinnon from St. Ann's Academy, the St. Ann's Academy Fine Arts students, especially Melissa Moses, Lyle Paul, Sage Thomas, and Lucinda Paul. We also thank the school administration for enabling the student art project. Kukwstsétselp.

## Notes

1. The city of Kamloops also has a significant urban Aboriginal population concentrated on the North Shore. While some of this urban Aboriginal population consists of off-reserve members of Secwepemc communities, at least half of this urban Aboriginal population consists of non-Secwepemc people from not only neighbouring Plateau nations, but also from the Plains, northern British Columbia, and other areas.

2. For a reflection on contemporary Secwepemc guardian spirit questing, see Marianne Ignace.

3. An immense popular and academic interest around graffiti art exists in North America, but even more so in Europe, where a World Congress on graffiti art was held in Vienna in 1997. Web searches reveal nearly 100,000 "hits" of web sites associated with graffiti.

4. For academic works on graffiti, see William Upski Wimsatt; Robert Reisner and Lorraine Wechsler.

5. Finding meaning in graffiti is not to support the desecration of public buildings through "bombing"; instead, we support the creation of public spaces that allow graffiti art.

6. See Russell A. Potter and Tricia Rose.

7. The artists are Melissa Moses, Sage Thomas, Lucinda Paul, and George Ignace.

## Works Cited

Bourdieu, Pierre. *Outline of a Theory of Practice.* London: Cambridge UP, 1982.

Ignace, Marianne. "Guardian Spirit Questing in the Nineties: A Mother's Thoughts." *Coyote U: Stories and Teachings from the Secwepemc Education Institute.* Ed. Peter Murphy, George Nicholas, and Marianne Ignace. Penticton, BC: Theytus Books, 1999. 184-188.

Indian and Northern Affairs Canada. *Report of the Royal Commission on Aboriginal Peoples.* Ottawa, 1996. Vol.4.

Potter, Russell A. *Spectacular Vernaculars: Hip-Hop and the Politics of Postmodernism.* New York: SUNY Press, 1994.

Reisner, Robert, and Lorraine Wechsler. *Encyclopedia of Graffiti.* New York: Macmillan, 1974.

Rosaldo, Renato. *Culture and Truth: The ReMaking of Social Analysis.* Boston: Beacon Press, 1989. 1-24.

Rose, Tricia. *Black Noise: Rap Music and Black Culture in Comtemporary America.* Middletown, CT: Wesleyan UP, 1994.

Wimsalt, William Upshi. *Bomb the Suburbs.* New York: Soft Skull, 2000.

# Change and Resistance: Kamloops' Civic Symbols and Identity in the 1990s

## Rachel Nash

As a child living in the city of Vancouver during the 1970s, I remember tracing that city's coat of arms as emblazoned on my school notebook: most memorably, two big men — a fisher and a lumberjack — bore the civic standard. Revealing volumes about changes in Vancouver and its hopes for the future, this dated image of a low-tech, resource-based economy now takes a back seat to Vancouver's newest symbol: the 2010 Vancouver Olympics emblem proudly marries the Olympic Rings with a stylized mountain and maple leaf. In this chapter I demonstrate how paying attention to these changes in official self-representations and trying to understand the motivation behind their shifting character provide a way of taking the pulse of a city, its values, and its identity. Civic symbols, however, are certainly not limited to official insignia, coats of arms, and similar materials put out by chambers of commerce, city governments, and various booster organizations. Civic self-representation occurs through a complex of different practices and mechanisms, including celebrations, mascots, and the language cities use to describe and promote themselves. In *The Homeless Mind*, W.F. Garrett-Petts and Donald Lawrence make the point that much of a city's self-representation falls outside of the regulation and control of city hall and similar institutions, noting that "official representations of place only tell part of the story; they leave out a more vernacular sense of personal place" ("Forward" 3). Artistic representations, as well, help places come to know themselves, whether through the work of locals, or from those outside the region. Ginny Ratsoy's "Away from Home, or Finding Yourself Back In Kamloops" documents how our case study small city, Kamloops, has found itself represented — and not represented — in Canadian literature.

This chapter supplements these works through an investigation into the representation of Kamloops in terms of its official iconography and controversy over a new architectural symbol. While the history of Kamloops, and its practices of self-representation, go back well over 100 years, this chapter focuses exclusively on recent developments in the history of Kamloops' self-representation during the 1990s, particularly around the year 1993. In 1993, the City of Kamloops marked its centenary and, most importantly, hosted the Canada Summer Games, a prestigious large-scale event, which garnered positive national attention and brought both visitors and infrastructure development to the city. More than just a year of major civic events and celebration, 1993 seemed also to function as a symbolic moment at which the fortunes of Kamloops were largely deemed to have turned for the better. This chapter examines representations of Kamloops during this period, as the community attempted the delicate task of fashioning a contemporary image, without completely abandoning its long-term identity in the process. Perhaps not surprisingly, given the changes afoot, Kamloops' self-representations from the 1990s reveal a place in flux as they attempt to foreground the city's vibrancy and modernity while simultaneously attempting to conserve unique, nostalgic, and stylized elements of the city's history and traditional identity. Briavel Holcomb notes that this catch-22 has faced other urban centres as modernization threatens to destroy their distinctiveness:

> Many cities today have major marketing campaigns to attract and retain businesses, investments, consumers, tourists and new residents. Considerable effort and resources are put into the creation and projection of urban images reflecting vibrant, growing places with accessible locations, reconstructed downtowns, and sunny business climates. However, an examination of these marketing materials reveals striking similarities in the images projected. Cities which are, in reality, distinctly different, become homogenized and virtually indistinguishable in their images. (114)

In order to track the tensions and motivations present during this difficult task of making symbols, which are simultaneously perceived as contemporary, unique, *and* representative, and what they might reveal to us about small cities — this chapter consists of two foci: an examination of Kamloops' civic iconography; and consideration of the debate

surrounding the design and appearance of an important new civic structure, the TNRD (Thompson Nicola Regional District) building, which opened its doors in 1998. The analysis of official civic emblems from this period reveals a conservative approach to the difficulty of changing symbolism: emblems introduce new versions of the city's identity but ultimately work within an established set of core Kamloops referents. In contrast, the public's initial antipathy towards the TNRD building demonstrates the impact of a more radical approach. The TNRD building as civic symbol challenges the limited traditional set of regional identity resources, and, instead, uses an alternative set of signs to represent the area. First, however, we turn to the background of this discussion, with an examination of the larger social situation which frames this chapter, particularly the rhetoric surrounding Kamloops during this historical period.

**Stories of a Turnaround**

While Kamloops' relatively diversified economy had protected the city from the extreme bust-and-boom cycle of many of British Columbia's single industry, resource-based towns and cities, the late 1960s, 1970s, and 1980s saw Kamloops' status as an important and desirable small city erode.[1] In his article "When the Travellers Come to Town," part of a Kamloops-themed book issued for the city's centenary, Wayne Norton examines the history of visitors to the area and their varying reactions. He reports on negative developments:

> By the mid-1960's [sic], as commercial and residential growth mushroomed, the favourable comments by tourists had diminished sharply. The change was both swift and dramatic. The same traveller who had found the city so contented and attractive in the early 1960's [sic]

returned in 1966. He was not impressed by the high-rise office and residential additions to the older parts of town. Nor did he find appealing the new homes that "spread untidily into the hills and through the valleys." His most severe criticism, however, was saved for the change in air quality.... The traditional sports fisherman, too, had complaints to make about the changes development brought to the area. One fisherman commented that, by the early 1970s, Kamloops had "lost much of its charm."... The city itself continued to draw negative comments from casual tourists. (25-6)

However, Norton concludes his examination of outsider attitudes towards Kamloops with the cautiously positive statement "that charm is once again associated with Kamloops" (27), a suitably upbeat sentiment for a work issued in the sunny atmosphere of the centennial year, 1993.

Media reports from multiple sources tell a similar story: Kamloops had been down on its luck, but the early 1990s represented a period of rejuvenation and growth as the city began to prosper. For example, a 1991 article, "Kamloops Thrives on New Attitude: New Investment and Opportunities Abound in City," published in *Trade and Commerce* spells out this touted transformation:

> Everyone agrees. A few years ago, Kamloops was in a rut. There had been a debilitating loss of jobs when Tranquille, a provincial institution for treatment of the mentally handicapped, closed and about 600 people found themselves out of work. The country was in the throes of a recession. Efforts at economic development — at a recovery — were stymied by an attitude that pervaded the populace. (Coyle 72)

The article then identifies the awarding of the Canada Summer Games as a rallying point, quoting a councillor who calls the

award "a renaissance, a rebirth of Kamloops" (72). Similarly, a 2001 article from the arch-conservative *BC Report* narrates much the same arc of improvement, opening with the statement: "Ten years ago, Kamloops was an ugly duckling. Its citizens inhaled sulphur from a large pulp mill within city limits. Travellers along the Trans-Canada Highway rarely stopped. Despite the hard times that have hammered the BC interior, the city of 80,000 has transformed itself in the past decade" (Byfield 32).

The people of Kamloops themselves share this perception of improvement: a municipal attitude survey from 1995, conducted every two years beginning in 1988, found that "A significant majority of the residents (93%) are satisfied or very satisfied with the quality of life in Kamloops. The quality of life rating steadily increased from 79% in 1988, 87% in 1991, 88% in 1993 and 93% in 1995" (City of Kamloops 1). Such positive changes in attitude towards Kamloops, both from within and outside the city, suggest a period of growth and improvement, and a time ripe for the active re-negotiation of civic symbols.

## Official Civic Symbols: Reading Kamloops' Iconography

Three civic symbols shared the spotlight during 1993 in Kamloops: the traditional City of Kamloops coat of arms; a design to commemorate the centenary, henceforth referred to in this discussion as the "centenary logo"; and the 1993 Kamloops Canada Summer Games logo (see Figures 1, 2, and 3). While these images have all been reproduced independently in various contexts, I first encountered them together, in this order, in a special 1993 issue of *Canadian Rail*, the magazine of the Canadian Railroad Historical Association, which focuses on the rail history of Kamloops. Another depiction of these symbols, also in the same order, occurs on the opening page of the 1993 calendar produced by the Kamloops Centennial Society. This order makes chronological sense, given the long-standing nature of the coat of arms, the centenary logo's reach from the past to the present of 1993, and the Games logo's grounding in the immediate present of these reproductions.

If, as I claim in the opening, interpreting the changes in civic symbols can be a way of taking the pulse of a city, what new insights might we gain from a reading of these symbols and the snapshot they provide of Kamloops' past, present, and future? If we consider these three symbols through a narrative lens — reading them as a trip through time — they produce evidence for which aspects of that identity have remained constant and valued over time, and which are subject to negotiation as the city attempts to fashion a current image. This set of Kamloops images tells a story of progress, culminating in the Canada Summer Games, and grounded in a continuing relationship between the city and its physical location. The first symbol, the Kamloops coat of arms, serves as the starting point and anchors the narrative.

Among its many details, the coat of arms features a coyote, salmon, and beaver and the Latin motto *salue et opes*.[2] Thus, the coat of arms represents an older, more established Kamloops symbol than the others offered in the sequence. Heraldry in general, and the whole notion of a coat of arms, arises from

Figure 1. Traditional coat of arms.

deeply established (though imported) medieval European traditions and values. The coat of arms' conventional styling and inclusion of Latin, a prestige language dead long before Kamloops was conceived as a city, further connect this image with the past, and with firmly established, traditional representations. While a small group, versed in the specific and detailed code of heraldry, would be able to extract more highly specific meaning out of this symbol, to the majority of its readers, the coat of arms implies, first and foremost, legitimacy and formality, authority, and seriousness.[3] Details such as the winged wheel, the shield trisected by fish-filled rivers, and the inclusion of a coyote and beavers all correspond with traditional historical notions of Kamloops as a frontier town, teeming with resources ready for extraction (and, indeed, echoing the overall message of the Vancouver coat of arms I remember as a child, with slight regional variations).

The second symbol, the centenary logo, evokes what seems initially to be a very different and thoroughly contemporary version of Kamloops, one far removed from the city's roots in the land so thoroughly recognized and celebrated by the coat of arms. Indeed, this symbol seems, in part, to represent an attempt to correct a Kamloops problem identified by Norton: he notices that during the 1970s "the image of a city … seemed to lack a clear, modern and positive definition" (26). As if in response to the problem noticed by

Norton, this emblem presents a highly stylized image of the hundred-year-old city as a series of high-rises, emerging from the side view of an open book, which clearly alludes — in a visual pun — to the meeting of the rivers. A prominent sun shines overhead. Accompanying text, this time in English, not Latin, names the city and marks the centenary dates. Additionally, the commanding centre position this symbol occupies, as well as its more substantial width, means that this symbol assumes a degree of prominence over the two flanking images.

As the central and, apparently, key link in the implied story of Kamloops told by these three images, the centenary logo signals a dramatic shift in sensibilities from the primitive grandeur evoked by the coat of arms. The order of these two images suggests that the early promise of rich natural resources, foregrounded by the coat of arms, has been fulfilled: the prominent series of skyscrapers represents highly urbanized prosperity and epitomizes generic 20th-century civic aspirations. As well, two metaphorical rivers of text meet in the centenary emblem, suggesting that Kamloops — as the meeting place of knowledge as well as rivers — forms the spine of a new information economy or superhighway so prevalent in late-20th-century rhetoric (although, ironically, in the form of an old technology, the book). Taken together, especially in the order in which they are presented, the coat of arms and the centenary image seem to indicate that the city has largely progressed past its resource-based origins and has arrived at a new stage of development, one distinguished by a wholesale and idealized modernity. Tellingly, while a few tall build-

Figure 2. Centenary logo (with book).

ings rise in the city's downtown, Kamloops does not boast such a dramatic skyline, nor does the current economic holy grail of information technology play a defining role in the city's economy. In other words, such imagery more closely reflects the desires and pretensions of the city than its reality in 1993 or since.

While the differences between these two civic symbols and the radical changes that they suggest seem to be the dominant characteristic of their relationship, the two also harbour an undercurrent of connection, indicating stable elements of the Kamloops identity. Most notably, the images both prominently reference the local landscape. The centenary emblem alludes to Kamloops' landscape through its metaphorical but clear reference to the rivers and the inclusion of a dominant sun, signalling the city's semi-desert location and frequent sunny days. As such, the second image echoes the more obvious landscape references in the coat of arms (e.g., the rivers and different types of native wildlife), albeit through a contemporary design idiom. Furthermore, the third emblem, that of the 1993 Canada Summer Games, again refers to the landscape, confirming its status as a defining characteristic of the city's identity. In the Canada Summer Games emblem, highly stylized mountainsides form a valley, in which hangs a multivalent sign: the sun doubles as a winning medal. The sun — a design element repeated in the two contemporary Kamloops symbols — refers again to the hot and sunny local climate. In contrast to the repetition of the sun motif, the mountain slope introduces a new element into the repertoire of Kamloops' nature and landscape

323

imagery. In terms of topography, mountain slopes define the Kamloops landscape to even the most casual observer; Kamloops emphatically sits in the Thompson valley and scrabbles up the adjoining mountainsides. While mountains are absent from the first two images, their presence in the third image, that of the Games, not only obviously evokes a formerly neglected aspect of the Kamloops landscape, but also corresponds to the growing importance of mountains. Mountains have become an increasingly valuable commodity, driven by high-priced tastes for wilderness recreation activities (for example, hiking, mountain biking, and, of course, all kinds of skiing and snowboarding). Tellingly, during the 1990s, a Kamloops-area ski hill, Tod Mountain, transformed into a significant ski resort, re-christened Sun Peaks.[4] As well, mountain slopes suggest speed and excitement, appropriate sentiments for a major athletic meeting. In short, the mountain imagery incorporated into the Games logo provides a successful blend of Kamloops' identity and sporting event, while foregrounding an increasingly valued aspect of the local landscape.

Figure 3: Canada Summer Games logo.

While the Games logo successfully blends traditional Kamloops identity with a new occasion and the newly-valued status of mountains, its position as the final image in this series — the implied conclusion to the story — presents some problems. The Canada Summer Games logo, then and now, also represents a fragile and limited vision for the city's overall future. In this arrangement, the symbol receives visual weight equal to that accorded to the coat of arms and a near equivalency to the slightly larger centenary symbol. However, in contrast to these two symbols, which express an enduring representation of Kamloops, the Games take place fleetingly, occurring only once, for two weeks of a single year. Indeed, the narrative suggested by these civic icons ends abruptly, framing the future in highly limited terms, with no clear through-line to the long-term future. In this choice of symbol, we find persuasive evidence of Kamloops' heavy investment in the Games themselves and a stalwart faith in the strength of the Games' legacy. Any suggestion of the city's future direction beyond the Games comes from reference in each of these symbols to the city's natural setting, especially the rivers and the sun. The role of natural setting as the connecting thread between the emblems suggests its on-going pivotal status in the overall configuration of Kamloops' identity.[5]

A recent interview with graphic artist Dennis Keusch reinforces this argument that Kamloops' natural setting provides the core of Kamloops' official civic identity, and, specifically, certain key elements of the city's landscape function as the city's primary signifiers. In early 1993, Keusch won a contest to design the medal awarded at the Kamloops Canada Summer Games. Keusch's simple, elegant design consists of a meeting of the three rivers (the

North Thompson, the South Thompson, and the Thompson), mountains in the background, and a large, vibrant sun. In an interview, Keusch described his initial immediate conviction that these three elements needed to form the design: "I knew it had to have hills, the sun, and the rivers." When pressed about why these elements seemed so self-evident, Keusch responded by discussing their interaction and how, together, they characterize Kamloops. He mentioned that the sun represented the good climate and steady sunshine of the area, and the light of the sun on the hills defined Kamloops to him. Likewise, the river valley exists in relation to the mountainsides. Keusch's instincts were clearly on target: he was told that his design "blew the others away." His success, I argue, was attributable to his graphic skill as well as to his clear grasp of the stable but gradually evolving set of representational resources for Kamloops, a group of selected natural images which has come to stand for the city. The easy victory of Keusch's design, and the connection between various official Kamloops emblems, demonstrate how civic symbols may evolve, gradually building from a consensus about an urban identity. The controversy over the TNRD building, discussed below, represents what happens when a symbol is perceived to violate a growing consensus about a city's identity.

## The TNRD Building as Civic Symbol

Official emblems such as those discussed above have the task of representing and symbolizing as their primary function; it is what they are intended to do. In contrast, other symbols may become symbols as a side function, sometimes intended, sometimes unintended. Such is the case with architecture. Buildings and other structures such as bridges and dams have a clear non-symbolic primary function: they are designed to house people

and things, to span water, to dam rivers, etc. However, civic architecture often takes on a symbolic role as well, significantly contributing to urban self-representation. Indeed, notable urban structures may come to represent the city as a whole more powerfully than official emblems: for example, the Eiffel Tower, Parthenon, and Golden Gate Bridge almost automatically stand in for Paris, Athens, and San Francisco. Just as houses become homes, the emotional centre of family life and domesticity, key civic buildings, usually public structures, often serve as the emotional centre of cities, the material embodiment of the values and shared life of a community. Embedded in the heart of downtown Kamloops, the newly erected, architecturally innovative TNRD building — a combination of regional headquarters, art gallery, and library — seemed destined for such an important role when it opened in 1998 (see Figure 4).

The TNRD building elicited minimal critique about its ability to perform the project's primary function: housing TNRD offices, the art gallery, and the library. Instead, public controversy focused almost entirely on the building's design aesthetic, a concern aligned with the building's secondary function as a symbol of Kamloops and the greater Thompson Nicola region. The building has had both its local proponents — for one, Jann Bailey, director of the Kamloops Art Gallery, has a long record of public appreciation for the structure, practically and aesthetically — and accolades from outside the region. In fact, the building has won a number of awards; most significantly it was among the eight winners of the 1998 Canadian Architect Award of Excellence. Even in the face of this positive recognition, the building's design faced great resistance from many in Kamloops. I argue that the controversy over the building's design reveals

Figure 4: Exterior of TNRD building. Photo by Kim Clarke.

a disjunction between what Kamloops has conventionally "meant" in the eyes of its citizenry and an alternative interpretation of Kamloops, radically expressed in the building's design. Despite the architects' thoughtful attention to the building's location, many of the people of Kamloops, at least initially, seemed to feel that the TNRD building abandoned too many of the signs of traditional Kamloops identity, misrepresenting the city and, consequently, violating the city's sense of self.

The TNRD building, long on the books as a needed addition to the region's public assets, began to seriously take shape in 1996, shortly after the 1993 Canada Summer Games had injected Kamloops with a dose of civic pride and energy.[6] The prestigious Governor General's Award-winning architectural firm of Peter Cardew and Nigel Baldwin won the bid with a striking and dramatic design characterized by its use of industrial materials and incorporation of open spaces.

While the inclusion of a bold and modern design into the cityscape might have seemed apt at this juncture in Kamloops' history — keep in mind the ambitious skyline of the centenary logo — the TNRD building's design evidently challenged the comfort level of many Kamloopsians. A *Kamloops Daily News* article from July 1998 focuses on public reaction to the design of the new, at that point, almost-complete TNRD building. The article's opening diction signals the reporter's own discomfort with the building's design and suggests a chaotic jumble; "Put together a pile of steel, bricks, and glass — with a few other elements thrown in — in the middle of downtown Kamloops, and you can sure get strong responses from residents" (Young). The article then reports on its poll of 23 people who happened to walk past the building. Significantly, eight of the interviewees said that they actively disliked the design. Their comments — noted in detail in the original article — mostly repeat the earlier concerns expressed by Cache Creek director John Ranta when the architectural model was first revealed (McRae B1): the building is repeatedly described as "cold," "industrial," and "ugly." Even the comments of those who like or are indifferent to the design pick up on these themes — one passerby comments that she's heard people say it looks like a trailer, and another notes that it reminds her of a grain elevator. The terms "boxy" and "industrial" find their way into even admiring remarks (Young).

The prevalent impression that the "cold" and "institutional" TNRD building has no place in Kamloops is deeply ironic, given that the building takes many of its design cues directly from the city itself. In her article "Conceptual Divide: Civic Reality in Kamloops," Elizabeth Shotton lavishly praises the building and lists many specific connections between the building and Kamloops, both in terms of its architecture and its setting. In Shotton's analysis, the mix of materials hostilely characterized as "a pile of steel, bricks, and glass — with a few other elements thrown in" by the *Kamloops Daily News* reporter actually reflect the

> quality of diversity [which] appears as central to the character of Kamloops. The very fabric of the city has developed as a peculiar mix of activities and building form which are all the more inspiring for their odd juxtaposition. Industrial storage buildings, invariably linked to the rail, with their rigorously functional forms and materiality sit incongruously near the gracious brickwork of more civic minded buildings. (n. pag.)

Later, Shotton explains the rationale behind the use of different exterior materials on the gallery/regional offices block and the library block. The office block is "constructed in a manner which recalls the industrial

sheds with their oddly shaped metallic protrusions and functionally austere elevators" (n. pag.). In contrast, the library block is sheathed in brick "to identify with other public buildings of the city, offering a graciously scaled and civically minded presence to Victoria Street" (n. pag.). In another description, Margaret Chrumka also identifies that the building incorporates echoes of existing Kamloops architecture: "Brick, commonly used on older buildings throughout Kamloops, was also used on the exterior, as was stucco" (17). Visual evidence strengthens the claims of Shotton and Chrumka. A number of photos accompany Shotton's article: shots of old sheds by the river, of a train passing a dilapidated grain elevator, of the trestle structure of the red bridge spanning the North Thompson, and of an architectural detail from an older Kamloops structure complement shots of the interior and exterior of the TNRD building. Placed together, the similarities are undeniable.

This mounting evidence poses a problem. If the TNRD building design so readily acknowledges and incorporates its particular location — Kamloops — why did the people of Kamloops find it so difficult to appreciate the building? Why was it rejected as a civic symbol? The answer, I hold, is not so simple, but may partially reside in a quotation Shotton uses in her discussion — though I might add that Shotton's article completely ignores the controversy over the building. She quotes Vittorio Gregotti from *Inside Architecture:* "a good work of civic realism is at once *familiar*, pluralistic, and critical" (my emphasis, qtd. in Shotton, n. pag.). The problem with the TNRD building may be that, although logically it should not lack this necessary familiarity, which Gregotti prescribes, it does. Even though the building clearly pays tribute to the surrounding cityscape, residents seem not to recognize the connection. Rather, they find the building unappealing and, even more problematic, unfamiliar.

Mel Rothenburger, the current mayor of Kamloops, was editor of the *Kamloops Daily News* when the building design was selected and the building was completed. He proved one of the design's most vociferous and high-profile critics, reportedly unable to meaningfully connect the building with the heritage architecture of the city that he values: "He could see little in the building that reflects other local heritage structures, such as the Old Fire Hall or the Old Courthouse" (Youds S7). Indeed, even the passerby cited above, who recognized that the building looks like a grain elevator, seemed to view the design echo as an unfortunate problem rather than a source of connection or a deliberate gesture.

The crux of this failure to recognize the familiar may lie in the way in which cities have come to focus on certain parts of their history, celebrating some aspects of the past as legitimate "heritage" while routinely minimizing others. Hilary P.M. Winchester, Pauline M. McGuirk, and Kevin M. Dunn examine the effects of place marketing, the use of publicity and promotion to sell cities, towns, and regions, on one industrial Australian city and conclude that partial representation and selections made in the process fundamentally misrepresent the city, ultimately doing it a disservice. One section of their argument focuses on how the push to promote the city tends to skew historical representations:

> In the place marketing of Newcastle, the city's richly layered vernacular heritage becomes a commodity to be advertised and sold to tourists and consumers. Parts of the heritage are, however, discarded or denied. The largely invisible heritage of the Awabakal[7], the embarrassing heritage of the convict era, and the unsightly legacy of coal and steel find no place in the re-figured landscape image. Instead the heritage that is commodified derives either from the commercial mercantile era or from the new post-industrial morphology. (55)

Much closer to home, Sherry Bennett has investigated the ways in which Kamloops has chosen to transform American train robber Bill Miner into a local folk hero, while virtually ignoring the McLean boys, a band of home grown criminals with an equally engaging story. I argue that this impulse, identified in an extreme form by Winchester et al. in Newcastle, also functions in Kamloops and extends beyond Bennett's example. Indeed, selective recognition of Kamloops history, one which minimizes the city's "vernacular heritage," even when the evidence stands all around the people of the town, accounts for much of the displeasure incurred by the TNRD building. The building's designers interpreted — and celebrated — a largely unacknowledged history of Kamloops. This working-class, industrial history has become generally unfamiliar to its own citizens, who do not recognize themselves in its representation, despite the city's ostensible pride in its blue-collar roots and optimistic claims such as "to live in the Thompson region is to be enveloped in the legacy of our Western Pioneers" (Rothenburger 16). This alienation is deepened by the presentation of those historical elements in a way that a layperson does not easily recognize because they fall outside of the received code of architectural representation, that is, the limited range of "heritage"[8] architecture, which in this part of the country generally celebrates genteel late-Victorian and Edwardian residences, and a few early public buildings. Railroad shacks, the tracks, rundown elevators, and the like, to which the TNRD building directly alludes, do not conventionally earn the appellation "heritage."

Peter Cardew, the building's architect,

commented on this tendency to recognize only a certain type of architectural heritage. Furthermore, he identified a definition of heritage with another region, the BC coast, suggesting the possibility of a kind of margin-centre dynamic or architectural colonialism at play in Kamloops' covert rejection of its own history:

> There is a robust quality in the older structures of Kamloops, which reflects the city's position as the nucleus of an economy nourished by the riches of the magnificent Canadian landscape. Unlike its older coastal cousin, which has distanced itself from the nature of the province and developed instead a soft-bellied veneer of sophistication, Kamloops is still very much of its own place. This same robustness and uniqueness is evident in the best cultural manifestations of the region. Yet at the same time, one sometimes senses an incomprehensible desire to emulate characteristics of coastal architecture, which one can only conclude in the cultural annexation of Kamloops into the suburbs of Vancouver. (qtd. in Youds S5)

Cardew's defence — written for the occasion of the Kamloops Art Gallery's 25th anniversary, and on the 5th anniversary of the building — also returns us to the issues raised at the outset of this chapter. How do cities represent themselves, or, more importantly, how do cities represent themselves *well*, eschewing the powerful influences of other places? How can civic symbols convey a modern, progressive spirit, while still capturing the unique qualities of a specific location? And how can we learn to recognize and celebrate such representation when it occurs, rather than negatively noting its difference from conventional choices, authorized elsewhere?

Holcomb, quoted earlier in this chapter, decried the homogenizing force of contemporary civic image-making, particularly when that practice is put in the hands of marketing experts. The TNRD building would seem to be the ideal corrective to such a bland, synthetic tendency. Although the civic symbols examined above do, arguably, successfully communicate the place's distinctive nature in a contemporary fashion, they nonetheless are confined to a narrow repertoire of representational units, a rigid equation of Kamloops with its surrounding landscape, in which the particulars and the stylization of the landscape shift slightly over time. In contrast to the relative adherence to an established group of choices that we find vis-à-vis the official civic symbols, the TNRD building challenges convention and conventional architectural choices. In effect, the building's design re-writes the possibilities for what Kamloops might mean (and meant), but does so with deference to the place and its history, examining and bringing to light neglected options such as the humble grain elevator. The maligned TNRD building works an agenda and, in doing so, predictably encounters resistance. In doing so it also prompts its users and observers to remember, re-acquainting and re-familiarizing us with the cityscape and the hidden vernacular histories within, pushing the envelope of our current gentrified definition of "heritage," by recalling other heritages, other stories of the city.

## Implications

I leave this discussion of Kamloops' practices of self-representation by speculating on how the ideas put forth here may specifically reflect the unique position of the small city, and their implications for other small cities beyond the extended example of Kamloops. A theme iterated throughout the Community-University Research Alliances project, and impetus for its creation, has been the absence of research on and representations of the small city. Instead we tend to find a focus split between the small towns and big cities.

Because the small city has commonly been less frequently represented — in Canadian literature, as Ratsoy demonstrates, for example — the small city has a relatively limited range of representational resources on which to draw. In other words, the big or "world-class" city is a rich and suggestive notion, as is the small town. In contrast, there are fewer established ways to discuss and describe the small city; the patterns are not as clear. Given these perceptual and representational restraints, the small city may encounter problems when self-representing. The exciting modernity and possibility associated with large cities, and the rural charm ideally associated with small towns are both inappropriate to the small city. Instead, the small city actively needs to invent itself, and, indeed, it has the opportunity to do so, turning its representational paucity into an opportunity to forge a unique identity for itself and for small cities in general.

Small cities may respond to their neither/nor status by attempting to become "both/and"; that is, the small cities may try to promote themselves as idealized places that combine the best of big cities and small towns, while transcending the limitations of both. I suggest, however, that this global and homogeneous strategy, one that might work for any small city, does not work equally well in every case. Rather, small cities, as the case of Kamloops demonstrates, have the opportunity to develop and sustain existing local identities without resorting to generic abstractions. The gradual evolution of Kamloops' official logos showcases the successful use of traditional symbols and how they gradually adapt over time, reflecting changes in the city's development. Kamloops' logos would not, for example, make sense for most other cities — rather, they reflect this particular city's unique characteristics. The TNRD building illustrates a more radical

approach to the same dilemma of small city self-representation; the building's design challenges architectural conventions, disputing the range of symbols which make up "heritage" and re-introducing elements of alternative vernacular heritages. As with the official Kamloops logos, the TNRD building would not make sense set in another location, even another small city. It takes its shape from the specific qualities of the small city around it. As reaction to the TNRD building illustrates, forging new identities, even those authentically grounded in the place itself, is not an easy task. People take their symbols seriously. However, the controversy over the building should not be taken as a sign of the building's failure to capture the public imagination and to gain acceptance as a civic symbol. Rather, the building brings to the fore the tensions always inherent in change, and, in this case, the change is active, intelligent, and meaningful, as Kamloops moves through time, making and re-making itself.

## Notes

1. See Mackinnon and Nelson for a historical overview of Kamloops' economy. This diversification is long-standing; for example, Wayne Norton notes that Kamloops did not suffer as much as other places during the depression because the local economy boasted Tranquille, the railways, and an active sex trade (86).

2. *Salue et opes* translates roughly into "safe and prosperous."

3. The coat of arms suggests, as well, the system of licensing and imperial power embodied in the Hudson's Bay Company, which for many years organized and maintained European settlement at the site of Kamloops.

4. In a 2001 article, Byfield notes that, "Nippon Cable bought Todd [sic] Mountain in 1992, renamed it Sun Peaks and has since injected almost $300 million. The payroll stands at 800. Last winter, Sun Peaks had 223,000 visits by skiers, some from as far away as Australia. Another $70 million is budgeted for the next two years" (32).

5. A set of standardized images such as those

described — the sun, rivers, and mountains — are both seductive and reductive. They come to seem like the *natural* or obvious choices to represent Kamloops. However, it is important to keep in mind that these images are selections from numerous possibilities, and represent ever-shifting, contextual values. Artists play an important role in reminding us of alternatives. For example, Laura Hargrave, an artist-researcher, represents a series of walks she takes along the rivers in Kamloops in her *River Walk Project*. While, like the standard images, she "identifies the river as the focal point for a series of walks and field sketches," she ultimately works with a much broader set of representational resources: "For the exhibition she constructs four small, wall-mounted shelves, each with a shallow lip, displaying sand and one or two objects collected while walking: dried leaves, a stick, a piece of rusted metal, tree bark, a broken cup, a fuel filter, a part of a tennis ball" (Hargrave).

6. See Chrumka for a description of the evolution of the Kamloops Art Gallery and a history of the funding of the new building.

7. The Aboriginal people of the area.

8. For an extended discussion of some of the politics surrounding current usage of the word "heritage," see my article "Legalizing Multiculturalism: Changes in Discourse, Changes in Attitude."

## Works Cited

Bennett, Sherry. "Upstaging History: Outlaws as Icons." *The Small Cities Book: On the Cultural Future of Small Cities*. Ed. W.F. Garrett-Petts. Vancouver: New Star Books, 2004. 255-277.

Byfield, Mike. "Kamloops Prepares for Take Off." *BC Report*. 28.1: 32-4.

Chrumka, Margaret. "Kamloops Art Gallery." *Artichoke*. 2.2: 14-1.

City of Kamloops. *Municipal Attitude Survey*. 1997.

Coyle, Allen. "Kamloops Thrives on New Attitude." *Trade and Commerce*. 86.1. 72-3.

Davies, David L. "The Railway History of Kamloops B.C.: A Century Old Story." *Canadian Rail*. Sept.-Oct. 1993. 151-171.

Garrett-Petts, W.F., and Donald Lawrence. "Foreword." *The Homeless Mind: An Exploration through Memory Mapping*. Ed. W. F. Garrett-Petts, Donald Lawrence, and David MacLennan. Kamloops: Cariboo Bookworks Press, 2003. 3.

Hargrave, Laura. Personal Interview. 2 Mar. 2003.

Holcomb, Briavel. "City Make-Overs: Marketing the Post-Industrial City." *Place Promotion: the Use of Publicity and Marketing to Sell Towns and Regions*. Ed. John R. Gold and Stephen V. Ward. Toronto: Wiley, 1994. 115-132.

Keusch, Dennis. Personal Interview. 15 Dec. 2003.

MacKinnon, Robert, and Ross Nelson. "Urban and Economic Change in Kamloops: Postindustrial Adjustments in a Staples Economy." *The Small Cities Book: On the Cultural Future of Small Cities*. Ed. W. F. Garrett-Petts. Vancouver: New Star Books, 2004. 23-47.

McRae, Allan. "Civic Centre Plans Endorsed by TNRD." *Kamloops Daily News* 8 March 1996: B1.

Nash, Rachel. "Legalizing Multiculturalism: Changes in Discourse, Changes in Attitude." *Textual Studies in Canada* 13/14: (Summer 2001): 113-130.

Norton, Wayne. "When the Travellers Come to Town." *Kamloops: One Hundred Years of Community 1893-1993*. Ed. Wayne Norton and Wilf Schmidt. Merritt, B.C.: Sonotek, 1992. 18-27.

Ratsoy, Ginny. "Away from Home, o Finding Yourself Back in Kamloops: Literary Representations of the Small City." *The Small Cities Book: On the Cultural Future of Small Cities*. Ed. W. F. Garrett-Petts. Vancouver: New Star Books, 2004. 205-220.

Rothenburger, Bernie. "Pioneer Heritage." *Kamloops: One Hundred Years of Community 1893-1993*. Ed. Wayne Norton and Wilf Schmidt. Merritt, B.C.: Sonotek, 1992. 12-17.

Shotton, Elizabeth. "Conceptual Divide: Civic Reality in Kamloops." 6 December 2003. <http://www.galleries.bc.ca/kamloops/conceptual.html>

Winchester, Hilary P.M., Pauline M. McGuirk, and Kevin M. Dunn. "Constructing Places for the Market: the Case of Newcastle, NSW." *International Journal of Heritage Studies* 2.1-2 (1996): 41-57.

Youds, Mike. "25 and Counting … And Painting and …" *Kamloops Daily News* 6 November 2003: S4-S5.

——— "Modernist Architecture Captures 20th-Century Design." *Kamloops Daily News* 6 November 2003: S7.

Young, Michelle. "Building Inspectors: Street Commentary on the TNRD's New Building Ranges from Good to Bad." *Kamloops Daily News* 11 June 1998: A3.

The Victory Inn, Kamloops.

# Kamloops: The Risk Society is In My Back Yard

## Linda Bell Deutschmann

This chapter is partly concerned with a failed attempt to place a halfway house for prison parolees in Kamloops, but it is mainly about the broader conditions that lie behind the events that took place in this city, and the role that community mapping can play in future events of this kind. The problem addressed here is faced by virtually every city in North America, and by many cities in Europe as well. The conditions of late modern society have created ever-increasing populations of unwanted people who are no longer supervised by accommodating extended families or placed in institutions or sent off to some frontier place of exile. At the same time, we have become an increasingly fortified society, where all but the most disorganized, anomic neighbourhoods are able to exercise considerable political power to ensure that LULUs (locally unwanted land uses such as halfway houses and skateboard parks) are held at bay. Transitional homes for alcoholics and drug addicts, group homes for the mentally challenged, hospices for AIDS patients, supportive accommodations for persons with FAS/FAE,[1] housing for low-income urban singles or for various categories of people facing multiple barriers to employment are increasingly treated with the same vigorous

rejection as nuclear power plants and toxic waste dumps.

The NIMBY ("Not in My Back Yard")/ siting problem is rooted in many streams of social change that affect the late modern societies of the western world. The two dominant forces of social change relevant here can be summarized under the headings of "risk society" and "dangerization." I will outline these issues first and then look at the specific situation where "Not in My Back Yard" emerges within these broader realities.

### Pre-Risk Society

Danger and fear are not new phenomena. Risk is, and always has been, "constitutive of the human condition" (Jaeger et al. 14). But the ways in which people deal with their feelings about danger have changed over time. In earlier periods, people dealt with danger through religious ritual, reliance on their social relationships, and reliance on religious, political, and military leaders. Gradually, this reliance came to be supplemented by reliance on medical and scientific experts, and eventually on actuarial experts who introduced the idea of "risk" management, and the language of risk. Leaders and experts were not always right, but they were still, overall, respected and relied upon. In the pre-risk society, constant obsession with risk factors was rare rather than typical (Douglas). Also, in the pre-risk society, it was the poor who carried the greatest burden of danger and actual harm. Whether the danger came from natural disaster, war, pestilential disease, the by-products of industry, or just the depredations of criminals and ne'er-do-wells, the poor suffered the most. On the whole, the poor in history have had little choice but to put up with conditions as they were, while the rich have secured and fortified themselves as much as possible away from the pains and incivilities of those below them.

### The Risk Society

The term "risk society" was introduced by Ulrich Beck to describe a new kind of society characterized by a pervasive anxiety and unrest about risk. Risk anxiety now affects all of us. It is no longer easy to place toxic waste or nuclear power plants in poor communities, or any communities. Wealthy people can no longer escape pollution by living farther up the hill. "Poverty is hierarchic, smog is democratic" (Beck "Modern Society" 36). Global warming and nuclear meltdown do not respect social class or national borders. A substantial literature has grown up concerning the "risk society" and its characteristic ways of understanding and responding to dangers (Beck *Rethinking Modernity*; *World Risk*; Giddens *Consequences*; *Modernity*; Stallings; Stern and Fineberg; Taylor-Gooby, et al.; Ungar).

In addition to the overall awareness of omnipresent risks, the "risk society" is characterized by a rapid decline in respect for, and trust in, leaders, experts, and elites. Declining trust in experts and authorities has been documented for all western societies. Rosenau, writing in the early 1990s, describes this phenomenon as "the puzzle of the 1980s" (403-

443), while Flanagan speaks of a shift from "a devotion to authority to cynicism and self-assertiveness" and Nevitte devotes his entire book to the topic of "the decline of deference" (306). The dramatic examples of Chernobyl (nuclear meltdown), thalidomide (a major drug scandal), Watergate (a major political scandal) and their after-effects have contributed to a climate of cynicism and distrust.

Many lesser exposures of malpractice and malfeasance have continued the relentless assault on naïve confidence in professionals and leaders. Less dramatic, but nonetheless significant, is the increasing awareness that the most that "experts" ever offer is a measure of the probabilities of risk, not an absolute protection against harm. For the most part, academics such as Beck welcome the legitimatization challenge posed by a distrustful, disrespectful citizenry (*Risk Society* 32-33). Beck recognizes the possibility that pervasive threats can be displaced onto scapegoats ("Modern Society" 75), even though he does not consider the impact that such "risk angst" (Rigakos) may have on the creation of demonized images of dangerous criminals and the disreputable poor, and the nearly paranoid rejection of most means of integration and inclusion that can flow from it. Thus, the "risk society" combines three very uncomfortable ideas: first, we are all surrounded by measurable and immeasurable risks at all times; second, such risks are potentially avoidable, so that we have responsibility to avoid them; and third, we cannot trust experts to guide us in avoiding them, because we believe that the experts will lie to us about these things. All of this is seen in a dramatic way when a NIMBY controversy breaks out.

### Dangerization

Dangerization is a term introduced by Michalis Liazos and Mary Douglas to refer to "the tendency to perceive and analyze the world through categories of menace" (261). In this view, our choices about when and where to go, when to go out, and when and where to use public transit are made on the same basis and "there is no later modern place without consciousness of dangerousness" (261). Liazos and Douglas argue that security in late modern society is achieved largely by amoral and impersonal means. We do not need to know the people we exclude. Examples of impersonal controls in action are security cameras, turnstiles, and magnetic tags. These automatic systems of security involve an increased tendency to focus on people as categories (such as club member or employee) instead of the older form of security which, involved getting to know people and making judgments of them in a holistic way; learning through face-to-face interaction or at least through systems of interpersonal references which people are trustworthy and which people are not.

Quite often, the "insiders" for automatic systems such as gated neighbourhoods and restricted clubs are people who can purchase membership. Inside the controlled spaces, there is order (or at least cleanliness and tidiness). Beyond them there seems to be disorder and danger. Despite the artificiality of this insider/outsider divide, it provides comfort. The more that we live within spaces created by these artificial systems of protection, the more the world outside them seems to be populated by dangerous outsiders who must be kept on the outside. We do not need to know whether they are actually detestable or not. According to Liazos and Douglas, they are disposable (263).[2] Dangerized populations are not just those people who cannot produce membership cards. They also include people who are identified to us by stigmatic categories such as "ex-offender" or "drug addict." Such categories preclude our

need to know anything else about the people they name.

## The Production of Dangerized Populations

It is impossible to exaggerate the rapid growth in numbers of those who fit into the stigmatized categories of people who are so very much unwanted in residential neighbourhoods. In part, they are the throw-offs and castaways of these very neighbourhoods, although they also come from other places.

We are producing more and more people with needs for supported supervised housing and sited social services. Children with special physical and psychiatric needs are surviving their childhoods and becoming adults who need supported living arrangements and assistance in daily living. Normal adults are living to be elderly people, sometimes having picked up substance abuse problems or having become afflicted with dementia.

We no longer favour long-term care in institutions for any but the most serious of mentally ill or the most dangerous of offenders. All others are treated and returned to the community, whether with supervision and support, or (at greater risk, mainly to themselves) without them. Governmental policies (tighter and more complex welfare conditions, for example) continue to place ever-greater numbers of marginal and unstable people onto the streets. This creates a demand for some means of keeping the streets predictable and sanitary for other citizens and their children. As these unwanted populations grow, their acceptability on the street or in neighbourhoods decreases still further.[3]

## Declining Space for Marginalized People
Just as we no longer have large penal institutions and asylums, we no longer have penal colonies or frontier places of exile. We are

also much less tolerant than our ancestors were of areas of cities that allow for all sorts of disorderly conduct, places where unwanted people could congregate away from the disapproving eyes of "decent folk."

It is rarer now to find families that are extended clans with many adult members and lots of space (farm families, for example). Families that have only one or two adult members are much less able to carry or reabsorb a member who is or has been "in trouble" or who has major needs. They are less likely to be both able and willing to take on the task, and they are likely to have neighbours who will be unfriendly about it if they try. There are also fewer families of this kind to "adopt" a needy person, even if paid to do so. The kind of work that Canadians do, and the competition for jobs, make the integration of offenders and other marginalized people much more difficult than in the past, when such people could more easily show themselves to be useful to the family and the community. When not taken in by a family, such people are at risk of homelessness and criminalization or re-criminalization (Fischer; Taylor).

As an example of the growth of just one of these marginalized categories, we can look specifically at the population of ex-offenders and parolees. First, there are more and more adjudicated offenders with substantial needs for supervision/support being released into the community. Factors entering into this situation include the intensifying reliance on formal justice procedures (i.e., criminalization) to deal with all sorts of social problems (including homelessness, mental illness, and cultural divergence) (Fischer; Taylor) and the downloading of responsibility from the central government level to the municipal and local levels, which effectively dumps these problems into neighbourhoods and streets. Second, there is an increasing likelihood that

the individual parolee will lack an intact extended family/community of his/her own, so that supervision and care are provided by strangers, if at all. Third, the rising costs of incarceration are fuelling increased interest in community justice alternatives, also mostly in neighbourhoods and on streets; and finally, late capitalism provides few jobs suitable for the skills of the prisonized population, even if a criminal record were not an additional barrier to employment.

With respect to this growing challenge to the community, there is greater public cynicism (much of it unwarranted) about "rehabilitation" (Martinson; Gendreau), and more support for zero-tolerance "anti-crime" initiatives. Offenders are increasingly "constructed" in the public mind as incurable moral monsters (Maruna; Sloop). With respect to offenders, this construction of danger is exacerbated by highly inflammatory community notification policies (Bedarf; Earl-Hubbard) and the tendency for media to treat every "parolee re-offends" story as a major headline event that makes re-entry much more problematic than it might otherwise be.[4] Exclusionary policies and the need for offenders to "keep hidden" mean that most of us get away with our TV images of "who" the criminals are. We do not see in our minds the former offenders living very quietly in the community right now.

## NIMBY

The designation "NIMBY" (Not in My Back Yard) is often used in the academic and planning literature to describe any citizen mobilization to resist the siting of a facility within or in close proximity to a particular street or community. The locally unwanted land use (LULU) may be a nuclear waste dump, a landfill, a residence for the homeless, a hospice for persons with AIDS, a halfway house for parolees, a needle exchange, or any other sited form of service. In some cases, the land use will be perceived as dangerous or stigmatizing by almost all observers: it is perceived as something no-one should be reasonably expected to accept as a close neighbour. In other cases, the undesirability of the facility may be more open to interpretation. Even churches, synagogues, and Sikh temples have been opposed by NIMBY neighbours.[5]

While academics and city planners tend to use the term NIMBY without apology, and with respect to all mobilizations against any kind of siting (justified or not), citizens involved in these disputes often reject the designation. They see NIMBY as lumping them in with people who are bigoted or selfish, or emotional and ignorant. They see themselves not as negative "rejecters," but as appropriately committed defenders of their community as it is, and as they believe it can be. They are asserting their right to be heard in decisions about their neighbourhood. They may point out other ways in which they have been good neighbours to worthy causes, "just not this one, and just not this street." They view the "unwanted land use" as one that is inconsistent with this view of their neighbourhood. "It's not NIMBY ... we just don't want high density ghettoizing of people."[6] They often see the proposed service as being imposed from the outside, or an inappropriate solution to community problems. As the solution proposed is not a natural "from within" response to the community's own needs, they argue that this is a violation of their rights as equal citizens.[7] Of course, there is a range within this thinking. Some NIMBYs *are* opposed to having stigmatized people anywhere near them and make little attempt to disguise this.[8]

Avoidance of the term NIMBY is difficult because there is no other terminology that is so readily understood when people simply do not want a facility placed in their neighbour-

hood or near where they live. There is no reason to identify a NIMBY movement as either negative or positive in the absence of its context. Most of these events are sufficiently complex that an overall moral evaluation is unlikely to be accurate or useful. There may well be times when NIMBY is the only appropriate response to the placement of a truly noxious hazard or an unwarranted change in land use. People who are against a sited project are almost always correct in asserting that they have not been given enough timely, valid information about the project, that the information that they have been given has been misleading and incomplete (whether intentionally or not), and that other neighbourhoods in the same city have not even been asked to carry the same load of stigmatized or demanding services as they have. (It is also sometimes true that the people who the project would serve are people who are more needy than dangerous, or that the street, community, and the city would be better off if the siting had been allowed.) Much of the literature about NIMBY has been written by planners[9] and those attempting to place sited services, so much of the discussion *has* been negative about the people who "get in the way" when placement is attempted. Nonetheless, most people, including myself, have been, or will be, on various sides of these controversies in their lifetimes. NIMBY is very much a problem of the late 21st century, and it is going to become more, not less, significant as the century unfolds.

NIMBY has not always been with us. It is largely a phenomenon emerging in North American cities in the 1970s and becoming loudly noticeable by the 1980s and into the millennium. Over this period we can trace the increasing spread of the "defended communities" (Suttles) and "privatopias" (McKenzie) within the "fortress society" (Blakely and Snyder). Physical space continues to become increasingly marketized: it is defined as either privately owned (as in malls and now even highways) or, if publicly owned, then sequestered for designated ("respectable") portions of the population. Even the lowest-income, ghettoized neighbourhoods have learned to use zoning, public pressure, and various kinds of exclusionary cooperatives and "homeowners associations" to protect what they perceive to be their space from elements that might detract from their social standing or threaten their security (Blakely and Snyder; Stark). Gentrification, the process whereby low-income local housing becomes displaced by remodelled, middle-class (even trendy) dwellings, has greatly added to this.

### Anatomy of NIMBY: The Kamloops Halfway House Controversy

I should make it clear that I write this not just as a researcher but also as a board member of the John Howard Society and a participant in the events described. While I attempt to be as objective as possible, I feel that there is no objective position possible in a controversy of this type. There is no "one story" that catches all of the events. I have been working towards strategies that will make further social service sitings more visibly open and fair as part of this research.

The justice system is designed to provide bureaucratic and academic expert ways of "handling" the crime problem. Citizens can consider imprisoned offenders as "out of sight, out of mind" until the day on which release is imminent and the problem returns to the community. The dominant research-supported theory of corrections at present maintains that the safest and most humane procedure for the return of offenders is gradual and supported release into the community through facilities such as halfway houses[10]

or day-reporting centres. The dominant view of "experts" is represented in a mixed discourse of reintegration: "therapy," de-marginalization, social bonds, and "geography of opportunity."[11] It ranges from the relatively reformist version — that halfway residences and similar initiatives provide helpful support and supervision — to much more radical proposals that shade into restorative justice, harm reduction, and reconstitutive replacement forms of justice practice (Blumenthal). Overall, these facilities are best sited away from the "downtown" core areas, and closer to or within residential areas that have public transportation for access to work/training/educational opportunities.

Although Kamloops is close to several correctional institutions, it is the only city of its size in British Columbia that does not offer a halfway house, or equivalent support, for the reintegration of adult offenders. At any one time, there are roughly 30 to 50 "federal" parolees living in private placement in the community. Even those who are potentially at high risk to re-offend are supervised primarily by visits to parole/probation officers, except in rare high-profile cases where the RCMP also "check up" on offenders' curfews. Nonetheless, there was little interest in the halfway house issue in any part of Kamloops before the halfway house controversy that broke out in September 1998. Despite more than ten years of effort, community agencies working with offenders, and government agencies charged with managing offender reintegration, had not been able to bring this issue forward for serious community consideration. By the 1990s, there was pressure on local agencies to cooperate with Correctional Service of Canada (CSC) to provide residential services for the reintegration of federal offenders in Kamloops. Criteria for such facilities favoured the format of a 12-bed, 24-

hour facility that would be placed in a residential area. Funding formulae meant that smaller units, such as a five-bed group home, would be less financially viable for the agency awarded the CSC contract.[12]

The John Howard Society began serious consideration of a halfway house project in May 1998, when the executive director of the John Howard Society met with senior personnel from the parole office to learn about the operation of halfway houses in other cities, and the protocol for establishing a facility in Kamloops.[13] While it was expected that there would be some initial opposition from any neighbourhood asked to accept this facility, the executive director and a majority of the board members of the Society felt that "information would cure the problem." There was ample evidence that, once established, such facilities are accepted within their settings. This had been the pattern for halfway houses in Toronto, Ottawa, Vernon, and Kelowna. Thus, it was felt that the evidence available would quickly defuse serious opposition. The board members were convinced that a halfway house would have a positive effect in the kind of neighbourhood where the agency could afford to buy. Once renovated to meet CSC and local ordinances, the halfway house would look better than most of the surrounding houses. It would produce no neighbourhood disturbances such as late-night partying, quarrelling partners, unsupervised children, or a garbage-strewn lawn. (Evidence from crime statistics indicates that the presence of such a facility may actually reduce local crime and is very unlikely to increase it.) As one John Howard insider stated: "I felt that we could swing it. I thought we could show them the evidence and convince them of our good faith. After all, we aren't out there to *hurt* the community. We aren't a for-profit company. We help

handle the crime problem. We don't make it worse. We've been in Kamloops for a long time."

The city government, and in particular the mayor, city council, and development services office were first informed of the plans in July of 1998. Near the end of July, the mayor of Kamloops wrote a column in a local paper in which he (neutrally) observed:

> Given the outcry that went up when the ... Mission considered taking federal parolees, it's going to be difficult, to say the least, to convince neighbours of potential residential facilities they should be permitted to open down the street. That's human nature, and it's hard to argue against. However, the reality is that a significant number of parolees are here now, and more will be coming. We have to ask ourselves if it's fair to insist that Kamloops residents who have committed crimes be sent elsewhere for reintegration into society. (*The Daily News* July 27 1998)[14]

By August, local papers were reporting on the presence of parolees in the community, and the fact that their numbers were expected to increase (Mehrer). By September of 1998, a duplex house in the residential neighbourhood of Brocklehurst, on the North Shore, had been selected as fitting the criteria for both neighbourhood and housing type. Following the legal procedure required by Kamloops zoning laws, the rezoning application was submitted within four days of purchase, and ten days later a large sign indicating the application for rezoning was placed on the lawn. And thus, the first stage of a NIMBY event was reached.

NIMBY events are incredibly similar, no matter where they occur and no matter whether the unwanted land use is toxic waste or unwanted people. Prior to the events, people in the affected community are not particularly interested in the issues that will later galvanize them. They are unlikely to have read very much on the subject or attended meetings, even if developers or social service agencies or the city have attempted to offer such events. When they learn that they already have a new neighbour (when rezoning has not been required) or that rezoning has been applied for, they respond with shock and anger. Somehow, they should have been told earlier. While other studies have shown that there is no such thing as notification that is early enough to prevent resistance, the lack of it does suggest "sneakiness" or lack of respect for the residents of the affected area.

A perceived lack of earlier notification helped to fuel the anger and resentment of the neighbours, as illustrated by comments made at the Kamloops Halfway House Forum, held in February 1999: "When John Howard first put the house on the street, I felt their approach was underhanded, and that they had betrayed the trust of our community. Many of the people here tonight feel the same way and you have to win back that trust." And: "I find it rather underhanded from the John Howard Society to buy houses without informing the neighbours about the purchase. I'd like to know how many other places have been bought in Kamloops." And again; "I honestly believe that this would never have fuelled, or escalated the way it has today, if the John Howard Society in Kamloops had been honest with the people on Joyce Avenue, and they weren't. You should not have to wake up in the morning and look across the street and see a rezoning application. They set panic on the street."

Even a supporter was critical:

"You sure mishandled this one. The first I heard about it on the news was when the house was already purchased, and the level of panic you

brought to our community and the people becoming entrenched instantly over the fear — without even listening — it was astounding the speed at which that happened." (Minutes)

In addition, a local paper commented:

People are naturally upset over a halfway house planned for their neighbourhood (one for teens already operates on the same street). There are 67 children living on the street where, if the project proceeds, men who committed armed robbery, sexual assault and attempted murder would dwell. Would similar opposition be encountered if the society canvassed the neighbourhood before buying the property? Probably. But the society should have more sense than to spring a halfway house on a neighbourhood as practically a fait accompli and expect it to cruise through rezoning like a houseboat on the Shuswap [Lake]. (*Daily News* 27 Sept. 1998)

This haste was partly a result of Kamloops' zoning regulations, which required purchase before a rezoning application. Notification before purchase was rejected by the John Howard board, as it was felt that some opposition was inevitable, and that this might well mean pressure on the owner not to sell. Even in retrospect it seems doubtful that earlier notification would have been early enough to prevent this sense of sudden bad news. Nonetheless, it did leave the impression that those who did not want the house to become a halfway house were facing a situation in which others had been planning for a long time "behind their backs."

The next stage of NIMBY is always "hot," and attempts to place a halfway house in Kamloops was no exception. On the same day as the sign announcing a zoning application was posted, two teams of John Howard representatives (involving two board members, the executive director, and two staff members) began visiting the neighbours. With 21 houses on the immediate block, the teams only managed to visit six before the situation became untenable, and they retreated to consider the safety of pursuing the matter further. The neighbours gathered for a community meeting on the same evening. The executive director and a male board member attended this meeting and attempted to answer questions. As they noted, "There were approximately 14, 16, people in this room, so 8 couples or so, who were adamantly against the implementation and establishing of the halfway house. To the point where one of the women spit on me and left the room. ... We solved nothing that night, short of entrenching the neighbourhood and the agency."[15]

Civility quickly deteriorated as a portion of the affected community mobilized to reject what they saw as an attack on their way of life, property values, women and children's safety, and other values. An organization was formed, eventually called the North Shore Community Advocates.[16] A mass meeting with approximately 200 participants (according to newspaper accounts) was held in a local backyard. John Howard representatives were at first expected to attend this meeting, but death threats were received at the office, and the local RCMP detachment suggested that they would prefer the society withdraw from participation in this meeting. A second mass meeting was held the following night. Both meetings were highly charged, night-time events lit by flares. They were emotional events, described by some observers as "like cross burnings."

Some of the literature on this subject suggests that there is a normal three-stage pattern to "locational conflict issues" (BC Housing Ministry). First, there is intense conflict, with opposition restricted to a small, vocal group living very near the proposed new land use. Then the debate moves into a wider public forum, in which "opposition becomes more rational and objective," and then "conflict resolution may occur." Increasingly, in the 1990s, evidence suggests that this pattern of increasing rationality, if it ever existed, is no longer typical. While more rational voices are heard as the conflict progresses, the smaller group directly affected by the siting of these facilities tends to become more, not less, entrenched in its distrust and opposition. Tactics of community relations, mediation, collaboration, incentives to communities, public forums, and court-based strategies are not effective in reducing this opposition (Balin). This latter pattern was the case in Kamloops. There was no "cooling out" of opposition, no move towards conflict resolution. (On the other hand, it may be incorrect to frame this as an issue of rationality and objectivity. It is easier to be "cool" if you are farther away and not directly affected.)

## City Dynamics

The size and nature of the city may have played a role in keeping the conflict from resolution. As discussed elsewhere in this volume, Kamloops is a small city whose neighbourhoods are self-conscious and mutually aware. The North Shore is currently the area demonstrating the greatest amount of resistance to the placement of new social service facilities,[17] and the controversy has typically been framed in terms of the North Shore being increasingly and unfairly disadvantaged relative to the expanding, and wealthier, South Shore neighbourhoods.

A comment that was repeated in various ways at the public meetings on the halfway house and social housing issues: "When you have something good, you put it on the South Shore; when it's bad you dump it on us." This expression of resentment was even more pronounced in private conversations, which often mentioned the way the "nighttime lights shine down on us from the hills of the South Shore, getting brighter every year." The university and the largest retail stores are "up the hill," in contrast to the many failed or threatened family-owned small businesses on the North Shore. While there are important pockets of poverty and social problems in other parts of the city (especially the downtown South Shore), the heaviest concentrations are found in North Shore communities. Allowing siting of housing and services for more "failures" (criminals and poor people) seems to add insult to these perceived injuries. Another way of looking at this, of course, is that services are being placed where they are needed.

Given the broader dynamics described in this paper, resistance to sited services should be expected in any neighbourhood, but the resistance will be greater where communities feel doubly threatened and marginalized but still retain their sense of community identity and political vitality. Although we learned many lessons in the process from the initial salvos of outrage to the eventual withdrawal of the halfway house proposal on November 20, 1999, two are worthy of further research and discussion.[18] These "lessons" are about "my map versus your map" and "voicelessness."

**My Map Versus Your Map**

Typically, one rather lengthy and frustrating phase of any NIMBY controversy is the "my map versus your map" phase. Those who are fighting the placement of the unwanted service (the halfway house or the subsidized housing or the needle exchange) provide arguments to the effect that their area is already carrying more than its share of "noxious" kinds of services and does not get the benefit of the "good" things that other parts of the city get. This argument may or may not have some truth in it because the placement of such services is often done according to the logic of putting the service where the need is, or finding the land for it where the land is affordable. However, it is not always true that these are the only solutions, or that the neighbourhood selected is in fact more burdened than all other neighbourhoods. This phase was particularly marked in the Kamloops controversy. While the evidence is not all "in" yet, there is considerable qualitative data to suggest that residents of North Shore communities feel quite strongly that their neighbourhoods are more burdened with "bad" things and last in line for the "good" things that Kamloops has to offer.

Typically, one problem the "my map versus your map" phase quite quickly runs into is manageability. You can only put so much on one map. Only by making the base map bigger and bigger can you put "everything" on it. Then some people complain that they want to look at what it would look like if certain things (senior citizen's housing, for example) were taken off the map. Each side produces maps that are favourable to its argument about where the social loads "really" are; the other side points out things left out or things added on and becomes even more suspicious and angry. Not only is the resulting map not very useful for problem solving, it is also not very useful for the researcher who wishes to preserve the various stages of the discussion.

GIS (Geographic Information Systems) is computerized software that allows for visual representation of social reality in ways that are more detailed and more accurate than allowed by any previously available technology. Above all, GIS allows for the infinite *layering* of mapped information. No longer do we risk "burying" our information by overloading one map with so much information that it becomes either too large to manage or unreadable. It is possible to have, for example, a map that includes a layer of a community's streets and homes, a layer of the community's schools and social service centres, a layer of the places where crimes occur (hot spots), and layers of the community's sports facilities, shopping malls, open spaces, neglected spaces, and any other classes of information that may interest the researcher or the community member at a particular time. The layers can be added together or taken apart as needed for different purposes. We can "save" what we have done and go back to it if we wish. If the community member wants to see all the bars and pawn shops added to the map, that can be done, not only for his/her community, but for all the communities in the city. GIS maps can be linked with photographs, satellite images, and other kinds of evidence such as charts, tables, and graphs. In other words, we can use GIS to combine data from many different sources. The maps can be interactive, and making them can be participatory.

GIS could add to the controversy by giving each side more ammunition (Obermeyer), but it has the potential to assist in diffusing the "my map versus your map" phase by providing accurate, timely, and comparable information to all participants. Not only can GIS be used when a conflict is underway; it can also be an important resource in planning to reduce the likelihood of serious conflict. If GIS had been available prior to the choice of the Joyce Avenue site for the halfway house, it is unlikely that that particular street would have been selected, given its particular combination of features.[19] The largest barrier to GIS use is technical competence. Learning GIS takes time and effort. The basics are not a problem, but the competence to combine the layers that are required for this work requires *really* skilled people, and most of these people are not trained for work outside of the physical sciences. The gap is slowly closing as more user-friendly programs are developed and more and more people learn to use them.

## Voicelessness

The following letter to the editor of *The Daily News* is from a member of the North Shore Community Advocates. This group emerged during the Victory Inn project, a social housing complex for low-income single people proposed by the John Howard Society in 2000. Many of the same people were involved in this controversy as in the first one. The North Shore Community Advocates succeeded in preventing the placement of Victory Inn on a street zoned for this use. The Victory Inn project, despite continued and vigorous opposition, was eventually completed farther north, next to the railway tracks. Although the letter was in response to Victory Inn, it is typical of much of the discourse of the halfway house controversy, particularly in its claim of "not being heard" and its reference to an increase in traffic, decline in property values, social services as burdens, other negative "loadings" in the area, and its problematic interpretation or unintentional parodying of expert knowledge:

> Are we just chopped liver? Have we nothing to say? We have collected over 500 signatures on a petition, over a 95% positive response rate, which says that this neighbourhood does not want a housing development at 440 Mackenzie Ave.! And this is not just a coverup for NIMBY type obstruction ...There are many reasons why the proposed complex should not be built there. Merely making it smaller will not do it. However, our efforts to be heard are going largely unnoticed. We have tried to communicate with anyone who seems to have any place in the decision-making hierarchy and mainly got the runaround.... The main fact is this is

not a simple issue. There are problems with site access, traffic and parking, revitalization plan conflicts, social services loading, and reduction of social opportunity. Studies show that crime rates are related to areas of low income…. At present the existing very high crime rate on the North Shore has been exacerbated by the switch of evening hours of operation in the liquor store on the South Shore to the new one in Northhills. Renewal efforts made in the older part of North Kamloops will be nullified as social problems increase with the resulting loss of residents who can afford to move…. The social planning council, which has dealt with this issue, has had no input from the residents of the affected neighbourhood…. To summarize, there are problems with the site, the consultative process is non-existent, and the official answer to the lack of low cost housing is simplistic: building where land is cheap and zoning seems appropriate. (Botham A7)

Observing the problem from the alternative viewpoint — and here I reveal my own contentious bias(es) to highlight the issues — we can see that a very small number of highly motivated people came up with a petition that included signatures from places such as Pritchard — a town well outside the city boundaries — and which thus reflected social networks rather than any kind of randomized sampling.[20] Taken in this context, the 95% response rate made no sense. About half — 486 — of the signatures on the petition came from dwellings outside of a two-kilometre radius of the proposed housing; 154 within one kilometre, and 185 within two kilometres. About 56 signatures were either duplicates or lacked an identifiable Kamloops address. In addition, the largest group of signatures came from a trailer park nearly two kilometres away. This type of housing is associated with more social problems than found around any assisted housing in the city.

Signatures were elicited in part by intimidation (a Doberman dog and "We'll be back") and the use of incorrect information (signers were allegedly told that the Victory Inn would have upwards of 70 parolees and mentally ill persons). Other claims, such as "crime rates are related to areas of low income," do not apply at all to the kind of social housing proposed. (Assisted housing in Kamloops is associated with lower crime rates than alternative housing for the needy.)[21] Finally, opponents of the Victory Inn project inundated every city office involved with daily multiple faxes; they had letters in the paper almost every day and were involved in several incidents of harassment of agency staff and volunteers.

It is doubtful that there were more than a handful of adults in Kamloops who were unaware that the Victory Inn issue existed. It is true that the North Shore Community Advocates were not consulted (they did not exist as a group) before the announcement of the assisted housing plans. Despite the fact that the area was already properly zoned, some consultation had taken place with local area businesses and other representatives, and when protest occurred, attempts were made to engage in a positive dialogue on the subject. The project was given approval in principle in letters to BC Housing from community groups such as the Kamloops Social Planning Council. The North Shore Business Improvement Association had originally written a letter to BC Housing in support of this initiative, but switched to a position of neutrality once the controversy broke out.

In response to the specific complaints of the North Shore Community Advocates, the Victory Inn project was scaled down from 35 to 26 beds, reoriented on its proposed lot, and made the subject of a community open-mike information meeting. Despite the fact that the Victory Inn project (1) represented long-term planning that was within the city plan; (2) was proposed in a properly zoned part of the city; (3) was only one of many social housing projects dispersed within the city (none of which has caused property value loss or other problems); and, (4) would bring construction money into a city that clearly needed it, the pressure from its opponents caused the city council to demand it be moved elsewhere.

The one voice that was not "heard," of course, was the collective voice of those who would live in Victory Inn. When people from the Lighthouse (a similar project run under the same agency aegis, but on the South Shore) took the risk of coming to a Victory Inn community meeting, anti-Victory Inn representatives decried the fact that these people from other forms of social housing were "used": "We are a little confused as to why the John Howard brought several people over from its Lighthouse project to stand and talk about how hard it is to be poor and publicly state they have never been in trouble with the law while never saying anything about the 33-per-cent occupancy for its own clients, who are by their own admission predominantly in conflict with the law" (Friesen A7). About six to eight places in the project would be "reserved" for John Howard agency clients (as is typically done in agency-run social housing), but these people would be the same people who are allowed to live anywhere in the community.[22] Again, other social housing in the city has the same mix of people and is associated with far fewer problems than the rooming-house/absentee-landlord buildings that constitute the main alternative.

## Conclusions

Kamloops, in most ways, is a typical North American city in its struggles with the problem of NIMBY and a growing crisis of social

service siting. The problem of NIMBY is exacerbated in Kamloops by tensions unique to the small city setting. Here, as in other cities, the problem of dangerization within the risk society has meant that labels such as "criminal" create dangerized categories of people who are constructed as demonized outsiders who must be kept away from our homes and families at all costs. Good citizens do not "hear" their voices and sometimes actively make sure that their voices are not heard. We do not trust experts who tell us that we would be safer with criminals living under supervision next door than living "somewhere else" unknown in the community. As a consequence, every victory for NIMBY means that more and more people needing supported, supervised housing remain at large, while the fortification of society progresses, making all of us prisoners in our own homes.

## Notes

1. FAS/FAE (Fetal Alcohol Syndrome/Fetal Alcohol Effect) are birth defects apparently caused by maternal alcohol consumption. Although highly variable in actual outcome, FAS/FAE are often associated with low IQ, high impulsiveness, and behaviours that are associated with "trouble" in the community.

2. Hidden Hills, formerly a suburb of Los Angeles, became the first U.S. gated city when, in 1961, it incorporated itself, but left its gates and private homeowners' association in place. City Hall stands outside the gates, partly so that outsiders will not have an excuse to enter the city. "If people could get into town just by saying 'we're going to city hall,'" explains city attorney Amanda Susskind, "then the residents of Hidden Hills would have no security" (Stark).

3. It is ironic, perhaps, that people who deny the role of experts in deciding when an offender is safe to be released on parole are often the same people to rely absolutely on the role of experts in identifying the individual as a criminal in the first place. Or it may simply be that there is an overriding pessimism at work. The average citizen is an essentialist when thinking about others. Those who were once dangerous are always and essentially dangerous. It is

only ourselves, and those we care about, who are capable of change, as is witnessed by the many shelves of self-help books on sale in any local bookstore.

4. If only we could have "ex-offender succeeds" stories every time an offender marks a five-year milestone or something of the sort, people might have a more realistic notion of the success rates for offenders and the system. Correctional Service of Canada is a government department advertised exclusively by its failures and most dramatically by its most spectacular failures. Very few companies could survive this way.

5. In Portland, neighbours belonging to Arlington Heights Neighbourhood Association voted to oppose a proposed Holocaust survivors memorial (a 50-foot long, 9-foot high basalt wall, to be set in Washington Park). The complaint, as usual, dealt with "negative externalities" (i.e., traffic), but there were also issues around reminding people of "bad things" (i.e., death) and commemorating dead Europeans (Young "Are a Bunch"). In Kamloops, a representative of a Sikh temple spoke out (at a public hearing) to oppose siting for Victory Inn (housing for the poor), saying that it was too close to the temple.

6. North Shore Community Advocates spokesperson (qtd. in Mehrer "John Howard" A1) concerning a 26-bed housing unit proposed in a downtown area.

7. Journalist Lisa Belkin catches some of the flavour of this in her discussion of neighbourhood resistance to the placement of homes for poor blacks within a middle-class white sector of Yonkers, New York. "They viewed their barriers and boundaries less as a way of excluding others, than as a way of defining themselves, providing a badge of belonging, a sense of place, a certainty of who they were and where they stood. ... This wasn't about race, they said. It was about their pride in overcoming the barriers this country places before all newcomers, and about the lives they had built — modest, perhaps, but theirs. Mostly it was about their fear that someone was trying to take it away" (Belkin 15).

8. A petition among businesses near the proposed Victory Inn social housing project, for example was signed by 45 businesses out of the 47 that were approached by one owner. He explained to a news reporter: "There's different levels of opposition. The businesses directly behind — there's all kinds of traffic and access issues. Other businesses are upset from an economic point of view: There won't be people getting any business from the project."

9. Planners, who are often frustrated by NIMBY and not usually sympathetic, have a list of acronyms that reflect this frustration: CAVE (Citizens Against Virtually Everything); NIMTOO (Not In My Term Of Office) PITBY (Put It In Their Backyard) BANANA (Build Absolutely Nothing Anywhere Near Anyone); and WHOA (We Have One Already). Of course, there's also DUDE (Developer Under Delusions of Entitlement) and NIRPY (Never In Rich People's Backyards). There is also NIWYE (Not Impressed With Your Expertise). This list is by no means exhaustive.

10. "Halfway" is a colloquial term for a range of community residential facilities (CRFs) provided by government or for government by various agencies. In Canada, nonprofit agencies such as the John Howard Society and the Elizabeth Fry Society (agencies mandated to assist people in conflict with the law) run much of this housing.

11. "Geography of opportunity" is a recent addition to the common concepts of NIMBY. It is most commonly found in literature about social housing initiatives that are intended to break up ghetto-like conditions. (Rubinowitz and Rosenbaum; Ihlanfeldt).

12. Given the increasing pressure on communities in relation to sited social services, this author believes that smaller units should be considered whenever possible. That is, government should consider contracting for small units when the placement is to be in purely residential settings. There should also be consideration for delivery of some benefit to the community through federal or municipal government in recognition that its setting is being "used" and other parts of the city (such as the gated communities and the "virtually gated" communities) are benefiting without contributing in this way.

13. Most of this information was obtained in an interview with the executive director of the John Howard Society. Other quotations within this section have preserved anonymity except in cases of letters to the editors of various newspapers.

14. The Kamloops New Life Mission's plans to treat drug- and alcohol-addicted federal parolees were not meant to be revealed until after the rezoning and after the mission's fund-raising campaign was underway. When the plans were exposed, there was a tremendous backlash, and the plans were shelved. This all occurred prior to the John Howard halfway house effort. Later, the mayor, who lived near the street, became a figurehead for those who were

opposed to the halfway house.

15. Being spat upon has been reported in similar controversies. Balin reports on how the mayor of Yonkers, New York, was treated this way by a NIMBY protester.

16. The North Shore Community Advocates eventually included residents from Brocklehurst (where Joyce Avenue is located) and two other North Shore areas, Westsyde and North Kamloops.

17. This is not just a question of the North Shore being the only place asked to take such facilities. For example, the Elizabeth Fry Society opened Elizabeth Court, a 46-unit apartment block, in May 2000 in an area on the South Shore that has much higher levels of social housing than are found in any of the North Shore communities. There was very little controversy with respect to this project.

18. Actually, there were many "lessons." I hope to develop this in further publications.

19. It is not appropriate to reveal the exact reasons why this would be so (confidentiality etc). We collect all sorts of data to include in maps — health, police, probation, parole — anything that is available.

20. Here I reveal my own contentious bias(es), in order to highlight the problem. I face a class in which many of the students agree with the letter writer. I am aware that there are many dimensions to these issues. Most people who are NIMBY argue that they are not racist, not poor-bashers, and not (unduly) selfish. Lisa Belkin catches some of the flavour of this when she writes about neighbours' resistance to social housing in Yonkers, NY: "They viewed their barriers and boundaries less as a way of excluding others, than as a way of defining themselves, providing a badge of belonging, a sense of place, a certainty of who they were, and where they stood" (Belkin 15). The bottom line is fear that such housing will take something away from the community, despite the increasing evidence that this effect does not occur.

21. Overall, the association between crime and poverty is compounded by discrimination against the poor and homeless. Harassment, arrest, and incarceration vie with social justice approaches to the "management" of the poor (Fischer).

22. The primary mandate of the John Howard Society is to serve men in conflict with the law. A very large proportion of John Howard clients, however, are not considered criminals (any more than

you are, when you get a traffic ticket), and many are people whose difficulties involve nonviolent and minor offences. Even with respect to clients who *have* had enough "trouble" to be imprisoned at some time in the past, no modern democracy considers every sentence to be a life sentence of social exclusion. It can be argued that the alternative policy, one that denies housing to those with any kind of criminal record, would not make any community safer.

## Works Cited

Adams, John. *Risk*. London: UCL Press, 1995.

Balin, Jane. *A Neighbourhood Divided: Community Resistance to an AIDS Care Facility*. Ithaca: Cornell UP, 1999.

Beck, Ulrich. "Modern Society as Risk Society." *The Culture and Power of Knowledge: Inquiries into Contemporary Societies*. Ed. N. Stehr and R. Ericson, 1992. Berlin: Walter de Gruyter, 199-214.

——. *Rethinking Modernity in the Global Social Order*. Trans. Mark Ritter. Cambridge: Polity Press, 1997.

——. *The Risk Society*. London: Sage, 1992.

——. *World Risk Society*. Cambridge: Polity Press, 1999.

Beck, Ulrich, Anthony Giddens, and Scott Lash. *Reflexive Modernization: Politics, Tradition and Aesthetics in the Modern Social Order*. Cambridge: Polity Press, 1994.

Bedarf, Abril. "Examining Sex Offender Community Notification Laws." *California Law Review* 83 (1995): 884-923.

Blakely, Edward, and Mary Gail Snyder. *Fortress America: Gated Communities in the United States*. Washington, DC: Brookings Institution Press, 1997.

Blumenthal, Heather. "Restorative Justice: Taking a New Approach to Crime and Corrections." *Let's Talk* (Correctional Service of Canada) 24.2 (1999): 1-5.

Botham, P.E.M. Letter. *The Daily News*. Kamloops. 13 May 2000. A5.

Couclelis, Helen, and Mark Monmonier. "Using GIS to Resolve Nimby: How Spatial Understanding Support Systems Can Help with the 'Not In My Back Yard Syndrome.'" *Geographical Systems 2.2* (1995): 83-101.

Earl-Hubbard, Michelle. "The Child Sex Offender Registration Laws: The Punishment, Liberty, Deprivation and Unintended Results Associated

with the Scarlet Letter Laws of the 1990s."
*Northwestern University Law Review* 90.2 (1996):
788-862.

Fischer, Pameal. "The Criminalization of the
Homeless." *Homelessness: A National Perspective.* Ed.
Marjorie J. Robertson and Milton Greenblatt. New
York: Plenum, 1992. 57-66.

Flanagan, Scott C. "Value Change in Industrial
Society." *American Political Science Review* 81
(1987): 1303-19.

Gendreau, Paul. *The Politics of Risk Society.* Oxford:
Blackwell, 1998.

Giddens, Anthony. *The Consequences of Modernity.*
Cambridge: Polity Press, 1990.

——. *Modernity and Self-Identity.* Oxford: Basil
Blackwell, 1991.

Ihlanfeldt, Keith R. "The Geography of Economic
and Social Opportunity in Metropolitan Areas."
*Governance and Opportunity in Metropolitan
America.* Ed. Alan Altshuler et al. Washington DC:
National Academy Press, 1999. 213-51.

Liazos, Michalis, and Mary Douglas. "Dangerization
and the End of Deviance." *British Journal of
Criminology* 40.2 (Spring 2000): 261-78.

Martinson, Robert M. "What Works? Questions
and Answers About Prison Reform." *The Public
Interest* 35 (1974): 22-54.

Maruna, Shadd. *Making Good: How Ex-Convicts
Reform and Build Their Lives.* New York: American
Psychological Association, 2000.

McKenzie, Evan. *Privatopia: Homeowner Associations
and the Rise of Residential Private Government.* New
Haven: Yale UP, 1994.

Mehrer, Ed. "John Howard Project Concerns
Residents." *Kamloops This Week.* 12 May 2000. A1.

——. "Year 2000: Half Released Parolees Coming."
*Kamloops This Week.* 1 August 1998. A1-2.

*Minutes of the Halfway House Task Force Held in the
Public Services and Operations Board Room.*
Kamloops, 1999.

Nevitte, Neil. *The Decline of Deference.*
Peterborough, ON: Broadview Press, 1996.

Obermeyer, Nancy J. "Spatial Conflicts in the
Information Age." Urban and Regional Information
Systems Association (1994): 269-282.

Rigakos, George S. "Risk Society and Actuarial
Criminology: Prospects for a Critical Discourse."
*Canadian Journal of Criminology* 41.2 (1999): 137-
50.

Rosenau, James. "The Relocation of Authority in a
Shrinking World." *Comparative Politics* 24.3 (1992):
253-71.

Rubinowitz, Leonard, and James Rosenbaum.
*Crossing the Class and Color Lines.* Chicago:U of
Chicago P, 2000.

Sloop, John M. *The Cultural Prison: Discourse,
Prisoners and Punishment. Studies in Rhetoric and
Communication*: U of Alabama P, 1996.

Stallings, Robert. "Media Discourse and the Social
Construction of Risk." *Social Problems* 37 (1990):
80-95.

Stark, Andrew. "America, the Gated?" *The Wilson
Quarterly* 22 (1998): 58-80.

Stern, Paul C. and Harvey V. Fineberg, eds.
*Understanding Risk: Informing Decisions in a
Democratic Society.* Washington DC: National
Academy Press, 1996.

Suttles, Gerald D. *The Social Construction of
Communities.* Chicago: U of Chicago P, 1972.

Taylor, David. "Social Control of Marginalized
Populations: The Los Angeles Aggressive
Panhandling Ordinance" *Criminology, Law and
Society.* Winter (1997). 7-14.

Taylor-Gooby, Peter, et al. "Risk and the Welfare
State." *The British Journal of Sociology* 50.2 (1999):
177-94.

Ungar, Shelly. *Moral Panic Versus the Risk Society.*
Toronto: Annual Meetings of the American
Sociological Association, 1997.

Young, Bob. "Are a Bunch of Neighbourhood
Activists Threatening the City?" *Willamette Week.* 18
Feb 1998. A4.

Young, Jock. "Cannibalism and Bulimia: Patterns of
Social Control in Late Modernity." *Theoretical
Criminology* 3.4 (1999): 387-407.

——. "Identity, Community, and Social Exclusion."
*Crime, Disorder and Community Safety: A New
Agenda?* Ed. Roger Matthews and John Pitts.
London: Routledge, 2001. 26-53.

——. *The Exclusive Society: Social Exclusion, Crime
and Difference in Late Modernity.* Thousand Oaks:
Sage, 1999.

# Cultural Heritage, Identity, and the Politics of Small Cities

## Mel Rothenburger, Mayor, Kamloops

When I speak to large gatherings of people at conventions or special events of any kind, I don't talk about representing "city council." Instead, I speak as a representative of "the government of Kamloops." And while I don't feel insulted on occasions when I am relegated to third on the speaking list after federal and provincial representatives, I'm finding more and more that the outdated protocol of putting "senior" governments first is no longer observed. Rather, the government most involved and responsible for an event speaks first, with other levels acknowledged as guests.

These small changes may seem insignificant, but they reflect a shift in the relationships and responsibilities of local, provincial, and federal governments. As the so-called senior governments continue to offload funding and service responsibilities onto local government, cities are fighting back, demanding and getting more authority in determining their own destinies. The disparities between large and small cities are often the subject of philosophical noodling among municipal politicians, but, in fact, small cities are more properly designated as small or medium.

The gulf between a medium-sized city such as Kamloops, and a small community such as Ashcroft or Merritt, is as broad as that between a Kamloops and a Vancouver or a Toronto. Medium-sized cities are in an enviable position to define their futures. Neither beset by the loss of vital services as small towns are, nor by the daunting issues of crime, traffic congestion, and urban decay that challenge major cities, we have the human resources to move ahead, and the experience of larger centres to draw upon.

Kamloops is truly a community of communities, both divided and connected by our river system and our geography. In 1967, Kamloops and North Kamloops, on opposite sides of the river, amalgamated. In 1972, the provincial government put an end to the proliferation of adjoining municipalities, forcibly amalgamating Kamloops, Valleyview, Dufferin, and Brocklehurst, plus the unincorporated areas of Dallas, Barnhartvale, Rayleigh, and Heffley Creek. We still haven't completely accepted this shotgun marriage, though we struggle valiantly with it. Maybe this urgency to find common ground is behind our many efforts to achieve a short, snappy mission statement for ourselves.

Only recently have we started to appreciate the strength of such a diverse city, where one can shop in the quaint art boutiques of the North Shore, enjoy the parks near our downtown or the university atmosphere in the growing southwest sector. We've come to realize that the quest for the all-encompassing one-line slogan approach to who we are doesn't make sense. God knows we've tried. Kamloops has, in various iterations, been "the Heart of the West," the "Hub City," the "Fisherman's Paradise," and now, the "Tournament Capital." The difference between the Tournament Capital program and previous brands is that the Tournament Capital has very clearly defined objectives for sports tourism and healthy lifestyles, and its results are easily measurable.

Yet we are also "BC's Adventure Destination." Doesn't having two marketing brands at the same time create confusion?

Not as long as our message is clear and consistent on each. Kamloops isn't just about sports, any more than it was just about fishing or cowboys. It's also about a vibrant arts community, a rich history from First Nations to exploration to the gold rush to cattle. It's about a growing and innovative technology sector and about pride in our university. It's about many things, too many to capture in one slick slogan. We need to approach our opportunities in several streams, yet understand that they converge at many points.

This, of course, can become a highly political discussion if we allow it to be, and success depends on our willingness as individuals to look beyond our own spheres of interest and to view community as more than the sum of its parts. There's nothing at all contradictory about being a sports capital and a cultural capital at the same time. What rule book says we can't have a national-level sports complex enjoyed by Olympic elite and recreational athletes alike, and a nationally recognized art gallery that exhibits renowned artists and local amateurs in the same building?

The answer is "none," because we make the rules. So the people of Kamloops put their tax dollars where their dreams are: into a performing arts theatre; a hockey arena; a visionary riverfront plan; a fibre network; essential infrastructure, such as a state-of-the-art water plant that incorporates a best-practices training centre; a Rivers Trail system; a fine museum and archives; an ambitious public art program focusing on heritage; a strategy for bringing back neighbourhoods; and a brand new cultural strategic plan.

At the same time, the quantum shift in the influence of levels of government has turned our attention to what were previously "no-goes" for city governments, like poverty, prostitution, and drug abuse.

In Kamloops, all of these issues and initiatives consciously or subconsciously emanate from our very name: "Meeting of the Waters," as translated from the Secwepemc language. We're a meeting place, and we focus on people, with all the strength brought by diversity of cultures, talents, and interests. We're blessed by our location, our natural resources, and the energy of our people.

The changing face of government in our country creates new challenges for cities of all sizes, to be sure. We need to continue to redefine the relationship between levels of government. "Senior" governments need to understand that both small and medium cities face limitations in developing local culture due to the fact that a smaller population base makes it tougher to get facilities and services of a standard enjoyed by the big guys. Federal and provincial governments have the ability to equalize such opportunities via funding and resources, but first they've got to accept that responsibility instead of using local government as a convenient receptacle for the fallout from budget cuts. We don't want a free ride; we want a level playing field.

Communities, on the other hand, face a challenge in providing both for the professionals who give inspiration, and for those still developing their talents. Our new cultural strategic plan emphasizes that point, referring to "recognition of the diversity of the cultural sector in Kamloops, from small to large, amateur to professional." The plan is built on encouragement of public involvement and on extending the role of arts and education in building a "learning community."

Our true identity, as it turns out, is not any single thing, but our ability to take advantage of the many opportunities afforded to us by our unique sense of place.

Rather than contradicting the ambition of becoming a cultural capital, the Tournament Capital of Canada program paves the way. We created the label first, then developed the programs and got funding approval. That might seem backward, but a $37.6 million referendum for new sports and recreation facilities was given the stamp of approval by voters because they understood what it was all about. Kamloops residents place a high value on quality of life, especially on our active lifestyle. More than 90% acknowledge quality of life as a fundamental reason they're here. They said, in effect, that if we want to be the Tournament Capital of the country we need to raise the bar.

So it can be with our goal of becoming a cultural capital. We already spend about $1.3 million annually on direct cultural funding, with a return of close to $8 million back into the economy. Yet, despite the overwhelming endorsement of our quality of life, the thousands of hours of volunteer time in arts and culture, and millions of dollars of investment, 84% of those surveyed said existing facilities are either "inadequate" or adequate "for now."

That's not something to be discouraged about. It means the energy is there. About three years ago, I proposed a new 1,000-seat stand-alone performing arts theatre and offered to champion it. The idea got nowhere, not because taxpayers rejected it, but because the arts community itself was reluctant. They were concerned about putting at risk what they already have by moving forward too aggressively. I'm convinced that's not the way it is today. Both our arts community and our community at large appreciate what we've got, but they see so much more.

We've set the goal, we've raised the bar, we have the strategy, and with support from our provincial and federal partners, we can make it happen.

# Index

big box stores 38, 43

big cities: and Aboriginal youth 307; arts as economic development strategy 111; compartmentalization 152; creative class 92, 99; as cultural centres 287-88; culture 1, 49, 66, 111; culture of participation 112; economies of scale 95; imposing on rural 135-36; lack of memory 142-43; in literature 205; modern 136-37, 138, 330; museum exhibits on 167-68; peripheral spaces 169; place of alienation 168; postindustrial economy 43; self-representation 9, 319, 320; valourization of the large 138

Biography of a Building 87, 88

Biography of a Street 49-50, 51

bissett, bill 21

Blaut, James M. 244

Bohemian class. See creative class; knowledge-sector workers

Bolin, Leslie 169, 180

Boris Karloff Slept Here 220, 280

Borsos, Phillip 257, 267

Bose, Chris 219

Bossenecker, John 266, 275n2

Bowering, George 16, 207, 208, 209, 212, 215-16, 219: McLean gang 216-17, 259, 271-72

Bowling Alone. See Putnam, Robert

Bradford, Neil 6

British Columbia: core-periphery structure 24, 28, 43, 329; cultural support 76, 77; early 1980s recession 35; fastest-growing areas 93; globalization 23, 92; meta-performance 297, 300; and Native policy 286, 288, 291, 305; reserve system 159, 306; staples economy 24, 42; theatre history 287-88, 297-300

Brocklehurst 26, 27, 30, 34, 51, 339. See also North Shore

Brooks, Arthur 66-67, 72, 82

Burke, Kenneth 258, 266, 270

Calgary 135-36

call centres 38, 42

camels 208, 209, 215, 216-17, 219, 220

Camille, Sam 310, 313

Campeau, Michel 167, 174, 176, 181

Camrose 139-42

Canada Summer Games (1993) 7, 11, 66, 75, 82, 319, 321: Bill Miner 267; logo 321, 323-25

Capone, Al 256

Caravan Farm Theatre 287

Cardew, Peter 326, 329

Cariboo College 33, 37. See also UCC

Chicago museums 222-23

Chief Louis 292

Chief Louis Centre 149. See also KIRS

Chilcotin War 261, 263

children: intelligences 232, 242; local culture 242-44; and maps 243-47; and rural-urban border 247; sense of place and self 248; in small cities 248; view of Kamloops 231, 233-34, 244-46, 247. See also education; museums; young people

children's museums. See museums: children's

Chrumka, Margaret 327

cities. See big cities; small cities

City of Kamloops 51, 55: Bill Miner as ambassador 257, 267; coat of arms 321-22; cultural funding 11, 65, 69, 70, 71, 72, 221, 290, 350; cultural support 76-79

civic iconography 9, 319

Clayton, Daniel 217

Cole, Douglas 216

collaboration: between Aboriginal and non-Aboriginal 298-99; community 4, 12, 49; cultural governance 78, 79; as organizational strategy 3; in Small Cities CURA 3-4, 50; social service facilities 343, 344; in theatre 280, 299, 300. See also arts; design charrettes; urban planning

college towns. See university towns

colonialism: Aboriginal people 284, 286, 288, 294, 305; architectural 329; and silence 292; small cities 292; and theatre 288, 297-300